AND
PANRE
QUESTION
BOOK

A QUESTION AND ANSWER REVIEW BOOK FOR THE PHYSICIAN ASSISTANT NATIONAL CERTIFYING EXAMINATION (PANCE) AND RECERTIFYING EXAM (PANRE)

FIRST EDITION

LCN: 2015904184
CreateSpace Independent Publishing Platform, North Charleston, SC

Printed by CreateSpace, an Amazon.com company.

DEDICATION

I would like to thank the Cornell University and the Long Island University Physician Assistant programs for believing in me as a clinical instructor and allowing me to enhance my craft. Thanks to my foundation teachers who inspired me: Stacey Hughes-Cleveland (I hope I make you proud), Marion Masterson, William Ameres and Sharon Verity. To all those who contribute to making this profession great and to all my fellow educators who contribute to this field on so many levels.

Thanks to all of the owners of the photos for helping me to make this book a visual experience. Your contribution is INVALUABLE.

Special thanks to my parents Winifred and Robert Williams. My second parents Xiomara and Froylan Flowers. Special thanks to my "hermanas" Mercedes Avalon & Gilda Cain (the best nurse in the world)! Much love to my big brother and inspiration Danilo Avalon.

To those who kept me focused when I wanted to quit this project with long phone calls, inspiring texts and encouraging words almost every day: Kwabena Omari, Tairu Crutchfield, Larry Romone Williams and Daran Thomas. You guys pulled me through this project.

To Kevin L. Young and Pamela Bodley, thank you for helping me promote the book and being there for me during the medical conferences. You guys are my "white hats".

Special thanks to all those who purchase or use this book. I hope that you find it educational, enjoyable, useful and practical.

HOW TO USE THIS BOOK

1. **Maximize your study time.** Many of us lead busy lives and many of us practitioners do not have a lot of time to spend hours and hours studying. I designed the book to maximize and optimize your study time. By making 5 possible choices instead of the normal 4, you refresh your mind about 5 different diseases or 5 different aspects of one disease. I highlight the differences and similarities of commonly paired possible choices to help learn how to better discern the most appropriate answer. The detailed answer explanations allow you to study while answering questions. In the "wrong answers", I italicize the buzzwords to look for when thinking about those disorders to improve your knowledge retention of those disorders as well.

2. **Improve application of knowledge.** In order to successfully pass the PANCE and PANRE, there are two important skill sets needed: retention and application of knowledge as well as test taking skills. You can know the material presented to you but if you don't answer what the question is asking or if you don't know how to use what you are given to pick the best possible answer then you can get a question wrong despite knowing the material. As a student, I would often just read the answer section just to see if I got the question right and would only read the explanations of the ones I got wrong. This is not the most effective strategy because sometimes, we can get a "right" answer for the 'wrong" reasons. You may have picked the correct answer but your train of thought was wrong. If you are given the same question in a different scenario, you may end up getting it wrong because you didn't truly understand the concept. I recommend reading all of the explanations as this will not only improve your application of knowledge but also maximize your time. In the answer section, I reference the page number to the topic content in Pance Prep Pearls so you can go easily go back to study any difficult or missed concepts.

3. **Enhance test-taking skills.** These questions, and more importantly, the answers are specifically designed to enhance your test taking skills by recognizing what in the question is clinically important information, making associations with history, physical examination findings, associated lab values and diagnostic studies. This approach improves your ability to effectively choose the best answer and eliminate other answers. In the explanation of many of the answers, I give you the reasoning as to why an answer is either right or wrong or how to eliminate an answer based on what is given or not given. For example more than one disease may present with bloody diarrhea but there is a clue in the stem that tells you it is ulcerative colitis instead of ischemic bowel disease or invasive diarrhea. By building great test taking strategies, you can enhance your score. In doing practice questions, keep in mind the potentially difficult question types. If you recognize them early, you are less likely to be tricked by them. These include:
   - The "2 step question" in which you have to know one thing to get the answer to the question
   - The best answer. Sometimes more than one or all of the choices may be appropriate for a particular disease, so look at the qualifiers: **"least likely", "most likely", "initial"** test, **definitive "gold" standard, "next" step.** Missing these qualifiers can make all the difference in picking the right answer. Make sure you are answering what the question is asking.
   - Notice patterns. If all the choices are in a specific pattern and one is not, that might be a clue that it may be the answer when you are not sure which one to choose.
   - Learning how to use the clues in the question to figure out the answer. Often when left between two answers, there are things in the question stem that make both possible. If the differentiating factor is not in the question asked of you, then that means there must be a clue in the question stem that makes one of those two choices more likelier than the other.

In addition, I recommend using a combination of study guides and practice questions to apply what you have been studying. There are tons of study guides, question banks and review books. Using a variety of them can help in this process. There are some great products available.

This book is set up as 6 exams (100 questions each exam) that you can take at different times in your studies.

An example on how to approach questions:

DURING EXAMINATION OF A PATIENT, A HARSH, SYSTOLIC, CRESCENDO-DECRESCENDO MURMUR IS HEARD. IT IS BEST HEARD AT THE RIGHT UPPER STERNAL BORDER AND RADIATES TO THE NECK. THE MURMUR DECREASES WITH INSPIRATION AND WITH THE VALSALVA MANEUVER. WHICH OF THE FOLLOWING IS THE MOST LIKELY DIAGNOSIS?

    A. PULMONIC STENOSIS
    B. AORTIC STENOSIS
    C. MITRAL STENOSIS
    D. AORTIC REGURGITATION
    E. HYPERTROPHIC CARDIOMYOPATHY

First, highlight or underline the important aspects of the question:
DURING EXAMINATION OF A PATIENT, A **HARSH, SYSTOLIC, CRESCENDO-DECRESCENDO MURMUR** IS HEARD. IT IS BEST HEARD AT THE **RIGHT UPPER STERNAL BORDER** AND **RADIATES TO THE NECK**. THE **MURMUR DECREASES WITH INSPIRATION AND WITH THE VALSALVA MANEUVER**. WHICH OF THE FOLLOWING IS THE MOST LIKELY DIAGNOSIS

One approach is to look directly for the answer. If you already know it, then you can choose it. If you are unsure of the answer, then use what you know to eliminate the ones you can to maximize the chance you pick the right one.

For example the murmur is systolic, so you can automatically eliminate all diastolic murmurs in the choices:
    A. PULMONIC STENOSIS
    B. AORTIC STENOSIS
    C. ~~MITRAL STENOSIS~~
    D. ~~AORTIC REGURGITATION~~
    E. HYPERTROPHIC CARDIOMYOPATHY

Now you are left with 3 systolic murmurs as possible choices. You can use different clues to reach the right answer now that you have fewer choices. You can use what you know to figure it out:

Option1
DURING EXAMINATION OF A PATIENT, A **HARSH, SYSTOLIC, CRESCENDO-DECRESCENDO MURMUR** IS HEARD. IT IS BEST HEARD AT THE **RIGHT UPPER STERNAL BORDER** AND **RADIATES TO THE NECK**. THE **MURMUR DECREASES WITH INSPIRATION AND WITH THE VALSALVA MANEUVER**. WHICH OF THE FOLLOWING IS THE MOST LIKELY DIAGNOSIS?

    A. PULMONIC STENOSIS
    B. AORTIC STENOSIS
    C. ~~MITRAL STENOSIS~~
    D. ~~AORTIC REGURGITATION~~
    E. HYPERTROPHIC CARDIOMYOPATHY

Now both aortic stenosis and pulmonic stenosis are harsh murmurs that can radiate to the neck, making them both possible answers. However, if you remember the fact that the murmur decreases with inspiration, you know that the murmur cannot be pulmonic stenosis. Using basic physiology, all right sided murmurs (pulmonic and tricuspid valves) increase with inspiration because with inspiration, blood shunts to the right side to get oxygenated, leaving less blood on the left side. So right-sided murmurs increase with inspiration and left-sided murmurs increase with expiration. Another helpful reminder is that pulmonic valve murmurs are best heard in the pulmonic area (left upper sternal border), which also makes pulmonic stenosis less likely. So we can safely cross off pulmonic stenosis.

A. PULMONIC STENOSIS
B. AORTIC STENOSIS
C. MITRAL STENOSIS
D. AORTIC REGURGITATION
E. HYPERTROPHIC CARDIOMYOPATHY

Now you are left with the last 2. There are a couple of clues that can help you figure out the answer:

DURING EXAMINATION OF A PATIENT, A **HARSH, SYSTOLIC, CRESCENDO-DECRESCENDO MURMUR** IS HEARD. IT IS BEST HEARD AT THE **RIGHT UPPER STERNAL BORDER** AND **RADIATES TO THE NECK**. THE **MURMUR DECREASES WITH INSPIRATION AND WITH THE VALSALVA MANEUVER**. WHICH OF THE FOLLOWING IS THE MOST LIKELY DIAGNOSIS

A. PULMONIC STENOSIS
B. AORTIC STENOSIS
C. MITRAL STENOSIS
D. AORTIC REGURGITATION
E. HYPERTROPHIC CARDIOMYOPATHY

1) The murmur of aortic stenosis radiates to the neck (but the murmur of hypertrophic cardiomyopathy does not), making aortic stenosis the likely answer.
2) Also, performing the Valsalva maneuver (having the patient bear down as if they are making a bowel movement) decreases venous return to the heart, which decreases the forward flow through stenotic valves and decreases the subsequent backflow of blood through regurgitant valves. Simply put, the Valsalva maneuver decreases ALL murmurs (both left and right-sided murmurs) with the 2 exceptions being the murmur of hypertrophic cardiomyopathy and the click of mitral valve prolapse (Valsalva increases the intensity of hypertrophic cardiomyopathy and increases the prolapse of the mitral valve, resulting in an earlier click). This makes aortic stenosis the most likely answer.

A. PULMONIC STENOSIS
B. **AORTIC STENOSIS**
C. MITRAL STENOSIS
D. AORTIC REGURGITATION
E. HYPERTROPHIC CARDIOMYOPATHY

To try this technique, I will give you 10 practice questions to get you warmed up.......

TABLE OF CONTENTS

CONTENT BLUEPRINT TASK AREAS	% OF EXAM CONTENT
HISTORY TAKING & PERFORMING PHYSICAL EXAMINATION	16
USING LABORATORY & DIAGNOSTIC STUDIES	14
FORMULATING MOST LIKELY DIAGNOSIS	18
HEALTH MAINTENANCE	10
CLINICAL INTERVENTION	14
PHARMACEUTICAL THERAPEUTICS	18
APPLYING BASIC SCIENCE & CONCEPTS	10

CONTENT BLUEPRINT BY ORGAN SYSTEMS	% OF EXAM CONTENT
CARDIOLOGY	16
PULMONARY	12
GASTROINTESTINAL/NUTRITIONAL	10
MUSCULOSKELETAL	10
EYES, EARS, NOSE AND THROAT	9
REPRODUCTIVE	8
ENDOCRINE	6
GENITOURINARY	6
NEUROLOGIC SYSTEM	6
PSYCHIATRY/BEHAVIORAL	6
DERMATOLOGIC	5
HEMATOLOGIC	3
INFECTIOUS DISEASE	3

1. A 45-year-old male presents to the emergency room. On physical examination, his skin is warm and flushed. There is decreased systemic vascular resistance. The patient has the following vital signs:
   Blood pressure: 119/50 mmHg
   Temperature: 99.9° F
   Respiratory rate: 30/min
   Pulse: 120 beats per minute. Bounding peripheral arterial pulses, capillary refill <2 seconds.
   Which of the following is the most likely diagnosis?
   a. hypovolemic shock
   b. obstructive shock
   c. cardiogenic shock
   d. hemorrhagic shock
   e. septic shock

2. A 42-year-old previously healthy male presents to the clinic with sudden onset of fevers, chills and blood-tinged sputum. On physical examination, there is evidence of a right lower lobar consolidation. He is otherwise healthy and had a negative PPD 3 weeks ago as part of his routine examination at work. He denies weight loss, recent travel or other symptoms. Which of the following would be the most likely results of a sputum culture in this patient?
   a. Gram negative rods
   b. Gram positive cocci in pairs
   c. Small, obligate, intracellular bacterium
   d. Gram positive cocci in clusters
   e. Intracellular aerobic bacterium gram negative rods

3. A 45-year-old male landscaper presents to the emergency room complaining of fever and a productive cough with thick brown sputum. Initial labs show eosinophilia and increased IgE levels. A CT scan of the chest shows mucous plugging, an atypical pulmonary infiltrate, lack of tapering of the bronchi and bronchial wall thickening. A fungal culture of the sputum grows mold with large, septate hyphae. Which of the following is the most likely etiologic agent?
   a. Cryptococcus neoformans
   b. Candida albicans
   c. Histoplasma capsulatum
   d. Mucor indicus
   e. Aspergillus fumigatus

4. Which of the following diuretics are associated with the development of gynecomastia?
   a. hydrochlorothiazide
   b. spironolactone
   c. furosemide
   d. acetazolamide
   e. mannitol

5. A 45-year-old male is diagnosed with hypertension. A kidney biopsy is performed, which shows nodules of pink hyaline material in the glomerular capillary loops. Which of the following medications is considered to be the management of the choice based on his comorbidities?
   a. hydrochlorothiazide
   b. enalapril
   c. terazosin
   d. metoprolol
   e. verapamil

6. A 38-year-old female is complaining of a gradual onset of increasing fatigue and weakness. Her history is unremarkable. She states she exercises regularly, she tries to eat healthy and has been a vegetarian for 5 years. On physical examination, skin pallor, stomatitis, an abnormal Babinski reflex, decreased proprioception and abnormal deep tendon reflexes are noted. There is no jaundice or other skin findings present. Abdominal examination is unremarkable. A complete blood count is performed, showing the following:

	PATIENT	NORMAL
WBC cells/mcL	6,900	3,500 – 10,500
Hemoglobin (grams/dL)	10.5	Male: 13.5 – 17.5 Female 12.0 – 15.5
Hematocrit (%)	32	Male: 38.8 – 50 Female 34.9 – 44.5
Platelet (/mcL)	240,000	150,000 – 450,000
MCV (fl/red cell)	116	80 – 100
Peripheral smear	Hypersegmented neutrophils	

Which of the following is the most likely diagnosis?
a.   Anemia due to hypothyroidism
b.   Iron deficiency anemia
c.   Vitamin B_{12} deficiency
d.   Folate deficiency anemia
e.   Thalassemia

7. A 32-year-old male presents to the emergency room with difficulty breathing and bilateral leg "heaviness" for 2 days. He states the weakness started in the legs but now the weakness is progressing to his arms. His symptoms started after having 4 days of nausea, vomiting and diarrhea. On physical examination, there is no abdominal tenderness. Neurologic exam shows symmetric weakness with 4/5 muscle strength in his arms and 3/5 muscle strength in his legs. There are decreased lower extremity deep tendon reflexes bilaterally. Stool cultures and gram stains are obtained. Which of the following is the most likely gram stain finding in this patient?
a.   Acid-fast positive rods
b.   Gram positive non spore-forming rods
c.   Gram positive cocci in clusters
d.   Gram positive cocci in pairs
e.   Gram negative oxidase-positive comma (S or seagull-shaped) rods

8. A 34-year-old male who works as a dishwasher in a restaurant is complaining of a bilateral, intensely pruritic hand rash. On physical examination, there are symmetrical, clear, tense vesicles on the palms with a "tapioca pudding" appearance extending to the lateral digits. There is no evidence of umbilication or erythema. Which of the following is the most likely diagnosis?
a.   Molloscum contagiosum
b.   Dishydrotic eczema
c.   Human papilloma virus
d.   Herpes simplex virus
e.   Nummular eczema

9. A 34-year-old female has been recently diagnosed with major depressive disorder. Upon questioning, she has had a few episodes of suicide attempts of which she tried to cut her wrists as well as tried to hang her herself. Which of the following medications is contraindicated in this patient?
    a.   Buspirone (Buspar)
    b.   Fluoxetine (Prozac)
    c.   Paroxetine (Paxil)
    d.   Amitriptyline (Elavil)
    e.   Escitalopram (Lexapro)

10. A 32-year-old woman presents to the clinic with cold intolerance and a 3-month history of weight gain despite having a decreased appetite. On physical examination, she has dry, rough and thick skin and a loss of the outer third of her eyebrows. There are decreased deep tendon reflexes. Which of the following is the most appropriate next step in the evaluation of this patient?
    a.   ACTH stimulation test
    b.   Free T4 level
    c.   Thyroid stimulating hormone levels
    d.   Radioactive iodine uptake scan
    e.   Thyroglobulin levels

QUESTION 1
Choice E (septic shock) is the correct answer. Septic shock is a type of distributive shock. Distributive shock is defined as excess vasodilation with shunting of blood flow from vital organs (heart, kidney) to non-vital organs (ex skin). *Early septic shock is associated with increased cardiac output (brisk capillary refill, warm, flushed skin), and decreased systemic vascular resistance* when compared to other types of shock.
SEPTIC SHOCK – MOST LIKELY (page 67)

Choice B (obstructive shock) is incorrect. *Obstructive shock is due to obstruction of blood flow from the heart or great vessels.* Common causes include massive pulmonary embolism, pericardial tamponade, tension pneumothorax and aortic dissection. Obstructive shock leads to a decreased cardiac output, increased pulmonary capillary wedge pressure and **increased systemic vascular resistance.**

Choice C (cardiogenic shock) is a *primary disorder of the myocardium* (ex myocardial infection, myocarditis, valvular, congenital heart diseases, and cardiomyopathy. Cardiogenic shock is associated with decreased cardiac output (cool, clammy skin), increased pulmonary capillary wedge pressure, and **increased systemic vascular resistance.**

Choice D (hemorrhagic shock) and choice A (hypovolemic shock) are due loss of blood or fluid volume. Hypovolemic shock is associated with decreased cardiac output (cool, clammy skin), decreased pulmonary capillary wedge pressure, and **increased systemic vascular resistance.**

QUESTION 2
Choice B (Gram positive cocci in pairs) is correct. *Streptococcus pneumoniae is the most common cause of community acquired pneumonia* (causing up to 65% of cases). Besides being the most common cause, clues in the vignette are a lobar consolidation (typical pneumonia) and *sudden onset of chills and blood-tinged sputum* which is hallmark for streptococcus. PULMONARY – PNEUMONIA – LABS/DIAGNOSTIC STUDIES (p 101).

Choice a is incorrect because gram negative rods, such as Pseudomonas, E. coli are associated with hospital acquired pneumonia. Other gram negative rods include Haemophilus influenza (the second most common bacterial cause of community acquired pneumonia), Legionella pneumophila and Klebsiella pneumoniae.

Choice C describes the bacteria *Mycoplasma pneumoniae*. It classically causes an atypical presentation with extrapulmonary symptoms (it is the *most common cause of walking pneumonia*) and is associated with blisters on the tympanic membrane (*bullous myringitis*) as well as *positive cold agglutinin autoimmune hemolytic anemia*. Mycoplasma lacks a cell wall, so *beta lactams (such as ceftriaxone & piperacillin/tazobactam) are ineffective against mycoplasma* (since the mechanism of action of beta lactams is inhibition of cell wall synthesis). *Macrolides or doxycycline are the drugs of choice for Mycoplasma pneumoniae infections.*

Choice D describes Staphylococcus aureus. Staphylococcus aureus is commonly associated with pneumonia after a viral infection, such as a complication of pneumonia (and may cause cavitary lesions). Cavitary lesions are often also seen with Klebsiella (a gram negative rod)

Choice E describes the bacteria chlamydia (Chlamydophila pneumoniae). It classically causes an atypical picture and is associated with pneumonia but also causes a concurrent sinusitis, laryngitis or viral symptoms.

QUESTION 3
Choice E (Aspergillus fumigatus) is the correct answer. This patient has radiologic evidence of *bronchiectasis (CT scan of the lungs showing lack of tapering of the bronchi and bronchial wall thickening).* *Allergic bronchopulmonary Aspergillosis is common in patients with bronchiectasis.* It is associated with the production of thick brown sputum, eosinophilia and increased IgE (reflecting the allergic component). *Aspergillus is a mold with large, branching (septate) hyphae.* ASPERGILLUS – MOST LIKELY (page 417). Aspergillus can present in 5 ways:
1. Allergic bronchopulmonary
2. Aspergilloma (fungus ball)
3. Chronic necrotizing pulmonary
4. Acute invasive
5. Chronic invasive (disseminated)

Choice A (Cryptococcus neoformans) can cause pneumonia and meningitis. Cryptococcus appears as encapsulated yeast.

Choice B (Candida albicans) usually causes esophagitis, oral thrush, intertrigo, vaginitis, fungemia and endocarditis. It presents as budding yeast and hyphae.

Choice C (Histoplasma capsulatum) is also a yeast.

Choice D (Mucor indicus) can present with sinusitis. It is a mold with nonseptate (non branching) hyphae.

QUESTION 4
Choice B (spironolactone) is the correct choice. *Spironolactone is a potassium-sparing diuretic* that works as an *aldosterone antagonist.* It blocks the aldosterone-mediated reabsorption of sodium, causing the retention of potassium simultaneously. Its chemical structure is similar to testosterone, but it blocks the testosterone receptor. This can lead to *gynecomastia to decreased androgen activity.* In some patients, its androgen-blocking side effect may be beneficial, for example spironolactone is used to block testosterone in hirsutism (such as women with polycystic ovarian syndrome) and in the management of acne. Its aldosterone blocking properties may be used to treat patients with hyperaldosteronism. SPIRONOLACTONE – PHARMACOLOGY (page 315)

Choice A (hydrochlorothiazide) side effects include: hypercalcemia, hyponatremia, hypokalemia, hyperlipidemia, hyperuricemia, hyperglycemia, metabolic alkalosis and sulfa allergies.

Choice C (acetazolamide) side effects include: hyperchloremic metabolic acidosis, hypokalemia, sulfa allergies and nephrolithiasis.

Choice D (mannitol) side effects includes pulmonary edema.

QUESTION 5

Choice B enalapril is correct. The biopsy description is classic for the ***Kimmelstiel-Wilson lesion*** (*nodular glomerulosclerosis) which is a pathognomic* lesion seen in patients with ***diabetic nephropathy***. This lesion is due to non-enzymatic glycosylation of proteins in patients with diabetes mellitus. This is usually the first evidence of proteinuria, leading eventually to microscopic proteinuria (evidence of renal damage and dysfunction). Over time this ***proteinuria*** and damage to the kidney will ultimately lead to end stage renal disease.   Diabetes is the most common reason patients end up on dialysis (hypertension is second). ACE inhibitors are considered renoprotective and agents of choice in patients with diabetes, chronic kidney disease or nephrotic syndrome due to their mechanism of action. ACE inhibitors preferentially dilate the efferent arterioles near the glomerulus, leading to a drop in glomerular filtration rate. A drop in glomerular filtration rate means less protein is lost at the glomerulus, reducing proteinuria. ACE INHIBITORS (page 479)

Choice A (hydrochlorothiazide) is incorrect.   Hydrochlorothiazides are often used in patients diagnosed with hypertension with no comorbidities, in African-American, patients (along with Calcium channel blockers) and in patients with isolated systolic hypertension. They do not have significant beneficial effects on proteinuria.

Choice C (Terazosin) is incorrect. Alpha blockers are not considered first line therapy in the management of hypertension due to its side effect profile (first dose hypotension and syncope). It is however considered a great choice in patients with both hypertension and benign prostatic hypertrophy. This is because alpha-1 receptor activation leads to contraction of the urethra and prostate, decreasing urinary outflow. ***alpha-1 blockers such as terazosin improve urinary outflow in patients with BPH by causing relaxation of the prostate and the bladder neck.*** Tamsulosin is the most uroselective of the alpha-1 blockers.

Choice D (Metoprolol) is a cardio selective beta blocker. Beta blockers are not usually first line medications in hypertension (but may be useful in patients with concurrent angina or post myocardial infarction).

Choice E (Verapamil) is a nondihydropyridine. In patients, Dihydropyridine calcium channel blockers (amlodipine, nicardipine etc. the 'pines") are preferred for hypertension because they have little effect on the heart but exerts its effect by causing dilation of peripheral arterioles. Nondihydropyridines, such as verapamil, may be useful in patients with hypertension and angina where you want the agent to work on the heart and the peripheral vessels.

QUESTION 6

Choice C (Vitamin B$_{12}$ deficiency) is the correct answer. Vitamin B$_{12}$ (Cobalamin) deficiency is associated with symptoms of anemia. *B$_{12}$ deficiency can cause spinal demyelination*, so neurologic symptoms are hallmark for Vitamin B$_{12}$ deficiency.   B$_{12}$ deficiency is associated with a *macrocytic anemia* (MCV >100 fl/red cell) and *hypersegmented neutrophils*. The most common cause of B$_{12}$ deficiency is pernicious anemia.   Other causes include strict vegan diet (as in this vignette due to the lack of B$_{12}$ from meat sources), Crohn's or malabsorption disorders (because B$_{12}$ is absorbed in the ileum), alcoholism and medications (such as H$_2$ receptor blockers, proton pump inhibitors, zidovudine and hydroxyurea). VITAMIN B12 DEFICIENCY – LABS/DIAGNOSTIC STUDIES (Page 453)

Choice A (anemia due to hypothyroidism) is a rare cause of macrocytic anemia.

Choice B (Iron deficiency anemia) does not classically present with neurological symptoms. *Iron deficiency is classically associated with a microcytic anemia* due to the decreased hemoglobin content of the red blood cells. Early iron deficiency may be normocytic but iron deficiency is not associated with a macrocytic anemia.

Choice D (*Folate deficiency anemia) can present very similar to B_{12} deficiency (including laboratory values of an MCV >100/fL and hypersegmented neutrophils)* but the key difference is the **absence of neurological symptoms in folate deficiency** (which is present in B_{12}). If you replace folate in patients with B_{12} deficiency anemia, you may correct the anemia but the neurological symptoms will persist.

Choice E (Thalassemia) presents with a microcytic anemia due to decreased hemoglobin production.

QUESTION 7
Choice E [Gram negative oxidase-positive comma (S-shaped) rods] is the correct answer. *Campylobacter jejuni is the most common bacterial cause of enteritis in the United States* and is also the *most common antecedent bacteria associated with post-infectious Guillain-Barré syndrome (GBS).* In this vignette, the patient had a recent GI infection. *Guillain Barré syndrome is a demyelinating polyradiculopathy with symmetric lower extremity weakness that is usually greater than upper extremity weakness.* On gram stain, Campylobacter jejuni is a gram negative oxidase-positive comma (S-shaped) bacillus. GUILLAIN BARRE SYNDROME – MOST LIKELY (page 158)

Choice A (Acid fast rods) includes mycobacterium organisms such as Mycobacterium tuberculosis.

Choice B (Gram positive non spore-forming rods) describes Listeria monocytogenes. L. monocytogenes is a facultative anaerobe (capable of cellular respiration by making ATP in the presence of oxygen and by fermentation in anoxic environments).
- **_L. monocytogenes:_ ↑ risk in newborn children, elderly, immunocompromised & pregnant women.**
  - **Bacteremia in pregnancy: most common in 3rd trimester. Bacteremia s CNS invasion* Nonspecific flu-like illness often with premature birth*, fetal death.** Often after ingestion of food such as soft cheeses, delicatessen meats and certain smoked foods.

  - **_Listeriosis (rare): sepsis or meningitis_**

Choice C (Gram positive cocci in clusters) describes Staphylococcus aureus. It is mostly part of the normal skin flora & mucous membranes (colonizes the nares). It can remain alive on dry surfaces for months. On gram staining, S. aureus stain as gram positive cocci in grape-like clusters.
- Diseases caused by Staphylococcus aureus:
  - Toxin production: food poisoning (enterotoxins), toxic shock syndrome, scalded skin syndrome (in infants)
  - Tissue invasion: septic arthritis, endocarditis, skin infections (pimples, abscess, impetigo, cellulitis), pneumonia, bacteremia.

Choice D (Gram positive cocci in pairs) describes Streptococcus pneumoniae. Streptococcus pneumonia is the most common cause of bacterial pneumonia; It may also cause meningitis, acute otitis media (AOM), sinusitis & peritonitis. Streptococcus pneumoniae proliferates in sites of inflammation and colonizes the nasopharynx.

QUESTION 8
Choice B (Dishydrotic eczema) is the correct answer. Dishydrotic eczema is a type of dermatitis characterized by *small, pruritic vesicles (blisters) with a "tapioca appearance"* most commonly seen on the palms and the soles (especially the lateral aspects of the fingers and toes). *Management of dishydrotic eczema includes topical corticosteroids* and other immunosuppressants. DISHYDROTIC ECZEMA – HISTORY AND PHYSICAL EXAMINATION (page 390)

Choice A (Molloscum contagiosum) is a benign viral infection (poxviridae family) most commonly seen in children, sexually active adults and in patients with HIV infection. It is classically characterized by *multiple, dome-shaped flesh-colored to pearly white, waxy papules with central umbilication.* *Curd-like material* can often be expressed if the center of the papule is squeezed.

Choice C (Human papilloma virus) causes warts (such as genital warts). The rash of HPV is classically described as *painless, non pruritic, soft, fleshy, cauliflower-like lesions* ranging in color from flesh colored to red.

Choice D (Herpes simplex virus) is classically described as *grouped vesicles on an erythematous base.*

Choice E (Nummular eczema) is a type of eczema described as *pruritic, sharply defined, coin-shaped lesions* most commonly seen on the dorsum of the hands, feet and extensor surfaces (such as the knees and elbows).

QUESTION 9
Choice D [Amitriptyline (Elavil)] is the correct answer. *Amitriptyline is a tricyclic antidepressant.* They are not used as first line in the management of depression due to their numerous side effects and their *potential toxicity in overdose cases.* In high doses, *TCA's function as sodium channel blockers,* leading to seizures, ventricular dysrhythmias and sinus tachycardia (from muscarinic blockade/anticholinergic activity). This sodium channel blocking activity is also thought to be one of the reasons that TCA's are helpful in pain syndromes. By blocking the sodium channels, it decreases the neurologic perception of pain (very similar to how lidocaine works). TCA's also have anticholinergic properties, which are most evident in toxicity. This anticholinergic property also explains its utility in the treatment of urge incontinence. Urge incontinence is due to detrusor muscle overactivity. The anticholinergic properties of TCA's may be helpful in this disorder. TRICYCLIC ANTIDEPRESSANTS – PHARMACOLOGY (page 492)

Choice A [Buspirone (Buspar)] is a drug used for anxiety disorders. *Buspirone does not cause sedation* like the other medications commonly used in anxiety disorders.

Choice B [Fluoxetine (Prozac)], Choice C [Paroxetine (Paxil)], and choice E [Escitalopram (Lexapro)] are selective serotonin reuptake inhibitors (SSRI's). SSRI's are less likely to cause severe toxicity, making *SSRI's the first line management of major depressive disorder.* They can, however, cause a prolonged QT interval.

QUESTION 10
Choice C (thyroid stimulating hormone) is the correct answer. The signs and symptoms of this vignette is classic for *hypothyroidism.* In evaluating both suspected hyperthyroid or hypothyroid disorders, *the first step is evaluation of TSH levels.* TSH levels are often abnormal way before serum free T4 and serum free T3 levels become abnormal, making *TSH levels the best screening test for thyroid function in suspected thyroid disease.*
THYROID DISORDERS – LABS/DIAGNOSTIC STUDIES (page 284)

Choice A (ACTH stimulation test) is the screening test in suspected adrenal insufficiency. Adrenal insufficiency classically presents with fatigue, muscle weakness and possible signs of hypoglycemia.

Choice B (free T4 level) is usually ordered (after the TSH levels) if the initial TSH levels are abnormal to determine what type of thyroid disorder is present.

Choice D (radioactive uptake scan) is ordered to help differentiate the possible causes of hyperthyroid or hypothyroid once the initial TSH and subsequent free T4 and free T3 levels are obtained.

Choice E (Thyroglobulin levels) are often used as a tumor marker for papillary and follicular thyroid carcinomas.

1. A 50-year-old male presents to the emergency room with 10/10 chest pain that is ripping and knife-like. On cardiac examination, there are no murmurs present. On peripheral vascular exam, there is a decreased left-sided femoral pulse compared to the right side. Blood pressure is 160/120 in the right arm and 110/90 in the left arm. Which of the following radiologic findings would most likely be present in this patient?
    a. cardiomegaly
    b. widening of the mediastinum
    c. rib notching and a "3 sign" of the aorta
    d. Kerley-B lines
    e. Batwing appearance of the hilum

2. A 21-year-old woman complains of headache, bloating, breast pain and swelling, irritability and noise sensitivity that occurs about 7-10 days before the onset of menstruation. The symptoms are usually relieved within 2-3 days after the onset of menstruation. She states that she has severe impairment of activities that causes her to have to use up all of her sick days. Which of the following is the most likely diagnosis?
    a. mittelschmerz
    b. premenstrual syndrome
    c. major depressive disorder
    d. premenstrual dysphoric disorder
    e. somatization disorder

3. A 55-year-old male with Cushing's disease presents with visual changes. A pituitary adenoma is seen on MRI compressing the optic chiasm. Which of the following visual deficits would most likely be seen in this patient?
    a. contralateral homonymous hemianopsia
    b. bitemporal heteronymous hemianopsia
    c. nasal hemianopsia
    d. decreased vision in the one eye
    e. quadrantopia

4. Which of the following is increased in patients with emphysema-dominant chronic obstructive pulmonary disease?
    a. Diffusing capacity of the lung for carbon monoxide (DLCO)
    b. Forced vital capacity (FVC)
    c. Forced expiratory volume in 1 second (FEV1)
    d. Residual volume (RV)
    e. Alpha-1 antitrypsin levels

5. A 40-year-old male is diagnosed with active tuberculosis. In educating the patient, he is told to avoid tyramine containing foods and the possibility of the development of hepatitis and peripheral neuropathy. Which of the following medication is the patient being educated about?
    a. rifampin
    b. isoniazid
    c. pyrazinamide
    d. ethambutol
    e. streptomycin

6. In evaluating a patient with progressive dyspnea, an echocardiogram is obtained, showing inadequate relaxation of the heart, a thickened pericardium and diastolic dysfunction. On physical examination, there is increased jugular venous distention, especially with inspiration. Which of the following is most consistent with the suspected diagnosis?
   a. pericardial knock
   b. bilateral atrial enlargement
   c. speckled myocardium
   d. vegetation on the mitral valve
   e. diastolic collapse of the cardiac chambers

7. A 7-year-old girl presents to the pediatric emergency department with left elbow pain after tripping and falling on an outstretched left hand. On physical examination, there is soft tissue swelling to the posterior left elbow with no prominence of the olecranon. She has decreased range of motion, especially noticeable with elbow extension. She refuses to use the arm. During neurologic evaluation, she is unable to abduct and oppose the left thumb. A radiograph is performed:

   Which of the following is the most likely diagnosis?
   a. nursemaid elbow
   b. radial head fracture
   c. posterior elbow dislocation
   d. supracondylar fracture
   e. lateral epicondylitis

   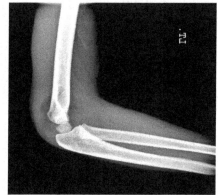

8. A 23-year-old female presents with double vision and drooping of the eyelids especially with upward gaze for the last 3 days. The weakness seems to worsen at the end of the day. She also complains of generalized body aches, weakness as well as dysphagia that is worsened with prolonged chewing. Her pupils are equal bilaterally and there is atrophy of the muscles of the arms or hand. Which of the following tumors are most commonly associated with the above symptoms?
   a. Non Hodgkin lymphoma
   b. Hodgkin Lymphoma
   c. Thymoma
   d. Small cell lung cancer
   e. Non small cell lung cancer

9. A 15-year-old female with a history of asthma and aspirin allergy presents to the pediatric clinic with a nontender, intensely pruritic rash. The lesions first started as tiny blisters but are now erythematous and scaly. There are sharply defined, coin-shaped lesions that are seen especially on the shins bilaterally. There are no satellite lesions. Which of the following is the most likely diagnosis?
   a. erythema migrans
   b. erythema nodosum
   c. nummular eczema
   d. lichen planus
   e. intertrigo

10. A 56-year-old male is being evaluated for anemia and has the following values:

		PATIENT	NORMAL
WBC	(cells/mcL)	9,800	3,500 – 10,500
Hemoglobin	(grams/dL)	12.2	Male: 13.5 – 17.5 Female 12.0 – 15.5
Hematocrit	(%)	32	Male: 38.8 – 50 Female 34.9 – 44.5
Platelets	(/mcL)	240,000	150,000 – 450,000
MCV		118	80 – 100
Peripheral smear		Hypersegmented neutrophils	

Which of the following is the most likely cause?
   a. Folate deficiency anemia
   b. Iron deficiency anemia
   c. Alpha thalassemia
   d. Lead poisoning
   e. Beta thalassemia

11. A 45-year-old male on chemotherapy develops substernal odynophagia, epigastric pain, nausea, vomiting and weight loss. He is afebrile. Routine blood bacterial and fungal cultures are negative. An upper endoscopy is performed, showing linear yellow-white plaques without ulcerations. A potassium hydroxide smear from brushings of the esophageal lesions reveals budding yeast and hyphae. Which of the following is considered the first-line management of choice in this patient?
   a. griseofulvin
   b. caspofungin
   c. nystatin
   d. fluconazole
   e. amphotericin B

12. A 48-year-old male with a history of diabetes mellitus is admitted for a pulmonary embolism that was seen on a spiral CT scan of the chest with IV contrast. 2 days later, he has sudden worsening of his creatinine levels. An arterial blood gas shows an anion gap metabolic acidosis with an increased lactate level. There are no signs of infection. Which of the following medications is the patient most likely prescribed to treat his diabetes mellitus?
   a. meglitinide
   b. acarbose
   c. metformin
   d. canagliflozin
   e. glyburide

13. An 8-year-old boy is recovering from an upper respiratory infection. His mother states that she noticed for the last 3 days, he has had swelling around his testicles and puffiness around his eyes, especially in the morning. The child denies any testicular or ocular pain. A urinalysis is performed, which shows 3+ proteinuria and Maltese cross-shaped oval fat bodies on polarized microscopic examination of the urine. Which of the following is the management of choice?
   a. prednisone
   b. cyclophosphamide
   c. simvastatin
   d. amoxicillin
   e. intravenous immunoglobulin

14. A 25-year-old female with a history of depression is brought into the emergency room by her friends after they found her sweating and mumbling on the floor of her dorm room. She now appears confused but is complaining of blurred vision, palpitations and "cotton mouth". She is febrile but her skin appears very dry and there is no evidence of piloerections. Her pupils are dilated and her bowel sounds are decreased. In evaluating the patient, an ECG is obtained, showing a QRS complex of 160 ms with a heart rate of 160 beats per minute. Which of the following is the most likely diagnosis?
    a. cannabis overdose
    b. oxycodone overdose
    c. ethanol intoxication
    d. tricyclic antidepressant overdose
    e. methadone overdose

15. A 43-year-old otherwise healthy male is referred to a gastroenterologist for chest pain and cough. He underwent cardiac workup, which was negative for cardiac disease. An esophagram is performed and shows a "bird's beak" appearance:
    Which of the following is the most likely
    diagnosis?
    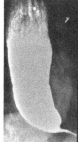
    a. Zenker's diverticulum
    b. Esophageal cancer
    c. Nutcracker esophagus
    d. Achalasia
    e. Diffuse esophageal spasm

16. Which of the following is a class I antiarrhythmic that has been shown to prolong ventricular repolarization and the refractory period?
    a. procainamide
    b. metoprolol
    c. amiodarone
    d. verapamil
    e. digoxin

17. A 43-year-old male presents after a near syncopal episode and is currently dizzy. The following rhythm is seen on ECG:
    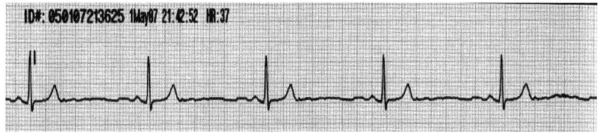
    Which of the following is management of choice?
    a. observation
    b. insertion of a permanent pacemaker
    c. IV epinephrine
    d. IV atropine
    e. IV amiodarone

18. During a neurological examination of a patient, tapping of the cheek over the facial nerve causes facial spasms. There are also carpal spasms with inflation of a blood pressure cuff. Which of the following electrolyte abnormalities is most likely responsible for the associated symptoms?
   a. hypernatremia
   b. hyperkalemia
   c. hypercalcemia
   d. hypomagnesemia
   e. hyponatremia

19. A 54-year-old male presents to the clinic with a history of chills, fever, malaise and nausea. Physical examination is remarkable for splenomegaly. A peripheral buffy coat smear shows morulae in the white blood cells. Which of the following is the most likely diagnosis?
   a. Leishmaniasis
   b. Trichinosis
   c. Ehrlichiosis
   d. Malaria
   e. Babesiosis

20. Which of the following is most consistent with meningiomas?
   a. they most often occur in the cerebral hemisphere and often cross the corpus callosum, causing a "butterfly" appearance on CT scan
   b. they most commonly occur in the convexities of the hemispheres and the parasagittal regions and are often attached to the dura
   c. they often occur in children and are most commonly seen in the 3rd or 4th ventricle
   d. they are associated with von-Hippel-Lindau syndrome especially if there is retinal involvement
   e. they are most common in the cerebellopontine area and are often associated with unilateral sensorineural hearing loss

21. Which of the following is the most common cause of secondary amenorrhea?
   a. premature ovarian failure
   b. pregnancy
   c. hypothalamic pituitary dysfunction
   d. androgen insensitivity
   e. Turner's syndrome

22. A sterile wisp of cotton to test corneal reflex is used in the evaluation of which of the following cranial nerves?
   a. III
   b. IV
   c. V
   d. VI
   e. VIII

23. A 35-year-old female presents with the fever, joint pain and the following facial rash after a 2-week vacation in the Dominican Republic. The rash spares the nasolabial folds:

Which of the following lab values would most likely be elevated?
a. Anti double stranded DNA antibodies
b. Anti centromere antibodies
c. Anti-Mi-2 antibodies
d. Anti smooth muscle antibodies
e. Anti endomysial IgA antibodies

24. A 44-year-old male is involved in a motor vehicle accident. On physical examination, he has distended jugular veins with decreased pulses only on inspiration. There are decreased breath sounds on the entire right side. The heart sounds are not muffled. Which of the following is the next most appropriate step?
a. chest tube thoracostomy
b. observation and oxygen therapy
c. insertion of large bore needle into the second intercostal pleural space followed by chest tube thoracostomy
d. insertion of a needle in the pericardial space
e. instillation of a sclerosing agent into the pleural space

25. Which of the following diseases classically presents with a pneumomediastinum?
a. Mallory-Weiss tears
b. Duodenal ulcer
c. Boerhaave syndrome
d. Pericardial tamponade
e. Zenker's diverticulum

26. In evaluation of a patient, an arterial blood gas is performed. The following ABG values are seen:
pH: 7.36
PaCO$_2$: 68 mmHg
HCO$_3$: 36 mEq/L
Which of the following is the most likely diagnosis?
a. Uncompensated respiratory acidosis
b. Uncompensated metabolic acidosis
c. Compensated respiratory acidosis
d. Compensated metabolic alkalosis
e. Compensated metabolic acidosis

27. Which of the following medications is the drug of choice to increase high density lipoprotein levels?
a. cholestyramine
b. ezetimibe
c. fenofibrate
d. nicotinic acid
e. simvastatin

28. A 26-year-old male with Down syndrome presents to the ophthalmology clinic with eye irritation and itching. On physical examination, there is erythema to the eyelid with crusting, scaling and red rimming. There is no conjunctival erythema. Which of the following is the initial management of choice?
   a.   oral cephalexin
   b.   warm compresses and eyelid scrubbing with baby shampoo
   c.   antibiotic eye drops
   d.   expression of the meibomian gland periodically
   e.   immediate ophthalmology consult

29. A 57-year-old male with a history of hypertension and diabetes mellitus presents with right-sided facial weakness and slurred speech that began 30 minutes ago as witnessed by his daughter while they were sitting on a park bench. On physical examination, there is upper extremity weakness that is more pronounced than the weakness in his lower extremities. Which of the following is the next most appropriate step in the management of this patient?
   a. have the patient chew an aspirin
   b. administer alteplase
   c. administer streptokinase
   d. obtain a non-contrast CT scan of the head
   e. obtain an MRI of the brain

30. A 23-year-old male recently returned from a camping trip in Utah. 4 days after his return, he presents to the urgent care center with fever, fatigue, severe body aches, headaches and hematuria. He is given antibiotics for a urinary tract infection and sent home. 3 days later, he presents to the emergency room with shortness of breath. On physical examination, there are crackles throughout the lung fields. Chest radiographs were obtained, confirming pulmonary edema. Upon further questioning, he states he noticed the smell of rodent urine when he arrived at the log cabin but he had to stay in the cabin for one night until there was a vacant cabin the next morning. His symptoms improved after 5 days of admission to the intensive care unit. Which of the following is the most likely etiology of his symptoms?
   a.   Hantavirus
   b.   Flavivirus
   c.   Coronavirus
   d.   Orthopox virus
   e.   Rhabdovirus

31. A 42-year-old male with a history of multiple episodes of major depression has occasions of elevated mood with irritability for a week at a time including racing thoughts, pressured speech and excessive involvement in pleasurable activities. He denies hallucinations and has no apparent delusions. He is still able to function at work and at home. Which of the following is the most likely diagnosis?
   a.   Bipolar disorder type I
   b.   Cyclothymia
   c.   Persistent Depressive Disorder (Dysthymia)
   d.   Bipolar disorder Type II
   e.   Schizoaffective disorder

32. Which of the following is most commonly seen on peripheral smear in patients with alpha thalassemia intermedia?
   a.   clumping of the red blood cells
   b.   hypersegmented neutrophils
   c.   Heinz bodies
   d.   macrocytosis
   e.   rouleaux formation

33. Which of the following physical exam findings is most consistent with a right middle lobe pneumonia?

    a. hyperresonance to percussion on the right side with tracheal deviation to the left

    b. dullness to percussion, bronchial breath sounds and egophony on the right side

    c. resonance to percussion, vesicular breath sounds and normal fremitus on the right side

    d. dullness to percussion, decreased breath sounds, and decreased fremitus on the right side

    e. hyperresonance to percussion, decreased breath sounds and decreased fremitus on the right side

34. A 27-year-old female at 37 weeks gestation with a longstanding history of hypertension is brought to the emergency room because she thinks she is having Braxton Hicks contractions. She states that she has been having abdominal pain preceded by painful contractions and thought her "water broke" because she saw dark red blood in the toilet. Her blood pressure is 150/90 mmHg; she is afebrile with otherwise stable vital signs. On physical examination, the uterus is tender & rigid. The vaginal pH is normal, a nitrazine test is negative, no ferning is seen and there is no maternal leukocytosis. Which of the following is the most likely diagnosis?

    a.   chorioamnionitis
    b.   placenta previa
    c.   vasa previa
    d.   abruptio placentae
    e.   mild preeclampsia

35. A 54-year-old female presents to the clinic with gradually worsening pruritus. The patient thought she had hives and took diphenhydramine (Benadryl) without relief of her symptoms. On further questioning, she states she has been having increasing fatigue. On physical examination, yellowing of the sclera is noted, and there is mild hepatomegaly. There is no right upper quadrant tenderness on palpation of the abdomen. Her vital signs are normal and she is afebrile. Liver function tests show a markedly increased alkaline phosphatase and GGT level. AST and ALT levels are only mildly elevated. A CBC is within normal limits. Anti-mitochondrial antibody testing is positive. Which of the following is the most likely diagnosis?

    a. autoimmune hepatitis
    b. acute cholecystitis
    c. acute cholangitis
    d. primary biliary cirrhosis
    e. primary sclerosing cholangitis

36. During a routine physical examination of a patient, an abdominal bruit is heard. Which of the following is the initial study of choice if abdominal aortic aneurysm is suspected based on the physical examination findings?

    a.   Angiography
    b.   Abdominal ultrasound
    c.   CT scan of the abdomen and pelvis
    d.   Magnetic resonance imaging of the abdomen and pelvis
    e.   Abdominal radiographs

37. A 43-year-old male presents with the following lesion that has increased in size over the last 6 months. Which of the following is the most important prognostic factor?

    a.   color variation
    b.   irregularity of the border
    c.   diameter greater than 6 millimeters
    d.   rapidity in the growth of the lesion
    e.   thickness of the lesion

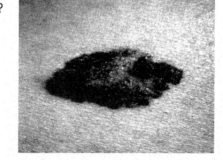

38. A 37-year-old female went camping and developed fever, headaches and body aches. A few days later, she developed a red, maculopapular rash first on the ankles and the wrists, spreading to her palms and soles before becoming generalized. She states she removed a tick from her shoulder 2 weeks ago. Which of the following is the most likely etiologic agent?
  a. Rickettsia rickettsii
  b. Borellia burgdorferi
  c. Babesia microti
  d. Ehrlichia chaffeensis
  e. Treponema pallidum

39. A 32-year-old male presents with weakness, acne and increasing weight. On physical examination, central obesity, positive supraclavicular fat pads and hypertension is noted. Endocrine tests are performed and shows the following:
  urinary free cortisol: 160 mg/dL (normal 10-100mg/dL)
  2 mg dexamethasone suppression: no suppression of cortisol levels
  8 mg dexamethasone suppression: positive suppression of cortisol levels
  Which of the following is the recommended management of this patient?
  a. transsphenoidal resection of the pituitary adenoma
  b. resection of the small cell lung cancer
  c. fludrocortisone replacement therapy
  d. prompt discontinuation of corticosteroid therapy
  e. surgical resection of the adrenal tumor

40. A 6-month-old male is brought into the pediatric emergency room. He was born full term via normal vaginal delivery. The first 6 months were uneventful but his mother brought him to the emergency room when she noticed he was "pale and yellow". A complete blood cell count is notable for severe anemia and hypochromic microcytosis. A peripheral smear shows numerous target cells and teardrop cells (dacrocytes). A hemoglobin electrophoresis is performed and shows the following:
  Hemoglobin A: decreased
  Hemoglobin A$_2$: increased
  Hemoglobin F: increased (90%)
  Which of the following is the most likely diagnosis?
  a. alpha thalassemia major
  b. beta thalassemia minor
  c. sickle cell trait
  d. beta thalassemia major
  e. sickle cell anemia

41. A 32-year-old female presents with weakness, fatigue and right eye pain with right-side color vision loss. On physical examination, there is muscle spasticity, an upward Babinski reflex and a positive Lhermitte's sign. Which of the following is the most appropriate management for the patient at this time?
  a. IV high-dose corticosteroids
  b. IV Glatiramer acetate
  c. IV cyclophosphamide
  d. SC beta-interferon
  e. Oral amantadine

42. A 55-year-old male presents with a persistent cough. A CT scan of the chest shows lack of tapering of the bronchi and bronchial wall thickening. Pulmonary function tests show a decreased FEV_1 and a decreased FEV_1/FVC ratio of 65%. Which of the following is the most likely diagnosis?

    a. Coal workers pneumoconiosis
    b. Emphysema
    c. Chronic bronchitis
    d. Idiopathic pulmonary fibrosis
    e. Bronchiectasis

43. A 36-year-old male with recent head trauma develops a stable epidural hematoma. He is placed on phenytoin seizure prophylaxis and is given hypotonic saline infusion.   After the saline infusion, he develops nausea, weakness and headache. A CT scan shows no change in the size of the bleed with no evidence of midline shift. Lab evaluation are as follows:

	PATIENT	NORMAL
Serum Sodium (mEq/L)	125	135 - 145
Serum Osmolarity (mOsm/kg)	268	280 - 290

The serum sodium should be corrected no faster than 0.5 mEq/L per hour to prevent which of the following complications?

    a. seizures
    b. cerebral edema
    c. vision loss
    d. vomiting
    e. central pontine myelinolysis

44. A 19-year old female with a history of systemic lupus erythematosus presents to the emergency room with uterine cramping and vaginal bleeding. On examination, the uterus size is compatible with the date of pregnancy and is nontender. She is afebrile and does not complain of chills. The cervix is dilated at 4 cm with some effacement. She has not passed any products of conception thus far nor is there any vaginal discharge. Which of the following is the most likely diagnosis?

    a. missed abortion
    b. septic abortion
    c. inevitable abortion
    d. incomplete abortion
    e. threatened abortion

45. Which of the following labs is most consistent with subclinical hypothyroidism

    a. normal TSH, decreased free T3, decreased free T4
    b. increased TSH, decreased free T3, decreased free T4
    c. increased TSH, normal free T3, normal free T4
    d. decreased TSH, decreased free T3, decreased free T4
    e. normal TSH, decreased free T3, normal free T4

46. A Positive McMurray's test is indicative of which of the following disorders?

    a. Iliotibial band syndrome
    b. Anterior cruciate ligamental tear
    c. Meniscal tear
    d. Posterior cruciate ligamental tear
    e. Patellar tendon rupture

47. A 63-year-old female presents to the clinic with a gradual onset of left-sided headache located near her temple described as throbbing, occasionally lancinating, unilateral and worse with eating. She has occasional scotomas. She states she does not have any prior history of headaches. On physical examination, there is a tender, throbbing left temporal artery. Which of the following is the first line management?
    a. ergotamine
    b. sumatriptan
    c. high-dose corticosteroids
    d. propranolol
    e. low-dose corticosteroids

48. A 43-year-old male with a history of hyperlipidemia, hypertension and type II diabetes mellitus presents with crushing, substernal chest pain of 45 minutes duration with radiation to the left arm. His prior ECG a month ago showed normal sinus rhythm with no abnormalities. Which of the following new ECG findings are considered an ST-elevation myocardial infarction equivalent?
    a. "m" shaped P waves in lead II, biphasic p wave in lead V1 (terminal component larger than initial).
    b. R waves larger than S waves in V1 with the R waves measuring >7mm
    c. Wide QRS complexes with broad, slurred R waves in V5 and V6 with a deep S waves in V1
    d. Deep S waves in lead I, isolated Q waves in lead III, inverted T waves in lead III
    e. Wide QRS complexes with an RsR' pattern in in leads V1 and V2. Wide S waves in V6

49. A 42-year-old male presents with left knee pain that he describes as being worse in the evening. He states that he occasionally gets the pain in the morning as well but it only lasts for 20 minutes. On palpation of the knee, the joint feels hard and bony with no bogginess, erythema and warmth. There is crepitus with range of motion. The following radiographs are performed on his knee and wrist:

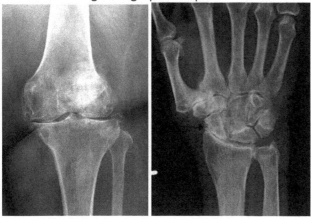

Which of the following is the most likely diagnosis?
    a. rheumatoid arthritis
    b. pseudogout
    c. gouty arthritis
    d. osteoarthritis
    e. reactive arthritis

50. Which of the following is considered a positive purified protein derivative (PPD) test?
    a. HIV positive female with a PPD of 4mm induration and 8mm erythema
    b. Physician assistant with a PPD of 11mm induration and 5mm erythema
    c. 45-year old male with a history of a granuloma on chest radiograph with a PPD of 4mm induration and 10mm erythema
    d. 40-year-old male with no identifiable risk factors with a PPD of 11mm induration and 5mm erythema
    e. 32-year-old prison inmate with a PPD of 8mm induration and 10mm erythema

51. A 23-year-old male presents with left-sided testicular pain and swelling for 2 days. On physical exam, the left testicle elevates when the inside of the thigh is grazed lightly. There is relief of the testicular pain when the testicle is elevated. A urinalysis is performed and is only significant for pyuria. There are visible intracellular organisms on peripheral smear. Which of the following is the management of choice?
    a. fluconazole
    b. ceftriaxone and azithromycin
    c. cephalexin
    d. levofloxacin
    e. clindamycin

52. A 43-year-old female vacationing in Panama suffers a bug bite. 3 weeks later, she develops unilateral periorbital edema on the same side of the bite. 2 months later, she develops dyspnea on exertion. Physical examination is significant for the presence of an S3 gallop. An echocardiogram shows evidence of dilated cardiomyopathy. Which of the following is the most likely etiology?
    a. Trichinosis
    b. Chagas disease
    c. Chikungunya
    d. Epidemic Typhus
    e. African sleeping sickness

53. A 63-year-old Caucasian male comes in for a well visit. The physician assistant notices a lesion on his nose. The lesion is a small, translucent papule with central ulceration, telangiectasias and rolled borders.
Which of the following is the next most appropriate step?
    a. Punch biopsy
    b. Avoid hot and cold weather, hot drinks, hot baths, spicy food and alcohol
    c. Avoid the sun and use sunscreen
    d. Apply acetic acid to look for whitening
    e. Topical corticosteroids

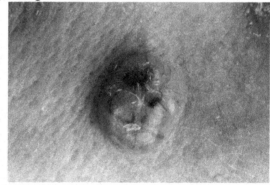

54. Which of the following is not considered part of the routine management of Meniere's disease?
    a. administration of meclizine
    b. administration of hydrochlorothiazide and triamterene
    c. avoidance of salt to reduce endolymphatic pressure
    d. alcohol abstinence
    e. increased usage of caffeine to reduce endolymphatic pressure

55. A 7-year-old male presents with fever, chills, neck stiffness, a purpuric rash and a positive Brudzinski's sign. A cerebrospinal fluid analysis is consistent with bacterial meningitis and gram stain shows gram-negative diplococci. Which of the following is the first line management based on the physical exam and the gram stain?
    a. IV Clindamycin
    b. IV Vancomycin
    c. IV Penicillin G
    d. IV Cephazolin
    e. IV Linezolid

56. In addition to Murphy's sign, which of the following is classically associated with acute cholecystitis?
   a. Kehr's sign
   b. Cullen's sign
   c. Psoas sign
   d. Dance's sign
   e. Boas sign

57. An intravenous drug user presents to the emergency room with persistent fever for the last 48 hours. On physical examination, there is a holosystolic murmur that radiates to the axilla. Echocardiogram shows vegetations on the mitral and tricuspid valves. Preliminary gram stain shows gram-positive cocci in clusters. Which of the following is the recommended management of this patient?
   a. IV ceftriaxone and gentamicin
   b. IV nafcillin and gentamicin
   c. IV vancomycin
   d. IV gentamicin
   e. IV penicillin G and gentamicin

58. A 43-year-old male develops sudden onset of fever, right upper quadrant pain that is persistent and jaundice. Labs are significant for an increased alkaline phosphatase with an increase in gamma glutamyl transpeptidase (GGT). Which of the following is the most likely diagnosis?
   a. acute cholecystitis
   b. choledocholithiasis
   c. acute cholangitis
   d. primary sclerosing cholangitis
   e. carcinoma of the head of the pancreas

59. Which of the following is not a sign of atropine poisoning?
   a. dry mouth
   b. urinary retention
   c. dry skin
   d. tachycardia
   e. miosis

60. Which of the following is not part of the routine management of atopic dermatitis?
   a. topical corticosteroids
   b. immediately drying the skin after showering to reduce irritation and keeping the skin dry
   c. the use of unscented hypoallergenic lotions
   d. topical antibiotics for secondary bacterial infections
   e. antihistamines for the itching

61. An 11-year-old boy who was recently diagnosed with Influenza A presents with recurrent epistaxis and petechiae. There is also recurrent bleeding of the gums. On physical examination, there is no evidence of splenomegaly. The patient is hemodynamically stable and there is no active bleeding seen. Labs show an isolated thrombocytopenia of 90,000 (Normal 150,100 – 450,000/mcL). Which of the following is the recommended management if clinical intervention is needed?
   a. plasmapheresis
   b. splenectomy
   c. intravenous immunoglobulin
   d. platelet transfusion
   e. fresh frozen plasma

62. A 3-day-old infant with Down syndrome fails to pass meconium. An abdominal radiograph shows dilated bowel loops with absent air in the rectum. Which of the following is the most likely diagnosis?
   a. Pyloric stenosis
   b. Meckel's diverticulum
   c. Intussusception
   d. Hirschsprung's disease
   e. Volvulus

63. A 37-year-old female undergoes an upper endoscopy for epigastric pain. A direct urease test was performed on the specimen and a direct urease test was positive. Which of the following is the management of choice in this patient?
   a. Lansoprazole 30mg + amoxicillin 500mg + clarithromycin 500mg
   b. Lansoprazole 30mg
   c. Lansoprazole 30mg + metronidazole 500mg + clarithromycin 500mg
   d. Lansoprazole 30mg + ranitidine 300mg
   e. Misoprostol 200mcg

64. A 40-year-old female presents with bilateral anterior shin redness that is tender to palpation. She is also complaining of eye pain and redness as well as the insidious onset of a nonproductive cough. A chest radiograph is performed, showing bilateral hilar lymphadenopathy. You notice a rash on her face consistent with lupus pernio. Which of the following describes the basic pathophysiology of the suspected diagnosis?
   a. the production of caseating granulomas with central necrosis of the granulomas
   b. small vessel vasculitis associated with granulomatous inflammation and necrosis
   c. idiopathic, exaggerated T cell response with the formation of noncaseating granulomas
   d. the presence of antibodies against Type IV collagen in the alveoli
   e. inflammatory reaction to an organic antigen

65. Which of the following is the most common reason hysterectomies are performed in the United States?
   a. ovarian cancer
   b. uterine cancer
   c. leiomyomas
   d. adenomyosis
   e. ectopic pregnancy

66. A 48-year-old female comes to the clinic for chronic headaches over the past year. She was particularly concerned because over the last two months, she has been experiencing some visual changes. She also complains of weight loss over the last 6 months and heat intolerance. Physical examination is positive for decreased vision in the outer half of both the right and left visual fields. Initial lab tests reveal the following lab values:

	PATIENT	NORMAL VALUES
TSH (mU/L)	6.9	0.9 - 5.0
Free T4 (nmol/L)	50	9-23
Free T3 (nmol/L)	4.8	0.8-2.4

Which of the following would is the best diagnostic study to confirm the suspected diagnosis?
   a. head CT without contrast
   b. head CT with contrast
   c. MRI of the sella turcica (pituitary gland)
   d. Skull X ray
   e. CT scan of the soft tissues of the neck

67. A 43-year-old male presents to the emergency room with a fever and joint pains. The patient was recently treated for a dental infection with oral penicillin VK. On physical examination, he is febrile and has a generalized maculopapular rash without a target lesion appearance. Physical examination is otherwise unremarkable. Labs show an increased BUN and creatinine with an elevated white blood cell count and eosinophilia. A urinalysis is performed and shows 2 RBC/high power field and the presence of many white blood cell casts. Which of the following is the most likely diagnosis?
   a. erythema multiforme minor
   b. erythema multiforme major
   c. acute tubular necrosis
   d. acute tubulointerstitial nephritis
   e. acute glomerulonephritis

68. A 32-year-old male presents with a 1-day history of eyelid pain. He denies any visual changes or ocular discharge. On physical examination, there is a painful, warm, swollen red lump at the margin of the eyelid without fluctuance. Slit lamp examination is unremarkable. Which of the following would be the next step in the management of this patient at this time?
   a. intravenous ampicillin/sulbactam
   b. bacitracin ophthalmic ointment
   c. warm compresses
   d. incision and drainage
   e. Trifluridine ophthalmic

69. A 25-year-old female presents with acute onset of nystagmus and double vision in the right eye. On physical examination, there is also delay of abduction of the affected eye. Both pupils constrict when a penlight is shone in the left eye but both dilate when the light is shone into the right eye. An MRI with gadolinium shows multiple white matter hyperdensities and plaques. Which of the following has been shown to decrease the progression of the relapsing-remitting form of this disease?
   a. glatiramer acetate
   b. methylprednisolone
   c. amantadine
   d. cyclophosphamide
   e. carbamazepine

70. A 6-year-old male presents with right knee pain and is unable to flex or extend the knee. Septic arthritis is suspected. Which of the following is the most likely gram stain finding?
   a. gram positive cocci in pairs and chains
   b. gram positive cocci in clusters
   c. gram negative rods
   d. acid fast bacilli
   e. gram negative diplococci

71. A 50-year-old male smoker presents to the clinic with painless gross hematuria that he says occurs from the start of urination through until the end of urination. He states he has no history of recent trauma. On physical examination, the prostate is firm and mobile with no nodules or tenderness. A urinalysis is performed, showing >10 red blood cells per high power field but otherwise unremarkable. Which of the following is the most appropriate next step in the evaluation of this patient?
   a. CT scan of abdomen and pelvis without contrast
   b. CT scan of the abdomen and pelvis with contrast and cystoscopy
   c. Fasting plasma glucose
   d. Observation and nephrologist follow up if hematuria persists
   e. Kidney biopsy

72. A patient with no noted risk factors for deep venous thrombosis develops unilateral right leg swelling. A venous Doppler is performed, showing non-compressibility of the superficial femoral vein. Which of the following is considered the management of choice for the first episode of idiopathic deep venous thrombosis?

    a. warm compresses and non steroidal anti-inflammatories
    b. initiation of heparin with warfarin. Warfarin therapy continued for less than 3 months.
    c. initiation of heparin with warfarin. Warfarin therapy continued for 3 to 6 months.
    d. initiation of heparin with warfarin. Warfarin therapy continued for 6 to 12 months
    e. initiation of heparin with warfarin. Warfarin therapy continued for greater than 12 months

73. A patient with a history of Type I bipolar disorder comes in for routine evaluation. The patient states he has been having some bone pain. Routine labs are as follows:

		PATIENT	NORMAL VALUES
TSH	(mU/L)	6.9	0.9 - 5.0
Free T4	(nmol/L)	6	9-23
Free T3	(nmol/L)	0.3	0.8-2.4
Calcium	(mg/dL)	12	8.5 – 10
Phosphate	(mg/dL)	2.0	2.5 – 4.5
iPTH	(mg/dL)	65	15 – 50

Which of the following medications is most likely responsible for these lab findings?

    a. Aripiprazole (Abilify)
    b. Quetiapine (Seroquel)
    c. Lithium (Lithobid)
    d. Haloperidol (Haldol)
    e. Clozapine (Clozaril)

74. Which of the following is classically associated with a negative Nikolsky sign?

    a. Toxic epidermal necrolysis
    b. Scalded skin syndrome
    c. Pemphigus vulgaris
    d. Steven Johnson syndrome
    e. Bullous pemphigoid

75. A 54-year-old male presents to the clinic with a 3-day history of redness to the face. He states he has been having four days of fever and chills. On physical examination, there is an erythematous, tender, sharply demarcated lesion on the right cheek and the nose with raised edges. There is no streaking, papules or pustules. There is no redness to the eye or ocular pain.

Which of the following is the most likely diagnosis?

    a. acne rosacea
    b. lymphangitis
    c. erysipelas
    d. intertrigo
    e. Chagas disease

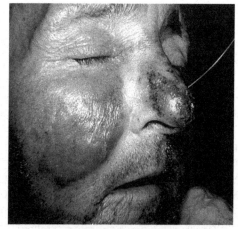

76. A 43-year-old male presents to the emergency room after being involved in a motor vehicle accident with neck pain after hyperflexion. On physical examination, he has bilateral upper and lower extremity weakness, but it is much more pronounced in the upper extremities with sensory loss of pain and temperature in a "shawl-like distribution over the extremities and the upper shoulders. There is preservation of position, light touch and proprioception. Which of the following is the most likely diagnosis?
   a. anterior cerebral artery infarction syndrome
   b. anterior cord syndrome
   c. central cord syndrome
   d. posterior cord syndrome
   e. Brown Sequard syndrome

77. A patient with longstanding bipolar disorder develops myocarditis. Which of the following medications is the most likely pharmacologic agent associated with myocarditis?
   a. Haloperidol
   b. Clozapine
   c. Buspirone
   d. Fluoxetine
   e. Amitriptyline

78. A 9-year-old male has had abdominal pain for 9 months, difficulty concentrating in school, intermittent headaches and weakness. A CBC shows anemia and microcytosis with basophilic stippling seen on peripheral smear. A radiograph of his knee is obtained:

Which of the following of the following tests should be ordered based on his symptoms?

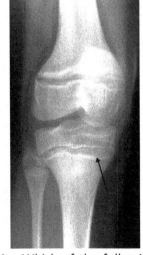

   a. serum iron
   b. serum B12
   c. serum lead
   d. serum folate
   e. serum ceruloplasmin

79. A 10-year-old girl is bitten by her neighbor's cat while trying to feed it. Which of the following is the most common organism associated with cat bites?
   a. Pasteurella multocida
   b. Bartonella henselae
   c. Brucella melitensis
   d. Coxiella burnetii
   e. Erysipelothrix rhusiopathiae

80. Which of the following is most commonly used in the diagnosis of suspected human papilloma virus infection?
   a. potassium hydroxide
   b. acetic acid
   c. India ink
   d. cold agglutinin test
   e. enzyme-linked immunosorbent assay test (ELISA)

81. A 6-month-old boy is brought into the office because his mother noticed he began wheezing and flaring his nose while breathing. Upon obtaining a history, his mother states he has never been diagnosed with asthma or reactive airway disease. She states he had runny nose, sneezing and cough 2 days prior to the worsening of the symptoms. On physical examination, you notice retractions. His oxygen saturation on pulse oximetry is 98% on room air. Acute bronchiolitis is suspected. Which of the following is the management of choice?
    a. observation
    b. supportive management include humidified oxygen
    c. intubation with mechanical ventilation
    d. corticosteroids
    e. palivizumab

82. A 45-year-old male presents to the emergency room with fever, nausea, vomiting and left lower quadrant pain. Which of the following is the most likely CT scan finding?
    a. inflammation of the appendix
    b. inflammation of a diverticulum
    c. inflammation of the gall bladder
    d. inflammation of the ileum
    e. irritable bowel syndrome

83. A 28-year-old male with a history of multiple endocrine neoplasia type IIA develops refractory hypertension. A CT scan of the abdomen shows the presence of pheochromocytoma. Which of the following medications is considered the first line management prior to surgical removal of the tumor?
    a. metoprolol
    b. atenolol
    c. hydrochlorothiazide
    d. phenoxybenzamine
    e. midodrine

84. Which of the following is not a classic manifestation of opioid withdrawal?
    a. piloerections
    b. small, pinpoint pupils
    c. rhinorrhea
    d. increased lacrimation
    e. tachycardia

85. A 34-year-old female with a history of sarcoidosis gets a tattoo with black and red dye. 4 days later, she develops painful, erythematous plaques on the anterior shins bilaterally. Which of the following is the most likely diagnosis?
    a. erythema migrans
    b. erythema marginatum
    c. erythema infectiosum
    d. erythema nodosum
    e. erythema multiforme

86. Which of the following is most consistent with malignant hypertension (grade IV hypertensive retinopathy)?
    a. venous compression at the artery-venous junction
    b. yellow spots with sharp margins that are circinate
    c. fluffy gray-white spots on the retina
    d. a detached retina
    e. blurring of the optic disc and cup

87. A patient is being evaluated for primary amenorrhea. On physical exam, she has a short stature, webbed neck, prominent ears, a broad chest with hypoplastic, widely-spaced nipples. Which of the following is the most likely diagnosis?
    a. Turner's syndrome
    b. Klinefelter's syndrome
    c. Down syndrome
    d. Fragile X syndrome
    e. Hypopituitarism

88. A 23-year-old female comes into the clinic because she has been having scanty periods with intermittent cessation of menstruation. On physical examination, she has coarse hair growth on her face, neck, abdomen and acanthosis nigricans. On pelvic examination, the ovaries are enlarged bilaterally but are smooth and mobile. Laboratory evaluation shows an LH: FSH ratio of 3:1 (normal FSH ratio 1.5:1). Which of the following is considered to be the first line management of this patient's condition?
    a. metformin
    b. danazol
    c. spironolactone
    d. estrogen + progesterone oral pills
    e. estradiol pills

89. Which of the following most reliably seen in peripheral venous disease?
    a. redness with dependency of the leg
    b. leg pain worse with ambulation
    c. thin, shiny skin with loss of hair on the foot
    d. cool extremities
    e. the presence of a medial malleolus ulcer with uneven ulcer margins

90. Which of the following is the most common cause of a transudative pleural effusion?
    a. nephrotic syndrome
    b. pulmonary embolus
    c. pneumonia
    d. cirrhosis
    e. congestive heart failure

91. A 34-year-old patient with a history of epilepsy is placed on anticonvulsant medication. He returns for a follow up visit and is noticed to have developed gingival hyperplasia. Which of the following medications is the most likely cause?
    a. lamotrigine
    b. valproic acid
    c. phenobarbital
    d. phenytoin
    e. ethosuximide

92. Which of the following dermatologic findings is pathognomic of dermatomyositis?
    a. the presence of Gottron's papules
    b. the presence of Lupus pernio
    c. the presence of erythema nodosum
    d. the presence of a malar rash that spares the nasolabial folds
    e. the presence of bullae and the sloughing off of the epidermis with gentle pressure

93. Which of the following medications are indicated in the management of nephrogenic diabetes insipidus?
    a. indomethacin
    b. amphotericin B
    c. desmopressin
    d. demeclocycline
    e. carbamazepine

94. Which of the following best describes the pathophysiology of thrombotic thrombocytopenic purpura?
    a. Autoantibodies against the glycoprotein IIb/IIIa receptor on platelets most commonly following a viral infection.
    b. Mutated Factor V that is resistant to breakdown by activated Protein C.
    c. Pathologic activation of the coagulation causing microthrombi and subsequent thrombocytopenia.
    d. Platelet activation by exotoxins (such as Shigella toxin or Shiga-like toxin released from Enterohemorrhagic Escherichia coli).
    e. Antibodies against ADAMTS 13 leading to large von Willebrand multimers, causing platelet activation.

95. A 15-year-old male with a history of sickle cell disease develops weakness, pallor and petechiae. Lab work shows a severe anemia, a decreased peripheral reticulocyte count and leukopenia. A bone marrow biopsy is done, showing hypocellularity with increased adipose tissue and decreased hematopoietic cells in the marrow space. Which of the following is the most likely preceding cause?
    a. Respiratory syncytial virus
    b. Parvovirus B-19
    c. Adenovirus
    d. Group A beta hemolytic streptococcus
    e. Staphylococcus aureus

96. A 32-year-old male returns from the Dominican Republic and develops cyclical fever every 72 hours, leukopenia and thrombocytopenia. A thin and thick peripheral smear shows intracellular parasites in the red blood cells consistent with plasmodium falciparum. Which of the following is the recommended first-line agent?
    a. Doxycycline
    b. Chloroquine
    c. Atovaquone
    d. Clindamycin
    e. Azithromycin

97. Which of the following radiographic findings is most specifically seen with asbestosis?
    a. Westermark's sign
    b. Pleural thickening
    c. Mediastinal widening
    d. Tram track appearance of the bronchi
    e. Bilateral hilar lymphadenopathy

98. Which of the following is not a classic finding in Bell's palsy?
    a. the ability to raise/wrinkle the forehead/eyebrow on the affected side
    b. loss of the nasolabial fold on the affected side
    c. hyperacusis and ear pain on the affected side
    d. the absence of upper and lower extremity involvement
    e. the loss of anterior 2/3 of sensation of the tongue on the affected side

99. Which of the following is not classically associated with pure prerenal azotemia?
   a.   increased specific gravity of the urine
   b.   fractional excretion of sodium >2%
   c.   the presence of Tamm-Horsfall proteins on urinalysis
   d.   blood urea nitrogen/creatinine ratio >20:1
   e.   decreased skin turgor

100.   A 45-year-old male with a history of type II diabetes mellitus presents with sudden onset of chest pain while shoveling snow. The following ECG is obtained

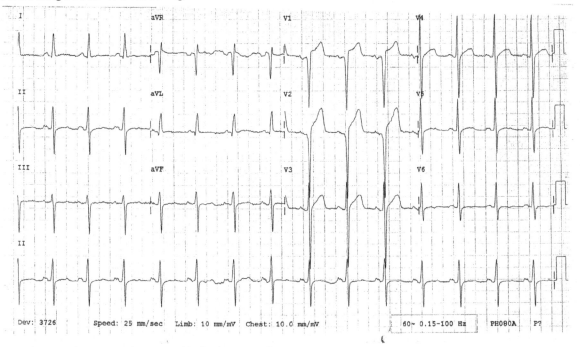

Which of the following is the most likely diagnosis?
   a.   lateral wall myocardial infarction
   b.   posterior wall myocardial infarction
   c.   Non ST elevation myocardial infarction
   d.   Inferior wall myocardial infarction
   e.   Anterior wall myocardial infarction

QUESTION 1

Choice B (widening of the mediastinum) is correct.   This is the classic description of aortic dissection in which a patient develops ripping chest pain due to a tear in the intima (innermost layer of the aortic wall). *A widened mediastinum may also be seen with pulmonary anthrax.* AORTIC DISSECTION – MOST LIKELY (page 56)

Choice A (cardiomegaly) is classically seen with systolic dysfunction (heart failure), dilated cardiomyopathy and with large pericardial effusions.

Choice C *(rib notching and a "3-sign") are signs of narrowing (coarctation) of the aorta.* Whenever there is significant variation of pulses between the left and the right, aortic dissection or Takayasu arteritis should be suspected. With coarctation of the aorta, there is usually the presence of a systolic murmur that radiates to the back. Coarctation usually present with signs of heart failure instead of acute chest pain.

Choice D and E (Kerley B lines and batwing appearance of the hilum) are associated with congestive heart failure. Pulmonary crackles (rales) would be most likely present in these patients and shortness of breath instead of knife-like pain is usually reported in congestive heart failure.

QUESTION 2

Choice D (premenstrual dysphoric disorder) is the correct answer. Premenstrual dysphoric disorder is a severe form of premenstrual syndrome (PMS) that is severe and disabling with extreme mood shifts that can cause severe functional impairment. PREMENSTRUAL DYSPHORIC DISORDER – MOST LIKELY (page 246)

Choice A (mittelschmerz), otherwise known as "ovulation pain" is lower abdominal or pelvic pain that occurs during ovulation (mid cycle). Mittelschmerz does not occur right before menstruation.

Choice B (premenstrual syndrome) is described as a *cluster of physical, behavioral or mood changes that occur during the luteal phase of the menstrual cycle* (7-14 days before the onset of menses and relieved 2-3 days after the onset of menses). It may cause discomfort but is not associated with functional impairment. If there is functional impairment (as seen in this vignette), it is termed premenstrual dysphoric disorder.

Choice C (major depressive disorder) is characterized by a *depressed mood and anhedonia with at least 5 associated symptoms almost every day for most of the days for at least 2 weeks.* It is not related to menstruation.

Choice E (somatization disorder) is a chronic condition in which the patient has physical symptoms *involving more than 1 body part but the symptoms are not associated with a physical cause.*

QUESTION 3

Choice B (bitemporal heteronymous hemianopsia) is correct. Cushing's disease (ACTH-producing pituitary adenoma) is the most common cause of endogenous Cushing's syndrome (signs and symptoms due to cortisol excess). Pituitary adenomas may be asymptomatic, nonfunctional, functional (producing hormones) or compressive (compressing local structures). Because of its close proximity to the optic chiasm, a pituitary adenoma can cause bitemporal heteronymous hemianopsia.
BITEMPORAL HEMIANOPSIA – HISTORY AND PHYSICAL EXAM (page 223 and 298)

Choice A (contralateral homonymous hemianopsia) may be seen if the lesion was at the optic tract or occipital lobe.

Choice C (nasal hemianopsia) may be seen if the lesion was lateral to the optic chiasm.

Choice D (decreased vision in the one eye) may be seen if the lesion was at the optic nerve or the retina (ex. Central artery or vein occlusion).

Choice E (quadrantopia) would be seen if the lesion was located at Meyer's Loop.

QUESTION 4

Choice D (residual volume) is the correct answer. Obstructive diseases (such as COPD & bronchiectasis) are associated with *increased lung volumes (including residual volume)* due air trapping (obstruction). All the others are decreased in emphysema. PULMONARY – EMPHYSEMA – LABS/DIAGNOSTIC STUDIES (page 80)

Choice A (diffusing lung capacity for carbon monoxide) is decreased. Any disease that decreases the alveolar total surface area will decrease the diffusing lung capacity for carbon monoxide (DLCO). Alveolar destruction in emphysema leads to a decreased DLCO.

Choice B (FVC) will be decreased. Forced vital capacity (FVC) represents the amount of air that can be forcibly exhaled from the lungs after taking the deepest breath possible. Because emphysema is an obstructive disorder (air cannot get out), there will be less air that can be forcibly exhaled from the lungs.

Choice C (FEV1) is decreased. Because emphysema is an obstructive disorder (air cannot get out), there will be less air that can be forcibly exhaled in 1 second. In obstructive disorders the FEV1 is decreased and the FEV1/FVC ratio is also decreased.

Choice E (alpha-1 antitrypsin) is also decreased. Alpha-1 antitrypsin is a protein in the lungs that prevents macrophage enzymes (such as elastase) from destroying the elastic tissue of the lung. Smoking increases alveolar white blood cells (inflammatory response to the particles in cigarettes) as well as causes a relative alpha-1 antitrypsin deficiency, leading to decreased elasticity (and increased compliance – meaning it is easier to expand the lung than it is for the lung to recoil back to its original shape). This leads to an increased residual volume.

QUESTION 5
Choice B (isoniazid) is the correct answer. *Isoniazid is associated with hepatitis* (especially in patients older than 35 years of age), and *peripheral neuropathy* (prevented with the coadministration of vitamin B6/pyridoxine). Patients may have interactions with tyramine-containing foods.
PULMONARY -TUBERCULOSIS – PHARMACOLOGY (page 108)

Choice A (rifampin) is associated with thrombocytopenia, orange colored secretions, hepatitis, fever, gastrointestinal upset and hypersensitivity reactions.

Choice C (pyrazinamide) is associated with hepatitis, hyperuricemia, gastrointestinal symptoms, arthritis, and a photosensitive dermatologic rash.

Choice D (ethambutol) is associated with optic neuritis, peripheral neuropathy and gastrointestinal symptoms.

Choice E (streptomycin) is an aminoglycoside. *Aminoglycosides are associated with nephrotoxicity and ototoxicity.*

QUESTION 6
Choice A (pericardial knock) is correct. This is a classical description of *constrictive pericarditis.* In constrictive pericarditis, the stiff, inelastic pericardium causes *diastolic dysfunction* by inhibiting the filling of the ventricles during diastole. The *pericardial knock* is due to sudden cessation of ventricular filling by the *stiff pericardium.*
CARDIOLOGY – CONSTRICTIVE PERICARDITIS – HISTORY AND PHYSICAL EXAMINATION (page 32)

Choice B (bilateral atrial enlargement) and choice C (speckled myocardium) are seen in restrictive cardiomyopathy. *Both constrictive pericarditis and restrictive cardiomyopathy are associated with diastolic dysfunction & impaired diastolic ventricular filling.* However, restrictive cardiomyopathy is associated with myocardial dysfunction, not a thickened or calcified pericardium. *A speckled myocardium is classically seen with amyloidosis* (the most common cause of restrictive cardiomyopathy).

Choice D (vegetation on the mitral valve) is classically associated with infective endocarditis

Choice E (diastolic collapse of the ventricles) is classic for pericardial tamponade. In tamponade, Kussmaul's sign (increased JVP with inspiration) may also be seen. *Cardiac tamponade is associated with Beck's triad* (muffled heart sounds due to the pericardial effusion), systemic hypotension (due to decreased forward flow) and increased jugular venous pressure (from increased backflow of blood). Tamponade by itself is not associated with thickening of the pericardium.

QUESTION 7

Choice D (Supracondylar fracture) is correct. The most common mechanism for supracondylar fractures is falling on an outstretched hand, especially in children 5-10 years old. The *"fat-pad sign"* is seen on X ray here. An **abnormal anterior or any posterior fat pad sign** (which represents hemarthrosis/bleeding into the joint) in children is most commonly associated with supracondylar fractures. *If an abnormal anterior (sail sign) or posterior fat pad is seen in ADULTS, then choice B (radial head fracture) would be the most likely answer.* The *most common complication of supracondylar fractures in children is median nerve or brachial artery injury (Volkmann's ischemic contracture).* Radial nerve injuries are also very common. The child is unable to abduct and oppose the left thumb, which indicates a motor deficit of the median nerve distribution. MUSCULOSKELETAL – SUPRACONDYLAR FRACTURES – MOST LIKELY (page 168).

Choice A (nursemaid elbow) is a subluxation and trapping of the annular ligament. The most common mechanism is lifting, pulling or swinging a child. The child usually presents with their arm slightly flexed and often will refuse to use the arm (or use it very minimally). There is usually NO swelling (as seen in this vignette). The radiographs of the elbow would be unremarkable, as it is due to the trapping of the annular ligament (soft tissue).

Choice C (posterior elbow dislocation) would be evident on radiographs and would show a noticeable deformity such as posterior displacement of the olecranon.

Choice E (lateral epicondylitis) is inflammation of the tendon insertion of the extensor carpi radialis brevis and is due to repetitive wrist extension (not trauma). This condition would be exceedingly rare in this age group. Radiographs are negative in lateral epicondylitis.

QUESTION 8

Choice C (Thymoma) is the correct answer. The *ocular weakness and generalized weakness that is worse with repeated use of the muscle is hallmark for myasthenia gravis.* Myasthenia gravis is an autoimmune disorder of the peripheral nerves due to *auto-antibodies against the POST-synaptic acetylcholine receptor*, causing progressive weakness that is worse with repeated muscle use. *Up to 75% of patients with myasthenia gravis have a thymus gland abnormality (such as a thymoma or hyperplasia).* In the neurologic exam, the reflexes are usually normal with Myasthenia gravis. NEUROLOGY – MYASTHENIA GRAVIS – BASICS (page 355).

Choice A (Non Hodgkin lymphoma) and Choice B (Hodgkin Lymphoma) are not associated with myasthenia gravis.

Choice D (Small cell lung cancer) frequently presents with paraneoplastic syndromes, one of them being Lambert-Eaton Myasthenic syndrome. This disorder is a malignancy-induced production of autoantibodies that prevent the PRE-synaptic release of acetylcholine. Lambert-Eaton Myasthenic syndrome is associated with weakness similar to Myasthenia gravis, however, patients with *Lambert-Eaton myasthenic syndrome have weakness that IMPROVES with repeated use* and may often have abnormal deep tendon reflexes.

Choice E (Non small cell lung cancer) may cause hypercalcemia and Pancoast syndrome but it is not commonly associated with myasthenia gravis. Pancoast syndrome affects the sympathetic chain, causing miosis on the side of the tumor. This patient has equal pupils bilaterally and no arm atrophy, making Pancoast less likely.

QUESTION 9

Choice C (Nummular eczema) is the correct answer. *Nummular eczema* is a type of eczema described as *sharply defined, coin-shaped, pruritic lesions* that are most commonly seen on the dorsum of the hands, feet and extensor surfaces (such as the knees and elbows). Patients with eczema often have other atopic diseases. *The presence of eczema, asthma and aspirin allergy is known as the atopic triad.*
DERMATOLOGY – ECZEMA – HISTORY AND PHYSICAL EXAMINATION (page 390).

Choice A (erythema migrans) is a rash that appears most commonly 1-2 weeks after an Ixodes tick bite. It is an *expanding, annular rash* that grows over days to weeks with central clearing, giving it the classic *"bull's-eye"* or target appearance. *Erythema migrans is associated with Lyme disease.*

Choice B (erythema nodosum) are *painful, erythematous, inflammatory nodules* seen especially on the *anterior shins.* It may also be associated with estrogen exposure (ex pregnancy), sarcoidosis, tuberculosis, and fungal infections (ex Coccidiomycosis) as well as inflammatory disorders.

Choice D (lichen planus) is an idiopathic cell-mediated dermatologic rash classically associated with the 5Ps: the rash is usually *purple in color, polygonal (irregularly shaped), planar (plaques), pruritic & papular with fine scales.* Patients often have nail dystrophy.   Oral involvement may include *Wickham striae* (lesions with lacy white/gray striae). There is an increased incidence of lichen planus in patients with chronic Hepatitis B and C infection.

Choice E (intertrigo) is a dermatologic manifestation in patients with candida infections. The rash is classically described as a *beefy-red rash with scalloped borders*, most often seen in *moist, dark areas (such as the axilla, the groin and under pendulous breasts).*

QUESTION 10

Choice A (Folate deficiency anemia) is the correct answer.   Folate deficiency causes a macrocytic anemia (MCV >100). On peripheral smear, hypersegmented neutrophils can be seen. Other causes of macrocytic anemia include B_{12} deficiency (which is associated with neurologic changes), alcoholism, liver disease & hypothyroidism.
HEMATOLOGY - FOLATE DEFICIENCY ANEMIA – LABS/DIAGNOSTIC STUDIES (page 453).

Choice B (Iron deficiency anemia) is associated with a microcytic anemia. Early iron deficiency anemia may be associated with a normocytic anemia.

Choice C (Alpha thalassemia), Choice D (Lead poisoning) and Choice E (Beta thalassemia) all will cause a microcytic anemia.

QUESTION 11

Choice D (fluconazole) is the correct answer.   Candida esophagitis presents classically with dysphagia, odynophagia. On Upper endoscopy, *linear lesions are hallmark of candida esophagitis.* Candida appears as *budding yeast with hyphae on potassium hydroxide smear.* Fluconazole is the first line management of esophagitis.
GASTROINTESTINAL/INFECTIOUS DISEASE - CANDIDA ESOPHAGITIS – CLINICAL INTERVENTION (page 127 and 416).

Choice A (Griseofulvin) is used for tinea fungal infections.

Choice B (Caspofungin) is used in severe, life threatening infections or in patients with Candidal infections resistant to amphotericin B and azole fungal drugs. The blood cultures in this vignette are negative, indicating there is no evidence of fungemia.

Choice C (*nystatin*) *is used as the first line management for topical treatment of candida infections* (such as vaginitis or oral candidiasis/thrush). It is not used in the management of esophagitis.

Choice E (amphotericin B) is used if the patient is not responsive to fluconazole or in cases of fungemia. Fluconazole can still be used in mild cases of fungemia.

QUESTION 12

Choice C (metformin) is the correct answer. Adverse effects of metformin therapy include macrocytic anemia, lactic acidosis (especially in patients with renal impairment), renal impairment, gastrointestinal complaints, and metallic taste. Contrast dye (given to this patient) can increase the risk for kidney damage and so, metformin is usually discontinued 48 hours before and after IV contrast is given. METFORMIN – PHARMACOLOGY (page 305).

Choice A (meglitinide) is associated with hypoglycemia.

Choice B (acarbose) is associated with the following adverse effects: hepatitis, and gastrointestinal symptoms.

Choice D (canagliflozin) is associated with thirst, abdominal pain and urinary tract infections.

Choice E (glyburide) is associated with hypoglycemia, gastrointestinal upset, disulfiram reactions, weight gain and cardiac dysrhythmias.

QUESTION 13

Choice A (prednisone) is the correct answer. The signs of *edema, proteinuria, and hyperlipidemia are hallmark of nephrotic syndrome. Minimal change disease causes 80% of nephrotic syndrome in children. Prednisone is the management of choice.* >80% of children with nephrotic syndrome will have remission with corticosteroid therapy after 3 months. GENITOURINARY – NEPHROTIC SYNDROME – CLINICAL INTERVENTION (page 317).

Choice B (cyclophosphamide) may be used in cases of resistant nephrotic syndrome or in children who fail prednisone therapy but is not first line for nephrotic syndrome.

Choice C (simvastatin) may be used to treat hyperlipidemia of nephrotic syndrome in certain populations but is not first line as it does not treat the underlying condition.

Choice D (amoxicillin) is not indicated in the management. The patient had a recent viral infection, so antibiotics are not useful in this patient.

Choice E (intravenous immunoglobulin) is not indicated in this vignette.

QUESTION 14

Choice D (tricyclic antidepressant overdose) is the correct answer. Signs and symptoms of *TCA overdose include strong anticholinergic side effects,* evident here by dry skin, dry mouth, pupillary dilation and decreased breath sounds (remember cholinergic activation of SLUDD-C which causes salivation, lacrimation, urination, digestion, defecation and pupillary constriction so anticholinergic effects would be the opposite of those). Due the *sodium channel blocking effect of TCA, cardiac toxicity and ventricular arrhythmias may occur.*
PSYCH/BEHAVIORAL – TRICYCLIC OVERDOSE – PHARMACOLOGY (page 377)

Choice A (cannabis overdose) may cause *dry mouth, conjunctival erythema,* narrow-complex tachycardia and hypotension. The strong anticholinergic and sodium blocking effects in this vignette is not classically associated with cannabis toxicity.

Choice B (oxycodone) and choice E (methadone) are narcotics. *Opioids and other narcotics often present with pupillary constriction (narcotics are miotics), respiratory depression, bradycardia, hypotension, coma, nausea and vomiting.* Choice C (ethanol intoxication) usually presents with lethargy, prolonged reaction time, muscular incoordination and facial flushing.

QUESTION 15

Choice D (Achalasia) is correct. Achalasia is a disorder that causes loss of Auerbach's plexus at the lower esophageal sphincter. Auerbach's plexus secretes nitric oxide (which leads to relaxation of the LES). Without Auerbach's plexus, there is increased LES pressure, leading to dysphagia. On a Barium swallow (esophagram), the increased LES tone leads to narrowing of the GE junction and pre narrowing dilation, leading to the classic ***"bird's beak"*** appearance. GI/NUTRITION – ACHALASIA – MOST LIKELY (page 129).

Choice A (Zenker's diverticulum) is an out pouching of the pharyngoesophageal pouch, which doesn't affect the lower esophageal sphincter. On esophagram, the contrast will collect in the diverticulum.

Choice B (Esophageal Cancer) would show a filling defect around the malignancy.

Choice C (Nutcracker) is associated with a normal esophagram.

Choice E (Diffuse esophageal spasm) would show a "corkscrew" appearance on esophagram due to strong, non-peristaltic contractions of the esophagus.

QUESTION 16

Choice A (procainamide) is the correct answer. Procainamide is a class I antiarrhythmic that has been shown to prolong repolarization and the refractory period. Class I antiarrhythmics block sodium channels. CARDIOLOGY – ANTIARRHYTHMICS – PHARMACOLOGY (page 480).

Choice B (metoprolol) is a beta blocker. Beta blockers are class II antiarrhythmics.

Choice C (amiodarone) is a class III anti-arrhythmic but it has properties of class I through class IV.

Choice D (verapamil) is a calcium channel blocker. Calcium channel blockers are class IV antiarrhythmics.

Choice E (digoxin) is a cardiac glycoside that is a negative chronotrope, dromotrope and inotrope.

QUESTION 17

Choice D (IV atropine) is correct. IV atropine is the first line treatment for symptomatic bradycardia. Most bradyarrhythmias are thought to arise from vagal hyperstimulation. Atropine is an anticholinergic drug that blocks the effects of acetylcholine released by the vagus nerve. It is the first line agent in most cases (except in patients with third degree AV block). CARDIOLOGY – BRADYCARDIA – PHARMACOLOGY (page 10).

Choice A (observation) is indicated for *asymptomatic* bradycardia

Choice B is the definitive management of persistent bradycardia. This may be used also in patients with third degree heart block.

Choice C (epinephrine) is the second line treatment for bradycardia. It increases the heart rate by directly stimulating the B_1 adrenergic receptor.

Choice E (amiodarone) is used for tachyarrhythmia not bradyarrhythmias.

QUESTION 18

Choice D (hypomagnesemia) is the correct answer. The symptoms described here are classically seen with hypocalcemia. Because magnesium is needed to make parathyroid hormone, *hypomagnesemia is often associated with hypocalcemia.* Hypocalcemia lowers the action potential threshold, leading to lower than normal stimulus causing contraction. *Chvostek's sign* (facial spasms with tapping of the facial nerve), perioral paresthesias, and *Trousseau's sign* (carpal spasms when a blood pressure cuff is inflated) are all manifestations of this lowered action potential threshold associated with *hypomagnesemia and hypocalcemia.*
RENAL/GU - HYPOMAGNESEMIA - HISTORY AND PHYSICAL (page 330).

Choice A (hypernatremia) usually causes neurologic symptoms from shrinkage of the brain cells.

Choice B (hyperkalemia) are associated with neuromuscular and gastrointestinal symptoms.

Choice C (hypercalcemia) is associated with decreased contractions and is associated with ileus and constipation (from decreased peristaltic contractions).

Choice E (hyponatremia) are associated with neurologic symptoms from cerebral edema.

QUESTION 19

Choice C (Ehrlichiosis) is the correct answer. Ehrlichiosis is caused by gram-negative intracellular bacteria that invades and destroys white blood cells. *Morulae are Ehrlichia clusters within white blood cells.*

Choice B (Trichinosis) is associated with the presence of *larvae in striated muscle on muscle biopsy.*

Choice D (Malaria) is associated with *intracellular red blood cell parasites* seen on *peripheral thin and thick smears.*

Choice E (Babesiosis) is associated with *pathognomic tetrad inclusions seen within red blood cells.*

QUESTION 20

Choice B (they most commonly occur in the convexities of the hemispheres and the parasagittal regions and are often attached to the dura) is the correct answer. Menigiomas are usually benign tumors that arise from the meningioepithelial arachnoid cells that cover the brain & spinal cord.
NEUROLOGY – MENINGIOMA – LABS/DIAGNOSTIC STUDIES (online chapter).

Choice A (they most often occur in the cerebral hemisphere and often cross the corpus callosum, causing a "butterfly" appearance on CT scan) describes *glioblastoma multiforme, the most common primary brain malignancy.* Glioblastomas are malignant astrocytomas, a tumor of the supportive glial cells of the brain.

Choice C (they often occur in children and are most commonly seen in the 3rd or 4th ventricle) describes an ependymoma. Ependymomas arise from the cells that line the ventricles and parts of the spinal column.

Choice D (they are associated with von-Hippel-Lindau syndrome especially if there is retinal involvement) describes hemangiomas. Hemangiomas are an abnormal buildup of blood vessels in the brain and other organs. 10% of patients with hemangiomas have associated von-Hippel-Lindau syndrome. VHL syndrome is an autosomal dominant genetic disease that leads to CNS tumors, hemangioblastomas, clear cell renal carcinoma, pheochromocytoma and pancreatic neuroendocrine tumors.

Choice E (they are most common in the cerebellopontine and are often associated with unilateral sensorineural hearing loss) describes a schwannoma. Schwannomas are tumors of cranial nerve VIII that lead to sensorineural hearing loss.

QUESTION 21
Choice B (pregnancy) is the correct answer.   Amenorrhea (the absence of menses) is divided into primary and secondary causes.   Secondary amenorrhea is defined as the absence of menses for at least 3 months in a patient with a previously normal menstruation (or >6 months in patients who was previously oligomenorrheic). Pregnancy is the most common cause of secondary amenorrhea so the first step in the workup of amenorrhea is to rule out pregnancy. REPRODUCTIVE – AMENORRHEA – BASICS (page 247).

Other causes of secondary amenorrhea include hypothalamic-pituitary dysfunction (Choice C), ovarian disorders such as choice A (premature ovarian failure) or uterine disorders.

Primary amenorrhea is defined as the failure of the onset of menarche (menstruation).   Primary causes of amenorrhea include androgen insensitivity (Choice D) and gonadal dysgenesis/Turner's syndrome (Choice E).

QUESTION 22
Choice C (cranial nerve V) is the correct answer. The trigeminal nerve has *both motor and sensory functions*. Sensory function is tested through light touch of the three branches & sensation of the corneal reflex with touch of the cotton wisp. To test motor function of the trigeminal nerve, the muscles of mastication can be assessed. NEUROLOGY – CRANIAL NERVES – BASICS (page 364).

Choice A (cranial nerve III) is assessed by testing the inferior rectus muscle during extra ocular movement examination.

Choice B (Cranial nerve IV) is assessed by testing the superior oblique rectus muscle during extra ocular movement examination.

Choice D (cranial nerve VI) is assessed by testing the lateral rectus muscle during extra ocular movement examination.

Choice E (cranial VIII) is assessed via auditory examination (gross hearing, Weber and Rinne testing).

QUESTION 23
Choice A (Anti double-stranded DNA antibodies) is the correct answer. This is the classic malar rash associated with lupus erythematosus. It presents with an *erythematous malar rash with sparing of the nasolabial folds. Anti-nuclear antibody testing is used to screen* suspected cases of systemic lupus erythematosus. Antibodies specific to SLE includes anti double-stranded DNA and Anti-Smith antibodies.   Suspect lupus in the differential in a *young woman presenting with fever, joint pain and a rash worsened with sun exposure.*
MUSCULOSKELETAL – SYSTEMIC LUPUS ERYTHEMATOSUS – LABS/DIAGNOSTIC STUDIES (page 201).

Choice B (Anti centromere antibodies) are seen with systemic sclerosis (scleroderma).

Choice C (Anti-Mi-2 antibodies) are classically seen with dermatomyositis. *Dermatomyositis can present with a malar rash similar to lupus but it does not spare the nasolabial folds.*

Choice D (Anti smooth muscle antibodies) are seen with autoimmune hepatitis.

Choice E (Anti *endomysial IgA antibodies) are seen in celiac disease.* The rash of celiac disease is classically *dermatitis herpetiformis*, a vesicular rash most commonly seen on the extensor surfaces, neck, trunk and scalp.

QUESTION 24
Choice C (insertion of large bore needle into the second intercostal pleural space followed by chest tube thoracostomy) is the correct answer. The distended jugular veins and decreased breath sounds indicate a tension pneumothorax. Tension pneumothorax is defined as a pneumothorax in which the increasingly positive pressure displaces or kinks the great vessels, leading to a marked decrease in cardiac output and forward flow. The blood that can't go forward backs up into the jugular veins, producing jugular venous distention. *Emergent management is needle decompression to restore cardiac output followed by chest tube placement.* PULMONARY – TENSION PNEUMOTHORAX – CLINICAL INTERVENTION (page 95).

Choice A (chest tube thoracostomy) is incorrect alone as it may take a long time before the air is absorbed, leading to progressive worsening of cardiac output. It is indicated alone for pneumothoraces >20%

Choice B (observation and oxygen therapy) may be used in the management of small pneumothoraces (ex <20%).

Choice D (insertion of a needle in the pericardial space) is used in the emergent management of pericardial tamponade. Pericardial tamponade is due to a pericardial effusion that exerts pressure on the heart, limiting the cardiac output. *It can also present with increased jugular venous pressure*, but muffled heart sounds would be heard on physical examination. *Beck's triad includes: increased jugular venous pressure, systemic hypotension and muffled heart sounds.* There would be normal lung sounds in tamponade as the lungs are not affected.

Choice E (instillation of a sclerosing agent into the pleural space) is used in pleurodesis (obliteration of the pleural space) in patients with recurrent effusions (such as malignant effusions). This can often be done with intrapleural administration of talc or bleomycin.

QUESTION 25
Choice C (Boerhaave syndrome) is the correct answer. Boerhaave syndrome is an esophageal rupture, causing the air in the esophagus to be absorbed into the soft tissues, leading to pneumomediastinum. GI/NUTRITION – BOERHAAVE SYNDROME – LABS/DIAGNOSTIC STUDIES (page 130).

QUESTION 26
Choice C (compensated respiratory acidosis) is the correct answer. The first step is to look at the pH. The pH is 7.36 (normal 7.35 – 7.45) which normal but closer to the acidic side than the basic side. Whenever the other values are abnormal but the pH is close to normal, suspect a compensated acid base disorder. An elevated $PaCO_2$ of 68 mmHg (normal 35 – 45) indicates a primary respiratory acidosis. Since the bicarbonate is increased and the pH is almost normal, it is compensated. If the bicarbonate remained within normal limits (22 -26 mEq/l) despite the acidosis, then uncompensated respiratory acidosis (Choice A) would have been the answer. RESPIRATORY – ACID BASE DISORDERS – LABS/DIAGNOSTIC STUDIES (page 117).

Choice B (Uncompensated metabolic acidosis) and Choice E (Compensated metabolic acidosis) are associated with a low pH and a low bicarbonate level (both of which are not present in this vignette).

Choice D (Compensated metabolic alkalosis) would be associated with a pH at or near 7.45.

QUESTION 27

Choice D (nicotinic acid) is the correct answer.   Niacin (nicotinic acid) is the best drug to increase HDL (high density lipoprotein) levels. CARDIOLOGY/ENDOCRINE – LIPID DISORDERS – PHARMACOLOGY (page 50 & 51).

Choice A (cholestyramine) is a bile acid sequestrant. It is associated with mild to moderate increases in HDL. It is also used to lower LDL. A side effect of bile acid sequestrants is that they may increase triglyceride levels.

Choice B (ezetimibe) is used to lower LDL levels.

Choice C (fenofibrate) does increase HDL levels but it is the best drug to lower triglyceride levels.

Choice E (simvastatin) is an HMG –CoA reductase inhibitor ("statin"). HMG-CoA reductase inhibitors are the best drugs to lower LDL levels and have been shown to reduce cardiovascular morbidity and mortality.

QUESTION 28

Choice B (warm compresses and eyelid scrubbing with baby shampoo) is the correct choice. This vignette is the classic description of anterior blepharitis (inflammation of the eyelids). It is common in patients with Down syndrome and eczema. HEENT – BLEPHARITIS – CLINICAL INTERVENTION (page 224).

Choice A (oral cephalexin) is the management of choice for skin and soft tissue infections thought to be caused by Staphylococcus aureus or Streptococcus species. Topical antibiotic ointments (Choice C) may be used as adjunctive treatment in some cases of infected blepharitis but oral antibiotics are not indicated.

Choice D (expression of the meibomian gland periodically) is the management for posterior blepharitis.

Blepharitis is not an ophthalmologic emergency so emergent ophthalmology consult (Choice E) is not indicated.

QUESTION 29

Choice D (obtain a non-contrast CT scan of the head) is the correct answer.   The signs and symptoms in this vignette are consistent with acute stroke with probable involvement of the *middle cerebral artery (since the weakness is more pronounced in the upper extremities compared to the lower extremities)*. A CT scan of the head is recommended to rule out hemorrhagic stroke because the patient presented in less than 3 hours from the symptoms onset so he may be a candidate for thrombolytic therapy (after a hemorrhagic stroke is ruled out). NEUROLOGY – ACUTE STROKE SYNDROME – LABS/DIAGNOSTIC STUDIES (page 360).

Choice A (chew an aspirin) is used in the management of acute coronary syndrome, it is not used in acute CVA.

Choice B (administer alteplase) can only be given after a CT scan of the head rules out hemorrhagic stroke.

Choice C (administer streptokinase) is incorrect because alteplase is the only thrombolytic used in the management of acute ischemic stroke syndromes and hemorrhagic stroke must be rules out via CT scan.

Choice E (obtain an MRI of the brain) can take a long time and so a CT scan is done for faster decision making in regards to whether or not to use alteplase.

QUESTION 30

Choice A (Hantavirus) is the correct answer. Rodents are the main vector for Hantavirus (especially the feces and the urine of deer mice). It is most common seen in Southwestern United States. There is a prodromal febrile phase including severe myalgias. It can progress to a *severe cardiopulmonary phase* and may cause renal failure. INFECTIOUS DISEASE – HANTAVIRUS – MOST LIKELY (page 438).

Choice B (Flavivirus) is associated with *Dengue Fever*.

Choice C (Coronavirus) is associated with *severe acute respiratory syndrome (SARS)*.

Choice D (Orthopox virus) is associated with *smallpox*.

Choice E (Rhabdovirus) is associated with *Rabies*. Rabies is transmitted by infected saliva from animal bites.

QUESTION 31

Choice D (Bipolar type II) is the correct answer. Type II Bipolar disorder is associated with major depressive disorder and hypomania. Type II Bipolar disorder is *not classically associated with impairment of social function.* PSYCH/BEHAVIORAL – BIPOLAR DISORDERS – BASICS (page 378).

Choice A (Bipolar disorder type I) is associated with major depressive disorder and hypermania. Bipolar disorder type I is associated with significant impairment of social function.

Choice B (Cyclothymia) is characterized by dysthymia with alternating episodes of mild elevation of the mood that doesn't meet the criteria for hypomania usually.

Choice C (Dysthymia) is characterized by a constant depressed mood for >2 and is usually milder than major depression. Patients doesn't usually cause impairment of function.

Choice E (Schizoaffective disorder) is characterized by the combination of schizophrenia and major depression.

QUESTION 32

Choice C (Heinz bodies) is the correct answer. Alpha thalassemia intermedia (Hemoglobin H disease) is associated with decreased production of hemoglobin alpha chains. There are 4 genes that encode for the alpha subunit. In patients with alpha thalassemia intermedia, there is only one functioning gene. The decreased alpha chain synthesis leads to excess beta chains that form insoluble tetramers called Heinz bodies that show up as red blood cell inclusions. These patients present with a severe anemia similar to beta thalassemia major (Cooley's anemia) characterized by severe anemia, hepatosplenomegaly, frontal & maxilla overgrowth, pigmented gallstones and iron overload. Heinz bodies can also be seen in G6PD deficiency.
HEMATOLOGY – ALPHA THALASSEMIA – LABS/DIAGNOSTIC STUDIES (page 454).

Choice A (clumping of the red blood cells) is associated with *autoimmune hemolytic anemia*, cryoglobulinemia or antigen-antibody reaction if transfused blood is not typed and cross matched.

Choice B (hypersegmented neutrophils) and choice D (macrocytosis) are associated with folate or vitamin B_{12} deficiency. *Thalassemia is associated with microcytosis* not macrocytosis.

Choice E (rouleaux formation) are aggregates of red blood cells that look like a *"stack of coins"* due to increase protein (ex. fibrinogen) in the serum. This is what causes an *increased erythrocyte sedimentation rate*. Common causes of rouleaux formation include infections, *multiple myeloma*, inflammatory disorders, connective tissue disorders and malignancies.

QUESTION 33

Choice B (dullness to percussion, bronchial breath sounds, egophony) is the correct answer. Lobar pneumonia is classically associated with bronchial breath sounds and egophony.
PULMONARY - PNEUMONIA – HISTORY AND PHYSICAL (page 102).

Choice A (hyperresonance to percussion on the right with *tracheal deviation* to the left) is associated with a *tension pneumothorax.*

Choice C (resonance to percussion, vesicular breath sounds, normal fremitus on the right side) is associated with a normal chest exam.

Choice D (dullness to percussion, decreased breath sounds, and decreased fremitus on the right side) is associated with a pleural effusion.

Choice E (hyperresonance on percussion, decreased breath sounds, decreased fremitus on the right side) is associated with a pneumothorax or hyperinflation (ex. severe emphysema).

QUESTION 34
Choice D (abruptio placentae) is the correct answer. Abruptio placentae is the premature separation of the placenta form the uterine wall, most commonly occurring in the third trimester. It is classically associated with *SEVERE ABDOMINAL PAIN, painful uterine contractions and a rigid uterus.* The most common predisposing factor for abruptio placentae is maternal hypertension (which is present in this patient).
REPRODUCTIVE – ABRUPTIO PLACENTAE – MOST LIKELY (page 273).

Choice A (chorioamnionitis) is an infection of the amniotic fluid and the membranes surrounding the fetus. *Although it may be associated with a tender, rigid uterus and abdominal pain*, it is also associated with *fever, maternal tachycardia, leukocytosis & the confirmation of premature rupture of membranes (ex fern test).*

Choice B (placenta previa) is associated with abnormal placental implantation on or close to the cervical os. It is associated with *painless vaginal bleeding*, and a *non tender uterus.*

Choice C (vasa previa) occurs when the fetal blood vessels traverse over the cervical os. It may cause a *painless vaginal bleed and fetal distress.*

Choice E (mild preeclampsia) is associated with *hypertension during pregnancy* but is not associated with vaginal bleeding unless it causes secondary complications.

QUESTION 35
Choice D (Primary biliary cirrhosis) is the correct choice. Most commonly seen in middle-aged women, PBC is associated with jaundice, pruritus & fatigue. Anti-mitochondrial antibodies are classic for the disease. PBC causes intrahepatic biliary obstruction, leading to a cholestatic pattern on LFTs (increased alkaline phosphatase and GGT).
GI/NUTRITION – PRIMARY BILIARY CIRRHOSIS – MOST LIKELY (page 144).

Choice A (autoimmune hepatitis) is associated with *anti-smooth muscle antibodies* and a hepatocellular damage LFT pattern (markedly elevated AST and ALT often 5 times the upper limit of normal) not a cholestatic pattern.

Choice B (acute cholecystitis) is associated with *fever, right upper quadrant pain* and is not classically associated with jaundice.

Choice C (acute cholangitis) is associated with the *triad of fever, right upper quadrant pain and jaundice.* It can present with jaundice but in this vignette the patient is afebrile and there is no right upper quadrant pain.

Choice E (primary sclerosing cholangitis) is associated with *inflammatory bowel disease*, particularly ulcerative colitis. PSC is associated with any age, intra and extra hepatic biliary involvement and a *positive perinuclear anti-neutrophil cytoplasmic antibodies (P-ANCA).*

QUESTION 36

Choice B (abdominal ultrasound) is the correct answer.   Abdominal ultrasound is the initial study of choice for suspected abdominal aortic aneurysms in stable patients.   CARDIOLOGY – AAA – LABS/DIAGNOSTIC STUDIES (page 55).

Choice A (*Angiography*) is the *definitive (gold standard)* test for suspected cases of abdominal aortic aneurysms. Choice C (CT scan of the abdomen and pelvis) can be used in the evaluation of suspected AAA but it is not the first line in asymptomatic patients with suspected AAA.

Choice D (Magnetic resonance imaging of the abdomen and pelvis) can be used in the evaluation of suspected AAA but it is not the first line in asymptomatic patients with suspected AAA.

Choice E (Abdominal radiographs) would only be positive if the abdominal aorta is calcified so it is not the first line diagnostic test for abdominal aortic aneurysms. It would more likely be seen as an incidental finding with this study.

QUESTION 37

Choice E (thickness of the lesion) is the correct answer.   Although all of the other answers are descriptive of malignant melanoma, *thickness of the lesion is the most important prognostic factor for malignant melanoma.* Malignant melanoma is the most common cause of skin cancer related death in the United States. Basal cell carcinoma is the most common type of skin cancer in the United States.

QUESTION 38

Choice A (Rickettsia rickettsii) is the correct answer. *R. rickettsii is the causative agent of Rocky Mountain spotted fever*, a potentially fatal but curable tick-borne disease. It is spreads primarily by the wood and dog ticks of the Dermacentor species. The classic presentation is *fever, chills & myalgias with a red maculopapular rash that starts on the wrists and ankles, spreading to the palms and the soles as well as centrally.* INFECTIOUS DISEASE – ROCKY MOUNTAIN SPOTTED FEVER – BASICS (page 426).

Choice B (Borrelia Burgdorferi) is the causative agent of Lyme disease spread by the Ixodes tick (deer tick) and classically presents with the rash of erythema migrans, arthritis, neurologic and cardiac symptoms.

Choice C (Babesia microti) is the causative agent of Babesiosis.

Choice D (Ehrlichia chaffeensis) is the causative agent of Ehrlichiosis.

Choice E (Treponema pallidum) is the causative agent of syphilis.

QUESTION 39

Choice A (transsphenoidal resection of the pituitary adenoma) is the correct answer. The patient has elevated cortisol levels and no suppression on screening test. There is suppression on high dose dexamethasone suppression test. Cushing's disease (pituitary ACTH hypersecretion) is associated with suppression on high dose dexamethasone suppression tests. ENDOCRINE – CUSHING'S DISEASE – CLINICAL INTERVENTION (page 298).

Choice B (resection of the small cell lung cancer) is associated ectopic ACTH production. Ectopic ACTH production is associated with no suppression of cortisol production on both low & high dose dexamethasone suppression tests. It is also associated with high levels of ACTH, since these tumors ectopically produce ACTH & are not responsive to the hypothalamus-pituitary-adrenal axis.

Choice C (fludrocortisone replacement therapy) is used in the management of adrenal insufficiency, not Cushing's syndrome.

Choice D (prompt discontinuation of corticosteroid therapy) and choice E (surgical resection of the adrenal tumor) are both associated with no suppression on both low and high dose dexamethasone suppression tests. They are also associated with low ACTH levels (due to pituitary suppression from the high levels of circulating cortisol via the negative feedback loop).

QUESTION 40

Choice D (beta thalassemia major) is the correct answer. Beta thalassemia major (Cooley's anemia) is a genetic disorder that leads to decreased beta globin chain synthesis. The three major types of hemoglobin are: "adult" hemoglobin (Hemoglobin A) which is composed of two alpha and two beta chains; "fetal" hemoglobin (Hemoglobin F) which is composed of two alpha & two gamma chains; and Hemoglobin A_2 (which is composed of two alpha and two delta chains). Hemoglobin A is the predominant hemoglobin produced after 6 months of life (about 95% of all total hemoglobin). In patients with Beta thalassemia major, the lack of beta chains lead to decreased Hemoglobin A synthesis. The other hemoglobins are produced in larger quantities to make up for the decreased percentage of Hemoglobin A. Hemoglobin F is particularly increased in beta thalassemia major (as it has a high affinity for oxygen). Thalassemia is associated with a microcytic hypochromic anemia (since there is decreased hemoglobin production). Because of the normal switch to production of majority of Hemoglobin A at 6 months, this is when most patients with beta thalassemia begin to manifest clinical manifestations. HEMATOLOGY – BETA THALASSEMIA MAJOR – MOST LIKELY (page 455).

Choice A (alpha thalassemia major) is associated with normal hemoglobin ratios. Because all three types of hemoglobin contain alpha chains, the ratio stays the same. "adult" hemoglobin (Hemoglobin A) is composed of two alpha and two beta chains; "fetal" hemoglobin (Hemoglobin F) is composed of two alpha and two gamma chains; and Hemoglobin A_2 is composed of two alpha and two delta chains.

Choice B (beta thalassemia minor) is also associated with decreased hemoglobin A, increased Hemoglobin A_2 and increased Hemoglobin F ratios. These patients are usually asymptomatic or may develop a mild anemia.

Choice C (sickle cell trait) is usually asymptomatic. These patients usually on become symptomatic in situations of severe hypoxia or dehydration. There would be evidence of Hemoglobin S on hemoglobin electrophoresis.

Choice E (sickle cell anemia) is associated with severe anemia. Hemoglobin electrophoresis would show high percentages of homozygous Hemoglobin S, increased fetal hemoglobin, and no Hemoglobin A.

QUESTION 41

Choice A (IV high-dose corticosteroids) is the correct answer. Multiple sclerosis is an autoimmune, inflammatory, demyelinating disease of the CNS white matter that usually present with *weakness, optic neuritis and upper motor neuron signs.* Corticosteroids reduce the inflammatory component as well as blunt the autoimmune response, making *corticosteroids the drug of choice for acute exacerbations of multiple sclerosis.*
NEUROLOGY - MULTIPLE SCLEROSIS – CLINCAL INTERVENTION (page 356).

Choice B (IV Glatiramer acetate) and choice D (beta-interferon) are used to *reduce the frequency* and *slow down the progression of the relapse-remitting type of multiple sclerosis* (not for acute exacerbations).

Choice C (IV cyclophosphamide) may also be used in the acute exacerbation phase, but it is not first line.

Choice E (Oral amantadine) can be used for the fatigue in patients with multiple sclerosis but it does not significantly affect the other symptoms.

QUESTION 42

Choice E (bronchiectasis) is the correct answer. Bronchiectasis is enlargement of the larger airways. The hallmark of bronchiectasis is lack of tapering of the enlarged bronchi and bronchial wall thickening, giving the airways a "tram track" appearance on imaging studies. As an obstructive disorder, it is associated with a decreased FEV_1 and a decreased FEV_1/FVC ratio of < 80%. PULMONARY – BRONCHIECTASIS – MOST LIKELY (page 83).

Choice A (Coal workers pneumoconiosis) is associated with obstruction (as seen in this vignette). It usually has a centrilobar emphysematous pattern with hyperinflation of the lungs and small upper nodules on radiographs.

Choice B (Emphysema) is associated with hyperinflation and the presence of bullae (due to enlargement of the terminal airways).

Choice C (Chronic bronchitis) is a clinical diagnosis.

Choice D (Idiopathic pulmonary fibrosis) is classically associated with diffuse reticular opacities giving it a "honeycombing" appearance on imaging studies.

QUESTION 43

Choice E (central pontine myelinolysis) is the correct answer. Demyelination occurs if hyponatremia (seen here with a low serum sodium) is corrected too rapidly. Hyponatremia causes cerebral edema (due to the hypotonicity) and the rapid correction leads to shrinkage of the brain cells with demyelination of the nerves, causing permanent neurologic deficits. GENITOURINARY – HYPONATREMIA – HEALTH MAINTENANCE (page 329).

Choice A (seizures) choice C (vision loss) and choice D (vomiting) can be seen as symptoms of hyponatremia, hypernatremia or the correction of either one, and are nonspecific.

Choice B (cerebral edema) occurs in rapid fluid correction of hypernatremia.

QUESTION 44

Choice C (inevitable abortion) is the correct answer. Inevitable abortion is defined as unsalvageable pregnancy before 20 weeks gestation in which the products of conception have not been expelled & cervical dilation is >3cm.

Choice A (missed abortion) is defined as an unviable pregnancy where there is no passage of products of conception but the cervix is closed. In this vignette, there is evidence of cervical dilation, making this an unlikely answer.

Choice B (septic abortion) is defined as retention of SOME of the products of conception. The cervix is usually closed and cervical motion tenderness is present (due to the presence of an infection of the retained products). It is classically associated with fever, a foul, brownish discharge, fever and chills.

Choice D (incomplete abortion) is defined as an unsalvageable pregnancy in which some of the products of conception have passed and the cervix is dilated. The uterus is often boggy in these patients.

Choice E (threatened abortion) is defined as a pregnancy that may be viable in which there is first semester vaginal bleeding with a closed cervix and no expulsion of the products of conception.

QUESTION 45

Choice C (increased TSH, normal free T3, normal free T4) is the correct answer. Remember that TSH levels change way before free T3 & free T4 levels will, making *TSH levels the best screening test for suspected thyroid dysfunction.* Increased TSH levels indicate a hypothyroid state. The normal free T3 and free T4 levels indicate a subclinical picture. In time, these patients may develop overt hypothyroidism. ENDOCRINE – HYPOTHYRODISM – LABS/DIAGNOSTIC STUDIES (page 284).

Choice A (normal TSH, decreased free T3, decreased free T4) is not a common thyroid combination but may be seen with euthyroid sick syndrome as one of the many ways this disease can present lab-wise.

Choice B (increased TSH, decreased free T3, decreased free T4) is consistent with primary hypothyroidism. Increased free T3 and free T4 will suppress pituitary TSH production via the negative feedback loop.

Choice D (decreased TSH, decreased free T3, decreased free T4) is consistent with secondary hypothyroidism (pituitary failure) or a much rarer tertiary hypothyroidism (hypothalamic failure). Secondary disorders (originating from the pituitary gland) are associated with TSH and free T4 going in the same direction.

Choice E (normal TSH, decreased free T3, normal free T4) is not a common thyroid disorder combination.

QUESTION 46

Choice C (Meniscal tear) is the correct answer. McMurray's test is used to evaluate possible meniscal injuries. MUSCULOSKELETAL – MENISCUS INJURIES – HISTORY AND PHYSICAL (page 183).

Choice A (Iliotibial band syndrome) is associated with a positive Ober test.

Choice B (Anterior cruciate ligamental tear) is associated with a positive Lachman or anterior drawer test.

Choice D (Posterior cruciate ligamental tear) is associated with a positive posterior drawer test.

Choice E (Patellar tendon rupture) is associated with inability to raise the straightened leg against gravity.

QUESTION 47

Choice C (high-dose corticosteroids) is the correct answer. This patient presents with classic symptoms of giant cell arteritis. *Giant cell arteritis* should be suspected in patients with *headache, scalp tenderness, jaw claudication, fever and visual loss.* CARDIOLOGY - GIANT CELL ARTERITIS – PHARMACOLOGY (page 58 & 209).

Choice A (ergotamine) and choice B (sumatriptan) are used in the abortive (symptomatic) management of migraines.

Choice D (propranolol) can be used in the prophylactic management of migraines.

Choice E (low-dose corticosteroids) is the management of choice for polymyalgia rheumatica, a disease that is closely related to giant cell arteritis but primarily causes a synovitis and bursitis of the proximal joints of the shoulder hip and neck.

QUESTION 48

Choice C (Wide QRS complex with broad, slurred R wave in V5 and V6 with a deep S wave in V1) is the correct answer. These findings are consistent with a left bundle branch block. *Left bundle branches are considered a myocardial equivalent* because myocardial infarctions can present with new bundle branch blocks. Preexisting left bundle branch blocks are already associated with ST elevations. The Sgarbossa criteria can be used to determine the possibility of ST elevation MI in patients with left bundle branch blocks.
CARDIOLOGY – ST ELEVATION – LABS/DIAGNOSTIC STUDIES (page 23).

Choice A ["m" shaped P waves in lead II with biphasic p wave in lead V1 (terminal component larger than initial component)] is the diagnostic criteria for left atrial enlargement.

Choice B (R wave larger than S wave in V1 with the R wave measuring >7mm) is the diagnostic criteria for right ventricular hypertrophy.

Choice D (Deep S wave in lead I, isolated Q wave in lead III, inverted T wave in lead III) is diagnostic criteria for right heart strain. S1Q3T3 syndrome may be seen in patients with a massive pulmonary embolism.

Choice E (Wide QRS complexes with an RsR' pattern in in leads V1 and V2. Wide S wave in V6) is the diagnostic criteria for right bundle branch block.

QUESTION 49

Choice D (osteoarthritis) is the correct choice. The patient has evening stiffness and morning pain less than 30 minutes. A hard, bony joint is classically seen with osteoarthritis. Radiographs show *asymmetric joint narrowing & osteophytes* (the hallmark of osteoarthritis).

Choice A (rheumatoid arthritis) is associated with *symmetric joint loss, osteopenia.* The joint is often *warm, boggy and swollen*. If the hand is involved, *ulnar deviation of the hand can be seen in severe cases.*

Choice B (pseudogout) is associated with chondrocalcinosis (calcification of the cartilage).

Choice C (Gout) is associated with a warm, red swollen joint and rat (mouse) bite lesions on X rays.

Choice E (reactive arthritis) is associated with an inflammatory arthropathy.

QUESTION 50

Choice B (a physician assistant with a PPD of 11mm induration and 5mm erythema) is the correct answer. In evaluation a PPD, the erythema is not part of the measurement, *only the transverse induration*. Because the patient is healthcare worker and is at risk of occupational tuberculosis exposure, ≥10mm induration is considered a positive finding, making this a positive PPD. PULMONARY – TUBERCULOSIS – LABS/DIAGNOSTICS (page 107).

Choice A (an HIV positive female with a PPD of 4mm induration and 8mm erythema) is incorrect. A PPD of ≥ 5mm induration is considered positive in a patient with HIV infection.

Choice C (a 45-year old male with a history of a granuloma on chest radiograph with a PPD of 4mm induration and 10mm erythema) is incorrect. A PPD of ≥ 5mm induration is considered positive in patients when granulomas are seen on chest X ray.

Choice D (a 40-year-old male with no identifiable risk factors with a PPD of 11mm induration and 5mm erythema) is incorrect. A PPD of ≥ 15mm induration is considered positive in patients with no risk factors.

Choice E (A 32-year-old prison inmate with a PPD of 8mm induration and 10mm erythema) is incorrect. A PPD of ≥ 10mm induration is considered positive in a prisoner who is at risk of possible tuberculosis exposure.

QUESTION 51

Choice B (ceftriaxone and azithromycin) is the correct answer. Chlamydia is the most common cause of acute epididymitis and orchitis in young men under the age of 35. Gonorrhea is also a common cause, so treatment for both is recommended. The positive Prehn's sign & the positive cremasteric reflex differentiates epididymitis/orchitis from testicular torsion. GENITOURINARY – EPIDIDYMITIS – CLINICAL INTERVENTION (page 332).

Choice A (fluconazole) may be indicated in fungal cases, which are relatively rare.

Choice C (cephalexin) has coverage against E. coli and H. influenzae.

Choice D (levofloxacin) and other fluoroquinolones is the management of choice for gram negative uropathogens.

Choice E (clindamycin) covers primarily gram positive organisms and anaerobes and is not the first line management.

QUESTION 52
Choice B (Chagas disease) is the correct answer. Chagas disease is caused by Trypanosoma cruzi and is most prevalent in Latin American countries and parts of Texas. The vector is the assassin bug and it causes an acute phase associated with the development of a *Chagoma (unilateral periorbital edema).* Complications can include toxic megacolon & esophagitis. It is the *most common cause of congestive heart failure in Latin America.* INFECTIOUS DISEASE – CHAGAS DISEASE – MOST LIKELY (page 428).

Choice A (Trichinosis) may also cause periorbital edema, but it is associated with muscle involvement. It is transmitted via wild boar and bear.

Choice C (Chikungunya) is caused by a virus transmitted by Aedes species of mosquito. It tends to cause biphasic fever, a rash and joint pains that persist for long periods of time.

Choice D (Epidemic Typhus) is caused by Rickettsia prowazekii and is transmitted by flying squirrels and the human body louse. It presents with arthralgia, back pain, delirium fever, headache and a rash that starts on the trunk and spreads to the extremities but spares the palms, closes and the face.

Choice E (African sleeping sickness) is transmitted by the Tsetse fly and causes a painless chancre at the bite site, generalized regional lymphadenopathy and daytime somnolence.

QUESTION 53
Choice A (punch biopsy) is the correct answer. Basal cell carcinoma is a malignant skin tumor. The lesion of basal cell carcinoma is usually described as a *small, raised, translucent, pearly papule with central ulceration and rolled borders.* Basal cell carcinoma most commonly occurs on the face, nose and trunk. *Basal carcinoma is the most common type of skin cancer in the United States* and is seen most commonly in fair-skinned individuals with prolonged sun exposure & patients with xeroderma. DERMATOLOGY – BASAL CELL CANCER – LABS (page 397).

Choice B (Avoid hot and cold weather, hot drinks, hot baths, spicy food and alcohol) are preventative measures in patients with Rosacea.

Choice C (Avoid the sun and use sunscreen) is used to prevent skin cancer and for normal health of the skin.

Choice D (Apply acetic acid to look for whitening) is used to diagnose human papilloma virus.

Choice E (Topical corticosteroids) are used for many autoimmune and inflammatory skin disorders.

QUESTION 54
Choice E (increased usage of caffeine to reduce endolymphatic pressure) is the correct choice. Caffeine INCREASES endolymphatic pressure and should be avoided in patients with symptomatic Meniere's disease. All of the other choices are part of the routine management. EENT – MENIERE'S DISEASE – HEALTH MAINTENANCE (p. 235).

QUESTION 55

Choice C (IV Penicillin G) is the correct answer. Neisseria meningitidis (a gram negative diplococcus) is the most common cause of bacterial meningitis in patients under the age of 18 years old. The drug of choice for Neisseria meningitidis is intravenous Penicillin G. NEUROLOGY – MENINGITIS – PHARMACOLOGY (p. 365).

Choice A (IV clindamycin) covers primarily gram positive and anaerobic organisms. N. meningitidis is a gram-negative organism.

Choice B (IV vancomycin) along with IV ceftriaxone is used in the empiric treatment of bacterial meningitis when the organism is not known. Vancomycin primarily covers gram positive and MRSA. Ceftriaxone primarily covers gram-negative organisms (it has some gram-positive coverage as well).

Choice D (IV cephazolin) is a first generation cephalosporin. 1st generation cephalosporins are used primarily for gram-positive coverage. N. meningitidis is a gram-negative organism. A 3rd generation cephalosporin (such as ceftriaxone) can be used in the management of N. meningitidis, not a first generation.

Choice E (IV Linezolid) has primarily gram-positive coverage (including MRSA and vancomycin resistant enterococcal infections). N. meningitidis is a gram-negative organism.

QUESTION 56

Choice E (Boas sign) is the correct answer. Boas sign is referred right shoulder pain seen in acute cholecystitis due to irritation of the phrenic nerve. GI/NUTRITION – CHOLECYSTITIS – HISTORY & PHYSICAL (p. 137).

Choice A (Kehr's sign) is left shoulder pain due to irritation of the phrenic nerve (ex due to splenic bleeding).

Choice B (Cullen's sign) is periumbilical ecchymosis most commonly seen with hemorrhagic pancreatitis.

Choice C (Courvoisier's sign) is a palpable non tender, distended gall bladder. It is associated with pancreatic cancer.

Choice D (Dance's sign) is a mass in the right upper quadrant or epigastrium with the absence of bowel in the right lower quadrant. Dance's sign is associated with intussusception.

QUESTION 57

Choice C (IV Vancomycin) is the correct answer. The patient presents with symptoms of infective endocarditis. Staphylococcus aureus is the most common cause of acute native valve bacterial infective endocarditis (and methicillin-resistant Staphylococcus aureus is seen especially in IV drug users). Staphylococcus aureus is seen on gram stain as gram-positive cocci in clusters. Management of choice in these cases include vancomycin (which covers gram positive organisms and MRSA). If the gram stain is not back before the initiation of treatment then gentamicin (Choice D) should be added until gram stain or cultures show the presence of gram-positive organisms. INFECTIOUS DISEASE - IVDA BACTERIAL ENDOCARDITIS – CLINICAL INTERVENTION (page 53)

Choice A (IV ceftriaxone and gentamicin) is not the recommended management of infective endocarditis with suspected MRSA.

Choice B (IV nafcillin and gentamicin) is the treatment of choice for the routine empiric management of acute, native valve infective endocarditis. Its coverage include beta lactamase producing staphylococcus aureus.

Choice E (IV penicillin G and gentamicin) is used in the routine empiric management of native valve subacute infective endocarditis.

QUESTION 58

Choice C (acute cholangitis) is the correct answer. Acute cholangitis usually presents with the *triad of 1: fever 2: right upper quadrant pain and 3: jaundice.* Cholangitis occur when a stone obstructs a bile duct, leading to a subsequent infection of the bile ducts and cholestasis. *An increased ALP with GGT is indicative of cholestasis.* GI/NUTRITION – ACUTE CHOLANGITIS – MOST LIKELY (p. 137).

Choice A (acute cholecystitis) may cause right upper quadrant pain but since the stone is in the cystic duct and bile can still travel down the hepatic ducts, it is not usually associated with jaundice or a cholestatic pattern on liver function testing.

Choice B (choledocholithiasis) is the presence of bile stones in the biliary tree. Choledocholithiasis can be asymptomatic or can cause episodic biliary colic. Choledocholithiasis is the predisposing factor to the development of acute cholangitis.

Choice D (primary sclerosing cholangitis) presents with progressive jaundice, pruritus, right upper quadrant pain and hepatomegaly. It is most commonly seen in patients with inflammatory bowel disease (such as Crohn's disease and Ulcerative Colitis). It is caused by autoimmune-mediated cholestasis with fibrosis of the intrahepatic and extrahepatic bile ducts. It is not due to hepatic vein thrombosis or occlusion.

Choice E (carcinoma of the head of the pancreas) can present with *Courvoisier's sign: a palpable distended NON tender gallbladder with associated jaundice and pruritus.*

QUESTION 59

Choice E (miosis) is the correct answer. Atropine is an anticholinergic agent. Acetylcholine causes SLUDD-C (increases salivation, lacrimation, urination, digestion, defecation and constriction of the pupils). Anticholinergics would cause the opposite of these findings, leading to mydriasis. ATROPINE TOXICITY – PHARMACOLOGY (Pediatrics extra chapter online).

QUESTION 60

Choice B (immediately drying the skin after showers to reduce irritation and keep the skin dry) is the correct answer. Dry skin exacerbates atopic dermatitis (eczema). Patients are often encouraged to use moisturizers as soon as they shower to maintain skin hydration. All of the other choices are part of the routine management of atopic dermatitis.

QUESTION 61

Choice C (intravenous immunoglobulin) is the correct answer. Idiopathic (immune) Thrombocytopenic Purpura is an acquired abnormal isolated thrombocytopenia. In children, it is most commonly seen after a viral infection with the subsequent development of antibodies against platelets with associated splenic destruction of platelets. The management in children is observation or intravenous immunoglobulin. In adults, the first line management is corticosteroids. HEMATOLOGY - IDIOPATHIC THROMBOCYTOPENIA PURPURA – CLINICAL INTERVENTION (page 462).

Choice A (plasmapheresis) is not used in the routine management of idiopathic thrombocytopenic purpura.

Choice B (splenectomy) can be used in children who are refractory to intravenous immunoglobulin or corticosteroid therapy.

Choice D (platelet transfusion) is reserved for management of severe thrombocytopenia: ex. platelet count of <10,000/mcL in patients with signs of clinically significant mucocutaneous or other bleeding.

Choice E (fresh frozen plasma) is indicated in the management in patients with coagulation factor deficiencies (especially when the specific factor concentrates are not available). Thrombocytopenia is a platelet disorder (primary coagulation pathway). The secondary coagulation pathway (clotting factor pathway) is not affected.

QUESTION 62

Choice D (Hirschsprung's disease) is the correct answer. Hirschsprung's disease is the congenital absence of ganglion cells especially in the distal colon & rectum. It may occur in other parts of the GI tract. There is an increased risk in children with Down syndrome. It presents with *neonatal intestinal obstruction: meconium ileus (failure of meconium passage >48h) in a full term infant.* Bilious vomiting and abdominal distention and toxic megacolon may also be seen. PEDIATRICS – HIRSCHSPRUNG'S DISEASE (Pediatrics extra chapter online).

Choice A (Pyloric stenosis) usually presents in early infancy with *projectile, nonbilious vomiting and an olive-shaped mass* (the pyloris).

Choice B (Meckel's diverticulum) is the *persistent portion of the embryonic Vitteline duct (yolk stalk).* It is usually asymptomatic but may present with painless rectal bleeding or ulceration.

Choice C (Intussusception) is an invagination of a portion of the intestinal segment. It presents with the classic *triad of vomiting, abdominal pain and passage of blood per rectum described as "currant jelly" stools.*

Choice E (Volvulus) is a twisting of any or part of the bowel on itself. It is most commonly seen at the sigmoid colon, and the cecum.

QUESTION 63

Choice A (Lansoprazole 30mg + amoxicillin 500mg + clarithromycin 500mg) triple therapy is the mainstay of H. pylori peptic ulcer disease. GI/NUTRITION – PEPTIC ULCER DISEASE – PHARMACOLOGY (p. 133).

Choice B can be used for H. pylori negative disease. Proton pump inhibitors (the "azoles') are the most effective drugs against acid production.

Choice C is an alternative in patients who are penicillin allergic (Metronidazole is substituted for Amoxicillin).

Choice E (Misoprostol) can be used to prevent ulcer recurrence particularly in patients with aspirin or NSAID-induced ulcers. Remember that *gastric ulcers are caused by decreased protective factors* (mucous and bicarbonate). Prostaglandins are responsible for those protective mechanisms. Aspirin and NSAID's exhibit their anti-inflammatory effects via prostaglandin inhibition. Misoprostol is a prostaglandin analog.

QUESTION 64

Choice C (idiopathic, exaggerated T cell response with the formation of noncaseating granulomas) is the correct answer. This describes the basic pathophysiology of sarcoidosis and also explains why corticosteroids are used in the management of sarcoidosis (they blunt the immune response and decrease the granuloma formation). *Sarcoidosis* is suspected based on the presence of *erythema nodosum* (bilateral anterior shin redness that is tender to palpation), *uveitis* (eye pain and redness) and *pulmonary involvement* (nonproductive cough with a chest radiograph showing *bilateral hilar lymphadenopathy*). *Lupus pernio* is the pathognomonic skin finding in patients with sarcoidosis. PULMONARY – SARCOIDOSIS – BASICS (p. 86).

Choice A (the production of caseating granulomas with central caseous necrosis in tissues) describes the pathophysiology of tuberculosis.

Choice B (small vessel vasculitis associated with granulomatous inflammation and necrosis) describes the pathophysiology of Wegener's granulomatosis (Granulomatosis with polyangiitis).

Choice D (the presence of antibodies against Type IV collagen in the alveoli) describes the pathophysiology of Goodpasture's syndrome.

Choice E (inflammatory reaction to an organic antigen) describes the pathophysiology of hypersensitivity pneumonitis

QUESTION 65
Choice C (leiomyomas) is the correct answer. Uterine fibroids are the most common indication for hysterectomy.

QUESTION 66
Choice C (MRI of the sella turcica) is the correct answer. The headache, visual changes (*bitemporal hemianopsia*) are suggestive of a *pituitary tumor*. Secondary hyperthyroidism is suggested by the labs because *both the TSH and free T4/T3 are going in the same direction* (both are elevated in this case). *MRI of the pituitary gland is the recommended diagnostic modality in suspect pituitary disorders.* ENDOCRINE – TSH ADENOMA – LABS (p. 300).

Choice A (Head CT without contrast), Choice B (head CT with contrast) and Choice D (skull X ray) are not the recommended test for suspected pituitary abnormalities.

Choice E (CT scan of the soft tissues of the neck) are not indicated since the symptoms and labs are indicative of a pituitary disorder.

QUESTION 67
Choice D (acute interstitial nephritis) is the correct answer. Acute tubulointerstitial nephritis is a type of intrinsic acute kidney injury. It is due to an *inflammatory or allergic response in the interstitium*. 70% of AIN is due to drugs (such as penicillin). AIN is associated with *fever, eosinophilia, arthralgias and a maculopapular rash* (as seen in this vignette). *White blood cell casts are hallmark for AIN.*
GENITOURINARY – ACUTE INTERSTITIAL NEPHRITIS – MOST LIKELY – (p. 320).

Choice A (erythema multiforme minor) and choice B (erythema multiforme major) can be caused by certain medications as well, but the *hallmark of erythema multiforme is the target lesion* (which is absent in this vignette).

Choice C (acute tubular necrosis) is usually indicated by the *presence of epithelial cell casts or muddy brown casts.*

Choice E (acute glomerulonephritis) is associated with *red blood cell casts & dysmorphic red blood cells.*

QUESTION 68
Choice C (warm compresses) is the correct answer. An *external hordeolum (stye)* is a local infection of the eyelid margin that presents with *localized eyelid pain and a warm tender swollen lump on the eyelid margin*. The treatment of choice is warm compresses as many of them point and drain spontaneously within 48 hours. If they don't after 48 hours, choice D (incision and drainage) may be indicated. In this vignette, there has only been one day of symptoms. EENT – HORDEOLUM- CLINICAL INTERVENTION (p. 224).

Choice A (intravenous ampicillin/sulbactam) would be indicated in moderate soft tissue infections, such as cellulitis & orbital cellulitis.

Choice B (bacitracin ointment) may be added if the hordeolum was actively draining.

Choice E (Trifluridine ophthalmic) would be used for herpes simplex keratitis. The absence of dendritic lesions or Hutchinson's sign makes herpes simplex keratitis less likely.

QUESTION 69

Choice A (glatiramer acetate) is the correct answer. The triad of *nystagmus, staccato speech and intentional tremor* are seen with multiple sclerosis. It often causes *optic neuritis* and eye pain with ocular movements. An *MRI is the test of choice* to confirm the diagnosis and often shows multiple white matter hyperdensities and plaques. *Glatiramer acetate or beta interferon both have been shown to decrease the progression of the relapsing-remitting form of this disease.* NEUROLOGY – MULTIPLE SCLEROSIS – CLINICAL INTERVENTION (p. 356).

Choice B (methylprednisolone) and other *high-dose corticosteroids are the drugs of choice for acute exacerbations with plasma exchange therapy often second line* if there is no response to corticosteroid therapy. Choice E (cyclophosphamide) may also be used as an immune modulator in acute exacerbations of multiple sclerosis.

Choice C (amantadine) has been shown to be *helpful for the fatigue symptoms* in multiple sclerosis but not for the other symptoms in this vignette.

Choice E (carbamazepine) is not used in the management of multiple sclerosis.

QUESTION 70

Choice B (gram positive cocci in clusters) is the correct answer. *Staphylococcus aureus is the most common organism associated with septic arthritis* and appears on gram stain as *gram-positive cocci in clusters.*

Choice A (gram positive cocci in pairs and chains) describes Streptococcus spp.

Choice C (gram negative rods) can cause septic arthritis, but they are not the most common cause.

Choice D (acid fast bacilli) is consistent with tuberculosis. Although it can cause arthritis, it is not the most common cause.

Choice E (gram negative diplococci) describes gonorrhea. This should always be in the differential in sexually active patients with septic arthritis (in addition to Staphylococcus aureus).

QUESTION 71

Choice B (CT scan of the abdomen and pelvis with contrast and cystoscopy) is the correct answer. In patients older than 40 years old who present with hematuria with a negative urinalysis, one should rule out a malignancy of the urinary tract. Cystoscopy allows for possible biopsy if bladder cancer is seen. GENITOURINARY – HEMATURIA – LABS/DIAGNOSTIC STUDIES (p 341).

Choice A (CT scan of abdomen and pelvis without contrast) is used to evaluate suspected nephrolithiasis. These patients usually present with renal colic and constant abdominal pain that may radiate to the testicles in males or the vulva in females.

Choice C (fasting plasma glucose) is used in the evaluation of suspected diabetes mellitus.

Choice D (observation and nephrologist follow up if hematuria persists) is not recommended in this age group because of the increased possibility for malignancy.

Choice E (Kidney biopsy) may be indicated if a lesion was seen during the workup of the CT scan.

QUESTION 72

Choice D (initiation of heparin with warfarin. Warfarin therapy for 6 to 12 months) is the correct answer. In the first event of deep venous thrombosis or pulmonary embolism in patients with no risk factors (idiopathic), it is recommended to teat for at least 6 months.   CARDIOVASCULAR – DEEP VENOUS THROMBOSIS – HEALTH MAINTENANCE (page 61).

Choice A (warm compresses and non steroidal anti-inflammatories) is used in the management of superficial thrombophlebitis. Remember that although it is called the "superficial' femoral vein, it is part of the deep venous system.

Choice B (initiation of heparin with warfarin. Warfarin therapy for less than 3 months) is not recommended in this case.

Choice C (initiation of heparin with warfarin. Warfarin therapy for 3 to 6 months) can be used for the 1st DVT or PE in patients with a reversible or time-limiting risk factor (ex immobilization, trauma, and post surgical).

Choice E (initiation of heparin with warfarin. Warfarin therapy for greater than 12 months) is recommended in patients with recurrent idiopathic DVT or PE or a continuing risk factor.

QUESTION 73

Choice C [Lithium (Lithobid)] is the correct answer. Lithium is used to treat bipolar disorder. Common side effects of Lithium therapy include hyperparathyroidism (manifested here by an increased intact parathyroid hormone, hypercalcemia and low serum phosphate). Lithium can also cause hypothyroidism (suggested here by the increased TSH, which is the screening test for any suspected thyroid disorder). PSYCH/BEHAVIOR – LITHIUM TOXICITY – PHARMACOLOGY (p. 383).

Choice A [Aripiprazole (Abilify)] side effects include: increased suicide rates in children, extrapyramidal symptoms, seizures, and hyperglycemia.

Choice B [Quetiapine (Seroquel)] is an atypical (2nd generation) anti-psychotic. Side effects include: diabetes mellitus, seizures, neuroleptic malignant syndrome, mild increases in prolactin levels, extrapyramidal symptoms, hyperglycemia, weight gain and hyperlipidemia.

Choice D [Haloperidol (Haldol)] is a typical (1st generation) anti-psychotic. Side effects include extrapyramidal symptoms, neuroleptic malignant syndrome (1st generation antipsychotics are associated with the highest incidence), increased prolactin, weight gain, seizures, and anticholinergic side effects to name a few.

Choice E [Clozapine (Clozaril)] is an atypical (2nd generation) antipsychotic. Side effects include agranulocytosis, myocarditis, diabetes mellitus, seizures, neuroleptic malignant syndrome, mild increases in prolactin levels, extrapyramidal symptoms, hyperglycemia, weight gain and hyperlipidemia.

QUESTION 74

Choice E (Bullous pemphigoid) is the correct answer. Bullous pemphigoid is a chronic, widespread, autoimmune, blistering skin disease primarily seen in the elderly. It is due to a Type II hypersensitivity autoimmune reaction against the basement membrane, leading to subepidermal blistering. Because it is subepidermal, it is usually associated with a negative Nikolsky sign. Nikolsky's sign is sloughing off of the epidermis with slight pressure applied to the skin. A positive Nikolsky's sign can be seen in toxic epidermal necrolysis (Choice A), Steven-Johnson syndrome (Choice D), pemphigus vulgaris (Choice C), and staphylococcal scalded skin syndrome (Choice B). DERMATOLOGY – BULLOUS PEMPHIGOID – HISTORY AND PHYSICAL EXAM (p. 401).

QUESTION 75

Choice C (erysipelas) is the correct answer. Erysipelas is a variant of cellulitis, distinguished by *well demarcated (sharp borders), marked erythema and warmth* (hence the nickname St. Anthony's fire). Erysipelas occurs most commonly on the face. INFECTIOUS DISEASE – ERYSIPELAS – MOST LIKELY – (p. 419).

Choice A (acne rosacea) is a papulopustular rash also associated with erythema. It would not cause systemic fever and chills (as it is infectious in nature).

Choice B (lymphangitis) is a cellulitis that begins to infiltrate the lymph vessels and presents with localized cellulitis and streaking, following the lymph vessels from the source towards the lymph nodes that drain the area.

Choice D (*intertrigo*) is most often cause by candida infections and presents with a *beefy red rash and satellite lesions.*

Choice E (Chagas disease) is a disease of the tropics that presents with circumorbital edema and may cause congestive heart failure.

QUESTION 76

Choice C (central cord syndrome) is the correct answer. Central cord syndrome is classically associated with *bilateral upper and lower extremity weakness (more pronounced in the upper extremity) with sensory loss of pain* and temperature in a *"shawl-like distribution over the extremities and the upper shoulders.* There is usually *preservation of position, light tough and proprioception* (since those are located posteriorly). NEUROLOGY – CENTRAL CORD SYNDROME – MOST LIKELY (extra chapter spinal cord injuries and CNS disorders online).

Choice A (*Anterior cerebral artery infarct syndrome*) would present with contralateral *hemiparesis greater in the lower extremity than the upper, urinary incontinence and personality changes* (including abulia) often with speech preservation.

Choice B (*anterior cord syndrome*) is associated with *complete paralysis as well as sensory temperature and pain loss especially in the lower extremities.* Preservation of proprioception and vibratory sensation is preserved.

Choice D (*posterior cord syndrome*) is associated with *loss of proprioception and vibratory sense only.* Pain, light touch and motor sensation is usually preserved.

Choice E (*Brown Sequard syndrome*) is classically associated *ipsilateral proprioception, vibratory, light touch and motor deficits with contralateral pain and temperature deficits.*

QUESTION 77

Choice B (clozapine) is the correct answer. *2 serious side effects of clozapine are agranulocytosis and myocarditis.* Clozapine is also associated with extrapyramidal symptoms, QT prolongation, arrhythmias, neuroleptic malignant syndrome, weight gain, hyperglycemia, and mild increases in prolactin levels. Other drugs associated with myocarditis includes doxorubicin, cyclophosphamide, penicillin, chloramphenicol, methyldopa & spironolactone. PSYCH/BEHAVIOR – CLOZAPINE – PHARMACOLOGY (p. 383).

QUESTION 78

Choice C (serum lead) is the correct answer. Lead poisoning (Plumbism) is most commonly seen in children (due to the increased permeability of the blood brain barrier). *In children the classic presentation is abdominal pain with constipation, varying neurologic symptoms, anemia and metabolic acidosis.* Patients may also be asymptomatic. Lab values include: increased serum iron, decreased total iron binding capacity, increased ferritin (*resembles an anemia of chronic disease picture except that the serum iron is elevated).* Lead lines (linear lead hyperdensities at the metaphyseal plates) are common findings on radiographs. HEMATOLOGY - LEAD POISONING – MOST LIKELY (p 455).

QUESTION 79

Choice A (Pasteurella multocida) is the correct answer as it is the most common organism associated with cat bites. Bite wounds tend to be polymicrobial, with different organisms of the oral flora of the animal. Coverage in cat bites should include Pasteurella multocida. *Amoxicillin/clavulanic acid is the drug of choice for cat bite wounds* because it has good gram positive, gram negative and anaerobic coverage. Doxycycline may be used in penicillin allergic patients. INFECTIOUS DISEASE – CAT BITES – CLINICAL INTERVENTION (p. 419).

Choice B (*Bartonella henselae*) is the agent that causes *cat scratch disease*.

Choice C (Brucella melitensis) causes brucellosis, which causes nonspecific flu-like illness. It is endemic to Mexico and animal vectors include goats, cheep, cattle and hogs. Transmission usually occurs with ingestion of unpasteurized milk and cheese.

Choice D (Coxiella burnetii) is a Rickettsial bacteria associated with Q fever.

Choice E (Erysipelothrix rhusiopathiae) is the causative agent of erysipeloid

QUESTION 80

Choice B (acetic acid) is the correct answer. Human papilloma virus infection can be diagnosed clinically, histologically or by the application of acetic acid, which causes whitening of the lesions). DEMRATOLOGY/INFECTIOUS DISEASE – HUMAN PAPILLOMA VIRUS – LABS/DIAGNOSTIC (p 396).

Choice A (potassium hydroxide) can be used in the diagnosis of candida fungal infections, or as part of vaginal mount testing in the diagnosis of suspected bacterial vaginosis, trichomoniasis and vaginal candidiasis.

Choice C (India ink) is used in the detection of Cryptococcus neoformans.

Choice D (cold agglutinin test) is used to detect cold agglutinin autoimmune hemolytic anemia. Secondary disorders that can cause a positive cold agglutinin test are Mycoplasma pneumoniae infections and infectious mononucleosis due to the Epstein-Barr virus.

Choice E [enzyme-linked immunosorbent assay test (ELISA)] has many applications such as part of the initial test for human immunodeficiency virus.

QUESTION 81

Choice B (supportive management and humidified oxygen) is the correct choice. Supportive management is the mainstay of management in acute bronchiolitis. PULMONARY – BRONCHIOLITIS – CLINICAL INTERVENTION (p. 110).

Choice A is not usually done in children with respiratory difficulty.
Choice C would be done if not responsive to treatment, severe cases or cyanosis.
Choice D (corticosteroids) are not usually used (unless there is a history of reactive airway disease).
Choice E (palivizumab) is used as prophylaxis not for treatment of acute bronchiolitis. Ribavirin may be given in severe cases of acute bronchiolitis.

QUESTION 82

Choice B (inflammation of a diverticulum) is the correct answer. The sigmoid colon (located in the left lower quadrant) is the most common site for diverticula formation. Classically diverticulitis presents with left lower quadrant pain. GI/NUTRITION – DIVERTICULITIS – BASICS (page 148).

Choice A (inflammation of the appendix) classically presents with right lower quadrant pain.

Choice C (inflammation of the gall bladder) usually presents with right upper quadrant pain.

Choice D (inflammation of the ileum) also classically presents with right lower quadrant pain.

Choice E (irritable bowel syndrome) can present with abdominal pain in any quadrant but it is not classically associated with fever.

QUESTION 83
Choice D (phenoxybenzamine) is the correct answer.   Nonselective alpha-blockers such as phenoxybenzamine or phentolamine are started for at least 2 weeks prior to surgery to prevent hypertension crisis during surgical removal of the tumor. ENDOCRINE – PHEOCHROMOCYTOMA – CLINICAL INTERVENTION (p. 299).

Choice A (metoprolol) and Choice B (atenolol) are beta-blockers. A very important point about presurgical medical management of *pheochromocytoma is that alpha-blockers must be initiated before beta-blockers* to prevent severe hypertension due to unopposed alpha constriction.

Choice C (hydrochlorothiazide) will not effectively reduce the hypertension as a solo agent. *Pheochromocytoma is a secondary cause of hypertension.*   Secondary hypertension may often be severe or refractory to multiple medications. Medications used to treat pheochromocytoma must be able to block sympathetic vasoconstriction.

Choice E (midodrine) is an alpha 1 agonist, which causes vasoconstriction. It is used to increase blood pressure in patients with severe orthostatic hypotension.   If used in the setting of pheochromocytoma, it will make hypertension worse.

QUESTION 84
Choice B (small, pinpoint pupils) is the correct answer. Narcotics are miotics, so narcotic intoxication will cause pinpoint pupils. Narcotic withdrawal will cause the opposite (mydriasis). All of the other choices are associated with narcotic withdrawal. PSYCH/BEHAVIORAL – OPIOID WITHDRAWAL – HISTORY AND PHYSICAL EXAM (extra chapter)

QUESTION 85
Choice D (erythema nodosum) is the correct answer. Erythema nodosum are *painful, erythematous, inflammatory nodules seen especially on the anterior shins.* It is associated with estrogen exposure (ex pregnancy), sarcoidosis, tuberculosis, fungal (ex. Coccidiomycosis) as well as inflammatory disorders and may rarely be seen in patients as a reaction to the red dye in tattooing. DERMATOLOGY – ERYTHEMA NODOSUM – MOST LIKELY (p. 396).

Choice A (erythema migrans) is associated with Lyme disease. The rash of erythema migrans is an expanding, warm, annular erythematous rash with central clearing and an inner erythema, giving it the *"bull's-eye' or target* appearance. In comparison to the multiple lesions seen in erythema marginatum, erythema migrans is classically one lesion around the site of the tick bite (however in disseminated disease, erythema migrans can present with multiple lesions).

Choice B (erythema marginatum) is one of the major Jones criteria in the diagnosis of rheumatic fever. Erythema marginatum is described as a *macular, erythematous, non-pruritic, annular rash with rounded, sharply demarcated edges (that may have central clearing).*

Choice C (erythema infectiosum) is the rash seen in patients with *fifth's disease.*   The rash of erythema infectiosum classically presents with an *erythematous rash with circumoral pallor, giving it a "slapped cheek"* appearance. The rash then progresses to a lacy reticular rash on the extremities (especially the upper extremities) and spares the palms and the soles.

Choice E (erythema multiforme) is a type IV hypersensitivity reaction that classically presents with dusty violet or red purpuric lesions with macules, vesicles or bullae in the center, giving it a classic *target appearance*. Besides the clinical scenario, erythema multiforme is distinguished from erythema migrans by the presence of pruritus and the presence of the central clearing in erythema multiforme.

QUESTION 86

Choice E (blurring of the optic disc and cup) is the correct choice. Stage IV (Malignant) hypertension is associated with *papilledema on fundoscopic exam*. Stage IV can show all the signs from stage I through stage IV, *but papilledema is most specific for Stage IV hypertension.* It is associated with end organ damage (a type of hypertensive emergency).

Choice A (venous compression at the artery-venous junction) describes *AV nicking which can be seen in stage II* and above hypertensive retinopathy, but is not specific for malignant hypertension.

Choice B (yellow spots with sharp margins that are circinate) describes the hard exudate pattern seen in diabetic retinopathy.

Choice C (fluffy gray-white spots on the retina) describes soft exudates seen in stage III hypertensive retinopathy.

Choice D (a detached retina) is associated with retinal detachment

QUESTION 87

Choice A (Turner syndrome) is the correct choice. Turner's syndrome (45,X) is due to the absence of all or part of a sex chromosome. This leads to gonadal dysgenesis and primary amenorrhea. Patients often develop premature ovarian failure. Classic physical exam findings include: short stature, webbed neck, prominent ears, a broad chest with hypoplastic, widely-spaced nipples. PEDIATRICS – TURNER'S SYNDROME – MOST LIKELY (p. 498).

Choice B (Klinefelter's syndrome) 47, XXY is due to an extra X chromosome. They are considered genetically male but may have a male, female or intersex phenotype. These patients often have gynecomastia and testicular atrophy.

Choice C (Down syndrome) is due abnormal cell division of chromosome 21. Some findings include: low set ears, flat facial features, upslanting palpebral fissures and single transverse palmar crease as well as other signs.

Choice D (Fragile X syndrome) is associated with alteration of the FMR1 gene. Classic presentation includes autism. Physical exam findings include: mitral valve prolapse, tall stature, hyperextensible joints, a long and narrow face, prominent forehead and chin, large ears, and macroorchidism.

Choice E (hypopituitarism) would be associated with decreased production of follicle stimulating hormone, luteinizing hormone, adrenocorticotrophic hormone, thyroid stimulating hormone and somatotropin.

QUESTION 88

Choice D (estrogen + progesterone oral pills) is the correct choice. Polycystic ovarian syndrome (PCOS) is associated with an elevated FSH:LH ratio, insulin resistance, increased androgen levels and the *triad of amenorrhea, hirsutism and obesity*. *Combination oral contraception is the mainstay of treatment* because it normalized bleeding and treats the hirsutism by reducing androgen levels.

Choice A (Metformin) may be used in PCOS for patients with abnormal FSH:LH ratio and may improve menstrual frequency in patients wishing to become pregnant by reducing insulin. Metformin is useful to improve fertility but is not used as a primary treatment for the majority of symptoms and signs associated with polycystic ovarian syndrome.

Choice B (danazol) is a medication that decreases estrogen levels and increases testosterone levels, so danazol would worsen the hirsutism associated with PCOS.

Choice C (spironolactone) is a potassium-sparing diuretic that, based on its structure, is similar to testosterone but it blocks the testosterone receptors, leading to anti-androgenic effects. It can be used for hirsutism and will may be helpful with hypertension associated with PCOS.

Choice E (estradiol pills) are not used as the primary treatment for polycystic ovarian syndrome as this disorder is already associated with unopposed estrogen. Using estradiol only in women with intact uterus may increase the risk for endometrial hyperplasia and endometrial malignancy.

QUESTION 89

Choice E (the presence of a medial ulcer with uneven ulcer margins) is the correct answer. Medial ulcers with uneven edges are classically associated with peripheral venous disease. Other physical exam findings include leg pain & cyanosis that is worse with dependency, stasis dermatitis with brownish pigmentation of the skin, and peripheral edema with normal temperature and pulses. All the other choices are classically associated with peripheral arterial disease. CARDIOVASCULAR – PERIPHERAL VENOUS DISEASE – HISTORY AND PHYSICAL (p. 62).

QUESTION 90

Choice E (congestive heart failure) is the correct choice. CHF accounts for 90% of transudative effusions. A transudative effusion is caused by fluid shift out of the capillaries either due to 1) increased hydrostatic pressure or 2) decreased oncotic pressure (albumin makes up the majority of oncotic pressure so if you don't make any albumin in cirrhosis or you lose it in the urine as in nephrotic syndrome) they will develop a transudate. But the qualifier here was the MOST COMMON, which made Choice A (nephrotic syndrome) and choice D (cirrhosis) incorrect in this vignette. Pulmonary embolism (Choice B) most often causes an exudate (but may cause a transudate). PULMONARY – PLEURAL EFFUSION – BASICS (p. 95).

Choice C (pneumonia) would cause an exudative effusion. Exudative effusions are caused by leaky capillary walls due to inflammation and/or infections. Besides plasma, exudative effusions contain proteins and cellular elements such as red blood cells, platelets, white blood cells and lactate dehydrogenase (LDH).

QUESTION 91

Choice D (phenytoin) is the correct answer. Side effects of phenytoin include gingival hyperplasia, rash, Steven-Johnson syndrome, nystagmus, slurred speech, hematologic complications, hypotension and arrhythmias with rapid IV administration. NEUROLOGY – ANTICONVULSANTS - PHARMACOLOGY (p. 368).

Choice A (Lamotrigine) side effects include: rash, Steven-Johnson syndrome, headache and diplopia.

Choice B (valproic acid) side effects include: pancreatitis, hepatotoxicity, GI disturbances and thrombocytopenia.

Choice C (phenobarbital) side effects include: permanent neurologic deficits if injected near peripheral nerves, depression, osteoporosis and increased irritability.

Choice E (ethosuximide) side effects include: drowsiness, ataxia, dizziness, headache, rash, GI upset and weight gain.

QUESTION 92

Choice A (Gottron's papules) is the correct answer. Gottron papules are raised, violaceous eruptions on the knuckles. *A purple, heliotrope rash around the eyelids is also pathognomonic for dermatomyositis.*

Choice B (the presence of *Lupus pernio*) is *pathognomonic for sarcoidosis.*

Choice C (erythema nodosum) is seen in sarcoidosis and other inflammatory diseases.

Choice D (the presence of a malar rash that spares the nasolabial folds) is classically seen with systemic lupus erythematosus. Note that in *dermatomyositis, you can develop a malar rash as well but the rash in dermatomyositis does not spare the nasolabial folds.*

Choice E (the presence of bullae and the sloughing off of the epidermis) describes *Koebner's phenomenon. It is classically associated psoriasis and pemphigus vulgaris.*

QUESTION 93
Choice A (indomethacin) is the correct answer. Nephrogenic diabetes insipidus is due to kidney insensitivity to ADH, leading to the *production of large amounts of dilute urine.* It is harder to treat than central diabetes insipidus. The *management of nephrogenic diabetes insipidus includes indomethacin and hydrochlorothiazide.* Indomethacin blocks prostaglandins (normally prostaglandins can block the action of ADH, so prostaglandin inhibition makes the patient more sensitive to ADH). Indomethacin also increases the concentration ability of the kidney, reducing the output of dilute urine. Hydrochlorothiazides block the distal diluting segment, causing the inability of the kidney to produce a dilute urine.

Choice B (amphotericin B), choice D (demeclocycline) are causes of nephrogenic diabetes and are not used in the treatment of diabetes insipidus.

Choice E (carbamazepine) increases ADH production so can be used as an adjunct to synthetic ADH/desmopressin (Choice C) in the management of central diabetes insipidus not the nephrogenic variant.

QUESTION 94
Choice E (Antibodies against ADAMTS 13 leading to large Von Willebrand multimers causing platelet activation) is the correct answer. These large Von Willebrand multimers adhere to platelets (leading to thrombocytopenia) & hemolytic anemia as red blood cells become sheared by the clots.

Choice A (Auto-antibodies against the glycoprotein IIb/IIIa receptor on platelets commonly following a viral infection) describes the pathophysiology of Idiopathic (Immune) thrombocytopenic purpura. This leads to platelet destruction by the spleen and an isolated thrombocytopenia.

Choice B (Mutated Factor V that is resistant to breakdown by activated Protein C) describes the pathophysiology of Factor V Leiden mutation. Protein C protects against coagulation, so this leads to a hypercoagulable state.

Choice C (Pathologic activation of the coagulation system causing microthrombi and subsequent thrombocytopenia) describes the pathophysiology of disseminated intravascular coagulation (DIC).

Choice D [Platelet activation by exotoxins (such as Shigella toxin or Shiga-like toxin released from Enterohemorrhagic Escherichia coli)] describes the pathophysiology of Hemolytic uremic syndrome.

QUESTION 95
Choice B (Parvovirus B-19) is the correct choice.   Aplastic crisis in patients with sickle cell disease can be precipitated by Parvovirus B-19 infections. HEMATOLOGY- SICKLE CELL DISEASE – HEALTH MAINTENANCE (page 457)

QUESTION 96

Choice B (Chloroquine) is the correct answer. Chloroquine is the drug of choice for management in chloroquine sensitive areas. For Chloroquine resistance, Atovaquone (Choice C) + Doxycycline (Choice A) or clindamycin (Choice D) can be used. INFECTIOUS DISEASE – MALARIA – CLINICAL INTERVENTION (p 427).

QUESTION 97

Choice B (pleural thickening) is the correct answer. Asbestosis classically causes fibrosis and thickening of the lining of the lungs (the pleura). *Pleural thickening (plaques) are commonly seen in asbestosis.* PULMONARY – ASBESTOSIS – LABS/DIAGNOSTIC STUDIES (p. 91).

Choice A (Westermark's sign) is classically seen with pulmonary embolism.

Choice C (Mediastinal widening) can be seen with aortic dissection, inhalation anthrax, cardiac tamponade, mediastinitis, hilar lymphadenopathy and aortic aneurysms.

Choice D (Tram track appearance of the bronchi) is seen with bronchiectasis.

Choice E (Bilateral hilar lymphadenopathy) is seen with sarcoidosis.

QUESTION 98

Choice A (the ability to raise/wrinkle the forehead/eyebrow on the affected side) is the correct answer. *Bell palsy is an idiopathic palsy of the facial nerve* (cranial nerve VII). Because the nerve is involved, all the facial muscles on the affected side will be involved, leading to the *inability to raise and wrinkle the forehead on the affected side.* In strokes, the contralateral innervation of the forehead and the dual innervation of the forehead will cause preservation of the upper facial muscles, leading to the ability to raise and wrinkle the forehead. If a patient is able to raise both eyebrows, it more likely means they may be having a stroke. All the other choices are classic presentations of Bell's palsy as the facial nerve has both motor and sensory functions. NEUROLOGY – BELL PALSY – HISTORY AND PHYSICAL (p. 363).

QUESTION 99

Choice B (fractional excretion of sodium >2%) is the correct choice. *Prerenal azotemia is due to reduced renal perfusion.* In prerenal azotemia, there is no structural damage to the nephron. Since there is no structural renal damage, the natural response is for the kidney to try to *maintain volume by increasing sodium reabsorption and water*, leading to a *fractional excretion of sodium characteristically less than 1%* and a *concentrated urine* (with a high specific gravity). GENITOURINARY – PRERENAL ACUTE KIDNEY INJURY – LABS/DIAGNOSTIC STUDIES (p. 320 & 321).

All of the other choices are seen with prerenal azotemia. Tamm-Horsfall proteins form hyaline casts that are nonspecific and can be seen in a normal urine specimen.

QUESTION 100

Choice E (Anterior wall myocardial infarction) is the correct answer. *Anterior wall myocardial infarctions* frequently involve the *left anterior descending artery.* It manifests on ECG as *ST elevations in leads V1 through V4* (as seen in this vignette). CARDIOLOGY – MYOCARDIAL INFARCTION – LABS/DIAGNOSTIC STUDIES (p. 23).

Choice A (*lateral wall myocardial infarction*) most commonly involves the *left circumflex artery.* It manifests on ECG as *ST elevations in the lateral leads: I, aVL, V5 and V6.*

Choice B (*posterior wall myocardial infarction*) most commonly involves the right coronary artery (and in some cases the circumflex artery branches). Because there are no leads that look directly at the posterior portion of the heart, the reciprocal changes (*ST depressions in the anterior leads V1 through V4*) makes this diagnosis highly suspicious (especially if there is also the presence of an inferior wall myocardial infarction (both inferior and posterior portions of the heart are supplied by the right coronary artery). Both inferior and posterior walls infarctions can occur separately.

Choice C (Non ST elevation myocardial infarction) is incorrect in this case as there are ST elevations in the anterior leads.

Choice D (Inferior wall myocardial infarction) most commonly involves the right coronary artery. It manifests on ECG as ST elevations in the inferior leads: II, III and aVF.

PHOTO CREDITS FOR EXAM 1

Basal cell carcinoma
> Wellcome Trust Library / CustomMedical (Used with permission)

Erysipelas
> By CDC/Dr. Thomas F. Sellers/Emory University [Public domain], via Wikimedia Commons

Melanoma
> Credit: J. Cavallini / CustomMedical (Used with Permission)

Lead lines
> By Dr Abhijit Datir (http://radiopaedia.org/cases/lead-poisoning) [GFDL 1.3 (www.gnu.org/licenses/fdl-1.3.html), GFDL 1.3 (www.gnu.org/licenses/fdl-1.3.html), CC BY-SA 3.0 (http://creativecommons.org/licenses/by-sa/3.0) or Attribution], via Wikimedia Commons

Achalasia:
> By Farnoosh Farrokhi, Michael F. Vaezi. [CC-BY-2.0 (http://creativecommons.org/licenses/by/2.0)], via Wikimedia Commons

Lupus Erythematosus
> By Doktorinternet (Own work) [CC BY-SA 4.0 (http://creativecommons.org/licenses/by-sa/4.0)], via Wikimedia Commons

Bradycardia
> By Glenlarson (Own work) [Public domain], via Wikimedia Commons

Osteoarthritis
> Credit: S. Needell / CustomMedical (Used With permission)

1. In a patient with normal blood urea nitrogen and creatinine levels, which of the following radiograph findings are most consistent with osteomalacia not due to renal disease?
    a. "salt and pepper" appearance of the skull
    b. "punched out lesions" appearance of the skull
    c. the presence of Looser zones
    d. "cotton wool" appearance of the skull
    e. pathologic fractures and radiologic evidence of kyphosis

2. A 45-year-old male with acquired immune deficiency syndrome is noncompliant with his antiretroviral therapy. He develops multiple nodulopapular, violaceous lesions on the skin consistent with Kaposi sarcoma. Which of the following is the most likely etiologic agent?
    a. Human papilloma virus
    b. Herpes simplex virus
    c. Human herpesvirus 8
    d. Epstein Barr Virus
    e. Cytomegalovirus

3. A 26-year-old female presents to the clinic with intermittent episodes of diarrhea and abdominal pain that is relieved with defecation. She has occasional episodes of constipation changes in frequency. There is no evidence of blood or mucous in the stools. Which of the following is the most likely diagnosis?
    a. diverticulitis
    b. diverticulosis
    c. irritable bowel syndrome
    d. chronic mesenteric ischemia
    e. volvulus

4. A 44-year-old woman is complaining of decreased vision and pain in the right eye especially when staring at lights. On physical examination, there is conjunctival erythema with the presence of a ciliary flush. A slit lamp reveals the presence of dendritic lesions. Which of the following is the most appropriate therapy?
    a. pilocarpine ophthalmic solution
    b. olopatadine ophthalmic solution
    c. prednisolone ophthalmic solution
    d. trifluridine ophthalmic drops and acyclovir orally
    e. polymyxin B/trimethoprim ophthalmic solution

5. Which of the following is not a side effect of erythromycin?
    a. prolonged QT interval
    b. cytochrome P450 inhibition
    c. diarrhea
    d. flushing with rapid IV administration
    e. increased potential for muscle toxicity if used with HMG coA reductase inhibitors

6. A 42-year-old male with a history of schizophrenia is being managed with Haloperidol (Haldol). He develops lip smacking, teeth grinding and rolling of the tongue. There are no signs of tremor, slowness of movement or other symptoms. Which of the following is the most likely diagnosis?
    a. neuroleptic malignant syndrome
    b. tardive dyskinesia
    c. acute dystonic reaction
    d. serotonin syndrome
    e. akathisia

7. A 32-year-old woman at 35 weeks gestation presents to the emergency room with painful contractions. A pelvic examination is done, revealing 4 cm cervical dilation with 81% effacement. There is a positive fern test and the L:S ratio is <2:1. There are no signs of fetal distress upon testing. She is afebrile and there is no uterine tenderness or vaginal discharge. Which of the following is the most appropriate management at this time?
   a. administration of prostaglandins
   b. administration of magnesium sulfate and corticosteroids
   c. administration of terbutaline
   d. observation until 85% effacement
   e. administration of oxytocin to induce labor

8. A 40-year-old male is complaining of exquisite pain and swelling to the right foot for 1 day. The patient states the pain started the day after Thanksgiving. He admits to having consumed large amounts of steak and beer for the holidays. On physical examination, the first metatarsophalangeal joint is tender, red, warm and edematous. A right foot radiograph is taken:

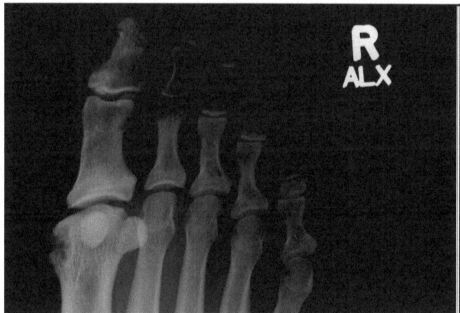

   Which of the following would be the most likely arthroscopic finding in this patient?
   a. less than 200 white blood cell/mm
   b. 21,000 WBC (90% PMN), negatively birefringent, needle shaped crystals
   c. 21,000 WBC (90% PMN), positively birefringent rhomboid shaped crystals
   d. 59,000 WBC (90% PMN), cloudy fluid
   e. 35,000 WBC (90% PMN) no crystals seen

9. A 43-year-old female with no significant past medical history is complaining of 8 months of generalized fatigue and weakness. Her symptoms include cravings to eat ice and clay. For 3 months, she has been having progressive dysphagia. Physical examination reveals pallor of the conjunctiva, atrophic glossitis, angular cheilitis and spooning of the nails. An upper endoscopy is performed to evaluate the dysphagia, revealing the presence of esophageal webs. Which of the following is the most likely panel found in this patient?
   a. decreased serum iron, decreased ferritin, increased total iron binding capacity
   b. decreased serum iron, increased ferritin, decreased total iron binding capacity
   c. increased serum iron, normal ferritin, decreased total iron binding capacity
   d. normal serum iron, normal ferritin, decreased total iron binding capacity
   e. increased serum iron, increased ferritin, decreased total iron binding capacity

10. A 45-year-old male with a history of diabetes mellitus and polycystic kidney disease is admitted to the intensive care unit for a subarachnoid hemorrhage. He is placed on stool softeners and phenytoin for seizure prophylaxis. His home medications are daily aspirin and chlorpropramide. He states over the last few days, he has developed nausea and fatigue. There are no signs of peripheral edema or decreased skin turgor. His vital signs are stable. Lab tests are as follows:

		PATIENT	NORMAL
Serum Glucose	(mg/dL)	128	64 – 128
Serum Sodium	(mEq/L)	129	135 – 145
Serum BUN	(mg/dL)	7	7 – 10
Serum Creatinine	(mg/dL)	0.7	0.8 – 1.4
Serum Osmolarity	(mOsm/kg)	257	280 – 290
Urine Osmolarity	(mmol/kg)	680	300 – 900
Urine sodium	(mEq/L)	35	20

Which of the following is considered the management of choice in this patient?
   a. hypertonic saline infusion with furosemide
   b. normal saline infusion
   c. fluid restriction
   d. fluid and sodium restriction
   e. demeclocycline administration

11. A 38-year-old male with a history of Type II diabetes mellitus presents to the clinic with sudden onset of slurred speech, drooping of the corner of his right mouth & inability to close the right eye fully. He also states that he had ear pain for a day that preceded the symptoms. The symptoms are not associated with visual changes, nystagmus or drop attacks. On physical examination, he has full range of motion with 5/5 motor & sensation of both the upper and lower extremities. Which of the following is the most likely diagnosis?
   a. right anterior cerebral artery occlusion
   b. right posterior cerebral artery occlusion
   c. Bell's palsy
   d. left anterior cerebral artery occlusion
   e. transient ischemic attack

12. Which of the following is increased in patients with emphysema-dominant chronic obstructive pulmonary disease?
   a. Diffusing capacity of the lung for carbon monoxide (DLCO)
   b. Forced vital capacity (FVC)
   c. Forced expiratory volume in 1 second (FEV1)
   d. Residual volume (RV)
   e. Alpha-1 antitrypsin levels

13. A 40-year-old male who works in the Fulton Fish Market in the Bronx, NY comes into the corporate clinic for a rash on his hands. He states he may have sustained a puncture wound while packing shellfish. On physical examination of the hand, there is non-pitting edema, purplish erythema and sharp, irregular margins from the possible puncture site extending peripherally with central clearing. There are neither granulomas present nor crepitus. A radiograph of the affected hand shows no evidence of fracture, retained foreign body or gas in the soft tissues. A wound culture is positive for growth of gram-positive bacilli after 3 days. Which of the following organisms is the most likely cause?
   a. Erysipelothrix rhusiopathiae
   b. Mycobacterium marinum
   c. Coxiella burnetii
   d. Clostridium perfringens
   e. Haemophilus ducreyi

14. A 43-year old male undergoes cholesterol screening and is found to have an abnormal cholesterol panel. After a trial of 6 months of rigid diet and exercise, his repeat cholesterol values are as follows:

	PATIENT	NORMAL VALUES
HDL	49 mg/dL	> 45 mg/dL
LDL	190 mg/dL	< 100 mg/dL
TRIGLYCERIDES	149 mg/dL	< 150 mg/dL

Which of the following medications is the most appropriate management for this patient?
   a.   simvastatin
   b.   cholestyramine
   c.   ezetimibe
   d.   fenofibrate
   e.   nicotinic acid

15. Depression is a side effect of which of the following anti hypertensive medications?
   a.   ACE inhibitors
   b.   Beta blockers
   c.   Hydrochlorothiazide
   d.   Angiotensin II receptor antagonist
   e.   Hydralazine

16. Which of the following most reliably distinguishes chronic primary adrenocortical insufficiency from secondary adrenocortical insufficiency?
   a.   the presence of fatigue
   b.   the presence of hyperkalemia
   c.   the presence of muscle weakness
   d.   the presence of hyponatremia
   e.   the presence of skin hyperpigmentation

17. A 23-year-old woman has a positive pregnancy test. She states that her last menstrual period was July 10 and that her periods are regular. Which of the following most accurately describes her estimated date of delivery according to Naegele's rule?
   a.   April 17
   b.   April 3
   c.   October 17
   d.   October 10
   e.   May 17

18. A 72-year-old male is admitted for status asthmaticus and is given ipratropium nebulizer therapy and oral corticosteroids. The nurse informs you the next morning that the patient is exhibiting signs of acute confusion in which the patient fluctuates between agitation and somnolence, with paranoid ideation. There are no visual hallucinations. Which of the following is the most likely diagnosis?
   a. dementia
   b. delirium
   c. Type II bipolar disorder
   d. Wernicke's encephalopathy
   e. Vascular dementia

19. A 37-year-old male with a history of chronic hepatitis B and Wilson's disease (for which he takes pencillamine) presents to the emergency room with shortness of breath. He denies any recent skin or throat infections. Physical examination reveals dullness to percussion, decreased fremitus and decreased breath sounds at the bases bilaterally with no crackles heard throughout the lung fields. The heart has a regular rate and rhythm. S1 and S2 are normal. No S3, S4, murmurs, rubs or other sounds are heard. There is bilateral peripheral and sacral edema. The labs are consistent with a hypotonic hypervolemic hyponatremia and hyperlipidemia. A urinalysis reveals proteinuria, oval fat bodies and fatty casts. A 24-hour urine protein collection shows proteinuria of 4 grams. Which of the following would most likely be seen on biopsy?
   a. IgA deposits in the glomerulus
   b. normal cellularity with thickened glomerular basement membrane
   c. nodular glomerulosclerosis with pink hyaline material around the glomerular capillaries
   d. hypercellularity with increased monocytes and positive immune humps
   e. hypercellularity with the presence of crescent-shaped collapse of the Bowman's capsules

20. A 43-year-old male presents with episodes of feeling as if the "room is spinning" that lasts for minutes to several hours over the last 2 days. This sensation is often accompanied with hearing loss, a ringing sensation in the ear and describes voices sounding as if he is "underneath water". Which of the following physical examination findings would most likely be present in this patient?
   a. bullae on the tympanic membrane
   b. horizontal nystagmus
   c. vertical nystagmus
   d. non fatigable nystagmus
   e. granulation tissue seen on the tympanic membrane

21. Which of the following accurately describes the primary pathophysiology of rheumatoid arthritis?
   a. degenerative wear and tear of the joint, leading to asymmetric joint narrowing
   b. T cell-mediated pannus formation with symmetric joint destruction and symmetric narrowing
   c. Joint damage due to enthesitis
   d. Imbalance in cartilage repair leading to more cartilage destruction than repair
   e. Joint damage as a result of peripheral neuropathy and repetitive microtrauma

22. Which of the following is not a side effect of long-term lithium therapy?
   a. hyperparathyroidism
   b. hypothyroidism
   c. syndrome of inappropriate antidiuretic hormone secretion
   d. arrhythmias
   e. seizures

23. A 21-year-old male is complaining of persistent swelling to the neck. He states the swelling has worsened over the last week when he celebrated his birthday and consumed large amounts of alcohol. On physical examination, there is nontender cervical lymphadenopathy. The swollen lymph node is excised. Which of the following biopsy findings are most consistent with Hodgkin's lymphoma?
   a. large B cells with bilobed or multilobar nuclei giving it an "owl eye appearance" due to eosinophilic inclusions in the nuclei.
   b. abnormal, fragile B-lymphocytes with a "smudged" appearance that occurs with slide preparation.
   c. crystalized granular elongated needles seen in the cytoplasm of immature white blood cells.
   d. red blood cell inclusions that are composed of denatured hemoglobin.
   e. reciprocal translocation between chromosome 9 and chromosome 22.

24. A 36-year-old woman with no past medical history presents to the emergency room with sudden onset of left-sided chest pain and shortness of breath. She denies any trauma but states that she recently drove 24 hours from Florida to New York in her car. She is on oral contraceptive pills and she smokes a half pack of cigarettes a day. Her vital signs are as follows: Temp: 98.6, HR: 128 and regular, BP 130/88, RR: 26, O2 sat 92% on room air. Her physical examination is unremarkable. Which of the following is the most appropriate next step in the evaluation of this patient?

    a. Pulmonary angiography

    b. Venous Doppler of the lower extremities

    c. Ventilation perfusion scan

    d. Spiral CT scan of the chest with contrast

    e. D-dimer

25. A 32-year-old sexually active male develops the following painless lesion:

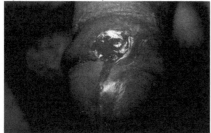

Which of the following is used in the diagnostic evaluation of this patient?

    a. India ink

    b. Tzanck smear

    c. Darkfield microscopy

    d. Potassium Hydroxide

    e. Polymerase chain reaction

26. A 55-year-old male with a history of myocardial infarction treated with triple bypass presents to the clinic with symptoms that are consistent with chronic mesenteric ischemia. Which of the following would be expected?

    a. dull abdominal pain worse with meals and associated with weight loss

    b. left lower quadrant pain and tenderness with bloody diarrhea

    c. severe abdominal pain out of proportion to physical examination

    d. right upper quadrant pain

    e. flank pain that radiates to the testicle

27. A 17-year-old newly diagnosed type I diabetic is placed on regular insulin and NPH insulin. His finger sticks in the morning before breakfast have been consistently elevated. He is instructed to record his fingersticks for the next 3 days and the fingerstick glucose levels are as follows:

11 PM	2AM	6AM	9AM after breakfast
89 mg/dL	40 mg/dL	180 mg/dL	98 mg/dL
90 mg/dL	52 mg/dL	240 mg/dL	101 mg/dL
92 mg/dL	47 mg/dL	278 mg/dL	101 mg/dL

(Normal fasting levels 80-110 mg/dL. Normal Post prandial levels <140 mg/dL)

Which of following is the most appropriate management of this patient?

    a. moving his NPH dose to the afternoon

    b. decreasing his bedtime NPH dose

    c. decreasing his evening regular insulin dose

    d. moving his last regular insulin dose from evening to bedtime

    e. avoiding a bedtime snack

28. A 19-year-old female presents to the emergency room with a sudden onset of blanchable, edematous, pink papules that forms irregular wheals. The patient states that on the way to the emergency room, some of the lesions disappeared and new lesions appeared. Which of the following signs are classically associated with this condition?
    a. Auspitz sign
    b. Koebner's phenomenon
    c. Dermatographism
    d. Nikolsky's sign
    e. Koplik's spots

29. A 43-year old female with a history of Ehlers-Danlos syndrome presents with a sudden onset of a thunderclap headache. A CT shows evidence of a subarachnoid hemorrhage. The patient is admitted to the ICU and is given phenytoin seizure prophylaxis along with bed rest. Which of the following electrolyte abnormalities are most likely to occur in this patient?
    a. hyperkalemia
    b. hypocalcemia
    c. hyponatremia
    d. hypokalemia
    e. hypernatremia

30. A 43-year-old patient is diagnosed with active tuberculosis. Ethambutol is one of the four drugs used to treat his active disease. A week into the treatment, he develops painless central blind spots in the right eye. On fundoscopic examination, there is a normal disc to cup ratio. During a swinging light test, when the light is shone from the left eye to the right eye, the pupil appears to dilate. The cornea looks normal in appearance and there is no conjunctival erythema. There is no blurring of the optic disc on fundoscopic examination. Which of the following is the most likely diagnosis?
    a. papilledema
    b. papillitis
    c. retrobulbar neuritis
    d. acute angle closure glaucoma
    e. chronic open angle glaucoma

31. Which of the following is most specific for differentiating schizophrenia from mania?
    a. inflated self esteem
    b. flat, blunted, emotional affect
    c. disorganized speech and thinking
    d. expansive or irritable mood
    e. impairment of social function

32. A 24-year-old woman presents with a 2-month history of leg pain when she walks more than 5 blocks. The pain is relieved shortly after rest. On physical examination, there are diminished pulses only affecting the left extremity. Blood pressure measurements between both arms are asymmetrical. An angiogram is performed and shows evidence of an aortic aneurysm. Which of the following is the most likely diagnosis?
    a. peripheral arterial disease
    b. Raynaud's phenomenon
    c. Takayasu arteritis
    d. Kawasaki disease
    e. Prinzmetal's angina

33. A 33-year-old male has been complaining of progressive shortness of breath with exertion. Physical examination reveals pursed lip breathing, increased anteroposterior diameter, decreased fremitus, hyperresonance to percussion and decreased breath sounds. Chest radiographs show darkened lung fields and flattened diaphragms. Upon questioning the patient, he says he has never smoked nor lived with smokers. Which of the following tests would most likely show the etiology of his symptoms?

  a. angiotensin converting enzyme levels
  b. Ig G antibodies to the type IV collagen of the alveoli
  c. anti-double stranded DNA antibodies
  d. sweat chloride test
  e. alpha-1 antitrypsin levels

34. A 31-year-old female had a normal vaginal delivery at 32 weeks gestation. 24 hours later, she has 3 episodes of uterine bleeding. She is afebrile with stable vital signs. There is no foul-smelling discharge from the vagina or uterine tenderness. She does not have any bruising of the skin. Prothrombin time and partial thromboplastin time are within normal limits.   Which of the following is the most appropriate treatment at this time?

  a. fresh frozen plasma
  b. IV Ceftriaxone
  c. IV oxytocin
  d. IV amoxicillin + gentamicin + metronidazole
  e. Obtain D-dimer levels

35. A 4-year-old boy is brought to the pediatric clinic by his mother after he developed a high fever, cough, conjunctivitis and a runny nose. He later developed small red spots in the buccal mucosa with a pale blue/white center opposite his first and second molars.   A brick-red rash began at his hairline and face, progressing to his extremities. The rash lasts 7 days. Which of the following is the most likely diagnosis?

  a. rubella
  b. rubeola
  c. fifth's disease
  d. mumps
  e. hand foot and mouth disease

36. A 53-year-old male with a history of adult polycystic kidney disease presents to the emergency room with a sudden onset of "the worse headache of my life" that was followed by a witnessed brief loss of consciousness. The patient is now experiencing headache, nausea, vomiting and nuchal rigidity. There are no focal neurological deficits and he is afebrile.   There is no papilledema present on fundoscopic examination.   A CT scan of the head shows no evidence of hemorrhage or mass lesion. A lumbar puncture is performed. Which of the following cerebrospinal fluid (CSF) findings would be most likely present?

  a. increased CSF opening pressure with an otherwise normal CSF examination
  b. high protein with normal white blood cell count
  c. increased oligoclonal IgG bands
  d. increased CSF opening pressure with xanthochromia that does not diminish from tube 1 to tube 4
  e. normal glucose with increased white blood cells (primarily lymphocytes)

37. A 43-year-old previously healthy female presents to the emergency room with chest pain and palpitations. The symptoms continue despite oxygen and IV fluid therapy. Her blood pressure is 80/60 mmHg. She is diaphoretic, dizzy and unable to speak in full sentences. Her pulses are palpable but rapid. An ECG is performed, showing a regular, narrow complex tachycardia at 180 beats per minute. There are no ST or T wave changes consistent with myocardial infarction and the patient has no significant cardiac risk factors. Which of the following is the recommended management of this patient?
   a. Atropine
   b. Synchronized cardioversion
   c. Adenosine
   d. Amiodarone
   e. Unsynchronized cardioversion

38. A 12-year-old boy presents to the pediatric clinic with facial swelling. He was treated three weeks ago for sinusitis and those symptoms have resolved. He is now complaining of unilateral eye edema with ocular discharge and decreased vision. There is pain with eye movement during the extra ocular exam. There are no cells or flare seen nor is there any fluorescein uptake. Which of the following is the most likely diagnosis?
   a. bacterial conjunctivitis
   b. anterior uveitis
   c. septal cellulitis
   d. dacrocystitis
   e. preseptal cellulitis

39. A 63-year-old woman is placed on Risedronate for osteoporosis. Which of the following should the patient be advised to do while on Risedronate therapy?
   a. Risedronate should be taken with milk to enhance its absorption
   b. The patient should remain upright for 30 minutes after taking Risedronate
   c. Risedronate reduces the risk of jaw osteonecrosis as well as osteoporosis
   d. Risedronate should be taken at night to maximize its effectiveness
   e. Risedronate should be taken with food to reduce the risk of pill induced esophagitis

40. A 43-year old female presents with flank pain and hematuria for the last 48 hours. A urinalysis is performed and shows the following:

	PATIENT	NORMAL
Urine pH	8.2	4.5 – 8
WBCs/hpf	15	≤ 2- 5
Leukocyte esterase	Positive	Negative
Protein	None	None
Nitrites	Positive	Negative
RBCs/hpf	8	≤ 3

A CT scan of the abdomen and pelvis without contrast shows the presence of staghorn calculi in the right kidney. A 1-mm stone is passed and is found to be composed of ammonium magnesium phosphate (struvite). Which of the following organisms is the most likely causative agent in the formation of these stones?
   a. Staphylococcus saprophyticus
   b. Escherichia coli
   c. Proteus mirabilis
   d. Enterococcus species
   e. Enterobacter species

41. Which of the following tests best differentiates nephrogenic diabetes insipidus from central diabetes insipidus?
   a. fluid challenge test
   b. dexamethasone suppression test
   c. fluid deprivation test
   d. desmopressin stimulation test
   e. Captopril test

42. Which of the following is the most likely diagnosis based on the rhythm strip?

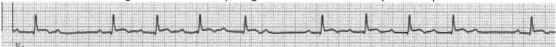

   a. First degree heart block
   b. Second degree heart block (Mobitz I)
   c. Second degree heart block (Mobitz II)
   d. Third degree heart block
   e. Ashman phenomenon

43. A 20-year-old thin female presents to the clinic with multiple episodes of chest pain, panic attacks, and dizziness whenever she exercises or exerts herself. On physical examination, there is the presence of a systolic ejection click. Which of the following is the recommended management of this patient?
   a. reassurance that the disease is self limiting
   b. education that she may develop the murmur of mitral stenosis
   c. propranolol for the autonomic symptoms
   d. aspirin to reduce the chest pain symptoms
   e. nitroglycerin as needed for the chest pain and other symptoms

44. In the evaluation of a 32-year-old female at 19 weeks gestation, a triple screen test is done and shows the following:
   Alpha-fetoprotein: low
   Beta hCG: high
   Estradiol: low
   Which of the following is the most likely cause of these findings?
   a. Open neural tube defects
   b. Trisomy 18
   c. Trisomy 21
   d. Multiple gestation
   e. Underestimation of gestational age

45. A 32-year-old physician who recently moved to the United States from mainland China presents to the clinic for yearly tuberculosis screening. The patient is asked during routine history about any symptoms and he denies chest pain, hemoptysis, weight loss, fever or chills. A PPD is placed, and 48 hours later, reveals 10 mm of induration and 5 mm of erythema. A chest radiograph shows no acute cardiopulmonary disease or granuloma. Which of the following is considered the management of choice?
   a. isoniazid + pyridoxine (B6) total duration of treatment for 9 months
   b. isoniazid + rifampin + ethambutol + pyrazinamide (total treatment duration of 9 months)
   c. isoniazid + rifampin + ethambutol + streptomycin (total treatment duration of 6 months)
   d. isoniazid + pyridoxine (B6) total duration of treatment for 12 months
   e. ceftriaxone + azithromycin

46. A 66-year-old male with chronic bronchitis has symptoms consistent with cor pulmonale. Which of the following medications have been shown to reduce overall mortality?
   a.   Theophylline
   b.   Oxygen
   c.   Ipratropium
   d.   Flunisolide
   e.   Albuterol

47. A patient has routine hepatitis B testing with the following lab values:
   Hepatitis B surface antigen: negative
   Hepatitis B surface antibody: positive
   Hepatitis B core antibody IgM: negative
   Hepatitis B core antibody IgG: positive
   Hepatitis E antigen: negative
   Which of the following is the most likely diagnosis?
      a.   The patient has acute hepatitis B infection
      b.   The patient is in the window period
      c.   The patient has been successfully vaccinated
      d.   The patient has full recovery of distant hepatitis B infection
      e.   The patient has chronic hepatitis B infection

48. A 53-year-old male has had chronic, intermittent, non-bloody diarrhea for the last 2 months associated with intermittent fever. He has had intermittent joint pains and describes a weird occurrence of twitching of his eye when he is chewing. Transglutaminase antibodies are negative. A small bowel duodenal biopsy is periodic acid-Schiff (PAS) stain positive and is positive for the presence of dilated lacteals. Which of the following is the most likely diagnosis?
   a. seronegative spondyloarthopathies
   b. Whipple's disease
   c. Crohn's disease
   d. ulcerative colitis
   e. Giardiasis

49. "H-shaped" vertebrae with central endplate depressions are seen with which of the following disorders?
   a.   Spondylolisthesis
   b.   Spondylolysis
   c.   Ankylosing spondylitis
   d.   Spinal stenosis
   e.   Sickle cell disease

50. Which of the following is the first line management of warm antibody type autoimmune hemolytic anemia in a patient with systemic lupus erythematosus?
      a.   Avoidance of the cold
      b.   Corticosteroids
      c.   Splenectomy
      d.   Deferoxamine
      e.   Hydroxyurea

51. Pulmonary fibrosis and thyroid disorders are classic side effects of which of the following medications?
    a. propranolol
    b. amiodarone
    c. adenosine
    d. procainamide
    e. verapamil

52. A 23-year-old male presents to the emergency room with high fever, headache, joint pain and chest pain. His ECG is positive for second-degree heart block, which was not present in prior ECGs. A lumbar puncture is performed and is consistent with Lyme meningitis. Which of the following is the treatment of choice?
    a. Oral Amoxicillin
    b. IV Ampicillin/sulbactam
    c. IV Ceftriaxone
    d. IV Gentamicin
    e. Oral Doxycycline

53. Which of the following classically describes the appearance of seborrheic keratosis?
    a. Red elevated nodule with adherent white scales with crusted blood at the margins
    b. dry, rough scaly, "sandpaper" like rash with hyperkeratotic plaques
    c. small papule or plaque with a velvety, warty, "stuck on" appearance
    d. small, raised translucent pearly papule with central ulceration and rolled borders.
    e. Asymmetric, multi-color, 7-mm lesion with irregular borders and rapid change in appearance

54. A 32-year-old male with no past medical or psychiatric history has a 2-month history of rapid functional decline as per his family. Today, he was found on the subway platform saying that "the voices in his head kept telling him to jump off the platform." He states he was contemplating jumping in an attempt to stop the sensation of "insects crawling on his body". He is sitting on the stretcher wearing a hat made of foil paper to protect his thoughts from being intercepted by the Chinese government. He seems to have a flat effect when communicating with the health care providers. Which of the following is the most likely diagnosis?
    a. schizophrenia
    b. Bipolar disorder
    c. Paranoid personality disorder
    d. Schizophreniform disorder
    e. Schizoid personality disorder

55. Which of the following describes myoclonus?
    a. rapid, involuntary, jerky, uncontrolled purposeless movements
    b. repetitive, non-rhythmic movements or vocals
    c. brief, sporadic single repetitive jerks or twitching of 1 or more muscle groups
    d. sustained contraction with twisting of the body and abnormal posturing
    e. repetitive, rhythmic jerking that usually lasts less than 2 to 3 minutes

56. Which of the following is classically seen in osteoarthritis?
    a. warm, boggy, and edematous joint
    b. positive rheumatoid factor, elevated C-reactive protein and erythrocyte sedimentation rate
    c. symmetric joint narrowing
    d. evening stiffness predominantly and morning stiffness lasting less than 30 minutes
    e. osteopenia

57. A 43-year-old male was ejected off of his motorcycle and had a witnessed brief loss of consciousness. He presents to the emergency room with headache, nausea, vomiting and dizziness. A CT scan of the head shows no evidence of fracture, midline shift, or evidence of intracranial bleed. He is not on aspirin or other anticoagulants. He remains lucid during his emergency room visit and upon discharge. Which of the following is the recommended management of this patient?

    a. raising the head of the bed, placing the patient in a dark, quiet room, supplemental oxygen and phenytoin seizure prophylaxis.

    b. cognitive and physical rest

    c. administer dexamethasone and mannitol

    d. immediate neurosurgery consult

    e. administer hypertonic fluids to reduce the neurologic symptoms

58. A 30-year-old woman with a history of Raynaud's Phenomenon presents to the clinic with difficulty swallowing. An esophagram shows esophageal motility abnormalities. On physical exam, she has clawed hands and some calcified lesions on her shins. Her skin is thin and shiny on the face and neck as well as distal to the elbows and the knees. Which of the following antibodies would most likely be seen in this patient?

    a. anti-La antibodies

    b. anti-centromere antibodies

    c. anti-smooth muscle antibodies

    d. anti-Mi2 antibodies

    e. anti-SRP antibodies

59. A 7-year-old girl presents with mild hearing loss and low-grade fever. On physical examination, there is erythema and an effusion of the tympanic membrane with decreased motility of the tympanic membrane on insufflation. There is absence of bullae on the tympanic membrane. Which of the following antibiotics are considered the first line management of choice?

    a. amoxicillin

    b. amoxicillin/clavulanic acid

    c. doxycycline

    d. ciprofloxacin

    e. metronidazole

60. A 54-year-old female is seen in the clinic for refractory hypertension. On physical examination, she has truncal obesity with thin arms and legs, striae on her abdomen and supraclavicular fat pads with facial redness and roundness. Which of the following is the most common etiology of her symptoms overall?

    a. Cushing's disease

    b. Exogenous corticosteroid use

    c. Adrenal tumor

    d. Ectopic ACTH-producing tumor

    e. Ketoconazole use

61. A 67-year-old male presents with weight loss, back and bone pain. Prostate specific antigen is 20 ng/mL (normal <4 ng/mL). Which of the following would be the most likely rectal examination finding?

    a. boggy nontender prostate gland

    b. smooth firm prostate

    c. hard nodular prostate

    d. enlarged symmetric firm prostate

    e. tender boggy prostate

62. A 35-year-old male comes to the clinic for a routine physical examination. During obtaining a history, he tells you his brother was diagnosed with colon cancer at 53-years-old. Which of the following describes the appropriate colon cancer screening guidelines for this patient?
   a. Fecal occult blood testing now and colonoscopy every 10 years
   b. Fecal occult blood testing at age 40 and colonoscopy every 10 years
   c. Fecal occult blood testing at age 50 and colonoscopy every 10 years
   d. Fecal occult blood testing at age 50 and colonoscopy every 5 years
   e. Fecal occult blood testing at age 40 and colonoscopy every 5 years

63. A 45-year-old male is being evaluated for a chronic cough. A chest radiograph is obtained, which shows honeycombing consistent with idiopathic pulmonary fibrosis. Which of the following pulmonary function test findings is most consistent with restrictive pulmonary disease?
   a. Increased total lung capacity
   b. Increased residual volume
   c. Increased FEV1/FVC ratio
   d. Increased lung compliance
   e. Increased functional residual capacity

64. A 43-year-old male went camping where he hunted and ate rabbits. 5 days later, he develops a headache, fever and nausea. On his hand, there is an ulcerated papule with a central eschar and tender regional lymphadenopathy. There is also splenomegaly and diarrhea. Which of the following is the most likely diagnosis?
   a. Cutaneous anthrax
   b. Tularemia
   c. Coccidiodomycosis
   d. Leishmaniasis
   e. Brucellosis

65. Which of the following is used in the treatment of acetaminophen toxicity?
   a. flumazenil
   b. naloxone
   c. N-acetylcysteine
   d. pralidoxime
   e. physostigmine

66. Which of the following describes the mechanism of action of argatroban?
   a. direct thrombin inhibitor
   b. potentiates antithrombin III as well as indirect thrombin inhibition
   c. inhibits Vitamin K dependent clotting factors II, VII, IX and X
   d. selective Factor Xa inhibitor
   e. inhibits adenosine diphosphate

67. Which of the following is not a side effect of lisinopril?
   a. teratogenicity
   b. hypotension
   c. hypokalemia
   d. azotemia
   e. dry cough and angioedema

68. A male is being evaluated. He states that he was a relatively normal height before puberty. After puberty, he developed a tall, thin stature. He has had issues in school with language comprehension. He later became obese. On physical examination, he has long limbs, gynecomastia and testicular atrophy as well as the presence of ataxia and scoliosis. Which of the following is the most likely diagnosis?
   a. Marfan syndrome
   b. Klinefelter's syndrome
   c. Turner's syndrome
   d. Ehlers-Danlos Syndrome
   e. Hypopituitarism

69. A 45-year-old female seeks medical therapy for her recurrent symptoms that occur multiple times over the last year. She has had a longstanding history of painful legs, difficulty swallowing, vomiting, intermittent dyspnea and dysmenorrhea. She has had multiple workups, of which no organic cause was found for her varied symptoms. She is convinced that surgery may be curative since "medicine doesn't seem to help". Which of the following is the most likely diagnosis?
   a. Body dysmorphic disorder
   b. Functional neurological disorder (Conversion disorder)
   c. Malingering
   d. Factitious disorder (Munchausen syndrome)
   e. Somatic symptom disorder (Somatization disorder)

70. A 54-year-old male presents with progressively worsening headaches. The headaches tends to be worse in the morning, waking the patient up at night. The patient also has some spatial disorientation. His vital signs are as follows: BP: 150/100, heart rate: 40 beats per minute, O_2 sat: 99% on room air, Respirations: Cheyne-Stokes breathing pattern. A CT scan shows a nonhomogeneous mass with a hypodense center, variable ring of enhancement with surrounding edema. The lesion crosses the corpus callosum giving it a "butterfly appearance". The lesion is not attached to the dura. Which of the following is the most likely diagnosis?
   a. glioblastoma multiforme
   b. oligodendroglioma
   c. ependymoma
   d. hemangioma
   e. meningioma

71. Which of the following is required in the diagnostic evaluation of a patient suspected of having osteoporosis?
   a. plain radiographs of the spine and the hip
   b. bone scan
   c. dual energy x-ray absorptiometry scan
   d. alkaline phosphatase levels
   e. magnetic resonance imaging of the spine and the hip

72. A 34-year-old male with a history of multiple endocrine neoplasia type 2B is being evaluated. Which of the following would most likely be elevated if thyroid biopsy were positive for medullary thyroid carcinoma?
   a. thyroid stimulating hormone levels
   b. thyroid stimulating antibody levels
   c. thyroid peroxidase antibody levels
   d. calcitonin levels
   e. parathyroid hormone levels

73. A 34-year-old female with a history of myasthenia gravis presents with respiratory muscle weakness and difficulty breathing that is worse towards the end of the day.   On physical examination, lungs are clear to auscultation bilaterally and there are no crackles heard. Edrophonium is given, which worsens the symptoms including sweating, diarrhea and miosis. Which of the following is the most likely diagnosis?

     a. Lambert-Eaton myasthenic syndrome
     b. Myasthenic crisis
     c. Cholinergic crisis
     d. Adult respiratory distress syndrome
     e. Congestive heart failure

74. A 45-year-old male presents with non-bloody diarrhea and crampy abdominal pain (especially in the right lower quadrant). Rovsing, Obturator and Psoas signs are negative. He undergoes an upper GI series with small bowel follow through and a "string sign" is seen in the terminal ileum. The patient is saccharomyces cerevisiae antibody positive. Which of the following lab findings would most likely be seen in this patient?

     a. increased alpha fetoprotein
     b. increased perinuclear anti-neutrophil cytoplasmic antibodies
     c. increased smooth muscle antibodies
     d. increased mean corpuscular volume of the red blood cells
     e. increased endomysial antibodies

75. A 43-year-old male is brought to the emergency room via ambulance. The patient is lethargic, hypotensive and has a decreased respiratory rate. His pupils are pinpoint and his ECG rhythm strip is as follows:

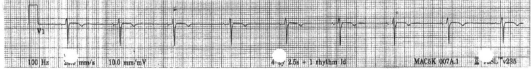

Which of the following is the most likely diagnosis?

     a. cocaine intoxication
     b. opioid intoxication
     c. tricyclic overdose
     d. amphetamine intoxication
     e. venlafaxine intoxication

76. A 32-year-old male presents to the clinic with focal, hard, nontender swelling to the eyelid on the conjunctival surface of the eyelid. There is no red rimming or flakes on the eyelid margin. Which of the following is the most likely diagnosis?

     a. hordeolum
     b. blepharitis
     c. dacrocystitis
     d. chalazion
     e. pterygium

77. A 45-year-old female presents with hand and wrist pain after falling on an outstretched hand. On physical examination, there is tenderness at the anatomical snuffbox. Radiographs of the hand and wrist show no evidence of fracture or dislocation. Which of the following is the most appropriate management?

     a. Observation and reassurance that it is only a wrist sprain
     b. Application of a volar splint
     c. Application of an ulnar gutter splint
     d. Application of a thumb spica splint
     e. Application of a posterior arm splint

78. A 32-year-old football player sustained a deceleration pivoting injury while playing football and felt a sudden pop with subsequent swelling of the left knee associated with buckling of the knee. He denies locking or popping of the knee. A radiograph of the knee is obtained and shows an avulsion of the lateral tibial condyle (Segond fracture). Which of the following tests would most likely be positive?
- a. Valgus stress test
- b. Varus stress test
- c. McMurray test
- d. Lachman test
- e. Posterior drawer test

79. Which of the following is the predisposing factor for the development of lichen simplex chronicus?
- a. human papilloma virus infection
- b. lichen planus
- c. urticaria
- d. erythema nodosum
- e. atopic dermatitis

80. A 42-year-old male presents with acute chest pain for 2 hours that is not relieved with rest. On physical examination, his vital signs are as follows:

Blood pressure: 88/60 mm/Hg
Pulse: 49 beats per minute
Respirations: 20 per minute
O2 sat: 97% on room air
Temperature: 98.9° F
ECG: 3 mm ST elevations in leads II, III and avF. ST depressions in leads V1, V2, V3 and V4.

Which of the following is the most appropriate management at this time?
- a. administration of IV nitroglycerin
- b. administration of IV morphine
- c. administration of IV fluids
- d. administration of IV labetalol
- e. administration of IV Furosemide

81. Which of the following is false regarding the classic chest pain associated with acute pericarditis?
- a. the chest pain is persistent
- b. the chest pain is sharp
- c. the chest pain is worsened with inspiration
- d. the chest pain is relieved with lying supine
- e. the chest pain radiates to the trapezius and the back

82. A 43-year-old female with a history of scleroderma (limited systemic sclerosis variant) develops episodes of color changes to her hands when she is exposed to the cold. She states that when she goes out in the cold, her fingers become swollen, white and painful with some areas turning blue. She states when she comes inside from the cold that her fingers turn red and the pain slowly subsides. Which of the following is the first line management of these symptoms?
- a. propranolol
- b. nifedipine
- c. aspirin
- d. clopidogrel
- e. ibuprofen

83. A 54-year-old male presents with hemoptysis and cough. He complains of intermittent episodes of wheezing, diarrhea, flushing and tachycardia. A bronchoscopy reveals a purple, well-vascularized central lesion. Which of the following is the most likely diagnosis ?
    a. bronchial carcinoid tumor
    b. non small cell lung carcinoma
    c. tuberculosis
    d. small cell lung carcinoma
    e. solitary pulmonary nodule

84. A 60-year-old male with a 50 PPY smoking history is evaluated for recent unintentional weight loss. A biopsy of a small mass found on chest radiograph is consistent with squamous cell carcinoma with no evidence of metastasis. Which of the following is the recommended management of choice?
    a. patient should undergo radiation only
    b. the patient should undergo surgical resection
    c. the patient is not a surgical candidate
    d. the patient should undergo chemotherapy and radiation therapy
    e. the patient should receive corticosteroids

85. A 45-year-old male presents with acute onset of right-sided chest pain and shortness of breath 7 days status post anterior cruciate ligament repair. His vital signs are as follows: Temp: 98.6, HR: 140 regular, BP: 130/82, RR: 29, O2 sat 92% on room air. An arterial blood gas is performed and shows the following:

    pH: 7.57   Normal: 7.35 – 7.45
    PaCO$_2$ = 26 mmHg   Normal: 38 – 42 mm Hg
    HCO$_3$ = 24 mEq/L   Normal 22 – 28 mEq/L

    Which of the following is the most common chest radiograph finding based on the most likely diagnosis?
    a. Pleural effusion
    b. Normal chest radiograph
    c. Wedge-shaped infarct in the lung
    d. Tram track markings
    e. Dilation of the pulmonary artery and collapse of the distal vessels with a sharp cutoff

86. Which of the following is not a recommendation in the management of pediculosis?
    a. bedding and clothing should be laundered in hot water with detergent
    b. bedding and clothing should be placed in a dryer on high for at least 20 minutes
    c. Permethrin lotion should be left on for 8 hours
    d. Toys that cannot be washed should be placed in an air-tight plastic bag for 14 days
    e. Lindane should be applied after a bath or shower to maximize its absorption

87. Which of the following describes the pathophysiology of pemphigus vulgaris?
    a. overgrowth of Malassezia furfur
    b. Type I IgE hypersensitivity reaction of the dermis and subcutaneous tissues
    c. Keratin hyperplasia in the stratum basale and spinosum due to T-cell activation
    d. Type II hypersensitivity reaction in the basement membrane
    e. Autoimmune disruption of the desmosome layer

88. A 36-year-old female presents with epigastric pain that is worse before meals and 2-5 hours after meals but is relieved with the consumption of food. There are no positional changes in the pain intensity. The symptoms tend to wake her up at night. She denies any weight loss or anorexia. On physical examination, the abdomen is nontender. Hemoglobin is in normal range. Which of the following is the most likely diagnosis?
    a. atrophic gastritis
    b. gastric ulcer
    c. duodenal ulcer
    d. acute pancreatitis
    e. pancreatic carcinoma

89. A 48-year-old male with no past medical history presents to the emergency room with an acute onset of painless vision loss. He describes the vision loss as a "curtain being lowered over his left eye". He states the visual loss began five hours ago and that floaters and flashing lights preceded it. On fundoscopic examination, there is a positive Schaffer's sign. Which of the following is the most likely diagnosis?
    a.   amaurosis fugax
    b.   central retinal artery occlusion
    c.   central retinal vein occlusion
    d.   papilledema
    e.   retinal detachment

90. A 53-year-old male with a history of diabetes mellitus complains of right auricular pain and discharge. There is noticeable tenderness, warmth and erythema to the right mastoid process. Which of the following organisms is most likely responsible for these symptoms?
    a.   Staphylococcus aureus
    b.   Pseudomonas aeruginosa
    c.   Rhizopus
    d.   Haemophilus influenzae
    e.   Moraxella catarrhalis

91. Which of the following is considered the first line management of polycythemia vera?
    a.   phlebotomy
    b.   imatinib
    c.   deferoxamine
    d.   red blood cell transfusion
    e.   cryoprecipitate

92. Which of the following is the first line management of heparin overdose?
    a.   Vitamin K
    b.   Deferoxamine
    c.   Protein C concentrates
    d.   Protein S concentrates
    e.   Protamine sulfate

93. Which of the following anti tuberculosis medications is associated with optic neuritis?
    a.   rifampin
    b.   isoniazid
    c.   pyrazinamide
    d.   ethambutol
    e.   streptomycin

94. A patient with severe B_{12} deficiency is being treated with intramuscular B_{12} supplementation. Which of the following electrolyte abnormalities is a common complication of B_{12} replacement therapy?
   a. hypercalcemia
   b. hypokalemia
   c. hyponatremia
   d. hyperkalemia
   e. hypocalcemia

95. Which of the following CSF findings is most consistent with Herpes Simplex Virus-associated encephalitis?
   a. increased opening pressure with otherwise normal CSF analysis
   b. increased protein with decreased glucose and increased lymphocyte count
   c. increased protein with normal glucose and increased lymphocyte count
   d. increased protein with IgG with oligoclonal bands
   e. increased protein with decreased glucose and increased polymorphonuclear neutrophils

96. Which of the following physical exam findings is most suggestive of an upper motor neuron lesion?
   a. muscle fasciculations
   b. flaccid paralysis
   c. decreased deep tendon reflexes
   d. muscle atrophy
   e. upward Babinski reflex

97. Which of the following is classically associated with mitral stenosis?
   a. bounding pulses with a wide pulse pressure
   b. weak, delayed carotid upstroke
   c. mid systolic ejection click
   d. opening snap
   e. increase in murmur intensity when then patient sits up and leans forward

98. Which of the following is the most common organism seen in cat scratch disease?
   a. Pasteurella multocida
   b. Bartonella henselae
   c. Coxiella burnetii
   d. Ascaris lumbricoides
   e. Francisella tularensis

99. Which of the following is the CNS histologic finding in a patient infected with rhabdovirus (Rabies)?
   a. Lewy bodies
   b. Pick bodies
   c. Negri bodies
   d. Mammillary bodies
   e. Neurofibrillary tangles

100. Which of the following skin conditions have the highest incidence of malignant transformation?
   a. oral lichen planus
   b. oral hairy leukoplakia
   c. erythroplakia
   d. Wickham striae
   e. aphthous ulcers

QUESTION 1

Choice C (the presence of Looser zones) is the correct answer. Osteomalacia is due to vitamin D deficiency in adults. It is associated with demineralization of the bone. In some areas, the demineralized bone (osteoid) can give the appearance of a fracture. This is called a Looser line or Looser zone.
ENDOCRINE - OSTEOMALACIA – LABS/RADIOGRAPHIC STUDIES (p. 294).

Choice A ("salt and pepper" appearance of the skull) is associated with *renal osteodystrophy*, a special type of osteomalacia seen in chronic renal disease. The secondary hyperparathyroidism associated with decreased vitamin D production causes increased bone resorption in the skull, leading to the salt and pepper appearance.

Choice B ("punched out lesions" appearance of the skull) is associated with *multiple myeloma.*

Choice D ("cotton wool" appearance of the skull) is associated with *Paget's disease of the bone.*

Choice E (pathologic fractures and radiologic evidence of kyphosis) is seen with osteoporosis.

QUESTION 2

Choice C (human herpesvirus 8) is the correct answer. Kaposi sarcoma is caused by infection of human herpes virus 8 and can be seen in patient with HIV and other immunosuppressive disorders. It is classically described as nodulopapular, violaceous lesions on the skin, gums and other areas.
INFECTIOUS DISEASE – KAPOSI SARCOMA – BASICS (p. 454).

QUESTION 3

Choice C (irritable bowel syndrome) is the correct answer. Irritable bowel syndrome is classically associated with the diarrhea, constipation and abdominal pain that is *classically relieved with defecation.*
GI/NUTRITION – IRRITABLE BOWEL SYNDROME – MOST LIKELY (page 149)

Choice A (ischemic colitis) usually presents with abdominal pain and bloody stools (due to bowel ischemia).

Choice B (diverticulosis) is the most common cause of lower gastrointestinal bleeding so it usually associated with bleeding.

Choice D (chronic mesenteric ischemia) usually presents with *abdominal pain that is worse with eating.* Chronic mesenteric ischemia is due to atherosclerosis of the arteries that supply the bowel. It can present with *"intestinal angina"* - abdominal pain worse with eating (due to the increased demand of blood to the bowel in the setting of a decreased supply). Patients frequently develop anorexia due the fear of the abdominal pain associated with eating.

Choice E (ulcerative colitis) often presents with left lower quadrant pain and bloody (or mucus-filled) stools.

QUESTION 4

Choice D (trifluridine ophthalmic drops and acyclovir orally) is the correct choice. The presence of dendritic lesions in this vignette indicates herpes ophthalmic keratitis. Keratitis is associated with visual changes and the presence of a limbic (ciliary) flush. Treatment for herpes keratitis includes the treatment with antiviral medications. EENT – HERPES KERATITIS – CLINICAL INTERVENTION (p. 230).

Choice A (pilocarpine drops) is used in *acute angle closure glaucoma or to treat Sjrogen's syndrome.* Pilocarpine is a cholinergic drug, which leads to pupillary constriction (reducing the angle closure in glaucoma). Pilocarpine causes increased tear and saliva production (treating the dry eye & mouth seen in Sjrogen's syndrome).

Choice B (olopatadine ophthalmic) is an antihistamine drop used to treat inflammation or chemosis in patients with allergic or viral conjunctivitis.

Choice C (prednisolone ophthalmic) can be used in patients with anterior uveitis. Which can also present with limbic (ciliary flush) as well as cells and flare on ophthalmic exam but would not be associated with dendritic lesions.

Choice E (polymyxin B/trimethoprim ophthalmic solution) is used in the management of conjunctivitis.

QUESTION 5
CHOICE D (flushing with rapid IV administration) is the correct answer. Red man syndrome is histamine-induced flushing of the skin associated with rapid IV administration of vancomycin. Slowing down the infusion can reduce the flushing. All of the other choices are associated side effects of erythromycin.
INFECTIOUS DISEASE – MACROLIDE ANTIBIOTICS – PHARMACOLOGY (p. 412 & 414).

QUESTION 6
Choice B (tardive dyskinesia) is the correct answer. The symptoms in this vignette are consistent with *tardive dyskinesia, a complication of long-term dopamine blocking agents such as Haloperidol. Symptoms include repetitive involuntary movements, mostly involving the extremities and the face. Symptoms include lip smacking, teeth grinding and rolling of the tongue.* PSYCH/BEHAVIORAL – TARDIVE DYSKINESIA – PHARMACOLOGY (p. 383).

Choice A (Neuroleptic malignant syndrome) is a condition seen due to decreased dopamine activity in patients on dopamine antagonists (such as anti-psychotic medications). It can also present with hyperthermia but these patients tend to be hyporeflexive, and often develop urinary incontinence.

Choice C (acute dystonic reaction) describes the reversible extrapyramidal symptoms that usually occur in hours to days after the initiation of a dopamine-blocking anti-psychotics (especially 1st generation anti-psychotics). The extrapyramidal symptoms include: intermittent spasms, trismus, protrusions of the tongue, facial grimacing, torticollis, and difficulty speaking.

Choice D (serotonin syndrome) is a potentially life-threatening condition due to increased serotonin activity. It is usually due to the potentiation between 2 serotonin agonistic drugs (including the natural herbal antidepressant St. John's Wort). Serotonin syndrome is characterized by autonomic dysfunction including tachycardia, blood pressure fluctuations, hyperthermia, hyperreflexia, myoclonus, dilated pupils, agitation and a hyperactive GI tract (due to the effect of serotonin on the enterochromaffin-like cells). Management includes serotonin antagonists such as cyproheptadine and benzodiazepines to decrease muscle contraction-induced hyperthermia.

Choice E (akathisia) describes the extrapyramidal symptoms of restlessness and the need to be in constant motion. Dopamine-blocking agents can lead to the development of akathisia.

QUESTION 7
Choice B (administration of magnesium sulfate and corticosteroids) is the correct answer. The positive fern test and cervical effacement suggests preterm labor (defined as regular uterine contractions and cervical dilation before 37 weeks gestation). An L:S ratio <2:1 indicates fetal lung immaturity so tocolytics (such as terbutaline or magnesium sulfate) can be given for 48 hours to delay delivery and allow for corticosteroid administration (to enhance fetal lung maturity). This is not used if there is suspected infection (in this vignette there is no foul discharge and the patient is afebrile). REPRODUCTIVE – PREMATURE LABOR – PHARMACOLOGY (p. 271).

Choice A (administration of prostaglandins) and choice E (oxytocin) would enhance uterine contraction and increase progression of premature labor.

Choice C (terbutaline) is a tocolytic, which can be used to delay premature labor, but the L:S ratio presented in this vignette makes the addition of the steroid and the tocolytic (Choice B) a more effective choice.

Choice D (observation until 85% effacement) is not the correct choice as the patient is already in premature labor.

QUESTION 8

Choice B (21,000 WBC (90% PMN), negatively birefringent, needle shaped crystals) is the correct answer. The presentation is classic for gouty arthritis. Gouty arthritis is due to uric acid deposition in the joints. *Exacerbations are frequently associated with the consumption of meat, seafood and alcohol (especially beer). Podagra (involvement of the 1st metatarsophalyngeal joint) is classic for gout.* Over time, inflammatory changes may cause bony destruction, leading to the classic *radiologic "rat bite" erosions* seen on this radiograph (at the first metatarsal head). MUSCULOSKELETAL – GOUTY ARTHRITIS – LABS/DIAGNOSTIC STUDIES (p. 204).

Choice A (less than 200 white blood cell/mm) is considered a normal joint fluid value.

Choice C [21,000 WBC (90% PMN), positively birefringent rhomboid shaped crystals] is classic for pseudogout.

Choice D [59,000 WBC (90% PMN), cloudy fluid] is seen with septic arthritis. *A white blood cell count in the joint fluid >50,000 is highly suspicious of septic arthritis.*

Choice E [35,000 WBC (90% PMN) no crystals] is consistent with any condition that causes inflammatory arthritis.

QUESTION 9

Choice A (decreased serum iron, decreased ferritin, increased total iron binding capacity) is the correct answer. The patient has *Plummer-Vinson syndrome*, which is characterized by the *triad: dysphagia, esophageal webs, and atrophic glossitis in patients with iron deficiency anemia.* Iron deficiency anemia is associated with a decreased serum iron, a *decreased ferritin* (ferritin is a protein that stores iron, in iron deficiency anemia the iron stores are used up). It is also associated with an *increased total iron binding capacity.* Iron binding capacity evaluates the blood's ability to combine iron with its carrier molecule transferrin.   In situations of low iron, more transferrin is produced, leading to a higher total iron binding capacity.
HEMATOLOGY – IRON DEFICIENCY ANEMIA – LABS/DIAGNOSTIC STUDIES (Page 454)

Choice B *(decreased serum iron, increased ferritin, decreased total iron binding capacity) is associated with anemia of chronic disease.* In anemia of chronic disease (due to chronic inflammation or infection), there is an increased ferritin because it is an acute phase reactant.   This increased ferritin sequesters iron.   The total iron biding capacity is decreased as there is less transferrin produced in anemia of chronic disease.

Choice E *(increased serum iron, increased ferritin, decreased total iron binding capacity) is seen with hereditary hemochromatosis.* Hereditary hemochromatosis is excess iron deposition in the parenchymal cells of the heart, liver, pancreas and endocrine organs.   This is associated with an increased serum iron (iron overload), increased transferrin saturation (transferrin is the iron carrying molecule, excess iron saturates the transferrin proteins) and a decreased total iron binding capacity (due to the higher serum iron levels). Lead poisoning may also present with similar lab findings. These disorders resemble anemia of chronic disease lab wise but the serum iron is elevated.

QUESTION 10

Choice C (fluid restriction) is the correct answer.   This patient has SIADH probably due to a combination of factors: the intracranial bleed, anticonvulsants such as phenytoin and chlorpropramide (a 1st generation sulfonylurea).   The absence of peripheral edema or hypovolemia indicates he is isovolemic. The low serum osmolarity and the low sodium make it a hypotonic isovolemic hyponatremia.   Hyponatremia is a problem of water overload not sodium. Therefore, the management of *hypotonic isovolemic hyponatremia is fluid restriction and to treat the underlying causes.* GENITOURINARY – HYPONATREMIA – CLINICAL INTERVENTION (p. 325).

Choice A (hypertonic saline infusion with furosemide) is the management of severe hyponatremia (ex. serum sodium <120 mEq/L) or severe neurologic symptoms.

Choice B (normal saline infusion) is indicated in hypovolemic hypotonic hyponatremia. In this vignette, there are no signs of hypovolemia: the creatinine is within normal limits, the BUN: creatinine ratio is less than 20:1 and there is no poor skin turgor.

Choice D (fluid and sodium restriction) is indicated in hypervolemic hypotonic hyponatremia. There are no signs of edema in this patient.

Choice E (demeclocycline administration) can be used in severe cases of SIADH.

QUESTION 11
Choice C (Bell's palsy) is the correct answer. Bell's palsy is an idiopathic, unilateral facial paralysis due to cranial nerve VII (Facial nerve) involvement. It classically presents with *ipsilateral hyperacusis* (which may be absent) followed by the onset of *unilateral facial paralysis and loss of the anterior 2/3 of taste* (because the facial nerve has both motor and sensory functions). *Since only the facial nerve is involved, the trunk and the extremities should not be affected.* NEUROLOGY - BELL'S PALSY – MOST LIKELY (p. 363).

Choice A (right anterior cerebral artery occlusion) and choice D (left anterior cerebral artery occlusion) would result in *contralateral hemiparesis* (weakness) that tends to be *greater in the leg than the arm.* It is also associated with urinary incontinence, personality changes and abulia (lack of will).

Choice B (right posterior cerebral artery occlusion) can result in *visual hallucinations, and "crossed symptoms"* – meaning ipsilateral cranial nerve deficits, contralateral muscle weakness, comas and *drop attacks.* This patient only has facial involvement, making posterior cerebral artery occlusion less likely.

Choice E (Transient ischemic attack) is an acute neurologic deficit involving the brain, spinal cord or the optic nerve and usually leads to clinical manifestations corresponding to one of the carotid arteries (such as amaurosis fugax) or the cerebral arteries. Symptoms classically resolve within 24 hours.

QUESTION 12
Choice D (residual volume) is correct. Obstructive diseases (such as COPD, Bronchiectasis) are associated with *increased lung volumes (such as residual volume),* reflecting air trapping (obstruction). All the other choices are decreased in emphysema. PULMONARY – EMPHYSEMA – LABS/DIAGNOSTIC STUDIES (p 80).

Choice A (DLCO) is decreased. Any disease that decreases the alveolar total surface area will decrease the DLCO. The alveolar destruction in emphysema leads to a decreased DLCO.

Choice B (FVC) will be decreased. FVC represents the amount of air that can be forcibly exhaled from the lungs after taking the deepest possible breath. Because it is an obstructive disorder (air cannot get out), less air can be forcibly exhaled from the lungs.

Choice C (FEV1) is decreased. Because it is an obstructive disorder (air cannot get out) there will be less air that can be forcibly exhaled in 1 second. In obstructive disorders the FEV1 is decreased and the FEV1/FVC ratio is also decreased.

Choice E (alpha-1 antitrypsin) is also decreased. Alpha-1 antitrypsin is a protein in the lungs that prevents destruction of the elastic tissue of the lung from enzymes such as elastase that are produced by macrophages. Smoking increases white blood cells (inflammatory response to the particles in cigarettes) as well as causes a relative alpha-1 antitrypsin deficiency, leading to decreased elasticity (increased compliance – meaning it is easier to expand the lung than it is for the lung to recoil back to its original shape, leading to increased residual volume).

QUESTION 13
Choice A (Erysipelothrix rhusiopathiae) is the correct answer. Erysipeloid is an occupational disease that usually follows a *skin abrasion or puncture wound from raw fish, shellfish, raw meat and poultry*. It presents with a localized cutaneous lesion that is usually limited to the hand, finger and web spaces. It is associated with *non-pitting edema and purplish erythema with sharp irregular margins extending peripherally while clearing centrally*. INFECTIOUS DISEASE - ERYSIPELOID – MOST LIKELY (p. 420).

Choice B (mycobacterium marinum) also known as "fish tank granuloma" is also associated with seafood handlers, marine workers and fisherman.   It classically presents with an *erythematous, bluish, raised papule or nodule at the site of trauma* and may develop subsequent *lesions along the path of lymphatic drainage*. As a mycobacterium species, the cultures are slow growing and may often take weeks before growing out in cultures. There were no granulomas present in this vignette.

Choice C (Coxiella burnetii) is the causative agent of Q fever.

Choice D (Clostridium perfringens) causes *gas gangrene*. On physical examination, there are usually *brownish bullae and crepitus* on physical examination of the affected tissues (from the gas produced by C. perfringens) with the presence of gas in the tissues on X ray.

Choice E (Haemophilus ducreyi) is the causative agent of chancroid, a sexually transmitted disease.

QUESTION 14
Choice A (simvastatin) is the correct answer. The patient has an elevated low density lipoprotein levels. HMG – CoA reductase inhibitors ("statins") are the best drugs to lower LDL levels and have been shown to reduce cardiovascular morbidity and mortality. CARDIOLOGY - LIPID DISORDERS – PHARMACOLOGY (p. 50).

Choice B (cholestyramine) is a bile acid sequestrant that can also be used to lower LDL but it is not the most effective. They also have the side effect of increasing triglyceride levels so it may not be the ideal medication to use in this patient with borderline triglyceride levels.

Choice C (ezetimibe) is also used to lower LDL but it is not the most effective LDL-lowering drug.

Choice D (fenofibrate) is the best drug to lower triglyceride levels. It has minimal LDL lowering properties.

Choice E (nicotinic acid) is the best drug to increase HDL (high density lipoprotein) levels. It does lower LDL.

QUESTION 15
Choice B (beta blockers) is the correct answer. Side effects of beta blockers include *fatigue, depression, impotence, hypotension, bradycardia, second or third degree heart block, and bronchospasms in patients with reactive airway diseases such as asthma & COPD*. Beta blockers may also worsen some peripheral vascular disease states, such as Raynaud's phenomenon. They may mask the symptoms of hypoglycemia (tachycardia, tremor and sweating).
PSYCH/BEHAVIORAL – DEPRESSION – PHARMACOLOGY (p. 46 & 479).

Choice A (ACE inhibitors) side effects include: *teratogenicity,* hypotension (it is used as an anti-hypertensive). Although ACE inhibitors are "renoprotective", they may cause azotemia in some patients with baseline kidney disease. *Dry cough and angioedema* are common side effects due to an *increase in bradykinin,* a potent vasodilator (as a result of ACE inhibition). The inhibition of aldosterone may lead to hyperkalemia.

Choice C (Hydrochlorothiazide) side effects include hyponatremia, hypokalemia, mild cholesterol elevations, hyperuricemia, hyperglycemia, hypercalcemia, sulfa allergies and metabolic alkalosis.

Choice D (Angiotensin II receptor antagonist) side effects include: hyperkalemia and teratogenicity.

Choice E (Hydralazine) side effects include: tachycardia, gastrointestinal symptoms, drug-induced lupus, neutropenia, myocardial infarction, blood dyscrasias and peripheral neuritis.

QUESTION 16
Choice E (the presence of skin hyperpigmentation) is the correct answer. Primary adrenal insufficiency is lack of the adrenal cortex production of cortisol, aldosterone (and androgen in females). The low levels of cortisol stimulate increased pituitary ACTH secretion. The increased ACTH levels causes increases in melanocyte stimulating hormone levels (both ATCH & MSH made from the same precursor molecule), leading to hyperpigmentation. In secondary, there is decreased ACTH production, so there is no hyperpigmentation. All of the other symptoms can be seen in both primary and secondary adrenal insufficiency.
ENDOCRINE – ADRENAL INSUFFICIENCY – HISTORY AND PHYSICAL EXAMINATION (p. 296).

QUESTION 17
Choice A (April 17) is the correct answer. Naegele's rule states that pregnancies last approximately 280 days (40 weeks) so to calculate it, use the first day of the menstrual period then subtract 3 months and add seven days to get a rough estimated due date. REPRODUCTIVE – ESTIMATED DELIVERY DATE – BASICS (p. 275).

QUESTION 18
Choice B (delirium) is the correct answer. Delirium is an acute, abrupt transient confused state due to an identifiable cause (in this vignette, anticholinergics can cause delirium in come patients as well as corticosteroids). There is usually full recovery within 1 week. NEUROLOGY – DELIRIUM – MOST LIKELY (p. 357).

Choice A (dementia) is a *progressive chronic intellectual deterioration.* The rapid onset of deterioration in this vignette suggests delirium is a more likely cause of the symptoms.

Choice C (Type II bipolar disorder) is associated with alternating *bouts of depression and hypomania.*

Choice D (Wernicke's encephalopathy) describes the *triad of gait abnormalities, ophthalmoplegia and mental confusion* due to Vitamin B1 (thiamine) deficiency. It is most commonly seen in patients with *alcohol abuse.*

Choice E (Vascular dementia) is a chronic disorder and is the second most common type of dementia (after Alzheimer's). It is due to chronic ischemia (such as *lacunar infarcts*).

QUESTION 19
Choice B (normal cellularity with thickened glomerular basement membrane) is the correct answer. Membranous nephropathy, which is one of the most common causes of primary nephrotic syndrome in adults, can often be caused by viral hepatitis (this patient has hepatitis B). Pencillamine can also cause membranous nephropathy. Membranous nephropathy is classically associated with *basement membrane thickening* on kidney biopsy. Nephrotic syndrome is characterized by *proteinuria, hypoalbuminemia, edema and hyperlipidemia.* The decreased oncotic pressure (from the hypoalbuminemia) may cause a transudative pleural effusion (in this

patient, there is decreased fremitus, decreased breath sounds and dullness to percussion, characteristic of a pleural effusion. GENITOURINARY – NEPHROTIC SYNDROME – LABS/DIAGNOSTIC STUDIES (p 317).

Choice A (IgA deposition in the glomerulus) is classically associated with *Berger's disease associated glomerulonephritis*. It would be associated with dysmorphic red blood cells, red blood cell casts, and hypertension.

Choice C (nodular glomerulosclerosis with pink hyaline material around the glomerular capillaries) is the classic description of the *Kimmelstiel-Wilson lesion, which is pathognomonic of diabetes mellitus-induced nephropathy.*

Choice D (hypercellularity with increased monocytes and positive *immune humps) is classically seen with post streptococcus glomerulonephritis.* Glomerulonephritis is associated with hypercellularity (increased inflammatory cells) hematuria, the presence of *red blood cell casts and dysmorphic red blood cells.*

Choice E (hypercellularity with the presence of *crescent-shaped collapse of the Bowman's capsules*) is classically associated with *rapidly progressing glomerulonephritis.* Glomerulonephritis is associated with hematuria and red blood cell casts.

QUESTION 20
Choice B (horizontal nystagmus) is the correct choice. The *4 cardinal symptoms of Meniere's disease are episodic peripheral vertigo, ear fullness, hearing loss and tinnitus. Peripheral vertigo causes horizontal nystagmus.* In peripheral vertigo, the nystagmus is usually fatigable. EENT – MENIERE'S – HISTORY AND PHYSICAL (p 235).

Choice A (*bullae on tympanic membrane) is classically seen with Mycoplasma pneumoniae infections.*

Choice C (vertical nystagmus) is seen with central vertigo. *Central vertigo is also associated with non fatigable nystagmus* (Choice D). Causes include: brainstem or cerebellar lesions, migraines and multiple sclerosis.

Choice E (granulation tissue seen on the tympanic membrane) is associated with cholesteatomas. *Cholesteatomas are associated with conductive hearing loss, peripheral vertigo and otorrhea.*

QUESTION 21
Choice B (T cell-mediated pannus formation with symmetric joint destruction and narrowing) is the correct choice. This is the classic description of the joint destruction associated with rheumatoid arthritis. MUSCULOSKELETAL – RHEUMATOID ARTHRITIS – BASICS (p. 206).

Choice A (degenerative wear and tear changes leading to asymmetric joint narrowing) and Choice D (Imbalance in cartilage repair leading to more cartilage destruction than repair) describes the pathophysiologic changes associated with osteoarthritis.

Choice C (Joint damage due to enthesitis) describes the pathophysiology of seronegative spondyloarthropathies such as reactive arthritis, psoriatic arthritis, and ankylosing spondylitis.

Choice E (Joint damage as a result of peripheral neuropathy and repetitive microtrauma) classically describes the pathophysiology of Charcot's joint associated with diabetes mellitus.

QUESTION 22
Choice C (syndrome of inappropriate antidiuretic hormone) is the correct answer. Lithium causes diabetes insipidus. Other side effects of lithium therapy include: increased thirst, seizures, arrhythmias, hypercalcemia, hyperparathyroidism, and hypothyroidism. PSYCH/BEHAVIORAL – LITHIUM – PHARMACOLOGY (p. 493).

QUESTION 23

Choice A (large B cells with bilobed or multilobar nuclei and an "owl eye appearance" due to eosinophilic inclusions in the nuclei) is the correct answer. This describes the *Reed Sternberg cell*, which is *pathognomonic for Hodgkin lymphoma.* HEMATOLOGY – HODGKIN LYMPHOMA – LABS/DIAGNOSTIC STUDIES (p 464).

Choice B (abnormal, fragile B lymphocytes with a *"smudged"* appearance that occurs with slide preparation) describes the smudge cells associated with *chronic lymphocytic leukemia.*

Choice C (crystalized granular elongated needles seen in the cytoplasm of immature white blood cells) describes the *Auer rod*, which is associated with *Acute myelogenous leukemia.*

Choice D (red blood cell inclusions that are composed of denatured hemoglobin) describes the Heinz body. *Heinz bodies are commonly seen in Hemoglobin H disease* (Thalassemia intermedia), *G6PD deficiency*, and other *thalassemias.*

Choice E (reciprocal translocation between chromosome 9 and chromosome 22) describes the *Philadelphia chromosome* with is *classically associated with chronic myelogenous leukemia.* The Philadelphia chromosome is hallmark of CML. Clinically however, it may be seen in a small percentage in cases of ALL and AML.

QUESTION 24

Choice D (Spiral CT scan of the chest) is the correct answer. This is the classic presentation of pulmonary embolism. All of the choices can be used in suspected pulmonary embolism so this question tests your ability to tell the indications and contraindications for each test. *Spiral CT scan of the chest with IV contrast is considered the best initial screening test for pulmonary embolism in a patient with moderate to high clinical suspicion.* There is a high clinical suspicion because she is a smoker, she is on oral contraceptives (hypercoagulability) and she had a car ride greater than 4 hours (venous stasis). PULMONARY – PULMONARY EMBOLISM – LABS/DIAGNOSTIC STUDIES (p 98).

Choice A (Pulmonary angiography) is indicated in patients in patients with a *high clinical suspicion in whom noninvasive testing such as Spiral CT scan and/or ventilation perfusion scan are either contraindicated and/or inconclusive. Pulmonary angiography is the gold standard (definitive diagnosis)* but because it is invasive, it is usually reserved for high probability patients in whom noninvasive testing is inconclusive. If the stem asked for the gold standard, this would have been the answer. Be sure to always answer what the question is asking.

Choice B (Venous Doppler of the lower extremities) can be done to look for the *source of the embolus as 95% of pulmonary emboli originate from the lower extremity or pelvic deep venous thrombi*, but in a case where pulmonary embolism is suspected, a negative Doppler does not exclude pulmonary embolism as there are other potential sources for thrombi formation.

Choice C (Ventilation perfusion scan) is often *indicated in patients with moderate to high risk in whom CT scan is inconclusive or contraindicated* (ex. patients who cannot tolerate IV contrast at increased risk of kidney injury).

Choice E (D dimer) is often used but it is *only clinical useful if the D-dimer is negative in low risk patients.* This patient is high risk (see choice D).

QUESTION 25

Choice C (Darkfield microscopy) is the correct answer. The picture in this vignette depicts a *chancre, the primary lesion of syphilis infection. Treponema pallidum* is a spirochete and the causative agent of syphilis. It is very difficult to grow Treponema pallidum in culture. *Darkfield microscopy is a direct method to diagnose syphilis in the presence of a chancre or condyloma lata.* An indirect method of using the *rapid plasma reagent* screening test (RPR) with a confirmatory *fluorescent treponemal antibody absorption test* (FTA-ABS) are used in all other presentations of syphilis. INFECTIOUS DISEASE – SYPHILIS – LABS/DIAGNOSTIC STUDIES (p 426).

Choice A *(India ink) is used in the diagnosis of Cryptococcus neoformans*. Other methods used in the diagnosis of Cryptococcal infections include Cryptococcal antigen (and blood cultures in cases of disseminated infection).

Choice B (*Tzanck smear*) can be used in the diagnosis of *Varicella Zoster and Herpes simplex virus infections*.

Choice D (Potassium Hydroxide) can be used in the diagnosis of candida fungal infections, or as part of the diagnostic vaginal mount testing in patients suspected of having bacterial vaginosis, trichomoniasis or vaginal candidiasis.

Choice E (Polymerase chain reaction) is used in many disorders, such as varicella zoster infections.

QUESTION 26
Choice A (dull abdominal pain worse with meals and weight loss) is the correct answer. Chronic mesenteric ischemia is due to atherosclerosis of the arteries that supply the bowel. It can present with *"intestinal angina"* (*abdominal pain worse with eating* due to the increased demand of blood to the bowel in the setting of a decreased supply). Patients frequently develop anorexia due the fear of the abdominal pain associated with eating. GI/NUTRITION – CHRONIC MESENTERIC ISCHEMIA – HISTORY AND PHYSICAL EXAMINATION (p 150).

Choice B (left lower quadrant pain and tenderness with bloody diarrhea) describes the pain of ischemic colitis.

Choice C (severe abdominal pain out of proportion to physical examination) describes the pain of acute mesenteric ischemia.

Choice D (diffuse abdominal pain relieved with defecation) describes the abdominal pain associated with irritable bowel syndrome.

Choice E (flank pain that radiates to the testicle) describes the pain associated with nephrolithiasis.

QUESTION 27
Choice B (decreasing his bedtime NPH dose) is the correct answer. This vignette describes the Somogyi effect. The Somogyi effect can be seen in patients who are started on insulin. It is characterized by nocturnal hypoglycemia (note the 2am low serum glucose levels) followed by a rebound hyperglycemic overshoot. The Somogyi effect is reduced by preventing the hypoglycemia by either decreasing the bedtime NPH dose, moving the NPH dose earlier or giving the patient a bedtime snack. ENDOCRINE – SOMOGYI EFFECT – CLINICAL INTERVENTION (p 304).

Choice A (moving his NPH dose to the afternoon) wouldn't affect the overnight hypoglycemia as the effects NPH peaks in 12 hours.

Choice C (decreasing his evening regular insulin dose) would be correct if the postprandial glucose levels were elevated.

Choice D (moving his last regular insulin does from evening to bedtime) wouldn't have a great effect on the 2 AM levels, as regular insulin peaks at about 2-3 hours.

Choice E (avoiding a bedtime snack) is used in the management of patients with the Dawn phenomenon. The Dawn phenomenon is caused by decreased insulin sensitivity and the nightly surge of counter regulatory hormones during overnight fasting.

QUESTION 28

Choice C (Dermatographism) is the correct answer. *Urticaria* is a type I hypersensitivity reaction associated with IgE and increased mast cells in the skin. It classically presents with *blanchable edematous pink papules that form irregular wheals.* These wheals may disappear, with the appearance of new lesions.
DERMATOLOGY – URTICARIA – HISTORY & PHYSICAL EXAM (p 393).

Choice A (*Auspitz sign*) is classically associated with *plaque psoriasis. Auspitz sign is punctate bleeding* (spots) when the plaques of psoriasis are unroofed.

Choice B (*Koebner's phenomenon*) is *new skin lesions appearing along the lines of trauma.* Koebner's phenomenon can be seen in many diseases: psoriasis, lichen planus, vitiligo, and some infectious diseases.

Choice D (*Nikolsky's sign) is sloughing off of the epidermis when slight pressure is applied to the skin.* A positive Nikolsky's sign can be seen in toxic epidermal necrolysis, Steven-Johnson syndrome, pemphigus vulgaris, and staphylococcal scalded skin syndrome.

Choice E (*Koplik's spots*) are *clustered, white lesions on the buccal mucosa with an erythematous rim* most commonly seen opposite the lower 1st and 2nd molars. They can be seen with *rubeola (measles).*

QUESTION 29

Choice C (hyponatremia) is the correct answer. Ehlers-Danlos syndrome is a connective tissue disorder that causes fragile connective tissue, which puts patients at increased risk for developing aneurysms. Berry aneurysms are small aneurysms that occur at the circle of Willis, making patients prone to developing subarachnoid hemorrhages. Syndrome of inappropriate ADH is often caused by CNS lesions (such as subarachnoid hemorrhage) as well as anticonvulsants (such as phenytoin, which this patient has been given here). The increased ADH causes increased free water retention, which lowers the serum sodium level. Remember that hyponatremia and hyponatremia are due to water problems not problem with sodium. GENITOURINARY – HYPONATREMIA – MOST LIKELY (p 325).

QUESTION 30

Choice C (retrobulbar neuritis) is correct choice. Ethambutol is a drug used to treat active tuberculosis and can cause optic neuritis (inflammation of the optic nerve). There are two types of optic neuritis, retrobulbar (optic nerve inflammation behind the eye) and papillitis (edema of the optic nerve at the eye). In this vignette, there is no blurring of the optic disc on fundoscopic exam, indicating retrobulbar neuritis. If there was evidence of blurring of the optic disc, then choice B (papillitis) would have been the correct answer.
EENT – OPTIC NEURITIS – MOST LIKELY (p 227).

Choice A (*papilledema*) is associated with blurring of the optic disc due to *increased cerebrospinal fluid pressure,* as seen with *benign intracranial hypertension or malignant hypertension.*

Choice D (acute angle closure glaucoma) is classically associated with blurring of the optic disc due to *increased intraocular pressure. Medications that can promote the development of acute angle closure glaucoma are anticholinergics and sympathomimetics* (because these medications cause dilation of the pupils which can close off the pre-existing narrow angle). Ethambutol is associated with optic neuritis.

Choice E (chronic open angle closure glaucoma) can cause blurring of the optic disc as well and is usually bilateral.

QUESTION 31

Choice B (flat, blunted emotional affect) is a negative symptom of schizophrenia that would not be seen in mania. All of the other choices can possibly be seen in both disorders. PSYCH/BEHAVIORAL – SCHIZOPHRENIA – HISTORY (p 382).

QUESTION 32

Choice C (Takayasu arteritis) is the correct answer. Takayasu arteritis is inflammation of the aorta, aortic arch and/or the pulmonary arteries. It most commonly presenting in women age 20-40y (especially Asian). The patients classically develop asymmetric blood pressure measurements (this finding is also classically associated with coarctation of the aorta and aortic dissection). MUSCULOSKELETAL – TAKAYASU ARTERITIS – MOST LIKELY (p 210).

Choice A (peripheral arterial disease) primarily involves the arteries of the lower extremities.

Choice B (Raynaud's phenomenon) is spasms of the peripheral end vessels in response to cold & emotional stress.

Choice D (Kawasaki disease) is seen in young children. It presents with fever and a variety of manifestations.

Choice E (Prinzmetal's angina) is vasospastic disorder of the coronary arteries.

QUESTION 33

Choice E (Alpha antitrypsin) is the correct choice. Suspect AAT deficiency in a young patient with emphysema who is not a smoker. PULMONARY – ALPHA ANTITRYPSIN DEFICIENCY – MOST LIKELY (p 80).

Choice A *(angiotensin converting enzyme) is elevated in sarcoidosis* (which is restrictive and associated with decreased lung volumes not increased lung volumes seen in this vignette).

Choice B (IgG in alveoli) is hallmark of Goodpasture's syndrome, causing hemoptysis & rapid kidney failure.

Choice C (anti-double stranded DNA antibodies) are seen with lupus.

Choice D (sweat chloride test) is used to diagnose cystic fibrosis.

QUESTION 34

Choice C (IV oxytocin) is the correct answer. The most common cause of post partum hemorrhage (up to 80%) is *uterine atony* (loss of uterine muscle tone). After delivery, uterine muscle contraction causes blood vessel compression and reduction of uterine blood flow. *Oxytocin causes rhythmic uterine contraction, improving uterine tone and reduces bleeding.* REPRODUCTIVE – POST PARTUM HEMORRHAGE – CLINICAL INTERVENTION (p 276).

Choice A *(fresh frozen plasma)* is used in patients *severe coagulation protein deficits* when the specific factor needed is unavailable. It may also be used in conjunction with plasmapheresis.

Choice B (IV ceftriaxone) is not used for post partum hemorrhage without signs of infection.

Choice D (IV amoxicillin + gentamicin + metronidazole) is used in the management of chorioamnionitis. The absence of uterine tenderness, fever or foul smelling discharge makes this diagnosis unlikely.

Choice E (obtain D-dimer levels) is indicated in patients with low suspicion of pulmonary embolism.

QUESTION 35

Choice B (rubeola) is the correct answer. Rubeola is the causative agent of measles. The vignette describes Koplik's spots. The rash of measles is classically described as a *brick-red rash starting on the face* and spreading to the trunk, *lasting 7 days*. It is often preceded by a prodrome of the 3 Cs: *cough, coryza and conjunctivitis*. DERMATOLOGY – RUBEOLA – MOST LIKELY (p 406).

Choice A *(rubella)* is associated with a *light red to pink spotted rash* that *lasts about 3 days*.

Choice C (fifth's disease) otherwise known as *erythema infectiosum* is associated with coryza, fever and the appearance of an erythematous rash with circumoral pallor giving the classic *"slapped cheek"* appearance. This rash is often followed by a lacy, reticular rash on the extremities (especially the upper extremities and the rash often spares the palms and the soles).

Choice D (mumps) is associated with parotid gland swelling.

Choice E (hand foot and mouth disease) classically presents with vesicular lesions on a reddened based with an erythematous halo in the oral cavity followed by vesicular rash involving the palms and the soles.

QUESTION 36
Choice D (increased CSF opening pressure xanthochromia that does not diminish from tube 1 to tube 4) is the correct answer. The neurological symptoms, nuchal rigidity, sudden onset of the *"worse of headache of my life"*, the *loss of consciousness with a lucid interval* followed by decompensation are hallmark for subarachnoid hemorrhage. Extrarenal manifestations of polycystic kidney disease include the presence of mitral valve prolapse and an increased propensity towards the development of berry aneurysms, which may rupture causing a subarachnoid hemorrhage. NEUROLOGY – SUBARACHNOID HEMORRHAGE – LABS/DIAGNOSTIC (p 361).

Choice A (increased CSF opening pressure with an otherwise normal CSF examination) would be seen with pseudo tumor cerebri/idiopathic intracranial hypertension. Pseudotumor cerebri usually presents with headache and may often develop *visual changes*. It is not associated with loss of consciousness.

Choice B (*high protein with normal white blood cell count*) is the characteristic CSF finding in patients with *Guillain Barré syndrome*. Guillain Barré classically presents with *symmetric lower extremity weakness that progresses to involve the upper extremities*.

Choice C (*increased oligoclonal IgG bands*) is the classic CSF finding in patients with *multiple sclerosis*.

Choice E [normal glucose with increased white blood cells (primarily lymphocytes)] is the classic CSF finding in viral meningitis, aseptic meningitis and encephalitis.

QUESTION 37
Choice B (synchronized cardioversion) is the correct answer. The patient has an *unstable tachycardia*, evident by chest pain, hypotension and persistent symptoms. *Synchronized cardioversion is the first line management of unstable tachycardia.* Synchronized cardioversion works by giving an electrical shock, which places all the cardiac cells in the absolute refractory period, terminating the tachyarrhythmia and allowing recovery of the sinoatrial node to become the dominant pacemaker. CARDIOLOGY – UNSTABLE TACHYCARDIA – CLINICAL INTERVENTION (p 10).

Choice A (*Atropine*) is used as the first line management for *symptomatic bradycardia*. Atropine *is an anticholinergic* drug that will increase the heart rate.

Choice C (*Adenosine)* can be used as first line management for *stable, regular, narrow complex tachycardia*, such as *paroxysmal supraventricular tachycardia*. Since the patient is unstable, this would not be the ideal choice.

Choice D (*Amiodarone)* is a class III antiarrhythmic (with class I through IV properties). It is used as first line management for *stable, wide complex tachycardia*.

Choice E (*Unsynchronized cardioversion*) otherwise known as *defibrillation* is indicated in only 2 instances: *ventricular tachycardia without a pulse or ventricular fibrillation.*

QUESTION 38

Choice C (septal cellulitis) is the correct choice. Orbital cellulitis is an infection of the cavity surrounding the eye. It is also associated with local superficial signs of infection. Due to the *involvement of the ocular muscles, it is associated with visual changes and pain with ocular movement.* EENT – SEPTAL CELLULITIS – MOST LIKELY (p 228).

Choice A (*bacterial conjunctivitis*) is associated with *conjunctival erythema* and may have *ocular discharge* but since there is no ocular muscle involvement, there should be no visual deficits nor pain with ocular movements.

Choice B (*anterior uveitis*) would be associated with *conjunctival erythema.* The hallmark of uveitis is the presence of *cells and flare* on eye examination.

Choice D (dacrocystitis) is an inflammation of the lacrimal gland. It is not associated with visual changes or eye pain with ocular movement. It is associated with local signs of infection on the nasal side of the lower eyelid.

Choice E (*preseptal cellulitis*) presents very similar to septal cellulitis with periorbital pain and swelling. The distinguishing factor is that *preseptal cellulitis is not associated with the ocular pain or visual changes* (that are seen in septal cellulitis since preseptal cellulitis does not involve the periorbital fat or the ocular muscles).

QUESTION 39

Choice B (The patient should remain upright for 30 minutes after taking Risedronate) is the correct answer. Risedronate is a bisphosphonate. Bisphosphonates should be taken in the morning with water on an empty stomach. Patients should remain upright to reduce the incidence of esophagitis commonly associated with bisphosphonates. Side effects of bisphosphonates include jaw osteoporosis and pathological femur fractures.

QUESTION 40

Choice C (Proteus mirabilis) is the correct answer. Staghorn calculi & struvite stones are composed of ammonium magnesium phosphate due to urea splitting organisms, which is most commonly associated with Proteus mirabilis. The splitting of urea (with ammonium as a byproduct) causes an increase in the urine pH >7. Other urea splitting organisms include: Klebsiella pneumonia and Pseudomonas aeruginosa. All the other organisms in this vignette do not produce the urease enzyme needed to split urea. GENITOURINARY – NEPHROLITHIASIS – BASICS (p 339).

QUESTION 41

Choice D (desmopressin stimulation test) is the correct answer. Central diabetes insipidus is the absence of ADH. Nephrogenic diabetes insipidus is kidney insensitivity to ADH. To distinguish between the two, desmopressin (ADH) is given and then urine osmolarity is measured. In central diabetes, the synthetic desmopressin will cause a gradual increase in urine osmolarity, indicating kidney responsiveness to ADH. In nephrogenic diabetes insipidus, the desmopressin is ineffective, leading to the continued production of dilute urine (indicating the kidney's unresponsiveness to ADH). GENITOURINARY – DIABETES INISPIDUS – LABS/DIAGNOSTIC (p 325).

Choice A (fluid challenge test) is used in patients with decreased urine output to see if there is an increased in urine output, which would indicate prerenal azotemia.

Choice B (dexamethasone suppression test) is used in the evaluation of suspected Cushing's syndrome.

Choice C (fluid deprivation test) is the screening test for suspected diabetes insipidus. After screening, a desmopressin test is done to distinguish central from nephrogenic diabetes insipidus.

Choice E (Captopril test) is used in the evaluation of patients with suspected renal artery stenosis.

QUESTION 42

Choice B [Second degree heart block (Mobitz I)] is the correct answer. Mobitz I second degree heart block (Wenckebach) is diagnosed by *progressive lengthening of the PR interval with occasional nonconducted ("dropped") QRS complexes.* In this rhythm strip, the second and seventh atrial impulses (P waves) were not conducted to the ventricles (absent QRS complexes).

Choice A (*First degree heart block*) is associated with a *prolonged PR interval* (greater than 0.20 seconds) but *every P wave is followed by a QRS complex* because all of the atrial impulses are conducted to the ventricles.

Choice C [*Second degree heart block (Mobitz II)*] is associated with a *PR interval of constant duration* and *occasional nonconducted impulses* ("dropped' QRS complexes) . The distinguishing factor between Type I and Type II is that in type I, the PR interval progressively lengthens before the nonconducted QRS whereas the PR interval remains the same duration in type II before the nonconducted QRS.

Choice D (Third degree heart block) is associated with atrioventricular dissociation. The P waves occur at regular intervals, the QRS complexes also occur at a regular intervals but the two are not connected (they operate independently of each other).

Choice E (Ashman phenomenon) is seen in patients with atrial fibrillation, which are occasional wide complex beats that occur with a right bundle branch morphology (due to aberrant conduction).

QUESTION 43

Choice C (propranolol for the autonomic symptoms) is the correct answer. In patients with *mitral valve prolapse with autonomic symptoms, beta blockers can be given to reduce the symptoms.* Otherwise, in the *majority of patients with mitral valve prolapse without significant autonomic symptoms, observation and reassurance is the treatment of choice* (Choice A). This is a key point to remember. Without significant autonomic symptoms, choose reassurance. CARDIOLOGY – MITRAL VALVE PROLAPSE – HEALTH MAINTENANCE (p 43).

Choice B (education that she may develop the murmur of mitral stenosis) is incorrect as mitral valve prolapse is not associated with mitral stenosis.

Choice D (aspirin to reduce the chest pain symptoms) and Choice E (nitroglycerin as needed for the chest pain and other symptoms) are not indicated in the autonomic symptoms associated with mitral valve prolapse in some patients.

QUESTION 44

Choice C (Trisomy 21) is the correct answer. In the triple screen test a low alpha-fetoprotein, a high beta HCG and a low estradiol is associated with a high likelihood of trisomy 21. REPRODUCTIVE – TRIPLE SCREENING – LABS (p 275).

Choice A (open neural tube defects), Choice D (multiple gestation) and choice E (underestimation of gestational age) are all associated with a high alpha fetoprotein.

Choice B (Trisomy 18) is associated with low alpha fetoprotein, low estradiol and low beta HCG levels. Infants with Trisomy 18 are often stillborn or die within the first year of life.

QUESTION 45

Choice A (isoniazid + pyridoxine (B6) total duration of treatment for 9 months) is correct. This is a 2-step question. The first step is determining if the PPD is positive or not. This is a common thing asked on the boards. First you have to determine your cut off rate by his risk factors. 10 mm or greater is considered positive in both health care workers (he is a physician) and immigrants (he is from China). Now that you determine he is positive, the next step is to obtain a chest radiograph to rule out active tuberculosis. Once active tuberculosis is ruled out, the diagnosis is **latent TB infection** (meaning he is infected but not infectious as evident by a positive PPD, the absence of symptoms and a negative chest radiograph). You can offer the patient prophylaxis for latent TB infection. Treatment of LTBI reduces the incidence of secondary (reactive) TB in the future if the patient's immune system wanes (ex. getting older, HIV, steroid use, or chemotherapy). *Treatment of latent TB infection is INH + B6 (to prevent peripheral neuropathy from the INH) for 9 months for the general population.* PULMONARY – LATENT TB INFECTION – CLINICAL INTERVENTION (p 108).

Choice B (isoniazid + rifampin + ethambutol + pyrazinamide total treatment duration of 9 months) is incorrect because 1) 4 drug treatment is used for active TB (which he does not have) and because active TB is usually treated for total 6 months duration.

Choice C [isoniazid + rifampin + ethambutol + streptomycin (total treatment duration of 6 months)] is the treatment for active TB (positive PPD, active symptoms and positive X rays for infection) not latent TB.

Choice D [isoniazid + pyridoxine (B6) total duration of treatment for 12 months] is the treatment of latent TB infection if the patient is HIV positive or has a granuloma seen on chest radiographs.

Choice E (ceftriaxone + azithromycin) is the treatment for community acquired pneumonia treated as an inpatient.

QUESTION 46

Choice B (oxygen) is the correct answer. In chronic bronchitis, chronic hypoxemia leads to hypoxemia-mediated vasoconstriction of the pulmonary bed, leading to pulmonary hypertension and increased afterload on the right side. The right side of the heart has to work against this pulmonary hypertension, causing right ventricular hypertrophy and eventually right sided heart failure. Oxygen has been shown to decrease mortality by reducing the hypoxemia-mediated vasoconstriction, decreasing the workload of the right side of the heart. All the other medications can be used but are not associated with a reduction of mortality in patients with cor pulmonale. PULMONARY – CHRONIC OBSTRUCTIVE PULMONARY DISEASE – PHARMACOLOGY (p 81).

QUESTION 47

Choice D (distant, resolved hepatitis B infection) is the correct answer. The presence of *positive surface antibodies and positive core IgG antibodies* indicates a distant resolved infection.

Choice A (acute hepatitis B infection) is incorrect. *Acute hepatitis B* infection is indicated by the presence of *positive Hepatitis B surface antigen with positive core IgM antibodies.*

Choice B (window period) is incorrect. The only positive marker in the *window period* is *the hepatitis B core antibody IgM.*

Choice C (The patient has been successfully vaccinated) is incorrect. *The only marker positive after successful vaccination is a positive surface antibody.* This is distinguished from distant resolved infection by the lack of the core antibody positivity in vaccinated individuals.

Choice E (The patient has chronic hepatitis B infection) is incorrect. Lab wise, chronic hepatitis B infection is associated with positive surface antigen and a positive core Ig G for 6 months. Hepatitis E is indicative of active replication.

QUESTION 48

Choice B (Whipple's disease) is the correct choice. Diarrhea, joint pain, fever are commonly seen in patients with Whipple's disease. CNS involvement may cause twitching of the eye muscles while chewing. Positive PAS macrophages and dilation of the lacteals on biopsy are hallmark of the disease. GI – WHIPPLE'S DISEASE – MOST LIKELY (p 160).

Choice A (seronegative spondyloarthropathies) can cause joint pain but diarrhea is not a common occurrence in these patients.

Choice C (Crohn's) disease can be associated with the symptoms. Biopsy would show transluminal inflammation.

Choice D (Ulcerative colitis) classically is associated with bloody diarrhea and is associated with diffuse erythema of the mucosa and submucosa.

Choice E (Giardiasis) can cause a chronic diarrhea but is not associated with Positive PAS macrophages.

QUESTION 49
Choice E (sickle cell disease) is the correct answer. This is a common radiograph finding due to micro infarctions leading to central endplate depression of the vertebrae. HEMATOLOGY – SICKLE CELL – LABS/DIAGNOSTIC (p 458).

Choice A (Spondylolisthesis) shows up on radiographs as *forward slipping of the vertebrae* on one another.

Choice B (Spondylolysis) is a *defect seen in the pars interarticularis.*

Choice C (Ankylosing spondylitis) is associated with a *bamboo spine* on radiographs.

Choice D (Spinal stenosis) is associated with narrowing of the spinal canal.

QUESTION 50
Choice B (corticosteroids) is the correct answer.   Corticosteroids are the first line agents in warm antibody autoimmune hemolytic anemia. Other immunosuppressant medications may also be used as well. Splenectomy (Choice C) may be used in refractory cases (as it removes the site of red blood cell destruction). HEMATOLOGY – AUTOIMMUNE HEMOLYTIC ANEMIA - PHARMACOLOGY (page 459).

Choice A (avoidance of the cold) is the treatment of *cold antibody autoimmune hemolytic anemia.*

Choice D (Deferoxamine) is chelation therapy used in states of iron overload.

Choice E (Hydroxyurea) can be used in severe pain in sickle cell crisis and in long-term management in some cases to reduce the frequency of pain crisis in patients with sickle cell anemia.

QUESTION 51
Choice B (amiodarone) is the correct answer. Amiodarone is a class III antiarrhythmic. Because it contains iodine, it may cause hyperthyroid or hypothyroid disorders. Other side effects include corneal deposits with long term use and pulmonary fibrosis. CARDIOLOGY – AMIODARONE – PHARMACOLOGY (p 480).

Choice A (propranolol) is a nonselective beta 1 and beta 2 antagonist. Side effects of beta blockers include depression, fatigue, impotence, second or third degree heart block, bradycardia, masking of the symptoms of hypoglycemia, bronchoconstriction in patients with asthma and chronic obstructive pulmonary disorders as well as unopposed alpha constriction if given to patients with cocaine-induced myocardial infarctions.

Choice C (adenosine) is the drug of choice in patients with supraventricular tachycardia and narrow complex tachycardia. Side effects include transient flushing, chest pressure/pain and bronchospasm.

Choice D (procainamide) is a class I antiarrhythmic that has been shown to prolong repolarization and the refractory period. Class I antiarrhythmics block sodium channels. Side effects include torsades de pointes, hypotension, tachycardia, tinnitus, and kidney injury.

Choice E (verapamil) is a nondihydropyridine calcium channel blocker. Side effects of calcium channel blockers include constipation, dizziness, bradycardia, second or third degree heart block and peripheral edema.

QUESTION 52

Choice C (Ceftriaxone) is the correct choice. IV Ceftriaxone is used in Lyme disease in patients who have *severe disease, neurologic disease (other than facial palsy), and cardiac disease* (such as second or third degree heart blocks). Other drugs used in the management of neurologic Lyme include cefotaxime and penicillin G. INFECTIOUS DISEASE – LYME DISEASE – PHARMACOLOGY (p 426).

Choice A (Amoxicillin) can be used in all other cases of Lyme disease (except noted above). Amoxicillin is the drug of choice in children under the age of 8 years (the tetracyclines can cause permanent staining of the teeth in children under the age of 8).

Choice E (Oral Doxycycline) is the drug of choice for Lyme disease in patients older than 8 years old in all other cases of Lyme disease than noted above in Choice C.

QUESTION 53

Choice C (small papule or plaque with a velvety, warty, "stuck on" appearance) is the correct answer. This is the classic description of seborrheic keratosis, a benign skin tumor most commonly seen in fair skinned elderly patients with prolonged sun exposure. DERMATOLOGY – SEBORRHEIC KERATOSIS – HISTORY AND PHYSICAL EXAM (p 395).

Choice A (red elevated nodule with adherent white scales and crusted blood at the margins) describes squamous cell carcinoma.

Choice B (dry, rough scaly, "sandpaper" like rash with hyperkeratotic plaques) describes actinic keratosis, a premalignant condition that may lead to squamous cell carcinoma.

Choice D (small, raised translucent pearly papule with central ulceration and rolled borders) is the classic description of basal cell carcinoma.

Choice E (asymmetric, multi-color, 7-mm lesion with irregular borders and rapid change in appearance) describes malignant melanoma.

QUESTION 54

Choice D (Schizophreniform disorder) is the correct choice. The patient meets the criteria for schizophrenia but the symptoms are *less than 6 months in duration,* making the diagnosis of Schizophreniform a more likely diagnosis. The criteria for schizophrenia are functional decline in addition to hallucinations and delusions. The main difference between the two is primarily the length of time.
PSYCH/BEHAVIORAL – SCHIZOPHRENIFORM – MOST LIKELY (p 382).

Choice A (schizophrenia) is a functional decline in addition to hallucinations and delusions. *The condition has to be present for greater than 6 months to meet criteria.*

Choice B (Bipolar disorder) is characterized by major depression alternating with episodes of hypermania or hypomania.

Choice C (Paranoid personality disorder) is characterized by distrust and suspiciousness of others. *Delusions can be present but hallucinations are not present.*

Choice E (Schizoid personality disorder) is characterized by *long pattern of voluntary social withdrawal, hermit-like behavior and a cold affect.*

QUESTION 55
Choice C (brief, sporadic single repetitive jerks or twitching of 1 or more muscle groups) is the correct answer. Myoclonus is an extrapyramidal symptom but can also be seen when a patient is falling asleep. Hiccups is a form affecting the diaphragm. NEUROLOGY – MYOCLONUS – BASICS (p. 352).

Choice A (rapid, involuntary, jerky, uncontrolled purposeless movements) describes chorea, which is another type of extrapyramidal symptom.

Choice B (repetitive, non-rhythmic movements or vocals) describes tics.

Choice D (sustained contraction with twisting of the body and abnormal posturing) describes dystonia, which is due to sustained contraction of antagonist muscles. Writer's cramp is an example of dystonia.

Choice E (repetitive, rhythmic jerking that usually lasts less than 2 to 3 minutes) describes clonus. *Clonus is rhythmic, myoclonus is not rhythmic.*

QUESTION 56
Choice D (evening stiffness predominantly and morning stiffness lasting less than 30 minutes) is the correct answer. All of the other choices are classically associated with rheumatoid arthritis.
MUSCULOSKELETAL – RHEUMATOID ARTHRITIS – HISTORY AND PHYSICAL (p 206).

QUESTION 57
Choice B (cognitive and physical rest) is the correct answer. The patient has trauma-induced neurological symptoms of altered mental status changes and loss of consciousness consistent with concussion syndrome since the head CT is negative. Cognitive and physical rest is the main management of concussion syndrome. NEUROLOGY – CONCUSSION SYNDROME – HEALTH MAINTENANCE (p 363).

Choice A (raising the head of the bed and placing the patient in a dark, quiet room), Choice C (administer dexamethasone and mannitol) , Choice D (immediate neurosurgery consult) are the management of subarachnoid hemorrhage. This patient remains lucid and has a negative CT scan. If there were a high suspicion for subarachnoid hemorrhage, then a lumbar puncture would be indicated to look for blood in the CSF.

Choice E (administer hypertonic fluids to reduce the neurologic symptoms) in addition to furosemide is the management of choice for severe, symptomatic hyponatremia.

QUESTION 58
Choice B (anti-centromere antibodies) is the correct answer. This is the classic description of CREST syndrome (Limited scleroderma). CREST is a mnemonic for Calcinosis cutis, Raynaud's phenomenon, Esophageal motility disorders, Sclerodactyly & Telangiectasia. Anti-centromere antibodies are associated with limited scleroderma whereas Scl-70 antibodies are more commonly associated with diffuse scleroderma.
MUSCULOSKELETAL – SCLERODERMA – LABS/DIAGNOSTIC STUDIES – (p. 201).

Choice A (*anti-La Antibodies*) are most commonly seen with *Sjrogen's syndrome.*

Choice C (*anti smooth muscle antibodies*) are classically seen with *autoimmune hepatitis.*

Choice D (*anti-Mi-2 antibodies*) are specific for d*ermatomyositis.*

Choice E (*anti-Signal Recognition Particle antibodies*) are seen in *polymyositis.*

QUESTION 59
Choice A (amoxicillin) is the correct choice. The erythematous tympanic membrane and decreased motility of the tympanic membrane are consistent with acute otitis media. Amoxicillin is considered the management of choice. Cephalosporins may also be used. Choice B (Amoxicillin/Clavulanic acid – Augmentin) is second line if not responsive to amoxicillin. EENT – OTITIS MEDIA – PHARMACOLOGY (p 232).

QUESTION 60
Choice B (exogenous corticosteroid use) is the correct answer. The vignette is describing the classic findings associated with Cushing syndrome (hypercortisolism). The most common cause overall is exogenous steroid use. ENDOCRINE – CUSHING'S SYNDROME – BASICS (p 290).

Choice A (Cushing's disease) is Cushing's syndrome due to increased pituitary ACTH secretion. Although this is the most common cause of ENDOGENOUS Cushing's syndrome, corticosteroid use is the most common cause overall. Cushing's disease causes 70% of endogenous causes. Endogenous causes include Cushing's disease, adrenal tumor (Choice C) and ectopic ACTH-producing tumor (Choice D). Many people confuse Cushing's syndrome and Cushing's disease. Cushing's disease one of the causes of Cushing's syndrome.

Choice E (Ketoconazole) is an antifungal medication that decreases cortisol production, so it used to medically treat Cushing's syndrome, it doesn't cause it.

QUESTION 61
Choice C (hard nodular prostate) is the correct answer. *Prostate cancer most commonly metastasizes to the bone,* so an elevated PSA with weight loss and bone pain may be highly suggestive of metastatic prostate cancer. The classic physical exam finding in prostate cancer is a *hard, nodular prostate gland* on digital rectal examination. GENITOURINARY – PROSTATE CANCER – HISTORY AND PHYSICAL EXAMINATION (p 337).

Choice A (*boggy nontender prostate gland*) is suggestive of *chronic prostatitis.*

Choice B (smooth firm prostate) describes a normal prostate gland.

Choice D (*enlarged symmetric firm prostate*) describes *benign prostatic hypertrophy.* BPH is commonly associated with elevations of *prostate specific antigen.* It would more likely present with obstructive or irritative symptoms but not weight loss or back pain.
Choice E (tender boggy prostate) describes acute prostatitis.

QUESTION 62
Choice E is correct. A first-degree relative is a parent, sibling or offspring. Because his brother was diagnosed at age 53, recommended age is to begin at age 40 (or 10 years before the person was diagnosed which would have been 43) so you use the lower number. The 10 year period comes from the thought it takes roughly about 10 years on average for a polyp to become malignant. GI – COLON CANCER – HEALTH MAINTENANCE (p 152).

	FOBT	COLONOSCOPY
Average Risk	Annually @ 50y	Colonoscopy q10y (flex sig q5y) (up to 80y)
1st degree relative >60y	Annually @ 40y	Colonoscopy q10y
1st degree relative <60y	Annually @ 40y	Colonoscopy q5y

Choice A is incorrect.

Choice B (Fecal occult blood testing at age 40 and colonoscopy every 10 years) is recommended in patients whose first degree relative was diagnosed with colon cancer over the age of 60.

Choice C (Fecal occult blood testing at age 50 and colonoscopy every 10 years) is the standard recommended guidelines in the general population.

Choice D is incorrect

QUESTION 63
Choice C (Increased FEV1/FVC ratio) is the correct answer. Idiopathic pulmonary fibrosis is a type of restrictive disorder. The scarring (fibrosis) "restricts" the movement of the lung. In restrictive disorders, both the forced expiratory volume in one second (FEV1) and forced vital capacity (FVC) are decreased. But the decrease in FVC is more than that of FEV1, resulting in a normal or higher than 80% FEV1/FVC ratio. Restrictive disorders are associated with decreased lung volumes (such as total lung capacity). Both restrictive and obstructive disorders are associated with a decreased functional residual capacity (for different reasons). Because lung movement is restricted, the lung compliance (ability to expand the lung) is reduced. PULMONARY – RESTRICTIVE DISORDERS – LABS/DIAGNOSTIC (p 84).

QUESTION 64
Choice B (Tularemia) is the correct answer. Tularemia is caused by Francisella tularensis, a gram-negative coccobacilli. It is transmitted via a *tick or insect bite or from handling rodent and rabbit tissues.*
INFECTIOUS DISEASE – TULAREMIA – MOST LIKELY (p 424).

Choice A (*Cutaneous anthrax*) is associated with a *black eschar.* It is normally found in *cattle, horses, goats, sheep and swine.* It presents with an *erythematous papule* that ulcerates into a *black eschar* with surrounding edema and vesicles.

Choice C (Coccidiodomycosis) may also present with an eschar. It grows in the soil of *arid/desert regions in Southwestern United States, Mexico, South and Central America.*

Choice D (Leishmaniasis) may also present with an eschar. It is most commonly associated with *bites from a female sand fly.* It presents with small erythematous papules.

Choice E (Brucellosis) is not classically associated with eschar formation.

QUESTION 65
Choice C (N-acetylcysteine) is the correct answer. N-acetylcysteine is the antidote in cases of acetaminophen toxicity. PSYCH/BEHAVIORAL – ACETAMINOPHEN TOXICITY – PHARMACOLOGY (pediatrics online chapter).

Choice A (flumazenil) is the antidote to benzodiazepine toxicity.

Choice B (naloxone) is the antidote for narcotics/opioid toxicity.

Choice D (Pralidoxime) is used in the management of organophosphate and acetylcholinesterase toxicity.

Choice E (Physostigmine) is an acetylcholinesterase inhibitor.

QUESTION 66

Choice A (direct thrombin inhibitor) is the correct answer. Direct thrombin inhibitors include argatroban, dabigatran and bivalirudin. HEMATOLOGY – ANTICOAGULANTS – PHARMACOLOGY (p 481).

Choice B (potentiates antithrombin III) describes the mechanism of action of unfractionated heparin and low molecular weight heparin. The heparins are an indirect inhibitors of thrombin.

Choice C (inhibits Vitamin K dependent clotting factors II, VII, IX and X) describes the mechanism of action of warfarin.

Choice D (selective Factor Xa inhibitors) includes fondaparinux, rivaroxaban and apixaban.

Choice E (inhibits adenosine diphosphate) describes the mechanism of action of the antiplatelets clopidogrel, ticlodipine and prasugrel.

QUESTION 67

Choice C (hypokalemia) is the correct answer. Lisinopril is an angiotensin converting enzyme inhibitor. Side effects of ACE inhibitors include teratogenicity & hypotension (it is used as an anti-hypertensive). Although ACE inhibitors are "renoprotective", they may cause azotemia in some patients with baseline kidney disease. Dry cough and angioedema are common side effects of ACE inhibition (due to an increase in bradykinin, a potent vasodilator). The inhibition of aldosterone leads to hyperkalemia. CARDIOLOGY – ACE INHIBITORS – PHARMACOLOGY (p. 479).

QUESTION 68

Choice B (Klinefelter's syndrome) is the correct answer. Klinefelter's syndrome (47, XXY) is due to an extra X chromosome. They are considered genetically male but may have a male, female or intersex phenotype. These patients often have gynecomastia & testicular atrophy. They also tend to have a tall thin stature but become obese later in life and issues with language comprehension. PEDIATRICS – KLINEFELTER'S SYNDROME – MOST LIKELY (online chapter).

Choice A (Marfan syndrome) is an autosomal dominant, genetic connective tissue disorder that leads to cardiovascular, ocular & musculoskeletal findings in addition to multi-systemic involvement.

Choice C (*Turner's syndrome*) 45,X is due to the absence of all or part of a sex chromosome. This leads to gonadal dysgenesis & primary amenorrhea. They often develop premature ovarian failure. Classic findings include: *short stature, webbed neck, prominent ears and a broad chest with hypoplastic, widely-spaced nipples.*

Choice D (Ehlers-Danlos Syndrome) is a genetic disorder of collagen synthesis leading to *skin hyperextensibility, fragile connective tissue & joint hypermobility.*

Choice E (Hypopituitarism) is associated with decreased production of follicle stimulating hormone, luteinizing hormone, adrenocorticotrophic hormone, thyroid stimulating hormone and somatotropin.

QUESTION 69

Choice E (Somatization disorder) is correct. Somatic symptom disorder (somatization disorder) is characterized by chronic physical symptoms involving more than 1 body part with no physical cause of the symptoms. PSYCH/BEHAVIORAL –SOMATIZATION DISORDER – MOST LIKELY (p. 384).

Choice A (body dysmorphic disorder) is characterized by an excessive preoccupation that a body part (or slight anomaly) is deformed, which often causes them to be ashamed.

Choice B (functional neurological disorder/conversion disorder) is a loss of motor or sensory neurologic function suggestive of a physical disorder but caused by psychological factors.

Choice C (malingering) is fabricating or exaggerating the symptoms of physical or mental disorders for a multitude of "secondary gains" (ex. financial compensation, avoiding work etc.).

Choice D (Munchausen syndrome) is an intentional, self-induced symptom or falsified physical or lab findings. This can include the seeking of multiple invasive procedures and operations even if they pose a serious life risk.

QUESTION 70

Choice A (glioblastoma multiforme) is the correct answer. Glioblastoma multiforme is the *most common primary brain malignancy* and classically shows up on CT scan as a *nonhomogeneous mass with a hypodense center and variable ring of enhancement with surrounding edema with a butterfly appearance* if it crosses the corpus callosum. NEUROLOGY – GLIOBLASTOMA MULTIFORME – MOST LIKELY (online chapter CNS tumors).

Choice B (oligodendroglioma) can be found anywhere in the brain but it is not as common as glioblastoma multiforme.

Choice C (ependymoma) often occurs in *children* and is most commonly seen in *the 3rd or 4th ventricle*.

Choice D (hemangioma) is most commonly found in the *cerebellum and the brainstem* (though they may occur in the cerebral hemispheres and the spinal cord. They are associated with von-Hippel-Lindau syndrome (especially if there is retinal involvement).

Choices E (meningioma) most commonly occurs in the convexities of the hemispheres and the parasagittal regions and are *often attached to the dura.*

QUESTION 71

Choice C (dual energy x-ray absorptiometry scan) is the correct answer. A *DEXA scan is the diagnostic test of choice for suspected osteoporosis* (defined as a T score of ≤ -2.5). All of the other choices may be used as adjuncts for osteoporosis or other suspected bone disorders but is not the diagnostic test of choice. ENDOCRINE – OSTEOPOROSIS – LABS/DIAGNOSTIC STUDIES (p 293).

QUESTION 72

Choice D (calcitonin levels) is the correct answer. Medullary thyroid carcinoma arises from the parafollicular C cells. The normal job of the parafollicular cells is to secrete calcitonin in response to hypocalcemia. Patients with medullary thyroid carcinoma will have elevated calcitonin levels so it can be used as a tumor marker in these patients to monitor tumor burden, effective treatment and tumor recurrence. ENDOCRINE – MEDULLARY THYROID CARCINOMA – LABS/DIAGNOSTIC (p. 290).

Choice A (thyroid stimulating hormone levels) is the first test ordered for suspected thyroid disorders. *Patients with thyroid malignancies are often euthyroid*, so thyroid function tests are often be normal.

Choice B (thyroid stimulating antibody levels) is classically associated with Graves' disease.

Choice C (thyroid peroxidase antibody level) is classically associated with autoimmune thyroiditis, such as Hashimoto's, silent lymphocytic or post-partum thyroiditis.

Choice E (parathyroid hormone level) is used to evaluate suspected parathyroid disorders.

QUESTION 73

Choice C (cholinergic crisis) is the correct answer.   Cholinergic crisis is a condition of excess acetylcholine (in this case due to acetylcholinesterase therapy).   Remember that muscarinic acetylcholine receptors cause "SLUDD-C" = Salivation, Lacrimation, Urination, Defecation and Digestion as well as Constriction of the pupil.   Signs and symptoms include acetylcholine excess (nausea, vomiting, salivation, diarrhea, miosis, bradycardia and respiratory failure).   The administration of a short-acting acetylcholinesterase inhibitor, such as Edrophonium, will aggravate the symptoms of cholinergic crisis.   NEUROLOGY – MYASTHENIA GRAVIS – MOST LIKELY (p. 355).

Choice A (Lambert-Eaton myasthenic syndrome) is a condition seen with small cell lung cancer. Patients develop weakness that *improves with repeated use.* It involves inhibition of presynaptic acetylcholine release.

Choice B (Myasthenic crisis) is a severe presentation of myasthenia gravis with respiratory failure. A *short-acting acetyl cholinesterase inhibitor such as Edrophonium will improve the symptoms of myasthenic crisis.*

Choice D (adult respiratory distress syndrome) and Choice E (congestive heart failure) will have positive pulmonary exam findings.

QUESTION 74

Choice D (increased MCV) is the correct answer.   The *string sign, non-bloody diarrhea and right lower quadrant pain is highly suggestive of Crohn's disease.*   The *terminal ileum is the most common site of Crohn's disease* and since it is located in the right lower quadrant, *RLQ pain is a common finding in patients with Crohn's.*   Both inflammatory bowel diseases (Crohn's and Ulcerative Colitis) are thought to arise from an inappropriate autoimmune response to the normal GI flora.   *Antibodies against the harmless saccharomyces cerevisiae* (Baker's/Brewer's yeast) is seen in about 70% of patients with Crohn's (and only 10-15% of those with ulcerative colitis so that also leads to the diagnosis of Crohn's).   Because Crohn's most commonly affects the *terminal ileum (where B12 is absorbed), patients may develop a B12 deficiency and a subsequent macrocytic anemia* with an increased mean corpuscular volume (MCV) of the red blood cell.
GI/NUTRITION – CROHN'S DISEASE – LABS/DIAGNOSTIC STUDIES (p. 151).

Choice A (*increased alpha fetoprotein*) is common in *hepatocellular carcinoma and germ cell tumors like nonseminomatous testicular cancer.* In utero, alpha fetoprotein is the dominant serum protein in the fetus (the fetal version of albumin). Alpha fetoprotein is normally produced by the yolk sac and the liver (which is why elevated levels can be seen in germ cell tumors & hepatocellular carcinoma).

Choice B (increased perinuclear anti-neutrophil cytoplasmic antibody) is commonly seen with ulcerative colitis (commonly associated with *bloody diarrhea and left upper quadrant* since it the inflammation has *contiguous spread from the rectum proximally* – affecting the left side first).   *Positive P-ANCA can also be seen in Churg-Strauss, primary sclerosing cholangitis & microscopic polyangiitis* (and in some cases of polyarteritis nodosa).

Choice C (increased *smooth muscle antibody*) is classically associated with *autoimmune hepatitis* (but can be seen in chronic hepatitis and cirrhosis). There was no mention of liver symptoms in this vignette.

Choice E (*endomysial antibodies) & transglutaminase antibodies* are classically associated with *Celiac disease* (which could cause a chronic diarrhea) but would be related to the consumption of gluten.

QUESTION 75

Choice B (opioid intoxication) is the correct answer.   Opioid intoxication is characterized by lethargy, respiratory depression, pinpoint pupils (narcotics are miotics), hypotension and bradycardia (the ECG shows sinus bradycardia of about 50 beats per minute).   PSYCH/BEHAVIORAL – OPIOID TOXICITY – MOST LIKELY (online chapter).

Choice A (cocaine intoxication) and choice D (amphetamine intoxication) can present with hyperthermia, increased motor activity, headache, tremor, flushing, hyperthermia, cold sweats, nausea, vomiting and seizures. SYMPATHETIC STIMULATION: sweating, tachycardia (arrhythmias), **pupillary dilation,** as well as peripheral vasoconstriction (which can cause hypertension and potentially myocardial infarction).

Choice C (tricyclic overdose) signs and symptoms include strong *anticholinergic side effects*. Due the *sodium channel blocking effect of TCA toxicity, ventricular arrhythmias are common*.

Choice E (venlafaxine intoxication) symptoms include sympathetic activation (leading to pupillary dilation), hypertension, serotonin syndrome and dizziness. Venlafaxine is a serotonin and norepinephrine reuptake inhibitor.

QUESTION 76

Choice D (chalazion) is the correct choice. A chalazion is a painless granuloma of the internal meibomian gland and presents with focal hard, nontender swelling to the conjunctival surface of the eyelid.
HEENT - CHALAZION – HISTORY AND PHYSICAL EXAMINATION – MOST LIKELY (p. 224).

Choice A (*Hordeolum*) is *painful* and would have *local signs of infection*.

Choice B (blepharitis) presents with *red-rimming and flakes on the eyelid margin*.

Choice C (dacrocystitis) presents with signs of *infection on the nasal side of the eyelid*.

Choice E (pterygium) presents with a *triangular-shaped painless growing mass on the conjunctiva* (not the eyelid).

QUESTION 77

Choice D (thumb spica splint) is the correct choice. Scaphoid fractures are associated with *tenderness to the anatomic snuffbox* located on the radial side of the wrist. Radiographs are often normal at the time of the initial injury and these fractures may not be evident until weeks later, so *immobilization with a thumb spica splint* is recommended *even in the setting of a negative radiograph*.
MUSCULOSKELETAL – SCAPHOID FRACTURES – CLINICAL INTERVENTION (p 173).

Choice A (observation and reassurance that it is only a wrist sprain) is not the recommended treatment for a patient with anatomic snuffbox tenderness on physical examination.

Choice B (application of a volar splint) is used for soft tissue injuries of the wrist and hand. It also provides wrist extension in the management for carpal tunnel syndrome and pisiform fractures.

Choice C (Application of an ulnar gutter splint) is classically used for injuries on the ulnar side such as soft tissue injuries and fractures of the fourth and fifth finger (ex Boxer's Fracture).

Choice E (posterior arm splint) is used in the immobilization of certain elbow injuries.

QUESTION 78

Choice D (Lachman test) is the correct choice. *Anterior cruciate ligament injuries are commonly associated with sudden deceleration, pivoting injuries*. It is classically associated with a *pop and then swelling from hemarthrosis*. Sometimes, the ruptured ACL can pull off a piece of the lateral tibial condyle at the ACL insertion site. This is known as a *Segond's fracture*. The Lachman's test is positive in patients with ACL injuries. An anterior drawer test may also be done but Lachman's test is more sensitive than the Anterior drawer test for ACL injuries.
MUSCULOSKELETAL – ANTERIOR CRUCIATE LIGAMENT INJURIES – HISTORY & PHYSICAL EXAM (p 183).

Choice A (*Valgus stress test*) is used to identify *medical collateral ligamental injuries.*

Choice B (*Varus stress test*) is used to identify *lateral collateral ligamental injuries.*

Choice C (*McMurray test*) is used to identify *meniscal injuries.* Meniscal injuries are classically associated with *locking and popping* of the knee.

Choice E (*Posterior drawer test*) is associated with *posterior cruciate ligamental injuries.*

QUESTION 79

Choice E (atopic dermatitis) is the correct answer. Lichen simplex chronicus (neurodermatitis) is a complication of atopic dermatitis in which the patients develop skin thickening due to repetitive itching and scratching of eczematous lesions. DERMATOLOGY – LICHEN SIMPLEX CHRONICUS – BASICS (p. 390).

QUESTION 80

Choice C (IV fluids) is correct. The *inferior ST elevations and the ST depressions in anterior leads* (which represents with reciprocal changes seen in posterior wall myocardial infarctions) reflect right coronary artery involvement. In patients with myocardial infarction, tachycardia is common but since the right coronary artery supplied the SA and the AV node in the majority of patients, patients with inferior and posterior myocardial infarctions may present with bradycardia. *Because right sided infarctions are preload dependent, IV fluids help to preserve preload, thereby protecting the cardiac output.*
CARDIOLOGY – MYOCARDIAL INFARCTION – CLINICAL INTERVENTION (p 26).

Choice A (IV nitroglycerin) is incorrect. Although IV nitroglycerin is helpful patients with myocardial infarction, patients with inferior and/or posterior wall MI's are preload dependent. IV nitroglycerin may decrease preload. In addition, a systolic blood pressure <90 mm Hg is a contraindication to the use of nitroglycerin. This question tests your knowledge of the indication and the contraindications of the drugs.

Choice B (IV morphine) can also decrease preload in these patients who are preload dependent (although often used in acute coronary syndrome). Because it can cause hypotension, IV morphine is contraindicated if systolic blood pressure is < 90 mmHg.

Choice D (IV labetalol) is also often used in the management of acute coronary syndrome. Contraindications to beta-blocker usage includes: pulse > 50 bpm & systolic blood pressure <100 mmHg. Beta blockers are also often routinely used in ACS. Be familiar with the indication and contraindications of beta blockers in these patients.

Choice E (Furosemide) is helpful in congestive heart failure, not inferior/posterior wall infarctions.

QUESTION 81

Choice D (the chest pain is relieved with lying supine) is the correct answer. The chest pain of pericarditis is classically pleuritic: sharp pain (Choice B) that worsens with inspiration (Choice C). The pain is usually persistent (Choice A) with radiation to the trapezius and back (Choice E). The pain is classically worse with the supine position but is relieved with sitting up and leaning forward. CARDIOLOGY – ACUTE PERICARDITIS – BASICS (p. 31).

QUESTION 82

Choice B (nifedipine) is the correct answer. Calcium channel blockers are the drugs of choice for Raynaud's phenomenon. Raynaud's phenomenon is due to vasospasms, so calcium channel blockers reduce vasospasms, increase vessel dilation, and improve blood flow.
MUSCULOSKELETAL – RAYNAUD'S PHENOMENON – CLINICAL INTERVENTION (p. 201).

Choice A (propranolol) is incorrect because *beta-blockers may worsen the symptoms of Raynaud's phenomenon* in some patients.

Choice C (aspirin), choice D (clopidogrel) and choice E (ibuprofen) are not routinely used in the management of Raynaud's phenomenon.

QUESTION 83

Choice A (bronchial carcinoid tumor) is the correct answer. Carcinoid tumors are neuroendocrine tumors and can *intermittently secrete serotonin* (causing diarrhea) and *histamine* (causing bronchoconstriction, flushing and hemodynamic instability). On bronchoscopy the classic finding is a *pink/purple well-vascularized lesion.* PULMONARY – CARCINOID TUMOR – MOST LIKELY (p. 92).

QUESTION 84

Choice B (surgical resection) is the correct choice. The treatment of choice for *localized non small cell carcinoma* (squamous cell, bronchoalveolar and large cell and adenocarcinoma) is *surgical resection.* PULMONARY – NON SMALL CELL LUNG CARCINOMA – CLINICAL INTERVENTION (p. 92).

Choice D (chemotherapy & radiation therapy) is indicated for *small cell carcinoma because it is usually associated with metastasis at the time of presentation.*

QUESTION 85

Choice B (normal chest radiograph) is the correct answer. The classic presentation of pulmonary embolism is a patient who suddenly develops *pleuritic chest pain, tachypnea and tachycardia* (in this case post operatively). The *most common chest radiograph associated with pulmonary embolism is a normal radiograph.* In fact, a patient with severe dyspnea with a normal chest radiograph and no other cause is a high clinical suspicion for pulmonary embolism. The pH is 7.57, which indicates alkalosis. The decreased $PaCO_2$ is indicative of a primary respiratory disorder. *Respiratory alkalosis is the most common arterial blood gas finding in early pulmonary embolism* due to hyperventilation, as *tachypnea is the most common sign of pulmonary embolism.* As it becomes severe, the patient may progress to developing respiratory acidosis.
PULMONARY – PULMONARY EMBOLISM – LABS/DIAGNOSTIC (p. 98).

Choice A (Pleural effusion) may be seen in pulmonary embolism but is not the most common radiograph finding.

Choice C (Wedge-shaped infarct in the lung) describes Hampton's hump, which is classically seen with pulmonary embolism. However, classic doesn't necessarily mean common so be careful to answer what the question is asking you.

Choice D (Tram track markings) is the classic radiographic finding in bronchiectasis.

Choice E (Dilation of the pulmonary artery and collapse of the distal vessels with a sharp cutoff) describes Westermark's sign, which is classically seen with pulmonary embolism. However classic doesn't necessarily mean common so be careful to answer what the question is asking you.

QUESTION 86

Choice E (Lindane should be applied after a bath or shower to maximize it absorption) is the correct answer. *Lindane is neurotoxic* and can cause *headaches and seizures in high doses.* It is *not to be used after a bath or a shower* because it will lead to increased absorption through the opened pores of the skin and a subsequent higher incidence of toxicity. All of the other choices are indicated in the management of pediculosis.
DERMATOLOGY – PEDICULOSIS – HEALTH MAINTENANCE (p. 399 and 400).

QUESTION 87

Choice E (Autoimmune disruption of the desmosome layer) is the correct answer. Autoimmune disruption of the desmosome layer describes the pathophysiology of pemphigus vulgaris. The desmosome disruption leads to positive Nikolsky's sign. DERMATOLOGY – PEMPHIGUS VULGARIS – BASICS (p. 401).

Choice A (*overgrowth of Malassezia furfur*) is associated with the development of *pityriasis (tinea) versicolor.*

Choice B (*Type I IgE hypersensitivity* reaction of the dermis and subcutaneous tissues) describes the pathophysiology of *urticaria* (an allergic response).

Choice C (*Keratin hyperplasia in the stratum basale and spinosum due to T-cell activation*) is the pathophysiology of *psoriasis.* Psoriasis is a chronic, multisystemic inflammatory immune disorder. It occurs due to keratin hyperplasia in the stratum basale and spinosum due to T-cell activation. This leads to greater epidermal thickness and continuous turnover of the dermis.

Choice D (Type II hypersensitivity reaction in the basement membrane) describes the pathophysiology of bullous pemphigoid. This leads to sub epidermal blistering (and the reason why it is classically associated with a negative Nikolsky's sign).

CHOICE 88

Choice C (duodenal ulcer) is correct. The classic presentation of *duodenal ulcers is epigastric pain that is relieved with food and worsened either before or 2-5 hours after meals.* Duodenal ulcers are relieved by food (due to the neutralization of acid in the duodenum from the increased duodenal bicarbonate release when food is consumed) GI/NUTRITION – PEPTIC ULCER DISEASE – MOST LIKELY (p. 133).

Choice A (*atrophic gastritis)* would classically cause a B_{12} *deficiency anemia* and subsequent *neurologic deficits.* The vignette specifically states there is no anemia, making this less likely.

Choice B (*gastric ulcer*) also causes *epigastric pain but it is usually worsened with food*. Gastric ulcers are worse with meals due to the *decreased protective factors* (such as mucous & prostaglandins in the setting of normal hydrochloric acid release.

Choice D (acute pancreatitis) is commonly also associated with *epigastric pain but it radiates to the back* and is not particularly associated with food. It is also often *positional (worsened with the supine position and relieved by sitting forward)*. There is pain change with changes in position in this vignette, making pancreatitis less likely.

Choice E (pancreatic cancer) often presents late in the course with *anemia, weight loss, jaundice.*

QUESTION 89

Choice E (retinal detachment) is the correct choice. Retinal detachment is classically associated with *photopsia (flashing lights)* when the retina detaches followed by progressive vision loss that is often described as *"curtain-like" beginning in the periphery and then progressing centrally. Schaffer's sign* is the visualization of clumps of the retinal pigment cells in the anterior vitreous humor on slit lamp examination.
EENT – RETINAL DETACHMENT – MOST LIKELY (p. 227).

Choice A (*amaurosis fugax*) can be seen with *temporary occlusion of the external carotid artery*. It may be described as a *"curtain going down"* but since it is transient, the *"curtain will go back up again"*.

Choice B (central retinal artery occlusion) has the classic fundoscopic appearance of *a pale retina with a "cherry red" macula*. It causes a sudden onset of *unilateral total vision loss.*

Choice C (*central retinal vein occlusion*) is associated with the fundoscopic appearance of *severe hemorrhaging, giving the retina a "blood and thunder" appearance.* It is *also associated with sudden onset of unilateral vision loss.*

Choice D (papilledema) would show blurring of the optic disc on fundoscopic examination

QUESTION 90
Choice B (Pseudomonas aeruginosa) is the correct answer. This is a classic presentation of malignant otitis externa, which is seen commonly in diabetics. *Pseudomonas aeruginosa is the most common cause of acute otitis externa as well as malignant otitis externa.* Choice A (staphylococcus aureus) is also a common cause of otitis externa. It can be caused by different bacteria and fungi (if due to fungal causes, Candida & Aspergillus usually predominate). EENT – MASTOIDITIS – BASICS (p. 233).

QUESTION 91
Choice A (phlebotomy) is the correct answer. Polycythemia vera is disorder of *increased red blood cell production, leading to hyper viscosity of the blood. Phlebotomy is the management of choice* as it reduces the red blood cell mass. HEMATOLOGY – POLYCYTHEMIA VERA – CLINICAL INTERVENTION (p 467).

Choice B (Imatinib) is an oral chemotherapeutic agent used in Philadelphia chromosome positive chronic myelogenous leukemia (and in relapsed or refractory Philadelphia-positive ALL).

Choice C (*deferoxamine*) is a *chelating agent used in iron overload states,* such as hereditary hemochromatosis and thalassemia.

Choice D (red blood cell transfusion) is used to increase red blood cell mass in patients with anemia. It would worsen the condition of polycythemia vera.

Choice E (cryoprecipitate) may be given to replace clotting proteins in deficient patients.

QUESTION 92
Choice E (Protamine sulfate) is the correct answer. Protamine sulfate is the antidote to heparin sulfate. Protamine sulfate is positively charged, so it binds to the negatively charged heparin.
HEMATOLOGY – HEPARIN OVERDOSE – CLINICAL INTERVENTION (p. 99).

Choice A (*Vitamin K*) is used as a reversal agent *for Warfarin (Coumadin).* Warfarin inhibits Vitamin K dependent clotting factors so vitamin K reverses its effects. Patients on warfarin should avoid food high in vitamin K.

Choice B (Deferoxamine) is chelation therapy used in states of iron overload.

QUESTION 93
Choice D (ethambutol) is the correct answer. Side effects of ethambutol include optic neuritis, peripheral neuropathy and gastrointestinal symptoms.

Choice A (*rifampin*) is associated with *thrombocytopenia, orange colored secretions, hepatitis,* fever, gastrointestinal upset and hypersensitivity reactions.

Choice B (*isoniazid*) is associated with *hepatitis (especially if older than 35 years of age),* and *peripheral neuropathy (prevented with the coadministration of vitamin B6).* Patients may have interactions with tyramine containing foods.

Choice C (*pyrazinamide*) is associated with *hepatitis, hyperuricemia*, gastrointestinal symptoms, arthritis, and a *photosensitive dermatologic rash*.

Choice E (*streptomycin*) is an aminoglycoside associated with *nephrotoxicity and ototoxicity*.

QUESTION 94
Choice B (hypokalemia) is the correct answer. With intramuscular B_{12} replacement, hypokalemia may result as new blood cells are being formed, since most of the body's potassium is found intracellularly. All of the other choices are not specifically caused by B_{12} replacement. HEMATOLOGY – B_{12} REPLACEMENT – HEALTH MAINTENANCE (Page 453).

QUESTION 95
Choice C (increased protein with normal glucose and increased lymphocyte count) is associated with HSV encephalitis. *Increased lymphocytosis is a common response to a viral infection. HSV is the most common cause of encephalitis.* These CSF findings are also seen with viral (aseptic) meningitis.
NEUROLOGY – ENCEPHALITIS – LABS/DIAGNOSTIC STUDIES (p 365).

Choice A (*increased opening pressure with otherwise normal CSF analysis*) is indicative of *idiopathic intracranial hypertension* (pseudotumor cerebri).

Choice B (*increased protein with decreased glucose and increased lymphocyte count*) is associated with *fungal meningitis and tuberculous meningitis.*

Choice D (*increased protein with IgG with oligoclonal bands*) is associated with *multiple sclerosis*, reflecting the increased CNS IgG production from the autoimmune inflammation of the central nervous system white matter.

Choice E (*increased protein with decreased glucose and increased polymorphonuclear neutrophils*) is the classic CSF finding in patients with *bacterial meningitis.*

QUESTION 96
Choice E (upward Babinski reflex) is the correct answer.   Upper motor neuron lesions classically cause *spastic paralysis, increased deep tendon reflexes, little to no muscle atrophy and an upward Babinski reflex* (think <u>U</u>pward Babinski = <u>U</u>pper motor neuron). It is not associated with fasciculations or flaccid paralysis. All the other choices are consistent with lower motor neuron lesions.
NEUROLOGY – UPPER MOTOR NEURON LESIONS – HISTORY AND PHYSICAL EXAMINATION (p. 359).

QUESTION 97
Choice D (opening snap) is correct. *Mitral stenosis is almost always caused by rheumatic fever.* It is classically associated with ruddy cheeks (mitral facies), atrial fibrillation (due to atrial enlargement), prominent S1 and an opening snap. CARDIOLOGY – MITRAL STENOSIS – HISTORY AND PHYSICAL EXAMINATION (p. 43).

Choice A (bounding pulses and wide pulse pressure) is classic for aortic regurgitation.

Choice B (weak, delayed carotid upstroke) is classic for aortic stenosis.

Choice C (mid systolic click) is associated with mitral valve prolapse.

Choice E (increased intensity of murmur when sitting up and leaning forward) is associated with aortic murmurs – aortic stenosis and aortic regurgitation. Mitral murmurs are increased when placed in the left lateral decubitus position.

QUESTION 98

Choice B (Bartonella henselae) is the correct answer. Bartonella henselae causes cat scratch disease, which may present with an ulcer at the inoculation site and flu-like symptoms progressing to lymphadenopathy. It is usually self-limiting and requires no treatment. If moderate or persistent, amoxicillin or doxycycline may be used. INFECTIOUS DISEASE – CAT SCRATCH DISEASE – BASICS (p. 423).

Choice A (Pasteurella multocida) is the most common organism in cat bite infections.

Choice C (Coxiella burnetii) is the causative agent of Q fever.

Choice D (Ascaris lumbricoides) is the cause of roundworm infections.

Choice E (Francisella tularensis) is the causative agent in Tularemia.

QUESTION 99

Choice C (Negri bodies) is the correct answer. Rabies is caused by rhabdovirus infection, leading to encephalitis. The definitive diagnosis is the presence of Negri bodies in the brain (especially in the hippocampus). Negri bodies are eosinophilic inclusions in the cytoplasm of neurons. INFECTIOUS DISEASE – RABIES – LABS/DIAGNOSTIC STUDIES (p. 436).

Choice A (*Lewy bodies*) are cytoplasmic protein aggregate inclusions in the neurons. In *Parkinson's disease* it is *localized to the substantia nigra*. They are seen diffusely in patients with Diffuse Lewy Body disease.

Choice B (*Pick bodies*) are random arrangements of tau proteins seen in patients with *frontotemporal dementia*.

Choice D (Mammillary bodies) are part of the normal limbic system.

Choice E (*Neurofibrillary tangles*) are aggregates of Tau proteins seen in *Alzheimer's disease*.

QUESTION 100

Choice C (erythroplakia) is the correct answer. 90% of patients with erythroplakia have evidence of dysplasia or malignancy. EENT – ERYTHROPLAKIA – BASICS (p 238).

PHOTO CREDITS

1. A 55-year-old male presents with symptoms and echocardiographic evidence consistent with infective endocarditis. On physical examination, there are painless macules that are seen on his palms and soles. Which of the following is the most likely diagnosis?
   a. Osler's nodes
   b. Janeway lesions
   c. Keratoderma blenorrhagicum
   d. Roth spots
   e. Erythema marginatum

2. An 11-year-old boy presents to the pediatric clinic with persistent temperatures. His mother states he has been having fever, runny nose and body aches. On physical examination of the head and neck, there is significant lymphadenopathy, giving the child a "bull neck" appearance. There are gray/white membranes on the posterior pharynx that bleeds when scraped as seen below:

   Which of the following is the management of choice?
   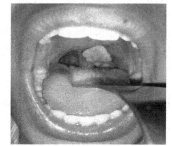
   a. nystatin oral
   b. IV fluconazole
   c. Diphtheria antitoxin + penicillin
   d. Diphtheria antitoxin + Gentamicin
   e. Botulism toxin + Penicillin G

3. A 32-year-old male with a history of hypertension presents to the clinic with abdominal and flank pain in addition to a 2-day history of dark urine. He has no significant past medical history. On physical examination, hepatomegaly and bilateral palpable kidneys are noted. There is the presence of a mid-systolic ejection click and a holosystolic murmur that radiates to the axilla. A urinalysis is positive for blood. There are no signs of anemia. Which of the following is the most appropriate next step in the evaluation of this patient?
   a. cystoscopy
   b. renal ultrasound
   c. renal biopsy
   d. 24 hour urine protein collection
   e. urine culture

4. A 10-year-old child presents to the pediatric clinic with fever, malaise and decreased appetite. His mother noticed that his gums became red and swollen. His gums bleed easily when he brushes his teeth. There were no rashes associated with these symptoms. On physical examination, there are yellow/grey vesicles on the oral mucosa, tongue and lips. There is also associated cervical lymphadenopathy. There are no exudates on the posterior pharynx or rashes seen. Which of the following is the most likely diagnosis?
   a. hand foot and mouth disease
   b. reactivation herpes simplex I
   c. acute herpetic gingivostomatitis
   d. acute herpetic tonsillopharyngitis
   e. Vincent's angina

5. A 33-year-old male presents to the emergency room with intermittent right-sided, pleuritic chest pain. The chest pain is not positional. There is dullness to percussion, decreased breath sounds and decreased fremitus all on the right side. An electrocardiogram shows no ST elevations or T wave changes. Which of the following is the most appropriate management of this patient?
    a. administration of ceftriaxone and azithromycin
    b. thoracentesis
    c. needle decompression followed by insertion of a chest tube
    d. insertion of a chest tube
    e. administration of aspirin

6. In evaluating a patient with oral thrush and odynophagia, which of the following endoscopic findings would be most likely seen in this patient?
    a. Large superficial ulcers
    b. Columnar cells in the lower esophagus
    c. Small deep ulcers
    d. Linear plaques
    e. Multiple corrugated rings

7. A 24-year-old male is involved in an altercation and suffered a direct blow to his left forearm while attempting to prevent being hit in the face with a bat. On physical examination, there is tenderness to the forearm with ecchymosis and a wrist drop.   The following radiograph is obtained:

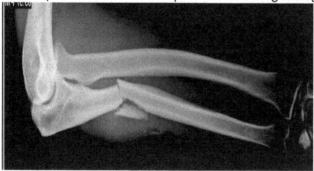

    Which of the following is the most likely diagnosis?
    a. Galleazzi Fracture
    b. Anterior elbow dislocation
    c. Posterior elbow dislocation
    d. Monteggia Fracture
    e. Nightstick Fracture

8. Which of the following is most commonly involved in rotator cuff injuries?
    a. teres minor
    b. infraspinatus
    c. subscapularis
    d. teres major
    e. supraspinatus

9. Which of the following is not a significant risk factor for the development of endometrial cancer?
    a. raloxifene therapy
    b. estrogen replacement therapy
    c. nulliparity
    d. chronic anovulation
    e. tamoxifen therapy

10. A 43-year-old male is found to have an incidental thyroid nodule. Radioactive iodine uptake scan reveals a cold nodule. A malignancy is seen on subsequent pathology. Which of the following is the most likely diagnosis?
   a. medullary thyroid carcinoma
   b. follicular cell thyroid carcinoma
   c. papillary thyroid carcinoma
   d. parathyroid carcinoma
   e. anaplastic thyroid carcinoma

11. A 34-year-old female with a history of bipolar disorder is being evaluated in the gynecology clinic because she is concerned that she may be pregnant. She is worried because she has not menstruated in the last 2 months despite having regular cycles before. She denies any weight gain. She thought she might have been pregnant because she noticed milky discharge from both breasts in the last 2 weeks. She states she also has not been interested in sex lately. A serum qualitative hCG is negative. Which of the following medications is most likely responsible for her symptoms?
   a. Olanzapine (Zyprexa)
   b. Haloperidol (Haldol)
   c. Quetiapine (Seroquel)
   d. Lithium (Lithobid)
   e. Bromocriptine (Parlodel)

12. A 20-year-old female with a history of hay fever and allergic rhinitis presents with tiny, erythematous, edematous, ill-defined blisters primarily on the antecubital and popliteal fossae bilaterally. The rash later dries and scales and is intensely pruritic. Which of the following is the most appropriate medical management?
   a. Oral acyclovir
   b. topical fluconazole
   c. topical metronidazole
   d. topical corticosteroids
   e. oral griseofulvin

13. A 30-year-old male presents with fatigue and weakness. On physical examination, there is conjunctival pallor and a normal neurological exam. Labs include:

   Serum iron: normal
   Serum ferritin: normal
   Total iron binding capacity: decreased
   MCV: 60 (Normal 80 – 100)
   Hemoglobin: 8.0 (Normal 13.5 – 17.5)

   Which of the following is the most appropriate next step in the evaluation of the patient?
   a. bone marrow biopsy
   b. urine electrophoresis
   c. a trial of iron therapy
   d. serum B_{12} levels
   e. hemoglobin electrophoresis

14. A farmer is brought into the emergency room by his wife. She states he was having headaches, muscle spasms and then developed tremors and convulsions. In the emergency room, he is complaining of visual changes, and chest tightness. On physical examination, there is diffuse wheezing, sweating and lacrimation. In addition to atropine, which of the following is used in the management of organophosphate poisoning?

    a. pralidoxime
    b. pyridostigmine
    c. pilocarpine
    d. phenoxybenzamine
    e. pyridoxine

15. Which of the following echocardiogram findings is most consistent with restrictive cardiomyopathy?

    a. diastolic dysfunction with marked dilation of both atria
    b. global systolic dysfunction
    c. thickened ventricular septal wall > 15 mm
    d. apical ballooning of the left ventricle
    e. diastolic collapse of the ventricles

16. Which one of the following HIV medications is associated with vivid dreams and neurologic disturbances?

    a. Efaviranz
    b. Zidovudine
    c. Indinavir
    d. Raltegravir
    e. Ritonavir

17. A 44-year-old male comes into the emergency room with crampy abdominal pain, nausea, vomiting and constipation. An abdominal radiograph shows the following:

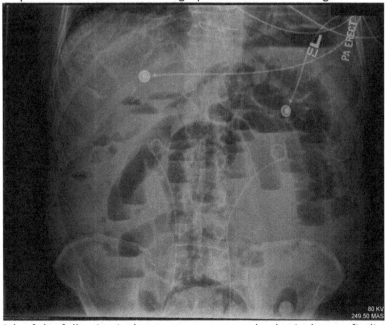

Which of the following is the most common early physical exam finding in this patient?

    a. Peritoneal signs
    b. Bowel sounds with gurgling at a rate of about 5-15 per minute
    c. No bowel sounds
    d. Hyperactive, high-pitched tinkling abdominal sounds
    e. Sausage-shaped mass

18. A 33-year-old female who is 2 weeks post partum presents to the clinic with right breast pain. On physical examination, there is local right breast tenderness, warmth and swelling with no palpable masses. The patient is afebrile and there is no evidence of axillary lymphadenopathy. There is no area of fluctuance. Which of the following is the management of choice in this patient?
    a. incision and drainage with the cessation of breast feeding from the affected breast
    b. warm compresses, dicloxacillin, and patient can continue to breastfeed
    c. ice packs, tight fitting bra and the avoidance of breast stimulation
    d. the administration of fluconazole
    e. warm compresses, the administration of gentamicin and the patient can continue to breastfeed

19. A 20-year-old male presents with severe throat pain and difficulty swallowing his secretions. He has a muffled, hot potato voice, trismus and his uvula is deviated to the left. There are no intraoral lesions. A CBC shows an elevated white blood cell count (primarily neutrophils and bands). Which of the following is the most likely diagnosis?
    a. Vincent's angina
    b. Ludwig's angina
    c. Acute herpetic tonsillopharyngitis
    d. Peritonsillar abscess
    e. Infectious mononucleosis

20. A 54-year-old male presents to the clinic with recurrent urinary tract infections and intermittent symptoms of hesitancy, straining to void and interruption of his urinary stream. He denies any perineal pain. On rectal examination, the prostate is nontender and boggy. Which of the following organisms is the most likely cause of these symptoms?
    a. Klebsiella pneumoniae
    b. Escherichia coli
    c. Pseudomonas aeruginosa
    d. Chlamydia trachomatis
    e. Proteus mirabilis

21. Which of the following is the most common inherited cause of hypercoagulability?
    a. Von Willebrand deficiency
    b. Protein C deficiency
    c. Antithrombin III deficiency
    d. Factor V Leiden mutation
    e. Protein S deficiency

22. An 11-year old previously healthy male with recent symptoms of myalgias and runny nose presents with a 3-week onset of gradual exercise intolerance, abdominal pain and shortness of breath. He has no recent travel history. On physical examination, rales are heard as well as a third heart sound. There is no periorbital edema or skin lesions. A chest radiograph shows cardiomegaly. Peripheral blood buffy coat smear is negative for motile parasites. A biopsy of the cardiac tissue shows infiltration of lymphocytes with myocardial tissue necrosis. Which of the following is the most likely cause of the symptoms?
    a. herpes simplex virus
    b. enterovirus
    c. adenovirus
    d. influenza virus
    e. trypanosoma cruzi

23. A 25-year-old male was struck while riding a motorcycle. He is complaining of lower back pain and paralysis but denies neck pain. On physical examination, there is flaccid paralysis with symptoms of anterior cord syndrome. Neurogenic shock is suspected. Which of the following is the hallmark of neurogenic shock?
   a. hypotension with tachycardia, decreased pulmonary capillary wedge pressure
   b. warm, flushed extremities with increased cardiac output
   c. hypotension with bradycardia and decreased pulmonary capillary wedge pressure
   d. cool, clammy skin. Decreased cardiac output with increased pulmonary capillary wedge pressure
   e. increased bicep jerk reflexes

24. A psychotherapist is evaluating a 36-year-old woman. She states that she suffers from frequent "temper tantrums" if she is not the center of attention. She goes out of her way to get attention at work from her male coworkers, such as wearing low-cut blouses and push-up bras to accentuate her cleavage. She believes she does this because she craves the attention of others to improve her self worth. In the initial evaluation, the psychotherapist notices she is overly emotional and dramatic in her description of her problems and cries and laughs almost at the same time. When she laughs, she makes sure to adjust her blouse in an attempt to show her cleavage to the psychotherapist. Which of the following is the most likely diagnosis?
   a. narcissistic personality disorder
   b. dependent personality disorder
   c. histrionic personality disorder
   d. borderline personality disorder
   e. schizotypal personality disorder

25. 52-year-old male presents with fever and a productive cough with brownish colored sputum. A chest radiograph shows a left lower lobe infiltrate with a left-sided pleural effusion. A thoracentesis is performed and fluid examination reveals a pH of 6.8, glucose: 32mg/dL, effusion to serum lactate ratio: 1.2, effusion to serum protein ratio 0.8. Which of the following is the most appropriate next step in management?
   a. obtain a chest CT scan
   b. administration of IV antibiotics and drainage of the pleural effusion
   c. administration of ceftriaxone and azithromycin
   d. repeat chest X rays to monitor the progression
   e. begin furosemide, oxygen, place the patient in sitting position, morphine and nitroglycerin

26. Which of the following is most consistent with moderate persistent asthma?
   a. Symptoms less than 2 times a day with a forced expiratory volume 81%
   b. Forced expiratory volume of 70% with daily symptoms, nighttime symptoms greater than 1 time a week
   c. Forced expiratory volume 59% with symptoms throughout the day
   d. The use of short acting beta 2 agonists greater than 2 days a week with a forced expiratory volume 85%
   e. Nighttime symptoms 3 to 4 times a month with an forced expiratory volume of 81%

27. In which of the following patients is the pneumococcal vaccine not indicated?
   a. A 7-year-old with sickle cell disease
   b. A 70-year-old patient who lives in a nursing home
   c. A 50-year-old with chronic renal failure
   d. A 40-year-old patient with history of hypertension
   e. A 45-year-old male with a history of diabetes mellitus

28. Which of the following is not used in the routine management of severe hyperkalemia?
   a. IV insulin with glucose
   b. IV calcium gluconate
   c. IV Metoprolol
   d. Oral sodium polystyrene sulfonate
   e. Nebulized albuterol

29. A 62-year-old male presents with anemia, headache and bone pain. Laboratory evaluation reveals an increased creatinine, hypercalcemia, and a normocytic anemia. Rouleaux formation of the red blood cells is seen on peripheral smear. A CT scan of the head reveals the presence of "punched out lesions" on the scout film of the skull. Which of the following is expected to be seen based on the most likely diagnosis?
   a. presence of basophilic stippling of the red blood cells
   b. presence of Heinz bodies in the red blood cells
   c. presence of kappa or lambda light chain proteins on urine electrophoresis
   d. presence of hyperchromic, sphere-shaped red blood cells
   e. presence of small, dense basophilic inclusions in the red blood cells

30. Which of the following medications functions to increase fetal hemoglobin levels, increase the water content of red blood cells and decrease the sickling deformity of red blood cells?
   a. Erythropoietin
   b. Deferoxamine
   c. Hydroxyurea
   d. Folic acid
   e. Vitamin B12

31. Which of the following tests is the gold standard (definitive diagnostic test) in a patient suspected of having a pulmonary embolism?
   a. chest radiograph
   b. ventilation-perfusion scan
   c. D-dimer levels
   d. pulmonary angiography
   e. Spiral CT scan with IV contrast

32. Which of the following is the most common premalignant skin condition?
   a. seborrheic keratosis
   b. rosacea
   c. lichen planus
   d. actinic keratosis
   e. chloasma

33. A 23-year-old male presents to the clinic with a single eschar. He states that he had local burning to the site for 4 hours before it became blanched. The blanching progressed to an erythematous margin with a red halo in the center and became a hemorrhagic bulla until the black eschar formed. He states it occurred after sleeping on a porch while visiting New Orleans. Which of the following is the most likely diagnosis?
   a. Rocky mountain spotted fever
   b. Lyme disease
   c. Brown recluse spider bite
   d. Ehrlichiosis
   e. Coccidiodomycosis

34. A 29-year-old male falls directly onto the left hip while ice-skating. He is complaining of sudden onset of left hip pain and is unable to bear weight. On physical examination, the left leg is foreshortened and externally rotated .   The following X rays are obtained:

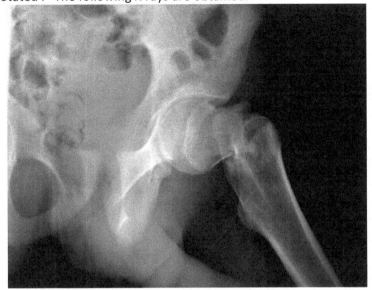

Which of the following is the most likely diagnosis?
- a.   Hip dislocation
- b.   Intertrochanteric fracture
- c.   Legg-Calve Perthe's disease
- d.   Sub trochanteric hip fracture
- e.   Osteonecrosis of the hip

35. Which of the following is not a side effect of propranolol?
- a.   depression
- b.   second degree heart block
- c.   impotence
- d.   masking of the symptoms of hypoglycemia
- e.   bronchodilation

36. Which of the following is classically associated with Crohn's disease?
- a. bloody diarrhea and left lower quadrant pain
- b. decrease of exacerbations with smoking
- c. granulomas and fistulas
- d. stovepipe sign on barium enema
- e. inflammation of the mucosa and submucosa only

37. A 2-week-old infant is brought into the emergency room for increasing lethargy. The infant has signs of dehydration. His mother states that after giving him his regular feeding, he seemed irritable and then had projectile, nonbilious vomiting.   After he vomited, she noticed and felt an olive-shaped mass in his abdomen. She states there has not been any blood or mucus in his stools. Which of the following is the most likely diagnosis?
- a.   Intussusception
- b.   Infant botulism
- c.   Meckel's diverticulum
- d.   Hirschsprung's disease
- e.   Pyloric stenosis

38. A 54-year-old male with a history of cirrhosis presents with an upper gastrointestinal bleed. Esophageal varices are found to be cause of the bleed. Which of the following is the first line management of choice in acute active esophageal variceal bleeding?
    a. propranolol
    b. vasopressin
    c. insertion of a transjugular intrahepatic portosystemic shunt
    d. endoscopic ligation of the bleeding vessel
    e. endoscopic sclerotherapy of the bleeding vessel

39. A 43-year-old male was admitted for a knee replacement. 4 days after successful surgery, the nurse calls the physician assistant to the floor because the patient is agitated and confused. The patient has pulled out his IV line, ripped the otoscope off the wall and tried to attack the patient care technician. The patient states he feels "as if ants are crawling all over my skin" as well as hearing voices. The patient has a noticeable tremor and is hyper reflexive. Which of the following is the most likely diagnosis?
    a. serotonin syndrome
    b. neuroleptic malignant syndrome
    c. alcohol withdrawal
    d. opioid withdrawal
    e. opioid intoxication

40. A 54-year-old male with a history of schizophrenia develops an acute leukopenia with a differential count showing a decrease in the neutrophil, basophil and eosinophil cell lines. Which of the following medications is the most likely cause?
    a. Clozapine (Clozaril)
    b. Lithium (Lithobid)
    c. Aripiprazole (Abilify)
    d. Risperidone (Risperdal)
    e. Ziprasidone (Geodon)

41. A 43-year-old male with a history of migraine disorder presents to the emergency room with headache, nausea and photophobia. He is given Promethazine (Phenergan) for the nausea as well as Ketorolac (Toradol) for the headache. About 30 minutes later, he develops slurred speech, torticollis and protrusion of his tongue. Which of the following is the recommended management?
    a. Cyclobenzaprine (Flexeril)
    b. Diphenhydramine (Benadryl)
    c. Metaxalone (Skelaxin)
    d. Clozapine (Clozaril)
    e. Lithium (Lithobid)

42. A 32-year-old male with a recent diagnosis of bipolar disorder is placed on lithium therapy. He is seen one month after initiation of medication for a well visit. He is complaining of an insatiable thirst in which he says he drinks about 5 liters of water a day and goes to the bathroom all the time. He now wakes up at least 6 times during the night to use the bathroom. Which of the following would be seen in this patient if lithium is the cause of his symptoms?
    a. hyponatremia
    b. increased arginine vasopressin levels
    c. decreased urine osmolarity
    d. elevated glucose levels
    e. peripheral edema

43. The triad of hemolytic anemia, venous thrombosis of large vessels and pancytopenia is hallmark of which of the following diseases?
    a. thrombotic thrombocytopenic purpura
    b. paroxysmal nocturnal hemoglobinuria
    c. idiopathic (immune) thrombocytopenic purpura
    d. hemolytic uremic syndrome
    e. autoimmune hemolytic anemia

44. A 32-year-old male presents with a painful left eye associated with a foreign body sensation, redness and tearing. There are no changes in visual acuity. A slit lamp examination is done, which shows an "ice-rink" sign. He states that he wears contact lenses. Which of the following is the best appropriate management?
    a. erythromycin ophthalmic ointment
    b. bacitracin ophthalmic ointment
    c. naphazoline ophthalmic ointment
    d. olopatadine ophthalmic ointment
    e. ciprofloxacin ophthalmic solution

45. A 68-year-old Asian woman presents to the clinic after slipping and falling on black ice with her hands outstretched while her wrist was extended. Radiographs of the wrist are obtained.
    Which of the following is the most likely diagnosis?
    a. Barton fracture
    b. Smith Fracture
    c. Colles fracture
    d. Rolando Fracture
    e. Scapholunate dislocation

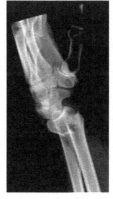

46. A 32-year-old woman presents to the labor and delivery unit at 34 weeks gestation complaining of right upper quadrant pain, headache. She develops a tonic-clonic seizure. Her blood pressure is 170/118. Which of the following is the most appropriate management at this time?
    a. administration of IV magnesium sulfate
    b. oxytocin and prompt delivery of the fetus
    c. administration of terbutaline
    d. administration of IV lisinopril
    e. administration of methyldopa orally and admission for monitoring

47. A 23-year-old woman at 19-weeks gestation and history of severe prolonged hyperemesis gravidarum presents to the emergency room after having painless vaginal bleeding and brownish discharge. Serum beta HCG levels are 120,000 mIU/ml. An ultrasound is performed, showing a "snowstorm" or "cluster of grapes" pattern. Which of the following is the management of choice?
    a. continue fetal monitoring and contraction stress test monitoring
    b. methotrexate
    c. uterine suction curettage
    d. admission to the hospital for close monitoring
    e. continued monitoring of the serum beta HCG levels to see if they double every 48 hours

48. A 56-year-old male with a history of Type II diabetes mellitus is found to have altered mental status. His blood pressure: 110/70 mmHg, pulse rate: 99 beats per minute, oxygen saturation: 98% on room air with a respiratory rate of 21 breaths per minute. A head CT without contrast shows no evidence of hemorrhagic stroke. Motor and sensory are both intact and there is no weakness. The following lab values are obtained:

		PATIENT	NORMAL VALUES
Plasma Glucose	(mg/dL)	630	80 - 110
Arterial pH		7.36	7.35 - 7.45
Serum Bicarbonate	(mEq/L)	17	21 – 28
Ketones (Urine/Serum)		Small	None
Serum Osmolarity	(mosm/kg)	410	275 – 295
Anion (Gap	mEq/L)	10	<11

Which of the following is considered first line in the management of this patient?
- a. intravenous insulin bolus followed by insulin drip
- b. IV administration of 0.9% sodium chloride solution
- c. IV administration of bicarbonate
- d. IV administration of IV glucagon
- e. IV administration of 5% dextrose and 0.45% sodium chloride solution

49. Which of the following is a side effect of methimazole?
- a. hyperthyroidism
- b. myelosuppression
- c. diabetes insipidus
- d. syndrome of inappropriate ADH secretion
- e. darkening of the tongue

50. A 23-year-old female presents with ocular weakness and generalized muscle weakness. Labs reveal positive acetylcholine receptor antibodies. Which of the following is the long-term management of choice?
- a. Plasmapheresis
- b. Pyridostigmine
- c. Carbamazepine
- d. Edrophonium
- e. Benztropine

51. Which of the following is a test used to assess for congenital hip dislocation/dysplasia?
- a. Ober test
- b. Barlow test
- c. Moro reflex
- d. McRoberts maneuver
- e. Woods maneuver

52. Dilated cardiomyopathy, alopecia and bone marrow suppression are side effects of which of the following medications?
- a. bleomycin
- b. vincristine
- c. methotrexate
- d. doxorubicin
- e. cisplatin

53. A 48-year-old male with a history of hypertension and hyperlipidemia is brought into the hospital by his brother for sudden onset of slurred speech and upper extremity greater than lower extremity weakness that began 40 minutes ago. By the time he presents to the hospital, the symptoms have completely resolved. The patient undergoes a stroke workup, which shows 81% stenosis of the internal carotid artery on carotid Doppler. Which of the following is the management of choice?

    a. IV alteplase
    b. IV streptokinase
    c. carotid endarterectomy
    d. lifestyle modification of risk factors
    e. admission to the hospital for observation of return of symptoms

54. Which of the following medications are contraindicated in the management of a cocaine-induced myocardial infarction?

    a. beta blockers
    b. aspirin
    c. calcium channel blockers
    d. benzodiazepines
    e. nitroglycerin

55. Which of the following exam findings is most consistent with isolated left-sided congestive heart failure?

    a. positive Kussmaul's sign
    b. peripheral edema
    c. nausea and vomiting
    d. positive hepatojugular reflex
    e. rhonchi

56. Which of the following is not a classic side effect of metformin?

    a. lactic acidosis
    b. macrocytic anemia
    c. radiocontrast-induced acute kidney injury
    d. hypoglycemia
    e. diarrhea

57. In comparison to emphysema, which of the following is most consistent with chronic bronchitis?

    a. hyperresonance to percussion
    b. decreased breath sounds on auscultation
    c. increased anteroposterior diameter
    d. pursed lip breathing
    e. rales, rhonchi, and wheezing

58. A 28-year-old male is brought into the emergency room for what is suspected to be an overdose on morphine. On physical examination, his pupils are pinpoint and in observing his breathing, you notice irregular respirations characterized by quick shallow breaths of equal depth with irregular periods of apnea. Which of the following describes this type of breathing?

    a. Cheyne Stokes respirations
    b. Biot's Respiration
    c. Kussmaul's respiration
    d. tachypnea

59. An 18-year-old male presents to the urgent care center with fever, headache and an expanding rash seen below.   He states he went camping in Connecticut 10 days ago.
Which of the following is the recommended management of choice?
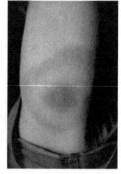
   a.   oral azithromycin
   b.   oral doxycycline
   c.   intravenous ceftriaxone
   d.   oral clindamycin
   e.   oral vancomycin

60. Which of the following is the most common clinical manifestation of chronic Q fever?
   a.   culture negative endocarditis
   b.   osteomyelitis
   c.   cirrhosis
   d.   pulmonary interstitial fibrosis
   e.   amyloidosis

61. A 32-year-old male with a history of Crohn's disease developed an inflammatory papule that progressed to a painful, necrotic ulcer with irregular, violet, undermined borders and a purulent base.   Which of the following is the most likely diagnosis?
   a.   furuncle
   b.   pyoderma gangrenosum
   c.   pyogenic granuloma
   d.   erythema infectiosum
   e.   carbuncle

62. A 43-year-old male diagnosed with a subarachnoid hemorrhage is admitted to the intensive care unit for observation.   He is given blood pressure control, phenytoin for seizure prophylaxis and a repeat head CT scan 24 hours later to monitor the bleed.   72 hours later, he develops an acute onset of fever and rash.   On physical examination, the rash is composed of dull, dusty-red, purpuric macules surrounded by a pale edematous rim and peripheral halo.   There are mucosal erosions and crusts on the lips and the buccal mucosa with a negative Nikolsky sign.   Which of the following is the most likely diagnosis?
   a.   Morbiliform drug rash
   b.   Erythema multiforme minor
   c.   Steven Johnson syndrome
   d.   Erythema multiforme major
   e.   Toxic epidermal necrolysis

63. A 22-year-old female presents to the emergency room with painful urination and pelvic pain.   On physical examination, she is febrile, there is lower abdominal tenderness to palpation with rebound tenderness and cervical motion tenderness.   There are no associated skin rashes or desquamation of the skin.   A CBC shows a white blood cell count of 15,000 cells/mm^3 (Normal 5,000 – 10, 000 cells/mm^3).   Beta hCG levels are undetectable.   Which of the following is the management of choice?
   a.   IV doxycycline + ceftriaxone
   b.   IV clindamycin + oxacillin
   c.   IV clindamycin + vancomycin
   d.   Oral methotrexate
   e.   IV ampicillin/sulbactam

64. A male with mild development disabilities is being evaluated and is noted to have a midsystolic ejection click on cardiac examination. Other physical exam findings include hyperextensible joints, a long and narrow face, prominent forehead and chin, large ears, and macroorchidism. Which of the following is the most likely diagnosis?
  a. Klinefelter's syndrome
  b. Fragile X syndrome
  c. Turner's syndrome
  d. Marfan's syndrome
  e. Ehlers-Danlos syndrome

65. A 60-year-old male presents headache and dizziness. Initial evaluation is positive for anemia, thrombocytopenia, and leukostasis. A bone marrow biopsy is performed, showing 28% blasts and the presence of Auer rods. Which of the following is the most likely diagnosis?
  a. acute myelogenous leukemia
  b. chronic lymphocytic leukemia
  c. acute lymphocytic leukemia
  d. multiple myeloma
  e. chronic myelogenous leukemia

66. A 65-year-old female with a history of a prior myocardial infarction presents to the ophthalmology clinic with a 2-day history of acute, sudden onset of right-sided visual loss. On fundoscopic exam, the retina is pale with a "cherry-red" colored macula. Which of the following is the most likely diagnosis?
  a. posterior uveitis
  b. amaurosis fugax
  c. retinal detachment
  d. central retinal vein occlusion
  e. central retinal artery occlusion

67. A 3-year old girl presents to the pediatric emergency room with drooling, dysphagia, muffled voice and difficulty swallowing her secretions. She is sitting in a tripod position. A lateral film shows a thumb print sign. Which of the following is the best next appropriate step in the management of this patient?
  a. visualize a cherry red epiglottis by using a tongue depressor
  b. initiate intravenous ceftriaxone and clindamycin
  c. protect the airway
  d. initiate supportive therapy and keep the child comfortable
  e. initiate botulism antitoxin and penicillin G

68. A 44-year-old male is brought in by his wife because she is concerned that the voices he hears are occurring with increased frequency. She states that over the last 8 months, he has been hearing voices and over the last month, he refused to have intercourse with her because he believes "the FBI has placed a microchip in my penis" to spy on him. His symptoms have caused him to lose his job and he hasn't been able to look for a new job or help her raise their children. Upon trying to ascertain a history, he has a cold, blunt affect and is very distrustful that the doctors at the hospital are "working for the FBI". Which of the following is the most likely diagnosis?
  a. schizophrenia
  b. Bipolar disorder
  c. Paranoid personality disorder
  d. Schizophreniform disorder
  e. Schizotypal personality disorder

69. A 56-year-old male with a history of chronic alcoholism and cirrhosis presents to the emergency room with confusion and disorientation to place and time. When performing a physical examination, ascites is noted and the patient has a flapping tremor when his wrists are extended. There is no ataxia or ophthalmoplegia. A CBC shows a mean corpuscular volume (MCV) of 85 (normal 80 – 100) and a mild normochromic normocytic anemia. Which of the following lab values are most consistent with the most likely diagnosis?

    a. increased amylase and lipase
    b. increased ammonia levels
    c. increased alkaline phosphatase with gamma glutamyl transpeptidase
    d. decreased thiamine levels
    e. decreased vitamin B12 levels

70. A 36-year-old male with a history of depression is placed on Sertraline (Zoloft). He develops sexual dysfunction that is thought to be secondary to drug therapy. Which of the following medications may be used to treat the depression with the least likelihood of the sexual dysfunction side effects?

    a. Citalopram (Celexa)
    b. Venlafaxine (Effexor)
    c. Bupropion (Wellbutrin)
    d. Amitriptyline (Elavil)
    e. Doxepin (Sinequan)

71. A 9-year-old male presents with fever, chills, neck stiffness, photophobia and headache. On physical examination, a positive Brudzinski's and Kernig's sign is elicited as well as the following rash:

Which of the following gram stains would most likely be seen based on the history and physical exam findings?

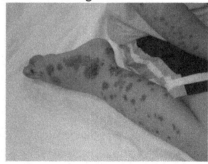

    a. gram negative rods
    b. gram negative diplococci
    c. gram positive cocci in pairs
    d. gram positive cocci in chains
    e. gram positive rods

72. A 7-year-old patient with a history of sickle cell disease develops osteomyelitis. A gram stain is performed and shows pink staining bacilli:

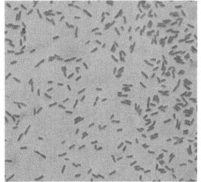

Which of the following is the management of choice in this patient?

    a. IV Oxacillin
    b. IV Ciprofloxacin
    c. IV Clindamycin
    d. IV Ceftriaxone
    e. IV Vancomycin

73. Which of the following is increased in patients with hemophilia B (Christmas disease)?
   a. prothrombin time
   b. fibrinogen
   c. bleeding time
   d. platelets
   e. partial thromboplastin time

74. A 10-year-old African-American male with no past medical history presents with symptoms of a urinary tract infection. He is placed on trimethoprim-sulfamethoxazole twice daily. A few days later, he develops abdominal and back pain. On physical examination, there is splenomegaly and pallor. A complete blood cell count shows a normocytic anemia. Peripheral smear is positive for shistocytes and Heinz bodies. Coombs testing is negative. Which of the following is the most likely diagnosis?
   a. Autoimmune hemolytic anemia
   b. Hereditary spherocytosis
   c. Glucose 6 phosphate-dehydrogenase deficiency
   d. Anemia of chronic disease
   e. Sickle cell anemia

75. A 7-month-old infant is brought into the emergency room for weakness and vomiting. His mother states she was trying to switch him from breast milk to formula. She states that he didn't seem to like the taste of the formula, so she placed a little honey in the bottle to make it more palatable for him. A few days later, he began to vomit the formula. On physical examination, the infant has flaccid paralysis, dry mouth, a feeble cry, and dilated, fixed pupils. Which of the following is the recommended management of this patient?
   a. diphtheria antitoxin + penicillin G
   b. tetanus immune globulin + metronidazole or penicillin
   c. botulism antitoxin with respiratory support
   d. botulism antitoxin + Penicillin G
   e. botulism antitoxin + Gentamicin

76. A 2-month-old infant is brought into the emergency room by his mother for fever and an erythematous rash that began centrally with fluid-filled blisters that ruptured with the application of light pressure. There is desquamation of the skin involving the palms and soles. Which of the following is the most likely diagnosis?
   a. hand foot and mouth syndrome
   b. staphylococcal scalded skin syndrome
   c. smallpox
   d. rocky mountain spotted fever
   e. Kawasaki's disease

77. A 34-year-old painter is complaining of anterior right shoulder pain when painting ceilings. He states he feels a similar pain when he is combing his hair or when reaching for his wallet. He states the pain is intermittent and denies any stiffness or weakness. On physical examination, there is no atrophy of the shoulder. There is increased pain to the anterior shoulder when the arm is abducted more than 90 degrees and exquisite pain when the Neer test is performed. There is increased shoulder strength and relief of the pain when subacromial lidocaine is administered. Which of the following is the most likely diagnosis?
   a. Rotator cuff tear
   b. Adhesive capsulitis
   c. Chronic unreduced shoulder dislocation
   d. Rotator cuff tendinitis
   e. Shoulder separation

78. A 54-year-old male presents to the clinic for recurrent sinus infections that are refractory to multiple trials of antibiotics. He complains over the years he has had severe sinusitis associated with fever. He states now for the last 2 days, he noted dark colored urine but denies hemoptysis. A chest radiograph is performed and shows a honeycombing appearance to the lungs and biopsy of the sinuses show necrotic tissue with granulomatous vasculitis. A urinalysis shows positive red blood cell casts and a renal biopsy reveals crescent-shaped glomerular inflammation and no linear IgG deposits on immunofluoroscopy. Which of the following would be classically positive in this patient?
   a. positive signal recognition protein antibodies
   b. positive perinuclear anti-neutrophil cytoplasmic antibodies
   c. positive anti cyclic citrullinated peptide antibodies
   d. positive anti-glomerular basement membrane antibodies
   e. positive cytoplasmic anti-neutrophil cytoplasmic antibodies

79. A 34-year-old male was placed on clindamycin for treatment of a MRSA-related abscess. On day 10, he develops severe diarrhea and is hospitalized. A CBC showed a white blood cell count of 25,000 cells/mcL (normal 5,000 – 10,000 cells/mcL) with a lymphocytosis. A colonoscopy is performed during the hospitalization, which demonstrates pseudomembranes and no evidence of toxic megacolon. He is otherwise stable. Which of the following is considered the initial first-line management of this patient?
   a. Vancomycin intravenously
   b. Vancomycin orally
   c. Erythromycin orally
   d. Metronidazole orally
   e. Ciprofloxacin orally

80. A 33-year-old female with a history of paroxysmal nocturnal hemoglobinuria complains of sudden onset of ascites, jaundice, hepatomegaly and right upper quadrant pain. Her only medications are combination oral contraceptive therapy. A urine pregnancy is negative. An ultrasound is performed, showing occlusion of the hepatic vein. Which of the following is the most likely diagnosis?
   a. primary biliary cirrhosis
   b. Acute cholangitis
   c. primary sclerosing cholangitis
   d. Wilson's disease
   e. Budd-Chiari syndrome

81. Which of the following is the classic description of a patient with an ascorbic acid (Vitamin C) deficiency.
   a. Diarrhea, dementia and dermatitis
   b. Ataxia, oculomotor palsies, global confusion
   c. The presence of looser lines (zones)
   d. Hyperkeratosis and perifollicular hemorrhages
   e. Magenta colored tongue, corneal lesions and scrotal dermatitis

82. An 18-year-old male presents to your clinic with intermittent shortness of breath while playing sports. The patient is otherwise healthy and states that his dad died at 24 years of age while playing sports. An echocardiogram shows asymmetrical septal wall thickening. Which of the following physical examination findings supports the most likely diagnosis?
   a. a systolic crescendo-decrescendo murmur that radiates to the neck
   b. the presence of a weak, delayed carotid upstroke
   c. a systolic crescendo-decrescendo murmur that decreases in intensity with squatting
   d. a systolic crescendo-decrescendo murmur that increases in intensity with handgrip
   e. a systolic crescendo-decrescendo murmur that decreases in intensity with Valsalva maneuver

83. A 24-year-old Asian male is admitted for pneumonia. An admission ECG is obtained. A peculiar pattern is noted especially in V1 and V2.

Which of the following is the most likely
   diagnosis?
   a. Hypothermia
   b. Brugada syndrome
   c. Takotsubo cardiomyopathy
   d. Kawasaki syndrome
   e. Left bundle branch block

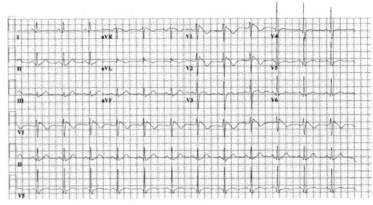

84. On cardiac examination, a holosystolic murmur is best heard at the apex and is accentuated when the patient is lying on the left side. The murmur radiates to the axilla and is associated with a mid-systolic ejection click. Which of the following is the most likely cause of this murmur?
   a. rheumatic heart disease
   b. mitral valve prolapse
   c. hypertension
   d. degenerative atherosclerotic disease
   e. congenital heart disease

85. A 54-year-old male is concerned about getting the influenza vaccine because he has allergies and does not want any interaction with the trivalent influenza vaccine. Which of the following would be a contraindication to the influenza vaccine?
   a. baker's yeast allergy
   b. pregnancy
   c. egg allergy
   d. gelatin allergy
   e. neomycin allergy

86. A 56-year-old male with a recent diagnosis of small cell lung carcinoma develops weakness that improves with repeated use of the muscle throughout the day. Which of the following describes the pathophysiology of the symptoms?
   a. dopamine depletion in the substantia nigra
   b. antibodies against the postsynaptic acetylcholine receptor
   c. antibodies against the presynaptic calcium-gated acetylcholine-releasing channels
   d. destruction and necrosis of both upper and lower motor neurons with progressive motor degeneration and preserved sensation
   e. prion-mediated degeneration of the brain

87. Which of the following is considered the best management for acute exacerbations of COPD?
   a. ipratropium bromide
   b. albuterol
   c. theophylline
   d. methylprednisone (solumedrol)
   e. ipratropium bromide and albuterol

88. A 54-year-old female states she has been having involuntary urinary leakage that is accompanied with a strong urge to urinate before she can make it to the bathroom. She also complains of increased urinary frequency and small volume voids when she urinates. In addition to bladder training, which of the following medications is considered first line medical management?
    a. midodrine
    b. oxybutynin
    c. pseudoephedrine
    d. mirabegron
    e. bethanacol

89. A 47-year-old male presents with right-sided flank pain. A CT scan of the abdomen and pelvis is obtained and shows an 11-mm struvite staghorn calculi. Which of the following is the recommended management?
    a. shock wave lithotripsy
    b. uretoscopy with stent
    c. observation
    d. alkalinization of the urine to dissolve the stones
    e. percutaneous nephrolithotomy

90. Which of the following is considered the first line management of myasthenic crisis?
    a. plasmapheresis
    b. corticosteroids
    c. azathioprine
    d. cyclosporine
    e. cyclophosphamide

91. Which of the following medications is used as the initial management of choice for heparin induced thrombocytopenia?
    a. enoxaparin
    b. argatroban
    c. dalteparin
    d. aspirin
    e. warfarin

92. Which of the following is the etiologic agent of chancroid?
    a. Erysipelothrix rhusiopathiae
    b. Chlamydia trachomatis
    c. Haemophilus ducreyi
    d. Anaplasma phagocytphilium
    e. Neisseria gonorrheae

93. A 41-year-old male is brought into the emergency room by his partner after what he thinks is an overdose of some drug. The patient is experiencing headaches, flushing and palpitations. Vital signs show an elevated blood pressure, tachycardia, hyperthermia and tachypnea. On physical examination, his pupils are dilated. Which of the following is the most likely diagnosis?
    a. opioid intoxication
    b. amphetamine intoxication
    c. cannabis intoxication
    d. benzodiazepine intoxication
    e. nicotine withdrawal

94. Which of the following is not commonly seen in hemolytic anemia?
   a. Increased haptoglobin
   b. Increased indirect bilirubin
   c. Increased lactate dehydrogenase
   d. Positive shistocytes
   e. Increased reticulocytes

95. A 32-year-old woman presents with a painless thyroid nodule after experiencing 6 months of weight gain, cold intolerance and fatigue. On physical exam, there is an enlarged, mobile, non-tender thyroid gland. She has generalized pitting edema and swelling of the face.   Initial lab values are as follows:

	PATIENT	NORMAL VALUES
TSH (mU/L)	7.8	0.9 - 5.0
Free T4 (nmol/L)	4	9 - 23
Free T3 (nmol/L)	0.2	0.8 - 2.4

Which of the following is the most likely diagnosis?
   a. DeQuervain's thyroiditis
   b. Acute suppurate thyroiditis
   c. Hashimoto's thyroiditis
   d. Reidel's thyroiditis
   e. Anaplastic thyroid carcinoma

96. A 43-year-old male is being treated for diabetes mellitus type II with oral therapy. He suddenly develops chest pain and 3-mm ST elevations in leads II, III and avF. There is also the presence of bilateral 2+ edema and crackles at the bases of the lungs on physical examination. Which of the following anti diabetic medications is most likely responsible for the chest pain and electrocardiogram findings?
   a. repaglinide
   b. rosiglitazone
   c. acarbose
   d. metformin
   e. exenatide

97. An 8-year-old male presents to the office with a rash on his face. His mother states the rash started out as fluid-filled blisters which ruptured, leaving a "honey-colored crust as pictured below:

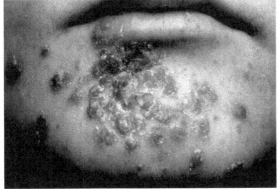

Which of the following is the most likely diagnosis?
   a. bullous impetigo
   b. Molloscum contagiosum
   c. non bullous impetigo
   d. ecthyma
   e. poison ivy

98. A 24-year-old male with a longstanding history of dandruff presents with erythematous plaques covered with fine white scales on his eyebrows, cheeks, and chest area. Which of the following is not the considered part of the routine management of this condition?

    a.   selenium sulfide
    b.   ketoconazole
    c.   corticosteroids
    d.   sodium sulfacetamide
    e.   metronidazole

99. A 53-year-old female presents to the urgent care clinic with eye redness for 2 days and a facial rash. On physical examination, there are grouped vesicles on an erythematous base on her nose. A slit lamp reveals dendritic lesions. Which of the following cranial nerves are most likely involved in this patient?

    a.   CN III
    b.   CN IV
    c.   CN V
    d.   CN VI
    e.   CN VII

100. A 42-year-old male presents with acute, constant, sharp chest pain worsen with inspiration and lying down.

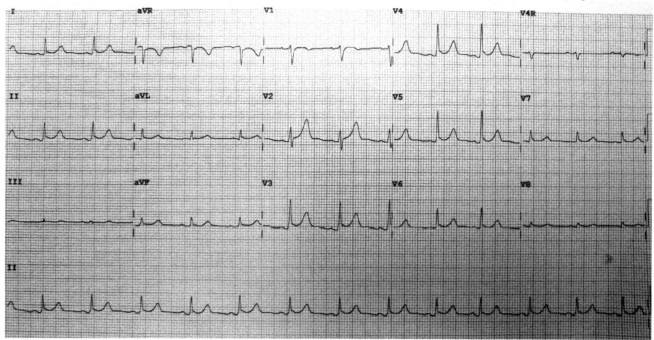

Based on the ECG, which of the following is the most likely diagnosis?

    a.   Brugada syndrome
    b.   Acute inferior wall myocardial infarction
    c.   Acute lateral wall myocardial infarction
    d.   Acute pericarditis
    e.   Unstable angina

QUESTION 1

Choice B (Janeway lesions) is the correct answer. Janeway lesions are seen in infective endocarditis and are classically described as *painless macules seen on the palms and the soles*, representing embolic and immune phenomena. They are part of the modified Duke criteria as a minor criterion for suspected infective endocarditis. CARDIOLOGY – INFECTIVE ENDOCARDITIS – HISTORY AND PHYSICAL EXAMINATION (p. 52).

Choice A (Osler's nodes) are tender, *painful nodules on the pads of the digits* that represent immunologic phenomena. They are part of the modified Duke criteria as a minor criterion for suspected infective endocarditis.

Choice C (Keratoderma blenorrhagicum) are *hyperkeratotic lesions on the palms and soles associated with reactive arthritis* (Reiter's syndrome).

Choice D (Roth spots) are retinal hemorrhages with pale centers. They are part of the modified Duke criteria as a minor criterion for suspected infective endocarditis.

Choice E (Erythema marginatum) are macular, annular rashes that are part of the major Jones criteria for rheumatic fever. Erythema marginatum is not associated with infective endocarditis classically.

QUESTION 2

Choice C (Diphtheria antitoxin + penicillin) is the correct answer. Corynebacterium diphtheria is a gram-positive rod that is transmitted from *inhalation of respiratory secretions*. It classically presents with ***pseudomembranes*** (described as gray/white membranes on the posterior pharynx that often bleeds if scraped). The pseudomembranes are made up of a combination of white blood cells, red blood cells, fibrin and bacteria. Patients may also have the classic *"bull neck"* due to enlarged cervical lymphadenopathy. Diphtheria may also be associated with myocarditis. Management includes the *diphtheria antitoxin* (with either *erythromycin or penicillin*) for 2 weeks. Prophylactic erythromycin is often given to close contacts as well. INFECTIOUS DISEASE – DIPHTHERIA – CLINICAL INTERVENTION (p. 420).

Choice A (nystatin oral) is the management of *oral candidiasis (thrush)*. Oral thrush usually presents on the tongue or the buccal mucosa with a *white coating that reveals erythema or bleeds when scraped*. It is not associated with the lymphadenopathy seen with diphtheria.

Choice B (IV fluconazole) is used in the management of fungal infections.

Choice D (Diphtheria antitoxin + gentamicin) is not used because gentamicin is an aminoglycoside that has gram-negative coverage (poor gram positive coverage). Corynebacterium diphtheria is a gram-positive bacillus.

Choice E (Botulism toxin + Penicillin G) is incorrect it is the treatment for wound botulism. *Botulism* usually presents with *dysphagia, drooling, muscle weakness, diplopia and fixed, dilated pupils*.

QUESTION 3

Choice B (renal ultrasound) is the correct answer. The hallmarks of *adult polycystic kidney disease* is *abdominal/flank pain, a palpable flank mass (enlarged cystic kidneys)* as well as cysts in other organs (such as the liver, causing hepatomegaly). Important *extra renal manifestations of PCKD are mitral valve prolapse* (described in this vignette as a systolic ejection click with the description of mitral regurgitation that often accompanies mitral valve prolapse) and the *development of berry aneurysms*, which can rupture, leading to subarachnoid hemorrhages. GENITOURINARY – POLYCYSTIC KIDNEY DISEASE – LABS/DIAGNOSTIC (p. 322).

Choice A (cystoscopy) is used to evaluate suspected bladder cancer.

Choice C (renal biopsy) is used to if renal carcinoma is suspected.

Choice D (24 hour urine protein collection) is used to evaluate the severity of proteinuria in patients with positive proteinuria on dipstick or urinalysis. This patient has no evidence of proteinuria.

Choice E (urine culture) is used in the evaluation of a patient suspected of having an infection of the urinary tract.

QUESTION 4
Choice C (herpetic gingivostomatitis) is the correct answer.   Herpetic gingivostomatitis is the primary manifestation of herpes simplex virus (type I) in children. It manifests as sudden onset of fever, anorexia, *gingivitis* (gum swelling, friable/bleeding gums) and *yellow grey vesicles on the oral mucosa, tongue and lips.* EENT – HERPETIC GINGIVOSTOMATITIS – MOST LIKELY (p. 239).

Choice A (*hand, foot and mouth disease*) is usually caused by *Coxsackie A virus*. It causes mild fever, *upper respiratory infection symptoms and progresses to vesicular lesions* on a reddened base in the *oral cavity, mucosa & tongue*. It is classically associated with a *vesicular rash that erupts on the body, including the palms and soles*. There is no associated rash in this vignette.

Choice B (reactivation herpes simplex – herpes labialis) is the secondary manifestation of a patient already infected with the herpes simplex virus. It is not usually associated with gingivitis (as seen in this vignette). *Herpes labialis* is associated with *prodromal symptoms often 24 hours prior to the eruption of the rash.* The rash is described as *painful, grouped vesicles on an erythematous base* along the lip and the surrounding external skin. The prodromal symptoms (such as burning, paresthesias) are due to the nerve stimulation by the virus.

Choice D (*acute herpetic tonsillopharyngitis*) is the *primary manifestation of Herpes Simplex Virus infection in adults.* It presents as vesicles that rupture, leaving ulcerative lesions with grayish exudates in the posterior pharyngeal mucosa.

Choice E (*Vincent's angina*) also known as *"trench mouth"* is an acute necrotizing ulcerative gingivitis that produces *profuse gingival bleeding, severe gingival pain and interdental papilla with ulcerative necrosis*. Malaise, fever and cervical enlargement are rare (those symptoms are prominent with herpes stomatitis).

QUESTION 5
Choice B (thoracentesis) is the correct answer. Decreased fremitus, decreased breath sounds and dullness to percussion are the classic physical exam findings of pleural effusion, so a thoracentesis can be both diagnostic and therapeutic. PULMONARY – PLEURAL EFFUSION – CLINICAL INTERVENTION (p. 95).

Choice A (administration of *ceftriaxone and azithromycin*) is the preferred management of *community acquired bacterial pneumonia* in a patient who will be admitted to the hospital and treated as an *inpatient*. Physical exam findings of *pneumonia* include: *bronchial breath sounds, egophony and increased fremitus* over the consolidation.

Choice C (*needle decompression followed by insertion of a chest tube*) is the treatment for *tension pneumothorax* Findings include: *hyperresonance to percussion, decreased breath sounds and tracheal deviation*.

Choice D (insertion of a chest tube) is treatment for *pneumothorax that is greater than 20% or large.*

Choice E (aspirin) is part of the initial treatment in acute coronary syndrome. The pain in acute coronary syndrome is usually done and not affected by inspiration. In many cases there would be an abnormal ECG.

QUESTION 6

Choice D (Linear plaques) is correct. Oral thrush is due to candida infection. *Candida esophagitis is associated with linear plaques in the esophagus.* GI/NUTRITION – CANDIDA ESOPHAGITIS – LABS/DIAGNOSTIC (p 127).

Choice A (*Large superficial ulcers*) is associated c *CMV esophagitis.*

Choice B (*columnar cells in esophagus*) is associated with *Barrett's esophagus* (a *pre malignant condition to esophageal adenocarcinoma*). In chronic reflux esophagitis, the normal squamous cells are replaced by columnar cells from the stomach (which are better suited for a higher acidic environment). There is no history of GERD in this vignette.

Choice C (*small deep ulcers*) is classic for *Herpes Simplex (HSV) esophagitis.*

Choice E (*corrugated rings*) is classic for *eosinophilic esophagitis.*

QUESTION 7

Choice D (Monteggia Fracture) is the correct choice. A *Monteggia fracture* is a *proximal ulnar shaft fracture* with *anterior radial head dislocation.* It may be associated with *radial nerve injury (manifested as a wrist drop).* This is often due to damage of the radial nerve by the radial head dislocation. MUSCULOSKELETAL – MONTEGGIA FRACTURE – MOST LIKELY (p. 171).

Choice A (Galleazzi Fracture) is a *mid-distal radial shaft fracture* with *dislocation of the distal radioulnar joint.*

Choice B (Anterior elbow dislocation) would show anterior displacement of the olecranon and Choice C (posterior elbow dislocation) would show posterior displacement of the olecranon.

Choice E (nightstick fracture) is an *isolated mid-shaft ulnar fracture.*

QUESTION 8

Choice E (supraspinatus) is the correct answer. *Rotator cuff injuries affects the SITS muscles & tendons. Supraspinatus involvement is most common.* The other muscles associated with the rotator cuff are choice B (infraspinatus), Choice A (teres minor), and Choice C (subscapularis).
MUSCOLOSKELETAL – ROTATOR CUFF INJURIES – BASICS (p. 165).

Choice D (teres major) has no impact on the rotator cuff.

QUESTION 9

Choice A (Raloxifene) is the correct answer. *Raloxifene is an estrogen antagonist in the breast and the endometrium.* Because it blocks estrogen effects in the uterus, it does not cause the unopposed estrogen needed to produce endometrial hyperplasia (and the subsequent development of endometrial cancer). All of the other choices increase the uterus' exposure to estrogen. *Tamoxifen (choice E) is an estrogen antagonist in the breast but it is also an estrogen agonist in the uterus, which can stimulate endometrial hyperplasia.*
REPRODUCTIVE – ENDOMETRIAL CANCER – HEALTH MAINTENANCE (p 250).

QUESTION 10

Choice C (papillary thyroid carcinoma) is the correct answer. *Papillary thyroid carcinoma is the most common thyroid malignancy.* Roughly 80% of all thyroid malignancies in men and women are papillary. Think "Papillary = popular".
ENDOCRINE – PAPILLARY THYROID CARCINOMA – MOST LIKELY (p 290).

QUESTION 11

Choice B [Haloperidol (Haldol)] is the correct answer. Typical (1st generation) antipsychotics work by *blocking the CNS dopamine (D_2) receptors.* Normally dopamine inhibits posterior pituitary prolactin release. *Dopamine blockade leads to increased prolactin levels,* which causes *galactorrhea, decreased libido, and amenorrhea* (prolactin inhibits the release of follicle stimulating hormone and luteinizing hormone).
PSYCH/BEHAVIORAL – ANTIPSYCHOTICS – PHARMACOLOGY (p 493).

Choice A [olanzapine (Zyprexa)] and choice C [Quetiapine (Seroquel)] are second-generation antipsychotics that are associated with mild increases in prolactin (they block CNS dopamine D4 receptors). 1st generation are associated with higher prolactin levels, so they would more likely cause the symptoms described in the vignette.

Choice D (Lithium) is not associated with increased prolactin levels.

Choice E (Bromocriptine) is not used in the management of bipolar disorders. Bromocriptine is a dopamine agonist that is often used to treat hyperprolactinemia by inhibiting prolactin release.

QUESTION 12

Choice D (topical corticosteroids) is the correct answer. Atopic dermatitis (eczema) is due to a *T-cell mediated immune response and IgE production.* Atopic dermatitis is *linked with other immune hypersensitivity disorders, such as hay fever and allergic rhinitis.* The classic initial rash presents with tiny *erythematous, edematous, ill-defined blisters seen primarily on the antecubital and popliteal fossae.* The rash later dries with scaling and is *intensely pruritic.* The initial management of choice is to reduce the immune and inflammatory response with topical corticosteroids. DERMATOLOGY – ATOPIC DERMATITIS – CLINICAL INTERVENTION (p 390).

Choice A (Oral acyclovir) is used in the management of *herpes simplex virus and varicella zoster virus.*

Choice B (topical fluconazole) is used for fungal infections.

Choice C (*topical metronidazole*) can be used in the *first line management for acne rosacea.*

Choice E (*oral griseofulvin*) is used in the first line management of *tinea capitus.*

QUESTION 13

Choice E (hemoglobin electrophoresis) is the correct answer. The patient has a microcytic anemia. Iron deficiency is the most common cause of anemia but the serum iron is normal, so there is no need to have a trial of iron therapy (Choice C) as it may lead to iron overload (since the body has no efficient way to excrete excess iron). Other causes of microcytic anemia are: thalassemia, lead poisoning and early anemia of chronic disease. *Thalassemia should often be suspected in a patient with microcytic anemia with normal (or increased) serum iron.* Hemoglobin electrophoresis and genetic testing can be done to evaluate for suspected thalassemia. HEMATOLOGY – THALASSEMIA – LABS/DIAGNOSTIC STUDIES (p. 454).

Choice A (bone marrow biopsy) is the gold standard diagnosis in the workup of anemia. It is invasive however and often other less noninvasive tests are done on the workup of anemia first.

Choice B (urine electrophoresis) is helpful if multiple myeloma is suspected. *Multiple myeloma* usually presents with *anemia, bone pain, renal failure, recurrent infections and elevated calcium.* Urine electrophoresis is done to look for lambda or kappa light chains (Bence-Jones proteins) in the urine.

Choice D (serum B_{12} levels) are used in the evaluation of macrocytic anemia to rule out Vitamin B_{12} deficiency. The patient in this vignette has a microcytic anemia.

QUESTION 14

Choice A (pralidoxime) is the correct answer.   Pesticides contain organophosphates. *Organophosphate poisoning is associated with acetylcholinesterase inhibition*, leading to nicotinic and muscarinic activation. These symptoms include: headaches, muscle spasms, convulsions, diffuse wheezing, increased sweating and lacrimation. Atropine is an anticholinergic given to reverse the muscarinic side effects. *Pralidoxime is also given to reactivate acetylcholinesterase* (which increases acetylcholine breakdown, reducing the symptoms).
NEUROLOGY – ORGANOPHOSPHATE POISONING – CLINICAL INTERVENTION (P. 476).

Choice B (pyridostigmine) is an acetylcholinesterase inhibitor similar to organophosphates and sarin gas. Administration of pyridostigmine in this patient would worsen the symptoms.

Choice C (pilocarpine) is a muscarinic cholinergic drug. Administration in this patient would worsen the symptoms.

Choice D (phenoxybenzamine) is a nonselective alpha 1 and alpha 2 antagonist. It is not used in the management of organophosphate poisoning.

Choice E (pyridoxine) is vitamin B6.

QUESTION 15

Choice A (diastolic dysfunction with marked dilation of both atria) is the correct answer. *Restrictive cardiomyopathy is increased ventricular rigidity* leading to *diastolic dysfunction* with preserved systolic function. Because the *ventricles are stiff and noncompliant*, it leads to some backup of blood in the atria, leading to *bilateral atrial enlargement* on echocardiography.
CARDIOLOGY – RESTRICTIVE CARDIOMYOPATHY – LABS/DIAGNOSTIC STUDIES (p 36).

Choice B (*global systolic dysfunction*) is seen with *dilated cardiomyopathy, systolic heart failure* or after a massive myocardial infarction.

Choice C (*thickened septal wall > 15 mm*) is the hallmark of *hypertrophic cardiomyopathy*.

Choice D (*apical ballooning of the left ventricle*) is seen with *Takotsubo cardiomyopathy*.

Choice E (*diastolic collapse of the ventricles*) is seen with *cardiac tamponade*.

QUESTION 16

Choice A (Efaviranz) is the correct answer. Efaviranz is a non-nucleoside reverse transcriptase inhibitor. Notable side effects of efaviranz are *vivid dreams and neurologic disturbances.* INFECTIOUS DISEASE – HIV – PHARMACOLOGY (p 440).

Choice B (*Zidovudine*) is a nucleoside reverse transcriptase inhibitor with the associated side effects of *bone marrow suppression, myopathy, hepatomegaly, and pancreatitis.*

Choice C (Indinavir) and Choice E (Ritonavir) are *protease inhibitors.* The most common adverse effects of protease inhibitors include nausea, vomiting, diarrhea, *lipodystrophy,* and hyperlipidemia. Indinavir is also associated with increased incidence of renal stones.

Choice D (Raltegravir) is an integrase inhibitor and is most commonly associated with hyperlipidemia and gastrointestinal symptoms.

QUESTION 17

Choice D (hyperactive bowel sounds) is correct. Crampy abdominal pain, nausea vomiting and constipation is the classic presentation of *small bowel obstruction*. Abdominal radiographs classically shows the *stepladder appearance* as fluid and air builds up in the obstructed bowel since it cannot go forward. In the *early stages of obstruction, there are hyperactive bowel sounds* as the bowel proximal to the obstruction fervently contracts to overcome the obstruction. Later in the disease, hypoactive bowel sounds (choice C) will prevail but the question specifically states early. GI/NUTRITION – SMALL BOWEL OBSTRUCTION – HISTORY AND PHYSICAL (p 147).

Choice A (peritoneal signs) is not specific to small bowel obstruction. It can also be seen with bowel ischemia Peritonitis can be seen with perforated viscous, appendicitis, abdominal trauma, fluid in the peritoneum, etc.

Choice B (gurgles about 5-15 per minute) are considered normal bowel sounds

Choice E (*sausage shaped ma*ss) is classically associated with *intussusception,* which is associated with vomiting & "currant-jelly" stools (contains mucus and blood). Intussusception is almost exclusively seen in infants. If it occurs in adults, it is often associated with a lead point (such as a malignancy) that causes the telescoping.

QUESTION 18

Choice B (warm compresses, dicloxacillin, and patient can continue to breastfeed) is the correct answer. This is the classic presentation of *infectious mastitis.* Infectious mastitis is an infection of the breast in lactating woman due to a break in the skin due to *nipple trauma from the suckling infant.* Infectious mastitis is associated with *unilateral breast pain with localized tenderness, warmth and swelling.* The management of choice is supportive management (warm compresses, breast pump), anti-staphylococcus antibiotics (such as dicloxacillin). Patients can continue to nurse if they so desire. REPRODUCTIVE – MASTITIS – CLINICAL INTERVENTION (p. 277).

Choice A (*incision and drainage* with the cessation of breast feeding from the affected breast) is the treatment of *breast abscesses.* In this case, there is no evidence of a palpable abscess, induration or fluctuance, making breast abscess less likely. An ultrasound can be done to look for a suspected breast abscess.

Choice C (*ice packs, tight fitting bra and the avoidance of breast stimulation*) is the management of choice for congestive mastitis. *Congestive mastitis is BILATERAL breast enlargement* often 2-3 days post partum.

Choice D (the administration of fluconazole) is the management of mastitis caused by Candida infections. Staphylococcus aureus is part of the normal skin flora, making Staphylococcus mastitis is more likely.

Choice E (warm compresses, the administration of gentamicin and the patient can continue to breastfeed) is not the treatment for infectious mastitis as Staphylococcus aureus is the most common causative agent and S. aureus is gram positive. Aminoglycosides, such as gentamicin, are generally ineffective against gram-positive organisms when used as a single agent. Aminoglycosides are used primarily for gram-negative coverage.

QUESTION 19

Choice D (Peritonsillar abscess) is the correct choice. Peritonsillar abscess is classically associated with dysphagia, pharyngitis, a *muffled "hot potato" voice*, difficulty handling oral secretions and trismus. The abscess often will *displace the uvula to the contralateral side.* EENT – PERITONSILLAR ABSCESS – BASICS (p 239).

Choice A (*Vincent's angina*) also known as *"trench mouth"* is an *acute, necrotizing, ulcerative gingivitis* that produces profuse gingival bleeding, severe gingival pain and interdental papilla with ulcerative necrosis.

Choice B (*Ludwig's angina*) presents with *swelling and erythema to the upper neck and chin.* Examination of the mouth will often reveal *pus on the floor of the mouth.*

Choice C (*acute herpetic tonsillopharyngitis*) is the *primary manifestation of Herpes Simplex Virus infection* in adults. It presents as vesicles that rupture, leaving ulcerative lesions with grayish exudates in the posterior pharyngeal mucosa.

Choice E (*infectious mononucleosis*) is associated with *posterior lymphadenopathy and exudative pharyngitis.*

QUESTION 20
Choice B (Escherichia coli) is the correct answer. The urinary tract *irritative symptoms* and the *obstructive symptoms* (hesitancy, straining to void and interrupted urine stream) and *boggy prostate* are indicative of *prostatitis.* Chronic prostatitis is associated with recurrent urinary tract infections and the absence of fever or perineal pain. On physical examination, a *boggy, nontender prostate* indicates *chronic prostatitis.* E. coli is the *most common organism in chronic prostatitis* (accounting for up to 80%). Other common gram-negative uropathogens that can cause prostatitis include: Klebsiella pneumoniae (choice A), Pseudomonas aeruginosa (Choice C), and Proteus mirabilis (Choice E). GENITORUINARY – CHRONIC PROSTATITIS – HEALTH MAINTENANCE (p 336).

Choice D (Chlamydia trachomatis) can cause prostatitis in older men, however, *Chlamydia trachomatis is the most common cause of acute prostatitis in younger men (especially under the age of 35 years).*

QUESTION 21
Choice D (Factor V Leiden mutation) is the correct answer. *Factor V Leiden is the most common inherited cause of hypercoagulability.* HEMATOLOGY – FACTOR V LEIDEN MUTATION – BASICS (p 469).

Choice A (*von Willebrand disease) is the most common inherited cause of bleeding.* It is associated with increased bleeding, not increased coagulation.

Choice B (Protein C deficiency), Choice C (Antithrombin III deficiency) and Choice E (Protein S deficiency) are other hypercoagulable disorders. They are not as common as Factor V Leiden mutation however.

QUESTION 22
Choice B is correct. Viruses are the most common cause of myocarditis, which is inflammation of the heart muscle. Of all the viruses the *Enteroviruses (Echovirus and Coxsackie* viruses – especially *Coxsackie B)* are the *most common causes.* CARDIOLOGY – MYOCARDITIS – BASICS (p 35).

Choice A (HSV) Choice C (adenovirus) and Choice D (influenza virus) may cause viral myocarditis, but they are not the most common viral etiologies.

Choice E (Trypanosoma cruzi) is a protozoal cause of *Chagas disease.* Chagas disease is associated with dilated cardiomyopathy as well but will often have a chagoma (swelling at the site of the bite by the Assassin bug – often on the face) and develops *ipsilateral periorbital swelling (Romaña's sign)* and evaluation of the blood will be positive for the parasitemia. The patient may develop toxic megacolon as a complication. The patient would usually have travel history or lived in Latin America (especially South America).

QUESTION 23
Choice C (hypotension with bradycardia, decreased pulmonary capillary wedge pressure) is the correct answer. In neurogenic shock, there is sympathetic chain disruption, leading to hypotension and bradycardia. The normal response to hypovolemia is tachycardia to maintain cardiac output. *The hallmark of neurogenic shock is hypotension with bradycardia.* CARDIOLOGY – NEUROGENIC SHOCK – BASICS (p 67).

Choice A (*hypotension with tachycardia, decreased pulmonary capillary wedge pressure*) is associated with *hypovolemic shock.*

Choice B (*warm, flushed extremities with increased cardiac output*) is associated with *early septic shock*.

Choice D (*cool, clammy skin, decreased cardiac output with increased pulmonary capillary wedge pressure*) can be seen with *cardiogenic or obstructive shock.* They both present the same.

Choice E (*increased bicep jerk reflexes*) is usually caused by an *upper motor neuron lesion.* Cervical injuries are usually associated with *flaccid paralysis.*

QUESTION 24

Choice C (histrionic personality disorder) is the correct answer. *Histrionic personality disorder* is characterized by *dramatic, overemotional, seductive & "attention-seeking' behaviors.* They are often self-absorbed, throw temper tantrums and crave to be the *center of attention.*   PSYCH/BEHAVIORAL – HISTRIONIC – MOST LIKELY (p. 380).

Choice A (*Narcissistic personality disorder*) is associated with *grandiose, often excessive, sense of self importance* in which the patients feel they are special, entitled and require extra attention but simultaneously have a *fragile sense of self esteem.* They often handle the aging process poorly.

Choice B (*dependent personality disorder*) is characterized by *dependent, submissive behavior* in which the patient needs constant reassurance, relies on others and has intense discomfort when they are alone.

Choice D (*borderline personality disorder*) is associated with *unstable, unpredictable mood swings, black and white thinking, relationship instability and self-harming behaviors.*

Choice E (*schizotypal personality disorder*) is a characterized by *strange, eccentric behavior, inappropriate affect* and "magical thinking" such as the belief in telekinesis and clairvoyance.

QUESTION 25

Choice B (antibiotics and pleural drainage) is the correct choice. This is an exudate pleural effusion based on Light's criteria (LDH ratio >0.6 and protein ratio > 0.5. A pH <7.2 and a glucose <40 mg/dL are indicative of empyema (bacteria consume the glucose). *The management of empyema is antibiotics and pleural fluid drainage* to speed up healing. PULMONARY – EMPYEMA – CLINICAL INTERVENTION (p 95).

Choice A (CT scan) may be obtained during the workup but it does not change the need for antibiotics & drainage.

Choice C (administration of ceftriaxone and azithromycin) is the treatment for inpatient community acquired pneumonia. It may be used in addition if there was an associated pneumonia with the effusion.

Choice D (repeat chest X rays to monitor the progression) may be included in the management of small effusions if empyema is not suspected.

Choice E is the management of congestive heart failure.

QUESTION 26

Choice B (Forced expiratory volume of 70% with daily symptoms, nighttime symptoms greater than 1 time a week) is the correct answer. *Moderate persistent asthma is defined as daily symptoms, daily use of short-term beta 2 agonists & nighttime awakenings greater once a week.* It is also associated with a *Forced expiratory volume of 60 – 80% predicted.* PULMONARY – ASTHMA – BASICS (p 79).

Mild persistent asthma is defined as *symptoms >2 days of the week, use of short-term beta 2 agonists > 2 days a week (bot not daily) and nighttime awakenings 3-4 times a month*. It is also associated with a *Forced expiratory volume greater or equal to 80% predicted*. (Choice D) and (Choice E) are examples of mild persistent asthma.

Severe persistent asthma is defined as *symptoms throughout the day, use of short-term beta 2 agonists several times a day, & nightly awakenings*. It is also associated with a *Forced expiratory volume less than 60% predicted*. (Choice C) is an example of severe persistent asthma.

Intermittent asthma is defined as *symptoms less than or equal to ≤ twice daily and ≤ twice weekly* with a normal FEV1. Choice A is an example of intermittent asthma.

QUESTION 27

Choice D (A 40 year old patient with history of hypertension) is the correct answer. Pneumococcal vaccine is recommended in patients *over the age of 65*. It is also recommended in patients between the ages *of 2-64 years* with *chronic diseases, such as congenital cardiac, pulmonary diseases, alcoholism, diabetes mellitus, asplenia, and immunocompromised patients.* PULMONARY – PNEUMOCOCCAL VACCINE – HEALTH MAINTENANCE (p 103).

QUESTION 28

Choice C (IV metoprolol) is the correct answer. Beta-blockers can cause potassium to shift out of cells so it can worsen hyperkalemia. Beta-$_2$ agonists can be used in the management of hyperkalemia to shift potassium into the cells. GENITOURINARY – HYPERKALEMIA – CLINICAL INTERVENTION (p 331).

Choice A (insulin with glucose) is used in the management of hyperkalemia. Insulin shifts potassium into the cells, reducing serum potassium levels. Glucose is added to prevent hypoglycemia from insulin administration.

Choice B (IV calcium gluconate) is used in the management of hyperkalemia in patients with significant ECG changes or severe hyperkalemia to stabilize the cardiac membrane and prevent arrhythmias.

Choice D (oral sodium polystyrene sulfonate) is used in the management of hyperkalemia by enhancing gastrointestinal potassium excretion, reducing serum potassium levels.

Choice E (Nebulized albuterol) can be used in the management of hyperkalemia by shifting potassium into the cell, reducing serum potassium levels.

QUESTION 29

Choice C (The presence of kappa or lambda light chain proteins on urine electrophoresis) is the correct answer. Multiple myeloma is *a malignancy of a single clone of plasma cells* that lead to an *increase in monoclonal antibody production*. The hallmark manifestations are: *bone pain, anemia, recurrent infections, renal failure, and hypercalcemia* (the increased bone resorption leads to the "punched out" lesions of the skull).
HEMATOLOGY – MULTIPLE MYELOMA – LABS/DIAGNOSTIC STUDIES (p. 464).

Choice A (*basophilic stippling of the red blood cells*) is coarse blue granules in the red blood cells due to residual RNA in the red blood cells. It is most commonly associated with *lead poisoning, sideroblastic anemia*, heavy metal poisoning, thalassemia, hemoglobinopathies, myelodysplasia and chronic alcoholism.

Choice B (*Heinz bodies* in the red blood cells) can be seen with *Thalassemia and G6PD deficiency*.

Choice D (*hyperchromic, sphere-shaped red blood cells*) can be seen in *hereditary spherocytosis and autoimmune hemolytic anemia.*

Choice E (The presence of small, dense basophilic inclusions in the red blood cells) describes Howell-Jolly bodies. *Howell-Jolly bodies are seen in splenectomized patients as well as severe hemolytic anemia.*

QUESTION 30

Choice C (Hydroxyurea) is the correct answer. *Hydroxyurea is used in the management of severe pain crisis in sickle cell disease, polycythemia vera,* refractory CML and some solid tumors. In sickle cell disease, it works by increasing fetal hemoglobin levels, increasing red blood cell water content and decreasing the sickling deformity of red blood cells.   HEMATOLOGY – HYDROXYUREA – PHARMACOLOGY (p. 457).

Choice A (*Erythropoietin*) is used in cases of *anemia due to renal failure* or *decreased bone marrow red blood cell production.*

Choice B (*deferoxamine*) is a *chelating agent used in iron overload states,* such as *hereditary hemochromatosis and thalassemia.*

Choice D (*Folic acid*) aids in the *synthesis of DNA and in erythropoiesis.* It is often used as adjunctive therapy in the management of certain anemias.

Choice E (Vitamin B$_{12}$) is needed to convert homocysteine into methionine for DNA synthesis.

QUESTION 31

Choice D (pulmonary angiography) is the correct choice. *Pulmonary angiography is the gold standard* (definitive diagnosis) *of pulmonary embolism* (PE). It is invasive and so it is usually not the first test done. Angiography is usually indicated in patients with a high probability of PE with negative or inconclusive, less invasive studies. PULMONARY – PULMONARY EMBOLISM – LABS/DIAGNOSTIC STUDIES (p 98).

Choice A (chest radiograph) may be obtained but is *chest radiograph is often normal in PE* so if you suspect a PE, another more informative test needs to be done.

Choice B (*VQ scan*) is often done in patients with a suspicion of PE and in whom a *CT with IV contrast is contraindicated (ex. a patient unable to receive IV contrast due to renal failure).*

Choice C (*D dimer) is only helpful if NEGATIVE in a patient with low suspicion.*

Choice E (*spiral CT scan*) is often *the best non-invasive tool* to determine if a pulmonary embolism is present

QUESTION 32

Choice D (actinic keratosis) is the correct answer. Actinic keratosis is a premalignant condition to squamous cell carcinoma and is the most common premalignant skin condition. All the other choices are benign skin conditions. DERMATOLOGY – ACTINIC KERATOSIS – BASICS (p 395).

QUESTION 33

Choice C (Brown recluse spider bite) is the correct answer. This is the classic description of a bite from a brown recluse spider bite. It classically begins with local burning at the site followed by blanching with a *red halo* around the ischemic center and then a *hemorrhagic bullae* that undergoes *eschar formation.*
DERMATOLOGY – BROWN RECLUSE SPIDER BITE – MOST LIKELY (p. 401).

Choice A (*Rocky mountain spotted fever*) is a potentially fatal tick-borne disease associated with a *red maculopapular rash first on the wrists and the ankles* the n spreading centrally over 2-3 days with palms and soles involvement characteristic.

Choice B (*Lyme disease*) is a tick-borne disease associated with the rash *erythema migrans*.

Choice D (Ehrlichiosis) is not usually associated with a rash.

Choice E (*Coccidiomycosis*) is associated with a *maculopapular rash*.

QUESTION 34
Choice B (Intertrochanteric Fracture) is correct choice. Hip fractures are classically associated with inability to bear weight. The fractured side is foreshortened and externally rotated. The fracture seen in the image involves the space between the trochanters and part of the neck. MUSCULOSKELETAL – HIP FRACTURE – MOST LIKELY (p 180).

Choice A (*Hip dislocation*) is classically associated with the affected leg *foreshortened and internally rotated.*

Choice C (*Legg Calve Perthe*) is *avascular necrosis of the femoral head* seen in children.

Choice D (Sub trochanteric fracture) would have a fracture site lower than the one seen in this picture.

Choice E (osteonecrosis of the hip) would show collapse of the femoral head.

QUESTION 35
Choice E (bronchodilation) is the correct answer.   Side effects of beta-blockers include fatigue, depression, impotence, masking of the symptoms of hypoglycemia (such as tachycardia, tremor and sweating), hypotension, bradycardia, second or third degree heart block, and bronchospasms in patients with reactive airway diseases such as asthma & COPD.   Beta-blockers may also worsen some peripheral vascular disease states, such as Raynaud's phenomenon. CARDIOLOGY – BETA BLOKCERS – PHARMACOLOGY (p. 479).

QUESTION 36
Choice C (granulomas and fistulas) is the correct choice. All the other choices are associated with ulcerative colitis. GI/NUTRTITION – INFLAMMATORY BOWEL DISEASE – MOST LIKELY (p. 151).

QUESTION 37
Choice E (pyloric stenosis) is correct.   Pyloric stenosis presents *most commonly in early infancy* with the classic presentation of *projectile, nonbilious vomiting* due to failure of pyloric sphincter relaxation, preventing food from entering the duodenum.   *An olive-shaped mass* is often present after vomiting.

Choice A (*Intussusception*) is classically associated with the *triad of 1. vomiting, 2. abdominal pain and 3. passage of currant jelly stools* (mucus and blood with the stool). In this scenario there was no blood or mucus.

Choice B (*Infant botulism*) most commonly associated with ingestion of spores in honey would present with *profound lethargy and loss of muscular tone (floppy baby syndrome).*

Choice D (*Hirschsprung's disease*) most commonly presents with *meconium ileus.*

QUESTION 38
Choice D (endoscopic ligation of the bleeding vessel) is the correct answer.   Endoscopic ligation is the management of choice for esophageal bleeding as it is associated with direct visualization, lower complications and lower re bleeding rates. GI/NUTRITION – ESOPHAGEAL VARICES – CLINICAL INTERVENTION (p 131).

Choice A (*propranolol*) is the *prophylactic treatment of choice to prevent re bleeding*. It is not the treatment of choice for an active bleed.

Choice B (vasopressin) is a pharmacologic vasoconstrictor used as an adjunctive treatment in the management of acute active esophageal variceal bleeds.

Choice C (insertion of a transjugular intrahepatic portosystemic shunt) is *indicated in active bleeds if the bleeding continues despite endoscopic or pharmacologic treatment.*

Choice E (*endoscopic sclerotherapy* of the bleeding vessel) can also be used in the management of acute variceal bleed but has a *higher complication and re bleeding rate compared to endoscopic rubber band ligation.*

QUESTION 39

Choice C (alcohol withdrawal) is the correct answer. This patient is exhibiting signs of *delirium tremens*, such as an *altered sensorium associated with tactile, visual, or auditory hallucinations* (ex something crawling on them), altered mental status, seizures coma and death. Patients who are alcoholics may be able to hide alcoholism but the symptoms end up occurring when they are hospitalized for a nonrelated illness and have no access to alcohol. PSYCH/BEHAVIORAL – DELIRIUM TREMENS – MOST LIKELY (online substance abuse chapter).

Choice A (serotonin syndrome) is a potentially life-threatening condition due to increased serotonin activity. It is usually due to the potentiation between 2 serotonergic agonists. *Serotonin syndrome is characterized by autonomic dysfunction* including tachycardia, blood pressure fluctuations, hyperthermia, hyperreflexia, myoclonus, *dilated pupils,* agitation and a *hyperactive GI tract* (due to the effect of serotonin on the enterochromaffin-like cells). Management includes serotonin antagonists such as cyproheptadine and benzodiazepines for hyperthermia to decrease muscle contractions.

Choice B (*Neuroleptic malignant syndrome*) is a condition seen due to *decreased dopamine activity* in patients on dopamine antagonist therapy (such as antipsychotic medications). It can also present with hyperthermia but these patients tend to be *hyporeflexive and may develop urinary incontinence.*

Choice E (opioid intoxication) *Narcotics are miotics*, so narcotic intoxication will cause pinpoint pupils. Narcotic withdrawal (Choice D) will cause the opposite, mydriasis

QUESTION 40

Choice A [Clozapine (Clozaril)] is the correct answer. Clozapine is an atypical (2nd generation) antipsychotic. *Side effects include agranulocytosis, myocarditis*, diabetes mellitus, seizures, neuroleptic malignant syndrome, mild increase in prolactin levels, extrapyramidal symptoms. hyperglycemia, weight gain and hyperlipidemia. PSYCH/BEHAVIORAL – CLOZARIL – PHARMACOLOGY (p. 493).

Choice B [*Lithium (Lithobid)*] is associated with *increased thirst, diabetes insipidus, seizures, arrhythmias, hypercalcemia, hyperparathyroidism, and hypothyroidism.*

Choice C [*Aripiprazole* (Abilify)] side effects include: *increased suicide rate in children,* extrapyramidal symptoms, seizures, and hyperglycemia.

Choice D [Risperidone] and Choice E [Ziprasidone (Geodon)] are partial dopamine D_2 receptor & serotonin receptor antagonists. Side effects include extrapyramidal symptoms, increased prolactin, sedation, weight gain and hypotension.

QUESTION 41

Choice B [Diphenhydramine (Benadryl)] is the correct answer. Promethazine works for nausea by *blocking dopaminergic receptors.* A potential side effect of dopamine blockade is *acute dystonia,* an extrapyramidal set of symptoms often occurring hours to days after the administration of a dopamine antagonist. Symptoms include *trismus, protruding of the tongue, facial grimacing, torticollis and difficulty speaking.* The symptoms are caused by an excess of acetylcholine in relation to dopamine. Acetylcholine is excitatory in the basal ganglia and dopamine is inhibitory. The decreased dopamine favors excitability, causing the symptoms. Diphenhydramine is an antihistamine, but many *antihistamines also have anticholinergic properties,* which is why they are useful in this setting. The anticholinergic benztropine may also be used. They restore the normal dopamine-acetylcholine balance towards normal. NEUROLOGY – DYSTONIC REACTION – CLINICAL INTERVENTION (p. 493).

Choice A [Cyclobenzaprine (Flexeril)] and choice C Metaxalone (Skelaxin) are muscle relaxers. They do not reverse the dopamine blockade.

Choice D [Clozapine (Clozaril)] is an antipsychotic that blocks dopamine, so this would make the condition worse.

Choice E [Lithium (Lithobid)] is used for bipolar disorders and acute mania as a mood stabilizer.

QUESTION 42

Choice C (decreased urine osmolarity) is the correct answer. *Lithium can induce nephrogenic diabetes insipidus,* which is an *insensitivity to ADH.* This leads to the *production of large amounts of dilute urine* with *decreased urine osmolarity.* Diabetes insipidus is associated with hypernatremia (if the patient's fluid intake does not match the increased fluid loss). Diabetes insipidus is also associated with *increased serum osmolarity* and the *absence of peripheral edema.* Note the urine osmolarity is DEcreased and the serum osmolarity is INcreased (leading to possible hypernatremia from the loss of fluids). GENITOURINARY – DIABETES INSIPIDUS – LABS (p 325).

QUESTION 43

Choice B (paroxysmal nocturnal hemoglobinuria) is the correct answer. PNH is a rare, acquired stem cell mutation that leads to a deficiency in red blood cell surface anchor proteins, leading to complement activation, *red blood cell destruction and thrombosis.* Because the protein deficiency affects red blood cells, white blood cells and platelets, it causes pancytopenia. The hemolytic anemia is associated with *dark colored urine that is worse at night with partial clearing during the day.* After the haptoglobin stores are used up from the severe anemia, the free circulating hemoglobin binds to nitric oxide, causing a hypercoagulable state.
HEMATOLOGY – PAROXYSMAL NOCTURNAL HEMOGLOBINURIA – BASICS (page 459)

QUESTION 44

Choice E (Corneal abrasion) is the correct choice. Corneal abrasions are seen as *uptake on fluorescein staining* (the ice rink sign). Because he wears *contact lenses, pseudomonal coverage* is important. Ciprofloxacin has excellent pseudomonal coverage. EENT – CORNEAL ABRASION – CLINICAL INTERVENTION (p. 228).

Choice A (erythromycin) & choice B (Bacitracin) can be used for prophylaxis in corneal abrasions in patients who are not contact lens wearers and when pseudomonal coverage is not needed.

Choice C (naphazoline) and Choice D (olopatadine) are used for allergic or viral conjunctivitis to reduce the redness and itching due to their antihistamine properties.

QUESTION 45

Choice C (Colles fracture) is the correct choice. The classic mechanism of injury is falling on an outstretched hand with the wrist extended. On lateral radiographs, *DORSAL angulation* of the distal segment is classically seen in *Colle's Fracture.* MUSCULOSKELETAL – COLLE'S FRACTURE – LABS/DIAGNOSTIC STUDIES (p 173).

Choice A (Barton's Fracture) is an *intraarticular distal radial fracture* that is associated with dislocation of the carpal bones.

Choice B (*Smith Fracture*) is a *distal radius fracture* (often cause the reverse Colle's because it is associated with a fall on the hand that is in hyperflexion). On lateral radiographs, *VENTRAL angulation* of the distal segment is classically associated with Smith's fracture. The ventral angulation distinguishes a Smith's fracture from a Colle's.

Choice D (*Rolando Fracture*) is a *comminuted fracture of the base of the first metacarpal bone*. Non-comminuted fractures of the first metacarpal bone are known as Bennett's fractures.

Choice E (Scapholunate dislocation) is associated with a widened space between the scaphoid and the lunate bones. This is best seen on the anteroposterior view not the lateral view.

QUESTION 46

Choice A (IV magnesium sulfate) is the correct choice. *Eclampsia* is defined as the *presence of seizures or coma* in a patient with preeclampsia (hypertension + proteinuria and edema after 20 weeks gestation – may be earlier than 20 weeks in twin gestations or molar pregnancies). *Magnesium sulfate will decrease seizures of eclampsia* (probably through multiple factors). REPRODUCTIVE – ECLAMPSIA – CLINICAL INTERVENTION (p 274).

Choice B (oxytocin and the prompt delivery of the fetus) is also part of the management of eclampsia but this is done after the mother is stabilized, making magnesium therapy the first step in the management.

Choice C (administration of terbutaline) is used as a tocolytic. It used to delay premature labor.

Choice D (administration of IV lisinopril) is not used in the management of hypertension of eclampsia because ACE inhibitors are teratogenic.

Choice E (administration of methyldopa orally and admission for monitoring) is not the management of the hypertension of eclampsia. IV hydralazine or labetalol is usually to emergently reduce blood pressure in pregnancy.

QUESTION 47

Choice C (uterine suction curettage) is the correct choice. *Gestational trophoblastic disease (hydatidiform molar pregnancy)* is an abnormal pregnancy in which a nonviable fertilized egg implants in the uterus. It is associated with *painless vaginal bleeding, uterine size/date discrepancies, a markedly elevated beta HCG for gestational age and a "snowstorm" or "cluster of grapes" pattern on ultrasound*. The management is *prompt removal of the uterine contents* of the molar pregnancy with suction curettage. REPRODUCTIVE - MOLAR PREGNANCY – CLINICAL INTERVENTION (p 268).

Choice A (continue fetal monitoring and contraction stress test monitoring) is not an option because molar pregnancies are nonviable.

Choice B (methotrexate) is not indicated in molar pregnancy because one must ensure all of the products of conception and intrauterine contents are removed to be sent to pathology to rule out choriocarcinoma.

Choice D (admission to the hospital for close monitoring) may be part of the management but removal of the products of conception is the primary management.

Choice E (continued monitoring of the serum beta HCG levels to see if they double every 48 hours) is a way to monitor viable pregnancies to look for possible abnormalities. Molar pregnancies are associated with abnormally increased levels of beta HCG.

QUESTION 48

Choice B (IV administration of 0.9% sodium chloride solution) is the correct answer. Patients with type II diabetes mellitus are at increased risk for developing hyperosmolar hyperglycemic syndrome (HHS), characterized in this vignette by the elevated glucose, increased serum osmolarity, pH >7.30. Intravenous normal saline is the mainstay in the management of Hyperglycemic hyperosmolar syndrome to help promote renal excretion of glucose, reduce serum osmolarity and restore hydration. ENDOCRINE – DIABETIC KETOACIDOSIS – CLINICAL INTERVENTION (p 306).

Choice A (intravenous insulin bolus followed by insulin drip) is part of the management of HHS but *insulin is usually started after saline therapy is initiated.*

Choice C (IV administration of bicarbonate) is only used in severe cases where there is *significant acidosis but is not part of the routine management of HHS.*

Choice D (IV administration of IV glucagon) will increase glucose levels, making the condition worse.

Choice E (IV administration of 5% dextrose and 0.45% sodium chloride solution) is part of the management of HHS but it is usually *used after initiation of normal saline when the glucose levels reach 250 mg/dL to prevent hypoglycemia from the co administration of insulin.*

QUESTION 49

Choice B (myelosuppression) is the correct answer. Methimazole is a drug used to treat hyperthyroidism. It prevents the production of thyroid hormone. The two most common *serious side effects of methimazole are hepatotoxicity and myelosuppression (especially agranulocytosis).* ENDOCRINE – METHIMAZOLE – PHARMACOLOGY (p. 286).

QUESTION 50

Choice B (Pyridostigmine) is the correct answer. Myasthenia gravis is an autoimmune disorder of the peripheral nerves due to *autoantibodies against the post-synaptic acetylcholine receptor,* causing *progressive weakness that is worse with repeated muscle use.* The first line long-term management of myasthenia gravis is an *acetylcholinesterase inhibitor,* such as *pyridostigmine & neostigmine.* They decrease the breakdown of acetylcholine in the synapse, allowing for longer acetylcholine-mediated activation of the nerves.
NEUROLOGY - MYASTHENIA GRAVIS – PHARMACOLOGY (p 355).

Choice A (Plasmapheresis) is indicated in myasthenia gravis crisis for rapid symptom relief.

Choice C (*Carbamazepine*) is used in the management of *seizure disorder and trigeminal neuralgia.*

Choice D (*Edrophonium*) is a *short-acting acetylcholinesterase inhibitor* that can be used to *diagnose myasthenia gravis* but not for long term.

Choice E (*Benztropine*) is an anticholinergic and thus *may worsen the symptoms of myasthenia gravis.*

QUESTION 51

Choice B (Barlow test) is the correct answer. In testing for development hip dysplasia/dislocation, the *Barlow test can be performed.* It involves adducting the hip with pressure placed on the knee pressing posteriorly. Once the hip dislocation is diagnosed, the *Ortolani maneuver can be used to reduce it.* REPRODUCTIVE – HIP DISLOCATION – DIAGNOSTIC STUDIES.

Choice A (*Ober test*) is used to evaluate *iliotibial band syndrome.*

Choice C (*Moro reflex*) is a test for fetal reflexes. The simulation as if the infant is falling will cause the infant to abduct their arms and crying.

Choice D (*McRoberts maneuver*) and Choice E (*Woods maneuver*) are used to maneuver infants during delivery when they present with *shoulder dystocia*.

QUESTION 52

Choice D (doxorubicin) is the correct answer. Doxorubicin is used in the management of acute myeloid leukemia, acute lymphoblastic leukemia and other solid tumors. *Doxorubicin use is associated with dilated cardiomyopathy, bone marrow suppression, gastrointestinal side effects & alopecia.* CHEMOTHERAPEUTIC AGENTS – PHARMACOLOGY (p 496).

Choice A (*Bleomycin*) is a chemotherapeutic agent that can also be used *intrapleurally for pleurodesis* in a patient with *recurrent malignant pleural effusions*. Talc may also be used. Bleomycin has been used in Hodgkin and Non Hodgkin lymphoma, testicular tumors and squamous cell carcinoma.

Choice B (vincristine) is used in the management of leukemia.

Choice C (methotrexate) is used in the management of Non Hodgkin lymphoma, trophoblastic tumors (choriocarcinoma and hydatidiform molar pregnancy), lung, breast, head and neck cancers as well as osteosarcomas.

Choice E (cisplatin) is associated with emesis, neurotoxicity, renal failure and hypomagnesemia.

QUESTION 53

Choice C (carotid endarterectomy) is the correct answer. Carotid endarterectomy is recommended in patients with internal or common carotid artery stenosis of greater than 70%.
NEUROLOGY – TRANSIENT ISCHEMIC ATTACK – CLINICAL INTERVENTION (p. 362).

Choice A (IV alteplase) and choice B (IV streptokinase) are contraindicated in the management of TIA. Only alteplase is approved for the use of ischemic stroke management but neither of them are used in TIA.

Choice D (lifestyle modification of risk factors) is also part of the management of TIA but carotid endarterectomy performed in patients with greater than 70% occlusion is associated with an 80% reduction in overall mortality.

Choice E (admission to the hospital for observation of return of symptoms) is incorrect. Patients are frequently admitted, but observation is not the management. A full work up for the cause of the TIA should be sought out.

QUESTION 54

Choice A (beta blockers) is the correct answer. Cocaine stimulates the sympathetic system, including the alpha 1 receptor (which causes arterial vasoconstriction). In patients with *cocaine-induced myocardial infarction, beta-blocker use may cause unopposed alpha 1 –mediated vasoconstriction* (because it blocks the beta-receptor's ability to compensate by increasing the heart rate). CARDIOLOGY – COCAINE INDUCED MYOCARDIAL INFARCTION – PHARMACOLOGY (p 26).

Choice B (aspirin) is part of the first line management in patients with suspected acute coronary artery syndrome as it prevents further platelet aggregation. It is safe to use in cocaine-induced myocardial infarctions.

Choice C (calcium channel blockers) are used in cocaine-induced myocardial infarctions because they decrease the vasoconstriction that leads to the symptoms.

Choice D (benzodiazepine) and choice E (nitroglycerin) are both used in the management of acute coronary syndrome and can be used in patients with cocaine-induced myocardial infarction.

QUESTION 55

Choice E (rhonchi) is the correct answer. *Left sided heart failure is characterized by increased pulmonary venous pressure due to fluid backing up into the lungs.* Pulmonary symptoms dominate left-sided heart failure. *Right-sided heart failure is associated with increased systemic venous pressure,* causing all of the other choices.
CARDIOLOGY – HEART FAILURE – HISTORY AND PHYSICAL EXAMINATION (p 28).

QUESTION 56

Choice D (hypoglycemia) is the correct answer. *Biguanides, such as metformin* work primarily by *decreasing hepatic glucose production.* They have no effect on pancreatic beta cell insulin secretion, so they are *not associated with hypoglycemia.*
ENDOCRINE – METFORMIN – PHARMACOLOGY (p 305).

QUESTION 57

Choice E (Rales, rhonchi, and wheezing) is the correct answer. The *hallmark of chronic bronchitis is cough. Rales, rhonchi and wheezing are classic signs of chronic bronchitis.* All of the other choices are associated with emphysema. Keep in mind that although in clinical practice, most patients have a combination of both emphysema and chronic bronchitis, they often want to assess that you know the difference between the two disorders. PULMONARY – CHRONIC BRONCHITIS – HISTORY AND PHYSICAL EXAMINATION (p 80).

QUESTION 58

Choice B (Biot's breathing) is the correct choice. Biot's respirations are characterized by irregular respirations characterized by quick, shallow breaths of **equal depth** with irregular periods of **apnea**. It can be seen with *opioid-induced respiratory depression.* PULMONARY – BIOT'S BREATHING – HISTORY & PHYSICAL (p 114).

Choice A (*Cheyne-Stokes*) respiration is characterized by *periods of deep breathing alternating with periods of apnea.* There is *smooth increases in the rate of breathing with smooth gradual decrease in the rate of breathing with a period of apnea.* Commonly seen during sleep as well as in patients with heart failure, respiratory depression, uremia & brain damage.

Choice C (*Kussmaul's respiration*) is *deep rapid continuous respirations.* Often as a result of *metabolic acidosis.*

Choice D (Tachypnea) is characterized by rapid shallow breathing.

QUESTION 59

Choice B (Doxycycline) is the correct answer. *Doxycycline is the first line treatment of Lyme disease.* Doxycycline, Amoxicillin and Cefuroxime have all been shown to have equal efficacy in the management of Lyme disease. *Amoxicillin is the drug of choice in children under the age of 8 years* (Tetracyclines can cause permanent staining of the teeth in children under the age of 8).
INFECTIOUS DISEASE – LYME DISEASE – CLINICAL INTERVENTION (p 426).

Choice A (Azithromycin) is not recommended as first or second line management for Lyme disease. Its role in the management of Lyme may be used as last line therapy in patients unable to tolerate doxycycline, amoxicillin or cefuroxime.

Choice C (*ceftriaxone*) *is used in Lyme disease in patients who have severe disease, neurologic disease (other than facial palsy), and cardiac disease (such as second or third degree heart blocks).* Other drugs used in the management of neurologic Lyme include cefotaxime and penicillin G.

Choice D (clindamycin) and Choice E (vancomycin) are not used in the management of Lyme disease.

QUESTION 60

Choice A (Culture negative endocarditis) is the correct answer as it is the most common chronic manifestation of Q fever. All of the other agents are less common clinical manifestations of chronic Q fever.

QUESTION 61

Choice B (pyoderma gangrenosum) is the correct answer. *Pyoderma gangrenosum is a skin lesion commonly seen in patients with inflammatory diseases, such as Crohn's, ulcerative colitis, rheumatoid arthritis and spondyloarthropathies.* It is classically described as an *inflammatory nodule or pustule* that later becomes a *painful necrotic ulcer with irregular purple or violet undermined borders and a purulent base.* It is a misnomer as it is not infectious cause or is it gangrenous. DERMATOLOGY – PYODERMA GANGRENOSUM – MOST LIKELY (p 407).

Choice A (*furuncle*) is a *deeper infection of the hair follicle* (in contrast to folliculitis which is superficial). It is characterized by a tender nodule with a fluctuant abscess and a central plug.

Choice C (*pyogenic granuloma*) also known as lobular capillary hemangioma, is a *solitary, glistening, friable red nodule or papule often seen especially after trauma.* There is an increased incidence in pregnancy (and can be seen in the gingiva in these patients). The name is a misnomer because it is not pyogenic (pus forming) nor is it a granuloma.

Choice D (*erythema infectiosum*) also known as *fifth's disease* classically presents as an *erythematous rash with circumoral pallor, giving it a "slapped cheek" appearance.* The rash then progresses to a *lacy reticular rash on the extremities* (especially the upper extremities) that spares the palms and soles.

Choice E (carbuncle) describes interlocking furuncles with multiple openings to the abscesses with cellulitis. They are larger and usually more painful than furuncles.

QUESTION 62

Choice D (erythema multiforme major) is the correct answer. Erythema multiforme is a *type IV hypersensitivity reaction* that classically presents with a *dusty violet or red purpuric lesions* with macules, *vesicles or bullae in the center, giving it a classic target appearance.* There are two types. *Erythema multiforme minor (the absence of mucosal involvement – Choice B)* and *Erythema multiforme major (the involvement of ≥1 mucous membranes, including oral, genital and ocular mucosa.*
DERMATOLOGY – ERYTHEMA MULTIFORME MAJOR – HISTORY AND PHYSICAL (p. 393).

Choice A (*Morbiliform drug rash*) is the most common type of cutaneous drug reaction. It is characterized by a generalized distribution of *"bright-red" macules and papules that coalesce to form plaques.* It is not associated with the appearance of target lesions (as seen in this vignette).

Choice C (*Steven Johnson syndrome*) is a cutaneous drug reaction. It usually *begins with sore throat, myalgias and fever.* It progresses to widespread ulcerative lesions and blisters on the mucous membranes. They also develop erythematous, pruritic macules on the skin *associated with epidermal detachment and detachment of the skin (positive Nikolsky's sign).* It *involves less than 10% total body surface area. If it involves greater than 30%, the diagnosis of toxic epidermal necrolysis* (Choice E) is the correct answer.

QUESTION 63

Choice A (IV doxycycline + ceftriaxone) is the correct answer. This is the classic presentation of pelvic inflammatory disease, an ascending infection of the upper reproductive tract. *Patients with PID usually present with pelvic/lower abdominal pain. Cervical motion tenderness (a positive Chandelier's sign) is hallmark of PID. Gonorrhea and chlamydia are two of the most common causes of PID,* so treatment will often cover these two organisms unless other organisms are suspected. REPRODUCTIVE – PELVIC INFLAMMATORY DISEASE – CLINICAL INTERVENTION (p 262).

Choice B (IV clindamycin + oxacillin) covers gram-positive and anaerobic organisms only. They are not reliable to treat chlamydia & gonorrhea effectively. This treatment however is suitable for toxic shock syndrome caused by exotoxin-producing Staphylococcus aureus. TSS is most commonly associated with tampon or diaphragm use, especially if left in for prolonged duration of time. *TSS is associated with high fever and an erythematous rash that resembles sunburn including the palms and soles as well as desquamation of the skin* (which is not present in this vignette). Choice C (IV clindamycin + vancomycin) would be used in these patients if MRSA is suspected.

Choice E (IV ampicillin/sulbactam) is most commonly used for skin and soft tissue infections such as cellulitis.

QUESTION 64
Choice B (Fragile X syndrome) is the correct answer. Fragile X syndrome is associated with alteration of the FMR1 gene. *Classic presentation includes autism.* Physical exam findings include: *mitral valve prolapse, tall stature, hyperextensible joints, a long and narrow face, prominent forehead and chin, large ears, and macroorchidism.* (online pediatrics chapter).

Choice A (*Klinefelter's syndrome*) 47, XXY is due to an extra X chromosome.   They are considered genetically male but may have a male, female or intersex phenotype. *These patients often have gynecomastia and testicular atrophy (not macroorchidism that is seen with Fragile X).* They also tend to have a *tall thin statures but become obese later in life and have issues with language comprehension.*

Choice C (*Turner's syndrome*) 45,X is due to the absence of all or part of a sex chromosome. This leads to gonadal dysgenesis & primary amenorrhea. They often develop premature ovarian failure. Classic physical exam findings include: *short stature, webbed neck, prominent ears, and a broad chest with hypoplastic, widely spaced nipples.*

Choice D (*Marfan's syndrome*) is an autosomal dominant genetic connective tissue disorder that leads to *cardiovascular, ocular & musculoskeletal findings* in addition to multi-systemic involvement.

Choice E (*Ehlers-Danlos syndrome*) is a genetic *disorder of collagen synthesis leading to skin hyperextensibility, fragile connective tissue & joint hypermobility.* It can present with *mitral valve prolapse, smooth and doughy skin, easy bruisability, positive Metenier's sign* and patients may develop *arterial aneurysms.*

QUESTION 65
Choice A (acute myelogenous leukemia) is the correct answer. *Acute myelogenous leukemia is classically associated with the Auer rods (*linear intracellular inclusions) and *greater than 20% blasts* (immature white blood cells) seen on peripheral smear. HEMATOLOGY – ACUTE MYELOGENOUS LEUKEMIA – MOST LIKELY (Page 466)

Choice B (*chronic lymphocytic leukemia*) is associated with *smudge cells* (fragile, well differentiated white blood cells that often smudge during slide preparation).

Choice C (*acute lymphocytic leukemia*) *most commonly presents in children* with a peak incidence between 2 to 5 years of age.

Choice D (*multiple myeloma*) is associated with a monoclonal protein spike on hemoglobin electrophoresis and *Bence-Jones (light chain) proteins on urine electrophoresis.*

Choice E (*Chronic myelogenous leukemia*) is most commonly seen in patients older than 50 years of age. It is associated with a *strikingly elevated white blood cell count*, increased LDH, an increased leukocyte alkaline phosphatase score. These white blood cells tend to be well differentiated (mature cells). Most patients are asymptomatic until they develop a blastic crisis. The *Philadelphia chromosome is classically associated with CML* (although in small amount of cases it can be seen in ALL and rarely in AML).

QUESTION 66

Choice E (central retinal artery occlusion) is the correct choice. Occlusion of the retinal artery is often due a thrombus or embolus in the retinal artery. *Patients often have atherosclerotic disease.* It presents with sudden *unilateral vision loss.* The classic fundoscopic exam finding is a *pale retina (due to the ischemia) with a cherry red macula.* EENT – CENTRAL RETINAL ARTERY OCCLUSION – HISTORY AND PHYSICAL EXAM (p 231).

Choice A (*posterior uveitis*) usually presents with *blurred vision and floaters.* Posterior uveitis is painless (unlike anterior uveitis which also presents with conjunctival erythema, ciliary flush and ocular pain). On examination, uveitis would reveal white blood cell and protein precipitates, the classic *"cells and flare" pattern* in the anterior chamber.

Choice B (*amaurosis fugax*) is a *transient loss of vision in one eye* and can also be seen in patients with atherosclerotic disease. It is classically described as a *"curtain or shade" coming down obscuring the vision.* It is usually transient, *lasting a few seconds or a few minutes* (but can at times, last a few hours). The patient in this vignette presents with a 2-day history of vision loss.

Choice C (*retinal detachment*) often presents with *flashing lights (photopsia) with PROGRESSIVE visual loss* (often also described as a *curtain or shade coming down on the visual fields*). On fundoscopic exam, the retinal tear will be seen. A positive Schaffer's sign (clumping of pigment cells in the anterior vitreous chamber) may be seen.

Choice D (*central retinal vein occlusion*) can also cause sudden onset of visual loss. Fundoscopic exam would show *extensive retinal hemorrhages,* the so-called *"blood and thunder" appearance of the retina.*

QUESTION 67

Choice C (protect the airway) is correct choice. This is the classic presentation of acute epiglottitis. The classic lateral radiograph finding is a *swollen epiglottis (thumb sign or thumbprint sign).* In children, airway compromise can occur if the child is agitated (such as attempting to visualize the epiglottis with a tongue depressor – choice A) or spontaneously, so *protection of the airway is paramount.*
PULMONARY – EPIGLOTTITIS – CLINICAL INTERVENTION (p 112).

Choice D (supportive therapy and keep the child comfortable) and Choice B (IV ceftriaxone and clindamycin) is part of the management, but protection of the airway is paramount.

Choice E is the management of choice for botulism.

QUESTION 68

Choice A (schizophrenia) is the correct answer. Schizophrenia is defined *as functional decline, hallucinations and bizarre delusions of greater than 6 months duration with 1 month of acute symptoms.* This patient has auditory hallucinations and control delusions. He also exhibits some *negative symptoms (cold, flat affect).* PSYCH/BEHAVIORAL - SCHIZOPHRENIA – MOST LIKELY (p. 382).

Choice B (*bipolar disorder*) is defined as *major depression plus episodes of mania.* Patients alternate between mania and depression (they usually don't have a flat affect), and the duration of the delusions make schizophrenia a more likely diagnosis.

Choice C (*paranoid personality disorder*) is associated with *distrust and suspicion as seen in this vignette but is not associated with hallucinations or marked impairment in functioning.*

Choice D (*Schizophreniform disorder*) shares all the *symptoms of schizophrenia but is less than 6 months in duration.* The patient in this vignette had the symptoms for at least 8 months.

Choice E (*Schizotypal personality disorder*) is associated with *odd, eccentric behavior and patterns suggestive of schizophrenia but patients with schizotypal disorder do not develop psychosis or delusions.*

QUESTION 69
Choice B (increased ammonia levels) is the correct answer. A common complication of cirrhosis is *hepatic encephalopathy*, which is manifested by *confusion and lethargy* (due to decreased liver clearance of ammonia byproduct of protein metabolism). The *increased ammonia levels* are toxic to neurological system. Physical exam findings of encephalopathy is *asterixis (flapping tremor) and fetor hepaticus*.
GI/NUTRITION – ENCEPHALOPATHY – LABS/DIAGNOSTIC (p. 143).

Choice A (increased amylase and lipase) is incorrect. Alcoholism is one of the most common causes of acute pancreatitis (in addition to gallstones). *Acute pancreatitis usually presents with abdominal pain (that often radiates the back) and is improved with leaning forward, sitting or lying in the fetal position.* Other symptoms include nausea, vomiting and fever.

Choice C (*increased alkaline phosphatase with gamma glutamyl transpeptidase*) is seen with *cholestasis*. These patients may often be asymptomatic or present with right upper quadrant pain (biliary colic).

Choice D (decreased thiamine levels) is incorrect. *Thiamine deficiency* is also commonly seen in alcoholics. It usually presents with *paresthesias, peripheral neuropathy and reflex impairment. Wernicke's encephalopathy presents with the triad of global confusion, ataxia and ophthalmoplegia* (which is absent in this vignette).

Choice E (*decreased vitamin B12 levels*) will often present with *paresthesias, gait abnormalities & memory loss.* B_{12} *deficiency is also associated with a macrocytic anemia and the presence of hyper-segmented neutrophils.*

QUESTION 70
Choice C [Bupropion (Wellbutrin)] is the correct answer. Bupropion has been shown to cause less GI & sexual dysfunction side effects when compared to SSRI's. PSYCH/BEHAVIORAL – DEPRESSION – PHARMACOLOGY (p 377).

Choice A [Citalopram (Celexa)] is a selective serotonin receptor reuptake inhibitor (SSRI) so it will be associated with sexual side effects as sertraline.

Choice B [Venlafaxine (Effexor)] is a serotonin and norepinephrine reuptake inhibitor (SNRI) that has a similar side effect profile as the selective serotonin reuptake inhibitors (SSRI's).

Choice D [Amitriptyline (Elavil)] and Choice E [Doxepin (Sinequan)] are tricyclic antidepressants. They are also associated with sexual dysfunction side effects.

QUESTION 71
Choice B (gram negative diplococci) is the correct answer. These are the classical physical exam findings of meningitis. A *petechial rash is hallmark for Neisseria meningitidis* (the most common cause of meningitis in children from 1 month until 18 years of age). On gram stain, Neisseria appears as *gram-negative diplococci*.
NEUROLOGY – NEISERRIA MENINGITIS – LABS/DIAGNOSTIC STUDIES (p 365).

Choice A (gram negative rods) may be seen if Escherichia coli or Haemophilus influenzae is the cause of meningitis. H. flu can be either rods or coccobacilli.

Choice C (gram positive cocci in pairs) or Choice D (gram positive cocci in chains) may be seen with Streptococcus pneumonia (pneumococcus), another common cause of meningitis in this age group. *Streptococcus pneumoniae is the most common cause of meningitis in patients 18 years and older.*

Choice E (gram positive rods) can be seen with Listeria monocytogenes. *L. monocytogenes can cause infections especially in young and elderly patients. Ampicillin has good L. monocytogenes coverage.*

QUESTION 72

Choice D (IV Ceftriaxone) is the correct answer.   Staphylococcus aureus is the most common organism in osteomyelitis in adults and children (including children with sickle cell disease). In patients with sickle cell disease, they are usually asplenic by adulthood (from either splenic crisis or from repeated micro infarctions to the spleen).   The spleen is responsible for recognizing encapsulated organisms such as: Salmonella, Streptococcus pneumonia and Haemophilus influenza, putting these patients at increased risk of infections with these organisms. *Patient with sickle cell disease have an increased incidence of Salmonella osteomyelitis* (a gram negative organism such as seen in this vignette by the pink staining rod-shaped bacteria).   *Third generation cephalosporins, such as Ceftriaxone,* have great gram-negative coverage and coverage of certain gram-positive organisms. MUSCULOSKELETAL – SICKLE CELL OSTEOMYELITIS – CLINICAL INTERVENTION (p. 195).

Choice A (IV Oxacillin) is anti-staphylococcal penicillin that is used in suspected staphylococcal or gram-positive infections.

Choice B (IV Ciprofloxacin) has great gram-negative coverage and *can be used in patients over the age of 18 in suspected salmonella infections. Fluoroquinolones can interfere with articular cartilage formation and health, so they are contraindicated in children under the age of 18* (the patient is 7 years old in this vignette).

Choice C (IV *Clindamycin*) is used primarily for *gram positive and anaerobic coverage "above the diaphragm".* The gram stain here shows gram-negative bacilli (pink staining, rod-shaped bacteria).

Choice E (*IV Vancomycin*) is used for *gram-positive infections* especially when *methicillin-resistant Staphylococcus aureus (MRSA) is suspected.* The gram stain here shows gram-negative bacilli (pink staining, rod-shaped bacteria).

QUESTION 73

Choice E (partial thromboplastin time) is the correct answer.   Hemophilia B is an *X-linked recessive* disorder leading to decreased *Factor IX, which is part of the intrinsic pathway,* leading to an *increase in partial thromboplastin time (PTT).* All of the other choices levels are normal in Hemophilia B.
HEMATOLOGY – HEMOPHILIA B – LABS/DIAGNOSTIC STUDIES (p 463).

QUESTION 74

Choice C (Glucose 6 phosphate-dehydrogenase deficiency) is the correct answer. G6PD deficiency is an X-linked recessive trait that appears primarily in *males (especially of African descent).*   Without the protection of G6PD, the hemoglobin in the red blood cells becomes denatured under oxidative stresses (leading to the development of *Heinz bodies).* Some *oxidative stresses include infections, fava (broad) beans & medications (such as sulfa drugs, antimalarials, methylene blue, isoniazid, nitrofurantoin, aspirin, and dapsone).*   This leads to *episodic hemolytic anemia.* HEMATOLOGY – G6PD DEFICIENCY – MOST LIKELY (p 456).

Choice A (Autoimmune hemolytic anemia) is associated with *sphere-shaped red blood cells and Coombs positivity.*

Choice B (Hereditary spherocytosis) is associated with *sphere-shaped red blood cells and Coombs negativity.*

Choice D (Anemia of chronic disease) is not associated with Heinz bodies. Shistocytes are not present anemia of chronic disease. Shistocytes indicate hemolysis.

Choice E (Sickle cell anemia) would have normally presented initially before the age of 10 years old. These patients have multiple chronic pain episodes throughout life and functional asplenia, so these patients usually have repeated infections, especially with encapsulated organisms (even if vaccinated).

QUESTION 75
Choice C (botulism antitoxin with respiratory support) is the correct choice. Clostridium botulinum is a gram-positive spore-forming rod. There are 2 forms: wound botulism and foodborne. *In infants, it most commonly due to ingestion of C. botulinum spores in honey.* The classic symptoms are the *7 D's: diplopia, dry mouth, dysphagia, dysarthria, dysphonia, decreased muscle strength and dilated but fixed pupils. Antitoxins are given in all cases.* Due to respiratory muscle weakness, the infant should receive respiratory support.
INFECTIOUS DISEASE – BOTULISM – CLINICAL INTERVENTION (p. 421).

Choice A (diphtheria antitoxin + penicillin G) is incorrect. The presentation of *diphtheria are flu-like symptoms with cervical lymphadenopathy and a pseudomembranes on the posterior pharynx.*

Choice B (tetanus immune globulin + metronidazole or penicillin) is incorrect because *tetanus infection presents with muscle spasms and increased contractions*, not muscle weakness.

Choice D (*botulism antitoxin + Penicillin G) is only used in wound botulism. In patients with foodborne botulism, antibiotics may release more toxins, worsening the condition.*

Choice E (botulism antitoxin + Gentamicin) is not used in the management. C. botulinum is a gram-positive organism. Aminoglycosides do not have reliable gram-positive coverage as a single agent.

QUESTION 76
Choice B (staphylococcal scalded skin syndrome) is the correct answer. *Scalded skin syndrome is an exfoliative staphylococcus infection* associated with a *painful, diffuse, erythematous rash that may develop fluid-filled blisters and may exhibit a positive Nikolsky sign. Desquamation of the palms and soles is common.*
INFECTIOUS DISEASE – SCALDED SKIN SYNDROME – MOST LIKELY (p 441).

Choice A (*hand foot and mouth syndrome*) classically presents with *vesicular lesions on a reddened based with an erythematous haloes in the oral cavity followed by vesicular rash involving the palms and soles.* Although it affects the palms and soles, it is not classically associated with a positive Nikolsky sign (seen here in this vignette).

Choice C (*smallpox*) is associated with *vesicles in the same stage* progressing to pustules with scarring.

Choice D (*rocky mountain spotted fever*) is classically associated with *fever, headache and the development of a red maculopapular rash first on the ankles and the wrists, progressing to the palms and the soles.* It is associated with a tick bite. Although it affects the palms and soles, it is not associated with a positive Nikolsky sign.

Choice E (*Kawasaki's disease) also involves the palms and the soles.* It is associated with *fever, strawberry tongue, and desquamation of the palms and soles.* Although it affects the palms and soles but it is not classically associated with a positive Nikolsky sign (seen here in this vignette).

QUESTION 77

Choice D (Rotator cuff tendinitis) is the correct choice. Rotator cuff tendinitis is more common in younger patients and is not associated with weakness, atrophy or continuous pain. Subacromial lidocaine injection into the area will lead to improvement in strength. Both rotator cuff tendinitis and tears may have pain and range of motion difficulties with overhead movements.

Choice A (*Rotator cuff tear*) is commonly associated with *weakness, atrophy and continuous pain.* Subacromial lidocaine injection will show continued weakness due to the tear in the rotator cuff.

Choice B (*Adhesive capsulitis*) is due to inflammation and is associated with *stiffness-pain cycles* and *decreased range of motion of the shoulder.*

Choice C (Chronic unreduced shoulder dislocation) would show a deformity and reduced range of motion.

Choice E (shoulder separation) is due to direct blow to the adducted shoulder. There is no history of acute or remote trauma to the shoulder in this vignette.

QUESTION 78

Choice E (positive cytoplasmic anti-neutrophil cytoplasmic antibodies – C-ANCA) is the correct answer. Necrotic sinusitis, lower respiratory tract involvement and rapidly progressing glomerulonephritis is the hallmark for Wegener's granulomatosis (granulomatosis with polyangiitis). It is classically associated with a positive C-ANCA. MUSCULOSKELETAL – WEGENERS GRANULOMATOSIS – LABS/DIAGNOSTIC STUDIES (p 211).

Choice A (*anti-SRP antibodies*) are classically associated with *polymyositis*, which usually presents with bilateral *proximal muscle weakness.*

Choice B (*P-ANCA*) is associated with *Microscopic polyangiitis, Ulcerative colitis, and pyoderma gangrenosum.*

Choice C (*anti-CCP Antibodies*) are specific with *rheumatoid arthritis.*

Choice D (*anti-GBM antibodies*) and *IgG linear deposits in the glomerular basement membrane* are associated with *Goodpasture's syndrome*, which usually presents with *hemoptysis and rapidly progressing glomerulonephritis.*

QUESTION 79

Choice D (Metronidazole orally) is the correct answer. C. difficile colitis is a result of *overgrowth due to a reduction of the normal flora by antibiotics. It is also spread by contact.* Although clindamycin is classically associated with it, any broad-spectrum antibiotic can potentially cause C. difficile colitis. A strikingly increased lymphocytosis is also commonly associated with C. difficile colitis (strikingly high lymphocytosis is also associated Pertussis). *Metronidazole is considered first line therapy.* The colitis classically causes a pseudomembrane appearance of the colon. GI/NUTRITION – CLOSTRIDIUM DIFFICILE – CLINICAL INTERVENTION (p. 157).

Choice A (Vancomycin IV) is not a treatment for C. difficile. IV vancomycin is used for gram-positive organisms and MRSA-related infections.

Choice B (*Vancomycin PO*) is the second line treatment for C. difficile colitis or is used first line in severe C. difficile infections. There is no evidence of toxic megacolon or severe disease in this vignette.

All the other choices are not used in the management of C. difficile colitis.

QUESTION 80

Choice E (Budd-Chiari syndrome) is the correct answer. Budd-Chiari syndrome is *hepatic vein thrombosis or hepatic vein occlusion.* It classically presents with the *acute onset of the triad of 1: ascites 2: hepatomegaly and 3: right upper quadrant pain.* Rapid onset of jaundice is also seen in this syndrome. Common causes includes paroxysmal nocturnal hemoglobinuria, idiopathic, hypercoagulable states, oral contraceptive use, malignancies and pregnancies. GI NUTRITION – BUDD CHIARI SYNDROME – MOST LIKELY (p. 136).

Choice A (*primary biliary cirrhosis*) is usually an incidental finding in patients with an *extremely high alkaline phosphatase.* Most patients are asymptomatic. *Fatigue is usually the first symptom followed by pruritus, jaundice, right upper quadrant pain and hepatomegaly.* Primary biliary cirrhosis is due to idiopathic, autoimmune involvement of the intrahepatic small bile ducts. It is not due to hepatic vein thrombosis or occlusion.

Choice B *(Acute cholangitis)* usually presents with the *triad of 1: fever 2: right upper quadrant pain and 3: jaundice.* Cholangitis is due to bile duct obstruction, not hepatic vein thrombosis or occlusion.

Choice C (*primary sclerosing cholangitis*) presents with *progressive jaundice pruritus, right upper quadrant pain and hepatomegaly.* It is most commonly seen in patients with *inflammatory bowel disease (such as Crohn's disease and ulcerative colitis).* It is caused by autoimmune-mediated cholestasis with fibrosis if the intrahepatic and extrahepatic bile ducts not due to hepatic vein thrombosis or occlusion.

Choice D (*Wilson's disease*) is due to free *copper accumulation in the liver, brain, kidney and cornea.* They may present with liver symptoms and will often have *corneal copper deposits (Kayser-Fleischer rings).*

QUESTION 81

Choice D (hyperkeratosis & perifollicular hemorrhages) is the correct answer. Vitamin C is needed for collagen synthesis. Scurvy (Vitamin C deficiency) is associated with the loss of collagen in blood vessels, leading to perifollicular hemorrhages & purpura among the other manifestations.
GI/NUTRITION – VITAMIN C DEFICIENCY – HISTORY AND PHYSICAL EXAMINATION (p. 154).

Choice A is classic for pellagra (Vitamin B3/Niacin) deficiency.

Choice B is classic for vitamin B1/Thiamin deficiency. *Ataxia oculomotor paralysis and global confusion is the triad of Wernicke's encephalopathy.*

Choice D (*Looser Zones*) are associated with adult onset vitamin D deficiency (Osteomalacia).

Choice E *ocular-oral-genital involvement* is classically associated with *riboflavin (Vitamin B2) deficiency.*

QUESTION 82

Choice C (a systolic crescendo-decrescendo murmur that decreases in intensity with squatting) is the correct answer. This vignette describes hypertrophic cardiomyopathy. Remember that *anything that makes the LV smaller (ex Valsalva, standing) or things that increase contractility (exercise, positive inotropes like Digoxin)* lead to a *more intense murmur with hypertrophic cardiomyopathy.*
CARDIOLOGY – HYPERTROPHIC CARDIOMYOPATHY – HISTORY AND PHYSICAL EXAMINATION (p 41).

Choice A, Choice B and Choice E are seen in aortic stenosis. Remember that Valsalva decreases venous return, reducing the amount of flow through a stenotic valve as well as regurgitation through a leaky valve. This means that ***Valsalva decreases all left and right-sided murmurs*** (AR, PR, AS, PS, MR, TR, MS, TS). ***The two notable exceptions to this rule are 1. hypertrophic cardiomyopathy*** (Valsalva increases the murmur of HCM) ***and 2. Valsalva leads to increase prolapse of the mitral valve (earlier occurrence of the ejection click).***

Choice D (a systolic crescendo-decrescendo murmur that increases in intensity with handgrip) is incorrect because the handgrip maneuver increases afterload. *Murmurs due to increased afterload (such as both aortic stenosis and hypertrophic cardiomyopathy) are decreased with the handgrip maneuver.*

QUESTION 83

Choice B (Brugada syndrome) is the correct answer. Brugada syndrome is seen most commonly in Asian males. Often found incidentally, *Brugada syndrome can lead to syncope, ventricular fibrillation and sudden cardiac death.* The hallmark of Brugada syndrome is a *right bundle branch block pattern seen in V1 and V2* (it is often incomplete), *ST elevations in V1 through V3 (with a sharp downsloping pattern).* There may be the presence of S waves in the lateral leads (I, aVL, V5 and V6). *Management includes implantation of a cardioverter defibrillator* to prevent sudden cardiac death. CARDIOLOGY – BRUGADA SYNDROME – LABS/DIAGNOSTIC STUDIES (p. 18).

Choice A (*Hypothermia*) may be suggested on an ECG by the presence of an *Osborne (J) wave*, which is elevation of the J point due to abnormal repolarization (especially seen in lead V2 through V5). Hypothermia is also associated with prolonged PR and QT intervals.

Choice C (*Takotsubo cardiomyopathy*) is a variant of dilated cardiomyopathy (often called the *Broken heart syndrome).* It is thought to follow an event that causes a *catecholamine surge* (ex emotional stress, family death, surgery). It is most common in menopausal women. Patients with Takotsubo cardiomyopathy usually present with symptoms of acute coronary syndrome. On ECG, it may manifest as ST elevations and/or T wave inversion with a mild elevation of cardiac enzymes. However, during the cardiac workup, the coronary arteries show no evidence of myocardial infarction. It classically shows up on echocardiogram with *left ventricular apical ballooning.*

Choice D (*Kawasaki syndrome*) is most commonly seen in children. A rare but devastating complication in *Kawasaki syndrome is myocardial infarction*, which would show up in the leads where the infarction is located.

Choice E (Left bundle branch) is associated with a wide QRS, a broad slurred R wave in V5 and V6 with a deep S wave in V1 and V2.

QUESTION 84

Choice B (mitral valve prolapse) is the correct answer. Mitral regurgitation is described as a holosystolic murmur that is best heard at the apex, accentuated when the patient is lying on the left side and radiates to the axilla. Mitral valve prolapse (the presence of an ejection click) is the most common cause of mitral regurgitation. CARDIOLOGY – MITRAL REGURGITATION – BASICS (p. 43).

Choice A (rheumatic heart disease) is the most common cause of mitral stenosis by far. Rheumatic heart disease can cause any of the valvular abnormalities.

Choice C (hypertension) is associated with most commonly associated with aortic regurgitation.

Choice D (degenerative atherosclerotic disease) is most commonly associated with the development of aortic stenosis in older patients.

Choice E (congenital heart disease) can cause any of the heart valvular abnormalities.

QUESTION 85

Choice C [egg allergy] is the correct choice. Both the trivalent influenza vaccine and the yellow fever vaccine is contraindicated in patients with egg allergies. Thimerosol (used in multi-dose vials as a preservative may also be a contraindication of the multi-dose vial is used). PULMONARY – INFLUENZA – HEALTH MAINTENANCE (p. 114).

Choice A is a contraindication to the Hepatitis B vaccine (Baker's yeast is used to mass produce the vaccine)

Choice B is a contraindication to any live attenuated vaccine

Choice D and choice E are contraindications to the MMR and the Varicella vaccine. These vaccines contain small amounts of neomycin to prevent bacterial contamination during the manufacturing process.

QUESTION 86

Choice C (antibodies against the presynaptic calcium-gated channels that release acetylcholine) is the correct answer. *Lambert-Eaton syndrome* is one of the paraneoplastic syndromes that may be seen with small cell carcinoma. This syndrome is caused by *malignancy-induced development of antibodies against the presynaptic calcium-gated channels that release acetylcholine.* Acetylcholine release stimulates muscle contraction, so the reduction of acetylcholine at the neuromuscular junction leads to weakness. *The hallmark of Lambert-Eaton syndrome is that the weakness IMPROVES with repeated use* (due to the increased number of subsequent action potentials increasing the calcium entry gradient, which overcomes the acetylcholine inhibition). This finding differentiates Lambert-Eaton from myasthenia gravis.
PULMONARY –LAMBERT-EATON SYNDROME – BASICS (page 92 and 355)

Choice A (*dopamine depletion in the substantia nigra*) describes the pathophysiology of *Parkinson disease*, which classically manifests as *tremor, bradykinesia and rigidity.*

Choice B (*antibodies against the post synaptic acetylcholine receptor*) describes the pathophysiology of *Myasthenia gravis.* Acetylcholine receptor antibodies decreases muscle contractions, leading to *weakness that WORSENS with repeated use.*

Choice D (*destruction and necrosis of both upper and lower motor neurons with progressive motor degeneration and preserved sensory*) describes the pathophysiology of *amyotrophic lateral sclerosis (ALS or Lou Gehrig's disease).* It classically presents with a *mixture of upper and lower motor neuron signs* with progressive motor deterioration with sparing of sensory.

Choice E (*prion-mediated degeneration of the brain*) describes the pathophysiology of *Creutzfeldt-Jakob disease.* The hallmark of CJD is rapidly progressing dementia, marked gait abnormalities and myoclonus (especially if the patient is startled).

QUESTION 87

Choice E (ipratropium + albuterol) is the correct choice. Unlike asthma, anticholinergics are preferred over short-term beta 2 agonists, but studies have shown that the *combination of the two show a greater response than using either alone (Choice B or choice A), making this the best choice.* PULMONARY – COPD – PHARMACOLOGY (p 81).

Choice C (theophylline) is a bronchodilator but its narrow therapeutic index and many side effects (GI, cardiac and neurologic) inhibits its use as a first line agent.

Choice D (methylprednisone) is incorrect. Unlike in asthma where steroids are effective, not all patients with COPD respond to steroids, so it is not first line treatment.

QUESTION 88

Choice B (oxybutynin) is the correct answer. This is the classic presentation of a patient with *urge incontinence* due to an *overactive bladder.* Acetylcholine causes contraction of the bladder so *anticholinergics (such as oxybutynin) are helpful to reduce bladder contraction and reduce bladder over activity.*
GENITOURINARY– URGE INCONTINENCE – PHARMACOLOGY (p. 342).

Choice A (midodrine) and choice C (pseudoephedrine) can be used to medically manage stress incontinence. Stress incontinence occurs when the intra-abdominal pressure rises above the urethral pressure, leading to leakage of urine. Alpha-1 agonists increases urethral pressure, reduce the symptoms of stress incontinence.

Choice D (mirabegron) is also used in the management of urge incontinence. It is a beta 3 agonist.

Choice E (bethanacol) is a cholinergic drug that will aggravate urge incontinence by stimulating further bladder contraction. *Bethanacol, however, can be used in patients with underactive bladder* as seen in some patients with *overflow incontinence. In these patients bethanacol can improve bladder activity.*

QUESTION 89
Choice E (percutaneous nephrolithotomy) is the correct answer. Percutaneous nephrolithotomy is an invasive procedure used for large stones >10-mm, struvite stones and staghorn calculi.
GENITOURINARY – NEPHROLITHIASIS - CLINICAL INTERVENTION (p. 339).

Choice A (*shock wave lithotripsy*) is used in larger stones to break them into smaller ones.

Choice B (*uretoscopy with stent*) provides *immediate relief to an obstructed or at-risk kidney*

Choice C (observation) can be used in small, asymptomatic stones.

Choice D (alkalinization of the urine to dissolve the stones) can be used to dissolve uric acid stones.

QUESTION 90
Choice A (plasmapheresis) is the correct answer. Myasthenic crisis is a severe presentation of myasthenia gravis with respiratory failure. Plasmapheresis or intravenous immunoglobulin is employed in the management of myasthenic crisis. NEUROLOGY – MYASTHENIC CRISIS – CLINICAL INTERVENTION (p. 355).

Choice B (corticosteroids), choice C (azathioprine) and choice D (cyclosporine) can be used as alternatives to acetyl cholinesterase inhibitors in the long term management of myasthenia gravis but is not first line for myasthenic crisis.

QUESTION 91
Choice B (argatroban) is the correct answer. Heparin induced thrombocytopenia is caused by a hapten complex formed with heparin + platelet factor 4. It causes *thrombocytopenia but clinically is associated with thrombosis. Initial management of choice is a direct thrombin inhibitor,* such as *argatroban and bivalirudin.*
HEMATOLOGY – HEPARIN INDUCED THROMBOCYTOPENIA – CLINICAL INTERVENTION (p 99 & 481).

Choice A (enoxaparin) and Choice C (dalteparin) are low molecular weight heparins. They are also associated with heparin-induced thrombocytopenia (though the incidence is less when compared to unfractionated heparin).

Choice D (aspirin) is an anti-platelet agent that is not used in treating heparin-induced thrombocytopenia.

Choice E (*warfarin) may be used in the long-term management of heparin-induced thrombocytopenia but only after proper management with a direct thrombin inhibitor* to prevent warfarin-induced thrombosis. Warfarin is associated with a procoagulant state in the first days of initiation of therapy due to a temporary induced protein C & S deficiency.

QUESTION 92
Choice C (Haemophilus ducreyi) is the correct answer. H. ducreyi is the causative agent in chancroid, which can present as painful genital ulcers with bubo formation. INFECTIOUS DISEASE – CHANCROID – BASICS (p 423).

Choice A (Erysipelothrix rhusiopathiae) is the causative agent of Erysipeloid.

Choice B (Chlamydia trachomatis) causes chlamydia urethritis/cervicitis, pelvic inflammatory disease, lymphogranuloma venereum and some cases of reactive arthritis.

Choice D (Anaplasma phagocytophilium) and Ehrlichia chaffeensis cause Ehrlichiosis.

Choice E (Neisseria gonorrheae) causes gonorrhea.

QUESTION 93
Choice B (amphetamine intoxication) is the correct answer. Amphetamine toxicity can present with hyperthermia, headache, flushing, nausea, vomiting, and seizures. It is associated with SYMPATHETIC STIMULATION: increased motor activity, sweating, tachycardia (arrhythmias), tremors, pupillary dilation & peripheral vasoconstriction (which can cause hypertension and potentially myocardial infarction).
BEHAVIORAL – AMPHETAMINE INTOXICATION – MOST LIKELY (online chapter)

Choice A (*Opioid toxicity) often present with pupillary constriction* (narcotics are miotics), *respiratory depression, bradycardia, hypotension*, coma, nausea and vomiting.

Choice C (cannabis) intoxication may cause dry mouth, conjunctival erythema, narrow complex tachycardia and hypotension.

Choice D (benzodiazepine intoxication) usually presents with lethargy, prolonged reaction time, muscular incoordination and facial flushing.

Choice E (nicotine withdrawal) may show signs of sympathetic hyperactivity.

QUESTION 94
Choice A (Increased haptoglobin) is the correct answer. In hemolytic anemia, increased red blood cell destruction leads to increased free hemoglobin, which is toxic. Haptoglobin binds free hemoglobin, so as the hemolytic anemia continues, the haptoglobin stores become depleted, leading to a decreased haptoglobin. All of the other choices are associated with hemolytic anemia. HEMATOLOGY – HEMOLYTIC ANEMIA – BASICS (page 452)

QUESTION 95
Choice C (Hashimoto's thyroiditis) is the correct answer. These signs and symptoms are consistent with hypothyroidism. The labs also indicate a primary hypothyroidism (an elevated TSH level and decreased free T3 and free T4 levels). Hashimoto's thyroiditis is the most common cause of hypothyroidism in the United States. ENDOCRINE – HASHIMOTO'S THYROIDITIS – MOST LIKELY (p. 287).

Choice A (*Deqeurvain's Thyroiditis*) can present with a hypothyroid or hyperthyroid profile depending on when the patient presents but is classically associated with *thyroid pain and tenderness* (which is not present in this vignette).

Choice B (acute suppurative thyroiditis) is also associated with pain. Patients usually appear sick and will often be febrile and may have leukocytosis.

Choice D (*Reidel's thyroiditis*) is fibrosis of the thyroid gland that is classically associated with a *"rock-hard, painful fixed nodular thyroid"* this physical examination description may also be used for *anaplastic thyroid carcinoma* (Choice E), which is a poorly differentiated aggressive thyroid malignancy.

QUESTION 96
Choice B (Rosiglitazone) is the correct answer. Rosiglitazone is a thiazolidinedione that works by increasing insulin sensitivity at the peripheral receptor sites in adipose tissue and muscles. Side effects of Rosiglitazone include cardiotoxicity, congestive heart failure (fluid retention, edema), hepatotoxicity, and fractures. ENDOCRINE – DIABETES MELLITUS – PHARMACOLOGY (p 305).

Choice A (Repaglinide) is associated with hypoglycemia.

Choice C (acarbose) is associated with hepatitis, diarrhea, abdominal pain, and flatulence.

Choice D (*metformin*) is associated with *lactic acidosis, renal impairment, GI complaints, macrocytic anemia, metallic taste & worsening of renal function if IV contrast is given within 48 hours of the last dose.*

Choice E (exenatide) is associated with delay of gastric emptying especially in patients with gastroparesis, hypoglycemia, and pancreatitis.

QUESTION 97
Choice C (non bullous impetigo) is the correct answer. Non-bullous impetigo is most commonly caused by *Staphylococcus aureus and Group A beta hemolytic Streptococcus (Strep pyogenes)*. Vesicles or pustules that develop the characteristic *honey-colored crusts* characterize it. DERMATOLOGY – IMPETIGO – MOST LIKELY (p. 398).

Choice A (*bullous impetigo*) is a rare form of impetigo associated with *vesicles that form large bullae* and rupture, leaving thin "*varnish-like*" crusts.

Choice B (*Molloscum contagiosum*) is classically characterized by *multiple, dome-shaped, flesh-colored to pearly white, waxy papules with central umbilication. Curd-like material can be expressed* if the center of the papule is squeezed.

Choice D (ecthyma) is a rare form of impetigo associated with an ulcerative pyoderma.

Choice E (*poison ivy*) initially begins an *erythematous, pruritic rash with the development of papules, plaques, vesicles and or bullae arranged commonly in linear or streak-like configurations* where a portion of the plant has made contact with the skin.

QUESTION 98
Choice E (metronidazole) is the correct answer. *Tinea versicolor classically presents with erythematous plaques and fine white scales common in the scalp, face, eyebrows, beard, nasolabial folds, chest and intertriginous regions of the groin.* Tinea versicolor is classically associated with *Malassezia furfur*, a yeast that is part of the normal flora but causes a reaction in some patients. All of the other choices can be used in the management of Tinea versicolor. DERMATOLOGY – SEBORRHEIC DERMATITIS – CLINICAL INTERVENTION (p. 392).

QUESTION 99
Choice C (CN V) is the correct answer. Herpes Zoster Ophthalmicus is a varicella zoster virus reactivation involving the trigeminal nerve. The Hutchinson sign are lesions on the nose that herald ocular involvement. Ocular involvement is evident by dendritic lesions seen on slit lamp exam. EENT– HERPES ZOSTER OPHTHALMICUS – BASICS (p 433).

Choice E (CN VII) causes Herpes Zoster Oticus (Ramsay-Hunt syndrome), which is facial nerve involvement.

QUESTION 100
Choice D (acute pericarditis) is the correct answer. The ECG shows *diffuse ST elevations with associated PR depression in the same leads.* In aVR, there is usually ST depression and PR segment elevation.

Choice A (*Brugada syndrome*) classically has a *right bundle branch block pattern with coved-appearing* ST elevations. Often seen in *young Asian males*, it can lead to *ventricular fibrillation* and so implantation of a cardioverter defibrillator is important for the long-term survival of these patients.

Choice B classically associated with ST elevations in inferior leads (I, II and aVF)

Choice C classically associated c ST elevations in lead I, aVL, V5 and V6

Choice E is classically associated with ST depressions and T wave inversion

PHOTO CREDITS

SMALL BOWEL OBSTRUCTION
B. Slaven / CustomMedical (Used with permission)

LYME DISEASE
Kallista Images / CustomMedical (Used With Permission)

DIPHTHERIA
By User: Dileepunnikri (Own work) [CC BY-SA 3.0 (http://creativecommons.org/licenses/by-sa/3.0)], via Wikimedia Commons

SALMONELLA
By Bobjgalindo (Own work) [GFDL (http://www.gnu.org/copyleft/fdl.html) or CC BY-SA 4.0-3.0-2.5-2.0-1.0 (http://creativecommons.org/licenses/by-sa/4.0-3.0-2.5-2.0-1.0)], via Wikimedia Commons

MENINGITIS
By Okwikikim at en.wikipedia (Transferred from en.wikipedia) [Public domain], from Wikimedia Commons

SICKLE CELL
By Y tambe (Y tambe's file) [GFDL (http://www.gnu.org/copyleft/fdl.html) or CC-BY-SA-3.0 (http://creativecommons.org/licenses/by-sa/3.0/)], via Wikimedia Commons

IMPETIGO
Wellcome Trust Library / CustomMedical (Used With Permission)

BRUGADA SYNDROME
By CardioNetworks: [ ] [CC BY-SA 3.0 (http://creativecommons.org/licenses/by-sa/3.0)], via Wikimedia Commons

PERICARDITIS
By James Heilman, MD (Own work) [CC BY-SA 3.0 (http://creativecommons.org/licenses/by-sa/3.0)], via Wikimedia Commons

1. An 18-year-old sexually active female presents to the clinic with vaginal discharge for 1 week. On inspection with a vaginal speculum, there is a frothy, yellow-green discharge that is malodorous. Many small punctate petechiae are noticed on the cervix. Which of the following is the management of choice?
    a. Clindamycin 300mg orally every 12 hours for 7 days
    b. Metronidazole 2g orally x 1 dose
    c. Ceftriaxone 250mg IM x 1 dose
    d. Azithromycin 1g orally x 1 dose
    e. Cephalexin 500mg orally x 7 days

2. A 24-year-old male presents with left anterior shoulder pain after for 1 hour after falling directly onto the left arm while playing basketball. On physical examination, the patient's left shoulder is held in abduction and externally rotated. There is a squared-off appearance to the left deltoid area. There is decreased range of motion at the shoulder joint but there is no skin tenting or ecchymosis. Which of the following is the most likely diagnosis?
    a. adhesive capsulitis
    b. posterior shoulder dislocation
    c. anterior shoulder dislocation
    d. Grade III shoulder separation
    e. Luxatio erecta

3. A 32-year-old female presents to the clinic with intermittent diarrhea, intolerable flatulence and intermittent abdominal pain. She states her symptoms seem to improve with fasting.   She has an anemia of chronic disease with a mean corpuscular volume of 84 (Normal 80-100). She has the following rash on her leg:
    Which of the following antibodies would be most
       likely seen in this patient?
    a. Smooth muscle antibodies
    b. Perinuclear anti-neutrophil antibodies
    c. Transglutaminase (Endomysial) antibodies
    d. Anti-mitochondrial antibodies
    e. ADAMTS13 antibodies

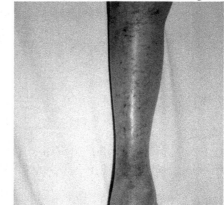

4. Patients taking streptomycin should be warned of which of the following side effects?
    a. ototoxicity and nephrotoxicity
    b. nonviral hepatitis and peripheral neuropathy
    c. retrobulbar neuritis
    d. orange discoloration of bodily fluids
    e. photosensitivity dermatitis or hyperuricemia

5.   Which of the following is classically seen in Parkinson disease?
    a. Lhermitte's sign
    b. an intentional tremor that predominantly affects the head, neck and voice
    c. Myerson's sign
    d. positive ice pack test
    e. increased deep tendon reflexes

6. A 42-year-old male was struck in the right eye with a blunt object. On physical examination, there is subconjunctival hemorrhage covering the entire right eye, the presence of a hyphema and an irregularly shaped pupil. Which of the following is considered to be the most appropriate management at this time?
    a. observation
    b. placement of a rigid eye shield with outpatient ophthalmology follow up
    c. topical bacitracin ointment and outpatient ophthalmology follow up
    d. placement of a rigid eye shield and immediate ophthalmology consult
    e. place the patient in a Trendelenburg position to avoid worsening of the hyphema

7. Which of the following is not seen in a patient with syndrome of inappropriate ADH secretion (SIADH)?
    a. hyponatremia
    b. urine sodium >20 mEq/L
    c. decreased serum osmolarity
    d. isovolemia
    e. decreased urine osmolarity

8. A 46-year-old male undergoes cholesterol screening and is found to have an abnormal cholesterol panel. After a 6-month trial of rigid diet and exercise, his repeat cholesterol values are as follows:

	PATIENT	NORMAL VALUES
HDL	46 mg/dL	>45 mg/dL
LDL	90 mg/dL	<100 mg/dL
TRIGLYCERIDES	350 mg/dL	<150 mg/dL

Which of the following medications is the most appropriate management for this patient?
    a. simvastatin
    b. cholestyramine
    c. ezetimibe
    d. fenofibrate
    e. nicotinic acid

9. A 33-year-old female is being evaluated for abnormal electrocardiogram findings. The electrocardiogram shows a prominent U wave and a prolonged QT interval. On physical examination, there are noticeable tooth enamel erosions and pitting of the teeth. She admits to having misused many laxatives and enemas to lose weight and drinks excess water to reduce her food intake. These activities are often done after episodes in which she goes on a 2-hour binge-eating spree. On physical examination, her body mass index is 19% (Normal 18.5 – 25%). Which of the following is the most likely diagnosis?
    a. body dysmorphic disorder
    b. anorexia nervosa
    c. functional neurologic disorder (conversion disorder)
    d. bulimia nervosa
    e. binge eating disorder

10. Which of the following is the most common presentation of sickle cell anemia in children under the age of 2?
    a. Dactylitis
    b. Osteomyelitis
    c. Meningitis
    d. Renal failure
    e. Hepatosplenomegaly

11. A 34-year-old male with a history of celiac disease develops a papulovesicular rash on the extensor surfaces including the back and the buttocks. Treatment with dapsone reduced the appearance rash.

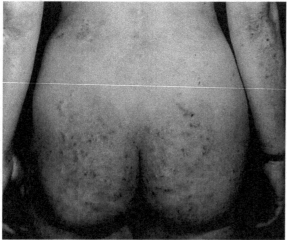

Which of the following is the most likely diagnosis?
a. varicella zoster reactivation
b. Molluscum contagiosum
c. dermatitis herpetiformis
d. Coxsackie virus infection
e. pyogenic granuloma

12. A 4-year-old male is brought into the pediatric clinic for fever and bilateral conjunctivitis. On physical examination, there is edema and desquamation of the palms and soles, a morbiliform rash that is not raised, bilateral nonsuppurative conjunctivitis, cervical lymphadenopathy, a strawberry tongue, and linear grooves in the nails. Which of the following is the best management?
a. Azithromycin
b. Penicillin VK
c. Aspirin
d. Aspirin and intravenous immunoglobulin
e. Corticosteroids

13. Which of the following set of physical exam findings are most consistent with Marfan syndrome?
a. low set ears, flat facial features, upslanting palpebral fissures, single transverse palmar crease
b. mitral valve prolapse, tall stature, hyperextensible joints, a long and narrow face, prominent forehead and chin, large ears, and macroorchidism
c. short stature, webbed neck, prominent ears, a broad chest with hypoplastic, widely-spaced nipples
d. mitral valve prolapse, smooth and doughy skin, easy bruisability, positive Metenier's sign
e. mitral valve prolapse, tall stature, arachnodactyly, pectus carinatum, joint laxity, ectopia lentis

14. A 65-year-old female with poor dentition presents to the clinic with a 4-week history of fever of unknown origin. During the workup, she is noted to have splinter hemorrhages and new onset of holosystolic murmur that radiates to the axilla (which was not present two months ago). She denies any IV drug use and there are no needle marks on the arms or the legs. Which of the following are the most likely echocardiogram and blood culture findings expected in this patient?
a. Staphylococcus aureus and pulmonic valve
b. Streptococcus viridans and mitral valve
c. Staphylococcus aureus and tricuspid valve
d. Staphylococcus epidermis and mitral valve
e. Enterococcus and aortic valve

15. A 45-year old male is on chronic medications including digoxin, amiodarone, carvedilol, spironolactone and hydrochlorothiazide. On physical examination, you notice a small, painless enlarged thyroid gland. Thyroid function tests are as follows:

	PATIENT	NORMAL VALUES
TSH	8.4 mU/L	0.9-5.0 mU/L
Free T4	7 nmol/L	9-23 nmol/L
Free T3	0.2 nmol/L	0.8-2.4 nmol/L
ESR	15 mmol/hr	F: 1-25mm/h M: 0-17mmol/hr

Which of the following medication is most likely responsible for the patient's physical exam findings?
a. digoxin
b. spironolactone
c. hydrochlorothiazide
d. amiodarone
e. carvedilol

16. A 44-year-old male who attended a hunter's convention a week ago in July presents to the emergency department with a 4-day history of fever (38.8° C), productive cough, nausea, diarrhea and progressive dyspnea. Lab tests reveal an increase in liver function tests and hyponatremia. A chest radiograph is obtained, showing an atypical infiltrate. He is told that numerous attendees who were sitting near the air conditioner also developed similar symptoms. Which of the following is the most likely diagnosis?
a. Chlamydia pneumophila (pneumoniae)
b. Mycoplasma pneumoniae
c. Pseudomonas aeruginosa
d. Klebsiella pneumoniae
e. Legionella pneumophila

17. A 50-year-old female with a history of longstanding hypertension and type I diabetes mellitus presents to the clinic with dysarthria, hand clumsiness and weakness especially when the patient is writing. There are no sensory deficits. A CT scan is performed and shows multiple hypodense "punched out lesions" near the basal ganglia. Which of the following is the most likely diagnosis?
a. Parkinson's disease
b. Lacunar infarct
c. Anterior cerebral artery infarct
d. Posterior cerebral artery infarct
e. Middle cerebral artery infarct

18. A 20-year-old male is accidentally hit in the head with a baseball. The coach states that he had a brief loss of consciousness and then he "seemed to be back to normal". After about 10 minutes, he develops nausea and vomiting. Upon evaluation of the patient, there are focal neurologic deficits and the right pupil is dilated. In addition to a fracture of the right temporal bone, which of the following are the most likely CT scan findings in this patient?
a. convex lens-shaped bleed that does not cross the suture lines
b. concave crescent-shaped bleed that crosses the suture lines
c. bleeding into the brain parenchyma
d. bleeding into the subarachnoid space
e. punched-out lesions near the basal ganglia

19. A 43-year-old male presents with sudden onset of right-sided ocular erythema and pain that started after watching a movie. He states when he left the movie theater, he noticed haloes around lights. On physical examination, the eye feels hard to palpation, the cornea appears hazy and the right pupil is mid-dilated. On fundoscopic exam, there is blurring of the optic disc. Which of the following is considered first line management for this patient?
    a. acetazolamide intravenous
    b. pilocarpine ophthalmic drops
    c. atropine ophthalmic drops
    d. prednisone orally
    e. dexamethasone intravenous

20. A 46-year-old male with a longstanding history of gastroesophageal reflux disease develops dysphagia to solids, weight loss and anemia. He does not smoke or drink and has not had any recent episodes of vomiting or retching. Which of the following is the most likely diagnosis?
    a. Barrett's esophagus
    b. Diffuse esophageal spasm
    c. Adenocarcinoma of the esophagus
    d. Squamous cell carcinoma of the esophagus
    e. Mallory Weiss tears

21. Which of the following describes the mechanism of action of Tamsulosin in the management of benign prostatic hypertrophy?
    a. alpha-1 agonist stimulating the alpha receptors on the bladder neck
    b. inhibits conversion of testosterone to dihydrotestosterone
    c. suppresses prostate gland growth
    d. provides rapid relief of symptoms by smooth relaxation of the prostate and bladder neck
    e. reduces the size of the prostate, increasing outflow of urine

22. A 35-year-old previously healthy male is admitted to the hospital for suspected infective endocarditis and is placed on nafcillin and gentamicin. A week later, he suddenly develops a drop in urine output and an increase in BUN and creatinine. A urinalysis with microscopic examination is done and shows epithelial cell casts, low specific gravity of the urine as well as a fractional excretion of sodium of 3%. Which of the following is the most likely diagnosis?
    a. obstructive uropathy
    b. acute interstitial nephritis
    c. acute glomerulonephritis
    d. acute tubular necrosis
    e. prerenal azotemia

23. A 19-year-old boy presents to the clinic complaining of left leg pain that is worsened when he plays sports as well as shortness of breath. On physical exam there is tenderness to the tibia with the swelling overlying the tender area. A radiograph is obtained and shows a "hair on end" and "sunburst appearance" to the diaphysis of the tibia. A chest radiograph is obtained and shows a mass in the left lung. The patient denies asbestos exposure or a smoking history. Which of the following is the most likely diagnosis?
    a. Osteochondroma
    b. Ewing sarcoma
    c. Osteosarcoma
    d. Chondrosarcoma
    e. Paget's disease

24. A 10-year-old boy is being transferred to another school for having academic and social difficulties in school. He was just transferred to the new school 3 months ago for issues in his previous school. He has had multiple fight with other students, has thrown multiple temper tantrums and recently, he set a trashcan on fire in the school when he was placed on detention. His mother states she has problems with him at home. She had to give away her beloved pets because he started doing cruel experiments with them. Which of the following is the most likely diagnosis?
    a. antisocial personality disorder
    b. attention deficit hyperactivity disorder
    c. oppositional defiant disorder
    d. conduct disorder
    e. Asperger syndrome

25. Which of the following best describes the primary mechanism of action of glyburide?
    a. decreases hepatic glucose production with no effect on pancreatic beta cells
    b. delays intestinal absorption of glucose
    c. increases insulin sensitivity at the peripheral receptor sites of adipose and muscle tissues
    d. lowers blood sugar by mimicking incretin
    e. stimulates pancreatic beta cell insulin release in a non glucose-dependent fashion

26. A 50-year-old male is being worked up for dilated cardiomyopathy and new onset diabetes mellitus. He does not have a history of alcohol abuse or hepatitis. On physical examination, there is testicular atrophy, abdominal ascites with a positive shifting dullness test and bronze-colored skin. Which of the following is not classically associated with the most likely diagnosis?
    a. increased serum ferritin
    b. decreased serum iron
    c. positive HFE C282Y genotype
    d. increased transferrin saturation
    e. positive hemosiderin deposition in the liver parenchyma on biopsy

27. A 43-year-old male presents with right knee pain. On physical exam, there is tenderness, erythema, swelling and decreased flexion of the right knee. A radiograph is performed and shows the following.

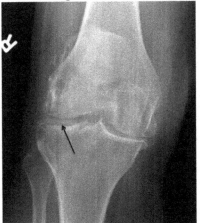

An arthrocentesis is performed, showing positively birefringent, rhomboid shaped crystals. Which of the following is considered the most likely diagnosis?
    a. Gouty arthritis
    b. Rheumatoid arthritis
    c. Osteoarthritis
    d. Pseudogout
    e. Paget's disease

28. A 65-year-old female who spent two months in Martha's Vineyard, Massachusetts presents to the urgent care center with a gradual onset of fever, chills and jaundice. There are no rashes present. Labs show evidence of a hemolytic anemia. She denies any overseas travel. A peripheral smear is obtained, showing parasites within the red blood cells in a tetrad formation. Which of the following is the most likely diagnosis?
    a. Ehrlichiosis
    b. Infectious Mononucleosis
    c. Malaria
    d. Babesiosis
    e. Typhus

29. Which of the following describes a chronic disease of the apocrine follicles, characterized by clusters of abscesses and/or epidermoid cysts, especially affecting the groin and the axilla?
    a. carbuncle
    b. folliculitis
    c. furuncle
    d. hidradenitis suppurativa
    e. Molluscum contagiosum

30. A 52-year-old female presents to the clinic with vaginal irritation, itching and what she describes as a "rash". She states she has also had some bleeding after sexual intercourse with her new partner. On vaginal examination, there is no vaginal discharge, petechiae or cervical abnormalities. The only positive finding is a red ulcerated, crusted lesion on the vulva with no satellite lesions. Which of the following is the most appropriate management at this time?
    a. Podophyllin topical
    b. acyclovir
    c. biopsy of the lesion
    d. fluconazole x 1 dose
    e. sodium bicarbonate sitz bath or douche

31. Which of the following is a contraindication for the use of methotrexate in the management of ectopic pregnancy?
    a. A patient with a blood pressure of 130/85 mmHg and a pulse rate of 80 bpm.
    b. A patient with a serum beta hCG >5,000
    c. the absence of fetal heart activity on ultrasound
    d. a patient with no free fluid in the retroperitoneum seen on ultrasound
    e. a patient who has a gestational sac of 3 centimeters

32. A 62-year-old male comes to the office complaining of a bilateral tremor of the hands and the forearm with certain movements. The tremor seems to worsen with stress but is shortly relieved with the ingestion of alcohol. On physical examination, a finger to nose test is performed and the tremor is intensified as his finger reaches nearer to his nose. His voice is shaky when he attempts to speak. His neurological exam is otherwise unremarkable and his legs are unaffected. Which of the following is considered first line medical therapy to help alleviate the tremors?
    a. prochlorperazine
    b. propranolol
    c. entacapone
    d. levodopa/carbidopa
    e. verapamil

33. A patient is being evaluated for progressive right-sided hearing loss. On physical examination, there is lateralization to the right ear and on Rinne test, and bone conduction is greater than air conduction on the Weber test. Which of the following is the most likely diagnosis?

a. Labyrinthitis

b. Acoustic neuroma

c. Meniere's disease

d. Cerumen impaction

e. Presbyacusis

34. A 48-year-old male complains of a sudden onset of right-sided facial weakness and weakness in the right arm greater than experienced in the right leg. On physical examination, Broca's aphasia is noted as well as a positive right arm drift test. The patient's speech is slurred but he is able to raise both eyebrows. Which of the following is the most likely diagnosis?

a. Bell's palsy

b. left middle cerebral artery occlusion

c. left posterior cerebral artery occlusion

d. left anterior cerebral artery occlusion

e. right middle cerebral artery occlusion

35. A 40-year-old male presents with the rapid onset of fever, chills, productive cough and chest tightness occurring 4-8 hours after working a new job. On physical examination, there is the presence of inspiratory crackles. A lung biopsy shows micronodular interstitial involvement with poorly formed noncaseating granulomas. Which of the following is the patient's most likely occupation?

a. ship builder

b. coal worker

c. bird breeder

d. sandblaster

e. demolition repair

36. Which of the following medications is used for the prophylactic management of esophageal varices to reduce fatal bleeding occurrences?

a. transjugular intrahepatic portosystemic shunt

b. octreotide

c. vasopressin

d. propranolol

e. endoscopic variceal ligation

37. A 43-year-old male with a history of primary hyperparathyroidism presents to the emergency room with left flank pain that is constant and radiates to the left testicle. There is no associated testicular erythema or swelling. Urinalysis is significant only for hematuria. A CT scan of the abdomen and pelvis is performed, showing a 3-mm stone in the left ureter. Which of the following is the recommended management of this patient?

a. Metoclopramide, toradol and nephrolithitomy

b. IV fluids, metoclopramide and shock wave lithotripsy

c. IV fluids, toradol, metoclopramide and tamsulosin

d. IV fluids and uretoscopy with stent

e. Alkalinization of the urine

38. A 45-year-old male who works in restaurant accidently trips with a hot oil vat and sustained burns to his legs, abdomen, chest and groin.   These burns are erythematous, moist, weeping with blistering and are very painful to the touch. Capillary refill is intact. Which of the following is the body surface area of the superficial partial thickness burn described?
   a.   27
   b.   37
   c.   28
   d.   54
   e.   55

39. Which of the following set of physical exam findings is most consistent with Trisomy 21?
   a.   low set ears, flat facial features, upslanting palpebral fissures, single transverse palmar crease
   b.   mitral valve prolapse, tall stature, hyperextensible joints, a long and narrow face, prominent forehead and chin, large ears, and macroorchidism
   c.   short stature, webbed neck, prominent ears, a broad chest with hypoplastic, widely-spaced nipples
   d.   mitral valve prolapse, smooth and doughy skin, easy bruisability, positive Metenier's sign
   e.   mitral valve prolapse, tall stature, arachnodactyly, pectus carinatum, joint laxity, ectopia lentis

40. A couple is attending psychotherapy because the female partner is unsure if they can salvage their relationship. She states she thinks he has a bad pattern that needs to be broken because he has had numerous failed relationships. He admits to being unable to maintain long-term relationships and enjoys his alone time but doesn't like being alone. He suffers from extreme mood swings and sometimes engages in reckless driving anytime he gets into a fight with his girlfriend. They seem to argue over issues because she accuses him of either seeing things all good or all bad with no middle ground. She wants to leave but states that she is nervous to leave because he has in the past threatened suicide if she left him. She states she cannot tolerate his incessant, erratic mood swings and aggression any longer. Which of the following is he most likely suffering from?
   a.   histrionic personality disorder
   b.   narcissistic personality disorder
   c.   dependent personality disorder
   d.   borderline personality disorder
   e.   avoidant disorder

41. A 24-year-old male is complaining of back pain with morning stiffness that decreases with exercise and activity. He has kyphosis and was diagnosed with sacroiliitis in the past. The patient is HLA B27 positive. Which of the following radiograph findings of the spine would most likely be seen in this patient?
   a.   squaring of the vertebral bodies
   b.   osteomyelitis
   c.   wedge shaped vertebrae
   d.   slipping of the vertebrae over another
   e.   defect fracture of the pars interticularis

42. A 40-year-old male presents with progressive swelling to the joints and difficulty performing daily activities. He develops fever on occasion.   On physical examination, there is diffuse swelling of the fingers. Radiographs show asymmetric arthritis with "pencil in cup" deformities. The patient is HLA B27 positive. Which of the following medical conditions is closely associated with this disorder?
   a.   Seborrheic dermatitis
   b.   Eczema
   c.   Psoriasis
   d.   Steven Johnson syndrome
   e.   Erythema multiforme

43. A 34-year-old patient presents with palpitations. The patient is hemodynamically stable. The following rhythm is seen on the monitor:

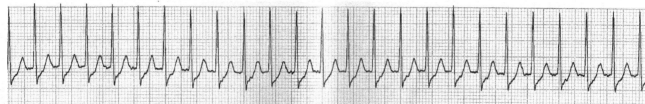

Which of the following is the management of choice
    a. synchronized cardioversion
    b. unsynchronized cardioversion
    c. amiodarone
    d. adenosine
    e. atropine

44. During cardiac examination, a continuous, machinery murmur is heard loudest at the left upper sternal border. Which of the following is the most likely diagnosis?
    a. Still's murmur
    b. Graham Steell murmur
    c. Austin Flint murmur
    d. Atrial septal defect
    e. Patent ductus arteriosus

45. A 22-year-old sexually active female presents to the clinic complaining of vaginal discharge. On physical examination, there is a copious, frothy, yellow-green, malodorous vaginal discharge. There are also punctate erythematous lesions on the cervix. Which of the following would also be seen in this patient?
    a. positive spirochetes on Darkfield microscopy
    b. the presence of clue cells on wet mount with few lactobacilli
    c. the presence of copious amounts of lactobacilli
    d. the presence of mobile protozoa on wet mount
    e. the presence of hyphae and yeast with potassium hydroxide application

46. Which of the following is considered to be the gold standard test for gestational diabetes?
    a. hemoglobin A1c >7.0
    b. 50g oral glucose challenge test
    c. random fasting blood glucose level
    d. ACTH stimulation test
    e. 3-hour glucose tolerance test

47. A 32-year old female at 36 weeks gestation goes to a family cookout and eats cold cut sandwiches and unpasteurized cheese that her mother brought her from the Dominican Republic. A few days later, she becomes febrile and goes into premature labor, undergoing a cesarean section. The child is born and in 3 days, the child develops fever and hypertonia. Blood cultures show gram-positive bacilli. Which of the following is the most likely etiologic agent?
    a. Streptococcus agalactiae bacteremia
    b. Listeria monocytogenes bacteremia
    c. Salmonella bacteremia
    d. Neisseria meningitidis bacteremia
    e. Shigella bacteremia

48. A 42-year-old male visiting Jordan brought a handmade wool turtleneck sweater while on his travels. 2 days later, he develops an erythematous papule on his neck that ulcerates, leaving a painless black eschar. 2 days later, he develops influenza-like symptoms. Which of the following is the most specific chest radiograph finding consistent with the suspected diagnosis?

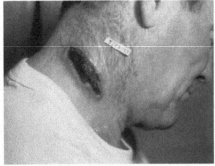

  a. widening of the mediastinum
  b. lobar infiltrate
  c. companion line
  d. atelectasis
  e. Westermark's sign

49. A 24-year old female has a puncture wound to the left foot through the sole of her tennis shoe after stepping on a rusty nail. Based on the mechanism of injury, which of the following organisms is associated with an increased incidence of infection?
  a. Haemophilus ducreyi
  b. Enterococcus species
  c. Strep agalactiae
  d. Pseudomonas aeruginosa
  e. Bartonella henselae

50. Which of the following is not seen in thrombotic thrombocytopenic purpura?
  a. Decreased ADAMTS 13 serum levels
  b. Positive neurologic symptoms
  c. Shistocytes on peripheral smear
  d. Increased partial thromboplastin time
  e. Normal prothrombin time

51. Which of the following is seen with pure nephrotic syndrome?
  a. hypertension
  b. sudden increase in blood urea nitrogen and creatinine
  c. red blood cell casts
  d. hypercellularity of the glomerulus on biopsy
  e. proteinuria greater than 3.5 grams/day

52. Which of the following most reliably distinguishes unstable angina from stable angina pectoris?
  a. chest pain radiating to the arm
  b. dull chest pressure
  c. shortness of breath
  d. chest pain lasting 55 minutes
  e. chest pain brought on by exertion

53. A 45-year-old is brought into the emergency room unresponsive. On physical examination, there is increased jugular venous pressure worsened with inspiration, a blood pressure of 90/60 mm Hg, muffled heart sounds and normal breath sounds. Which of the following is the recommended management of this patient?
   a. chest tube thoracostomy
   b. pericardial window
   c. pericardiocentesis
   d. pericardiectomy
   e. administration of IV furosemide

54. A 43-year-old male presents to the office for a well visit. During routine examination, there is an elevated superficial, fleshy, triangular-shaped mass on nasal side of the left eye. He states he noticed it before and that it has been growing slowly over time. He denies any ocular itching, tearing or changes in vision. On eye examination, his visual acuity is 20/20 bilaterally and his pupils are round and reactive to light with a normal red reflex. Which of the following is the most likely diagnosis?
   a. retinoblastoma
   b. pterygium
   c. pinguecula
   d. hordeolum
   e. chemosis

55. A 29-year-old male presents with swelling of the neck and pain on swallowing. On physical examination, there is no tonsillar swelling. There is swelling and erythema to the upper neck and chin with noticeable pus on the floor of the mouth. There is no bleeding of the gums or ulcerations of the interdental papillae. Which of the following is the most likely diagnosis?
   a. Vincent's angina
   b. Ludwig's angina
   c. Acute herpetic tonsillopharyngitis
   d. Peritonsillar abscess
   e. Infectious mononucleosis

56. A 67-year-old male presents with epigastric pain that radiates to the back. In taking a history, he describes having months of intractable itching, 30-pound weight loss and anorexia. On physical examination, there is a palpable, nontender gall bladder and jaundice. Which of the following is the most likely diagnosis?
   a. Colorectal carcinoma
   b. Acute cholecystitis
   c. Acute cholangitis
   d. Acute pancreatitis
   e. Pancreatic carcinoma

57. A 45-year-old female presents to the dermatology clinic with a very pruritic rash. On physical examination, there are multiple purple, polygonal, flat papules with fine scales and irregular borders primarily on the shins and scalp. Her nails are atrophic. On physical examination of her mouth, there is a papular rash in the mouth with white striations seen on the buccal mucosa. Which of the following infectious etiologies is most commonly associated with this dermatologic disorder?
   a. Hepatitis C virus
   b. Epstein Barr virus
   c. Group A beta hemolytic streptococcus
   d. Paramyxovirus
   e. Togavirus

58. Which of the following describes the primary mechanism of action of ondansetron?
    a. it activates dopamine receptors
    b. it is a dopamine receptor antagonist
    c. it is antagonizes cholinergic receptor
    d. it antagonizes serotonin receptors
    e. it antagonizes histamine receptors

59. A 15-year-old female is treated for suspected methicillin resistant Staphylococcus aureus cellulitis with cephalexin and trimethoprim-sulfamethoxazole. After 5 days, she developed runny nose, body aches and fever. The next day, she developed a painful rash that started on the face and chest and involved the palms and soles. The rash later that progressed to vesicles and bullae formation, covering 37% of her body. There are no target lesions present. There are also painful hemorrhagic erosions in the mouth including the buccal mucosa with a grayish-white membrane. There is sloughing of the skin with gentle application of pressure. Which of the following is the most likely diagnosis?
    a. Toxic epidermal necrolysis
    b. Erythema multiforme major
    c. Morbiliform drug rash
    d. Steven Johnson syndrome
    e. Erythema multiforme minor

60. A 43-year-old male survived a horrific plane crash 3 weeks ago. As the lone survivor, he expresses extreme guilt about not being able to save anyone else. His wife states that he often wakes up at night in a "cold sweat" at least 3 times a week and states he keeps having the same recurring nightmare of the night of the crash and has since started working from home to avoid taking flights despite having to commute as part of his job. Which of the following is the most likely diagnosis?
    a. generalized anxiety disorder
    b. panic attack
    c. acute stress disorder
    d. post traumatic stress disorder
    e. conversion disorder

61. A 43-year-old female with a long history of depression is being treated with Venlafaxine (Effexor). She decides she wants to be "all-natural" & begins to take St. John's Wort in an attempt to eventually "wean off pills". 3 weeks later, she develops a temperature of 103°F, tremors, nausea, vomiting, abdominal cramps & diarrhea. On physical examination, she appears very agitated & diaphoretic. Her pupils are dilated, her deep tendon reflexes are increased & the nurse witnessed an episode of myoclonus in her right leg. An ECG is performed, showing sinus tachycardia. Which of the following is the most likely diagnosis?
    a. Neuroleptic malignant syndrome
    b. Acute dystonia
    c. Tardive dyskinesia
    d. Serotonin syndrome
    e. Panic attack

62. Which of the following medications is considered to be the first line for prophylactic management of cluster headaches?
    a. amitriptyline
    b. lithium
    c. verapamil
    d. propranolol
    e. aspirin

63. Which of the following cerebrospinal fluid findings are most consistent with multiple sclerosis?
   a. increased white blood cells (primarily lymphocytes) with decreased glucose
   b. high protein with normal white blood cell count
   c. increased oligoclonal IgG bands
   d. high protein with increased white blood cells (primarily polymorphonuclear neutrophils) with decreased glucose
   e. normal glucose with increased white blood cells (primarily lymphocytes)

64. Which of the following is considered the first line management of a women at 18 weeks gestation with hyperemesis gravidarum, a 9% weight loss and hypochloremic metabolic alkalosis?
   a. observation and reassurance that the vomiting is due to oversensitivity to the hormones of pregnancy
   b. Promethazine
   c. Dimenhydrinate
   d. Pyridoxine with doxylamine
   e. The administration of high protein foods with small frequent meal intake

65. A 43-year-old male presents to the clinic with a 5-day history of profound diarrhea. He describes his bowel movements as grey, with no odor, blood or pus. In obtaining a history, he states he returned 2 days ago from a Mardi Gras festival in New Orleans and ate local crawfish and other shellfish. On physical examination, there is no rash. His vital signs show a high-grade veer and a pulse rate of 128 beats per minute. Which of the following is the most likely diagnosis?
   a. Campylobacter enteritis
   b. Salmonella gastroenteritis
   c. Vibrio cholera
   d. Shigella enteritis
   e. Staphylococcus enteritis

66. A 43-year-old female has a history of epigastric pain that is worse with food. She has had multiple ulcers in the past that took longer than 8 weeks to heal. She also complains of intermittent diarrhea that is not relieved with fasting. A secretin test is done and there is no inhibition of gastrin levels. Which of the following is the most likely diagnosis?
   a. H. pylori gastritis
   b. Proton pump induced hypergastrinemia
   c. Atrophic gastritis
   d. Zollinger Ellison syndrome
   e. Meckel's diverticulum

67. A 70-year-old male with no past medical history presents to the emergency room with flank pain. On physical exam, there is a palpable mass on the left side as well as a left sided varicocele. Urinalysis shows hematuria. An abdominal CT scan is done to rule out kidney stones. There is no evidence of kidney stones but a solid mass in the left kidney can be seen. The right kidney appears normal. A biopsy is done, revealing renal cell carcinoma. A full workup is done and is negative for metastatic disease. Which of the following is the management of choice?
   a. chemotherapy
   b. radical nephrectomy
   c. interleukin
   d. partial nephrectomy
   e. radiation therapy

68. A 32-year-old patient has a right index finger injury after sustaining a sudden blow to the tip of the finger with forced flexion. He denies any finger pain but on physical examination, he is unable to straighten the distal portion of his finger. Radiographs show a small avulsion at the base of the distal phalanx. The proximal interphalangeal joint is unaffected. Which of the following is the most likely diagnosis?
   a. Jersey finger
   b. Boutonniere deformity
   c. Swan neck deformity
   d. Finger sprain
   e. Mallet finger

69. A 36-year-old male presents to the office with low back pain radiating down the anterior aspect of his left leg. On physical exam, there is no midline tenderness. There is weakness with left ankle dorsiflexion and a loss of the left knee jerk reflex. There is no saddle anesthesia, urinary or bowel incontinence. Which of the following is the most likely diagnosis?
   a. A vertebral compression fracture at L5
   b. Herniated disc at S1
   c. Lumbosacral strain
   d. Herniated disc at L4
   e. Cauda Equina syndrome

70. A 6-year-old boy presents to the pediatric urgent care center for 3 days of low-grade fever, runny nose, sore throat and nonproductive cough. On physical examination, the lung exam is unremarkable for lobar consolidation. HEENT examination reveals a mildly erythematous pharynx and fluid-filled blisters on the tympanic membrane. A rapid strep test is performed and is negative. He is stable for discharge. Which of the following is considered the management of choice in this patient?
   a. doxycycline
   b. levofloxacin
   c. ceftriaxone
   d. azithromycin
   e. ceftriaxone + azithromycin

71. A 23-year old thin male with a 5 PPY smoking history presents to the emergency room with sudden onset of sharp chest pain worsened with inspiration and shortness of breath. A chest radiograph is obtained which shows a pneumothorax occupying 35% of the lung field and an otherwise unremarkable X ray. Which of the following is the next most appropriate step?
   a. chest tube thoracostomy
   b. observation and oxygen therapy
   c. insertion of large bore needle into the pleural space through the second intercostal space
        followed by chest tube thoracostomy
   d. avoid high altitudes or unpressurized aircrafts
   e. instillation of a sclerosing agent into the pleural space

72. Which of the following is the most commonly associated cardiac abnormality seen in patients with coarctation of the aorta?
   a.   bicuspid aortic valve
   b.   ventricular septal defect
   c.   atrial septal defect
   d.   mitral stenosis
   e.   thickened septal wall

73. A 70-year-old female has an echocardiogram performed for follow up evaluation after having positive cardiac enzymes with a negative angiography. The echocardiogram shows apical left ventricular ballooning. Which of the following is the most likely diagnosis?
   a.   unstable angina
   b.   Brugada syndrome
   c.   Takayasu arteritis
   d.   Takotsubo cardiomyopathy
   e.   Restrictive cardiomyopathy

74. Which of the following describes the mechanism of action of nedocromil?
   a. blocks leukotriene-mediated neutrophil migration and smooth muscle contraction in patients with allergic asthma
   b. inhibits mast cell mediated degranulation in patients with exercise or cold air induced asthma
   c. inhaled corticosteroid that blunts the immune system response
   d. anticholinergic that dilates the central airways in patients with acute asthma
   e. beta 2 agonist that dilates the peripheral airways in patients with acute asthma

75. Hemorrhagic cystitis and an increased risk of bladder cancer are side effects of which of the following medications?
   a.   cisplatin
   b.   doxorubicin
   c.   gemcitabine
   d.   5-fluorouracil
   e.   cyclophosphamide

76. A 43-year-old male is being managed for peptic ulcer disease. Cytochrome P450 inhibition, gynecomastia and impotence are side effects of which of the following medications?
   a.   misoprostol
   b.   sucralfate
   c.   sorbitol
   d.   cimetidine
   e.   omeprazole

77. A 3-year-old is brought into the pediatric clinic by his mother for the sudden onset of spontaneous grunts, blinking, shoulder shrugging, blurting out of repetitive phrases as well as repeating intermittent obscene words. He does not have a recent history of sore throat, skin or gastrointestinal infections. Which of the following is the most likely diagnosis?
   a. Sydenham's chorea
   b. Tourette's syndrome
   c. Huntington's syndrome
   d. Guillain-Barré syndrome
   e. Parkinsonism

78. A 32-year-old male sustained a crush injury to the left middle finger. Radiographs of the finger did not reveal a fracture or dislocation. The patient recovered fully. 3 weeks later, a bright-red, friable, moist, raspberry-like 5-mm nodule appears at the site of injury.

Which of the following is the most likely diagnosis?

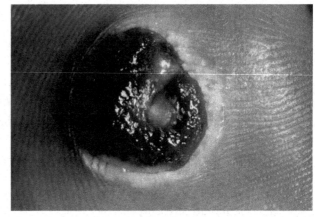

  a. pyogenic granuloma
  b. pyoderma gangrenosum
  c. erythema nodosum
  d. malignant melanoma
  e. cellulitis

79. A 68-year-old male develops headache, fever and a purpuric rash. The cerebrospinal fluid is positive for gram-negative diplococci. A few hours later, the patient develops spontaneous bleeding at the venipuncture site. Initial labs show an elevated prothrombin time, partial thromboplastin time, international normalized ratio with a decreased fibrinogen level. Which of the following is the most likely diagnosis?
  a. idiopathic thrombocytopenic purpura
  b. disseminated intravascular coagulation
  c. thrombotic thrombocytopenic purpura
  d. hemolytic uremic syndrome
  e. Von Willebrand disease

80. Which of the following is most consistent with diffuse, large B-cell Non-Hodgkin lymphoma?
  a. History of Epstein Barr infection
  b. Bimodal distribution of increased incidence in the 3rd and 6th decades
  c. The presence of the Reed Sternberg cell on lymph node biopsy
  d. Painful lymph nodes with the ingestion of alcohol
  e. Noncontiguous, extranodal spread of the disease

81. Which of the following is not classically associated with diabetes insipidus?
  a. isovolemia
  b. low urine specific gravity
  c. increased thirst
  d. decreased urine osmolarity
  e. hyponatremia

82. A 38-year-old male undergoes a thyroidectomy for Grave's disease. On his follow up visit 2 weeks later, he states he has been having occasional episodes of numbness around his lips, and audible wheezing. On physical examination, there is facial spasm with tapping on the facial nerve and increased deep tendon reflexes. Which of the following lab value sets is most consistent with this presentation?
  a. increased calcium, increased PTH levels, decreased phosphate levels
  b. decreased calcium, increased PTH levels, increased phosphate levels
  c. decreased calcium, decreased PTH levels, increased phosphate levels
  d. decreased calcium, increased PTH levels, decreased phosphate levels
  e. decreased calcium, decreased PTH levels, decreased phosphate levels

83. A 32-year-old sexually active male presents with left knee pain. A knee radiograph is performed and is negative for fracture, dislocation or periosteal reaction. An arthrocentesis is performed and shows the following:

	PATIENT	NORMAL
COLOR	Cloudy	Colorless, straw-colored
Viscosity	Absent	High
Cell count	57,000 WBCs 94% Neutrophils	<150 WBCs
Glucose	28	0-10
Crystals	Negative	Negative
Gram stain	Gram negative diplococci	Negative

Which of the following is the first line management of choice?

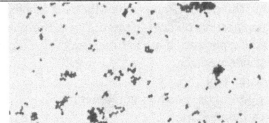

    a. IV Nafcillin
    b. IV Vancomycin
    c. IV Ceftriaxone
    d. IV Penicillin G
    e. IV Azithromycin

84. A 5-year-old boy is brought to the pediatric clinic with a five-day history of nonproductive cough, runny nose, stuffy nose and sneezing. This has progressed to severe coughing fits that can occur spontaneously or when he yawns sometimes accompanied by posttussive vomiting. On physical examination, you notice that when the child coughs, there is a whooping sound on inspiration. Which of the following is the most likely etiologic agent?

    a. Haemophilus influenza type B
    b. Bordetella pertussis
    c. Paramyxovirus
    d. Parainfluenza type B
    e. Coxsackie virus

85. A 54-year old male is admitted for a knee replacement. 2 days after the surgery, he suddenly develops tachycardia, tachypnea, pleuritic chest pain and shortness of breath. A D-dimer is obtained and is elevated. Which of the following radiograph findings are classic for this disorder?

    a. Hampton's hump
    b. hyperinflation of the lung
    c. Kerley B lines
    d. companion lines
    e. reticular-nodular honeycombing pattern

86. Which of the following is considered the first line long-term management for mild, persistent asthma?

    a. inhaled albuterol
    b. inhaled salmeterol
    c. inhaled fluticasone
    d. ipratropium and albuterol
    e. oral prednisone

87. In evaluation of a patient, which of the following values would be most consistent with a patient chronic hepatitis B?

	HB surface antigen	HB surface antibody	HB core antibody	HB envelope antigen	HB envelope antigen
A.	NEGATIVE	POSITIVE	POSITIVE (Ig G)	NEGATIVE	NEGATIVE
B.	POSITIVE	NEGATIVE	POSITIVE (Ig G)	NEGATIVE	NEGATIVE
C.	POSITIVE	NEGATIVE	Positive (Ig M)	POSITIVE	NEGATIVE
D	NEGATIVE	POSITIVE	NEGATIVE	NEGATIVE	NEGATIVE
E.	NEGATIVE	NEGATIVE	POSITIVE (Ig M)	NEGATIVE	NEGATIVE

88. A 44-year-old male presents to the emergency room with severe sharp, stabbing pain behind the right eye. The patient states the episodes last about an hour on average and happens a few times a day over the last month. The patient states when the pain comes, it is associated with runny nose, tearing of the eye and nasal congestion on the affected side. The pain seems to be worse with alcohol and at night. He is currently experiencing a painful episode now. Which of the following is the treatment of choice for the current symptoms?
   a. verapamil
   b. 100% oxygen via nonrebreather mask
   c. carbamazepine
   d. sumatriptan
   e. propranolol

89. Which of the following is an indication for the administration of 300 micrograms of RhoGAM (Rh immunoglobulin)?
   a. Rh positive mother and Rh negative father
   b. Rh negative mother and Rh negative father
   c. Rh positive mother and RH status of the father unknown
   d. Rh negative mother and Rh status of the father unknown
   e. Rh positive mother and RH positive father

90. An 18-year-old Caucasian male presents with testicular pain, a negative Prehn's test, a negative cremasteric reflex and the absence of the "blue dot" sign. No testicular masses are palpated. Which of the following is the most likely diagnosis?
   a. torsion of the appendix of the testicle
   b. epididymitis
   c. orchitis
   d. testicular torsion
   e. testicular cancer

91. A 24-year old woman is complaining of fatigue, joint pain and intermittent fever. On returning from Jamaica, she developed an erythematous rash that spares the nasolabial folds. She is otherwise healthy and is not currently on any medications. A preliminary chest radiograph shows a pleural effusion. Which of the following is considered the screening test in this patient based on her symptoms?
   a. anti-histone antibodies
   b. anti-nuclear antibodies
   c. anti-Ro antibodies
   d. rheumatoid factor
   e. anti-mitochondrial antibodies

92. A 34-year-old woman presents with extreme pain to the left wrist after falling on an outstretched hand. She sustained a triquetral fracture and was placed in a splint. She states that 7 days later, she had a gradual onset of lightning-shock sensations of the left arm, intermittent left arm color changes with increased nail and hair growth on the left upper extremity. Which of the following is the most likely diagnosis?
   a. Mononeuritis multiplex
   b. Complex regional pain syndrome
   c. Acute arterial insufficiency
   d. Raynaud's phenomenon
   e. Chronic peripheral arterial disease

93. Which of the following medications have been known to increase the incidence of myasthenic crisis?
   a. edrophonium
   b. gentamicin
   c. azathioprine
   d. prednisone
   e. neostigmine

94. A 32-year-old male is being managed for status epilepticus in which repeated doses of lorazepam fails to break the seizure. Which of the following is the next most appropriate step in the management of this patient?
   a. continue giving lorazepam until the seizure breaks
   b. begin IV phenytoin
   c. begin IV phenobarbital
   d. cool the patient to decrease the muscle contraction
   e. perform a prolactin level

95. A 42-year old male was involved in a car accident and came to the hospital in cardiac arrest. The patient was intubated during the arrest. After about 2 weeks of being in the intensive care unit, he develops oxygen desaturation. A portable chest radiograph shows a right lower lobe pneumonia. Which of the following is the most appropriate management of this patient?
   a. azithromycin
   b. doxycycline
   c. ceftriaxone + azithromycin
   d. metronidazole
   e. piperacillin/tazobactam + gentamicin

96. A 45-year-old patient with a recent bout of sepsis is thought to have developed acute respiratory distress syndrome. Which of the following is most consistent with the acute respiratory distress syndrome?
   a. Pulmonary capillary wedge pressure >18 mm Hg
   b. PaO_2/FIO_2 < 200mm Hg on ABG
   c. Increased B-type natriuretic peptide
   d. rapid response to oxygen therapy
   e. normal chest x ray

97. A 32-year old male wants to make an appointment to see a psychiatrist because he is very concerned about how his habits are affecting his relationship. He states he is a perfectionist who feels he must have complete order and control or else things don't go right. He states that he is a "complete stickler for the rules" and finds it very frustrating to complete a project if the rules are not strictly adhered to. He states he does not feel anxious or depressed at this time. Which of the following is the first line management of this condition?
   a. Propranolol (Inderal)
   b. Sertraline (Zoloft)
   c. Nortriptyline (Pamelor)
   d. Lithium (Lithobid)
   e. Psychotherapy

98. A 23-year-old female comes in for medical evaluation. She states "I feel fine but my dance company requires I gets a medical evaluation in order to continue dancing with them". Physical examination reveals lanugo, salivary gland hypertrophy, and multiple dental erosions. She states she has a normal appetite but watches what she eats carefully to avoid becoming overweight. She states she uses laxatives to help prevent obesity. Laboratory evaluation reveals BUN: creatinine ratio of 25:1, an increased TSH level and hypokalemia. Her body mass index is 16 kg/m^2 with a body weight <70% of ideal weight. Which of the following is the most likely diagnosis?
   a. Bulimia nervosa
   b. Factitious disorder (Munchausen syndrome)
   c. Anorexia nervosa
   d. Binge eating disorder
   e. Conversion disorder

99. An 8-year-old African-American male was seen by his pediatrician for a lesion near his lips described as fluid-filled blisters that ruptured spontaneously, leaving behind honey-colored crusts. He was treated with mupirocin topically. 2 weeks later, he returns with his mother to the pediatrician because she was worried that he had 3 episodes of scanty "cola-colored" urine and puffiness to his eyes especially in the morning. Which of the following most likely be seen in this patient?
   a. positive cytoplasmic anti-neutrophil cytoplasmic antibodies (C-ANCA)
   b. positive anti-streptolysin titers
   c. positive perinuclear anti-neutrophil cytoplasmic antibodies (P-ANCA)
   d. positive anti glomerular basement membrane antibodies
   e. positive IgA deposits in the mesangium

100. A 43-year-old otherwise healthy female has been having recurrent episodes of episodic dull chest pain that usually occurs at rest or awakens her at night. She denies any pain currently and is asymptomatic. Chest radiology shows no acute cardiopulmonary disease. A 12 lead electrocardiogram shows normal sinus rhythm at 88 beats per minute with no ST-T wave changes. An exercise stress test is performed and showed no acute ST depressions, ST elevations of T wave inversions. Which of the following is the most likely diagnosis?
   a. acute pericarditis
   b. stable angina
   c. unstable angina
   d. prinzmetal's angina
   e. Non ST elevation myocardial infarction

QUESTION 1

Choice B (metronidazole 2g orally x 1 dose) is the correct choice. *Frothy, green-yellow discharge and small punctate petechiae on the cervix (strawberry cervix) are classic for trichomoniasis.* The management of choice is Metronidazole. REPRODUCTIVE – TRICHOMONIASIS – PHARMACOLOGY (p. 260).

Choice A (Clindamycin) is used in the management of bacterial vaginosis,

Choice C (Ceftriaxone) is used in the management of gonorrhea.

Choice D (azithromycin) is used in the management of chlamydia.

Choice E (cephalexin) is used in the management of cellulitis.

QUESTION 2

Choice C (anterior shoulder dislocation) is the correct choice. *Anterior shoulder dislocations are the most common type of shoulder dislocation.* The *shoulder is often held in abduction and external rotation* with loss of the deltoid prominence (leading to a squared-off shoulder since the humeral head is dislocated anterior and inferior). MUSCULOSKELETAL – ANTERIOR SHOULDER DISLOCATION – MOST LIKELY (p. 164).

Choice A (*Adhesive capsulitis – Frozen shoulder*) is *shoulder stiffness* due to inflammation not trauma. There is no shoulder deformity in patients with adhesive capsulitis.

Choice B (*Posterior dislocation*) most commonly presents with prominence of the humeral head posteriorly. It is usually due to severe trauma or seizures and the hand may be *held in adduction* instead of abduction.

Choice D (*Grade III shoulder separation*) is a rupture of both the acromioclavicular and the coraclavicular joints, which would lead to *significant joint widening, tenting of the skin and a deformity at the AC joint*, not the deltoid area. With shoulder separations, there may be associated ecchymosis if there is soft tissue injury.

Choice E (luxatio erecta) is an *inferior dislocation* that is rare (<1% of all shoulder dislocations). It has a dramatic presentation as the patient presents with the arm *HYPERabducted and locked higher than their head* as if they were raising their hand.

QUESTION 3

Choice C (Endomysial antibodies) is the correct answer. *Celiac disease is due to an autoimmune reaction to gluten* (gluten hypersensitivity). The endomysium is the layer of connective tissue that surrounds the muscle fiber. Tissue transglutaminase is contained in the endomysium and these antibodies are classically associated with Celiac disease. In addition *dermatitis herpetiformis*, a papulovesicular rash (hence the name herpetiformis), is thought to be caused by epidermal transglutaminase antibody deposition. These antibodies destroy the intestinal villi, leading to malabsorption symptoms worsened after eating gluten-containing foods.
GI/NUTRITION – CELIAC DISEASE – MOST LIKELY (p. 148).

Choice A (*smooth muscle antibodies*) are classically associated with *autoimmune hepatitis* and cirrhosis.

Choice B (*P-ANCA*) is classically associated with *ulcerative colitis, microscopic polyangiitis, primary sclerosing cholangitis and Churg-Strauss,* none of which are described in this vignette.

Choice D (*Anti-mitochondrial antibodies*) are seen with *primary biliary cirrhosis.*

Choice E (*ADAMTS 13 antibodies*) are antibodies against the protein that cleaves von-Willebrand factor, leading to large multimers that causes the hemolytic anemia seen in *thrombotic thrombocytopenic purpura*. It presents with the *pentad of fever, neurologic signs, thrombocytopenia, hemolytic anemia and renal failure.*

QUESTION 4
Choice A (ototoxicity and nephrotoxicity) is the correct choice. Streptomycin is an aminoglycoside. Remember that ami**NO**glycosides primarily cover gram **N**egative **O**nly (most reliable for gram negative coverage unless added with another antibiotic) and side effects are **N**ephrotoxicity and **O**totoxicity.

Choice B (*hepatitis and peripheral neuropathy*) are classically seen with *isoniazid (INH).*

Choice C (*optic neuritis*) is seen with *Ethambutol (think E for Eyes).*

Choice D (*orange colored secretions*) are classically seen with *Rifampin.*

Choice E (*photosensitive dermatitis or hyperuricemia*) is seen with *pyrazinamide.*

QUESTION 5
Choice C (Myerson's sign) is the correct answer. Myerson's sign a sustained blink when the bridge of the nose is tapped repetitively in patients with Parkinson's disease.
NEUROLOGY – PARKINSON'S DISEASE – HISTORY AND PHYSICAL EXAMINATION (p. 353).

Choice A (*Lhermitte's sign*) and Choice E (*increased deep tendon reflexes*) are seen often in patients with *Multiple sclerosis.* They usually present with weakness, optic neuritis and upper motor neuron signs.

Choice B (an *intentional tremor that predominantly affects the head, neck and voice*) is the classic description of *essential familial tremor.*

Choice D (*positive ice pack test*) is a test often done in the emergency room in patients suspected of having *myasthenia gravis.* An ice pack is placed over the eye and will cause improvement of the weakness. The classic symptoms of myasthenia gravis include ❶ *ocular symptoms: diplopia* (double vision), ptosis (droopy eyelids); ❷*generalized weakness* including respiratory muscle weakness and ❸ *bulbar weakness*: slurred speech & dysphagia.

QUESTION 6
Choice D (rigid eye shield and immediate ophthalmology consult) is the correct choice. This is a classic presentation of a *globe rupture*, which is ophthalmologic emergency. *A rigid shield is placed to protect the eye from further damage.* EENT – GLOBE RUPTURE – CLINICAL INTERVENTION (p. 225).

QUESTION 7
Choice E (decreased urine osmolarity) is the correct answer. SIADH is associated with increased ADH secretion, which leads to free water overload. This leads to increased urine osmolarity as water is reabsorbed in the collecting tubule via ADH activation. GENITOURINARY – SIADH – BASICS (p. 325).

The increased ADH causes increased free water reabsorption, leading to an isovolemic hypotonic hyponatremia (Choice A) and (Choice C). There is usually the absence of peripheral edema because the edema is usually prevented by the renal sodium loss (Choice B).

QUESTION 8
Choice D (fenofibrate) is the correct answer. This patient has an isolated hypertriglyceridemia. *Fibrates are the most effective drug to lower triglyceride levels* (up to 60% reduction). CARDIOLOGY – FIBRATES – PHARMACOLOGY (p. 51).

Choice A *(simvastatin) is the best drug to lower LDL.*   It can reduce triglyceride levels between 10-20%. Statins have been shown to be cardioprotective.

Choice B *(cholestyramine) is used to reduce LDL levels.* Side effects of the bile acid sequestrants *include increases in triglyceride levels, and thus, may worsen this patient's elevated triglyceride levels.* Bile acid sequestrants are usually used to lower LDL in patients with normal triglyceride levels.

Choice C (ezetimibe) is used to lower LDL levels.

Choice E (nicotinic acid) is the second best drug to reduce triglyceride levels (between 20-50% reduction). *Nicotinic acid is the best drug to increase HDL* and, like statins, have been shown to decrease cardiovascular risk.

QUESTION 9
Choice D (bulimia nervosa) is the correct answer. Bulimia nervosa is characterized by *binge eating and purging*. These patients tend to be *normal weight or overweight*. The patient in this vignette has a normal BMI.

Choice A (*body dysmorphic disorder*) is characterized by an *excessive preoccupation that a body part (or slight anomaly) is deformed, which often causes them to be ashamed.*

Choice B (*anorexia nervosa*) is the refusal to maintain a normal body weight. These patients have a *BMI of <17.5.*

Choice C (*focal neurological disorder/conversion disorder*) is a *loss of motor or sensory neurologic function suggestive of a physical disorder but caused by psychological factors.*

Choice E (binge eating disorder) is *binge eating without the associated purging* seen in bulimia nervosa.

QUESTION 10
Choice A (Dactylitis) is the correct answer.   Dactylitis due to microthrombosis is the most common initial presentation of sickle cell in infants and young children. All of the other choices are also possible presentations in patients with sickle cell disease. HEMATOLOGY – SICKLE CELL DISEASE – HISTORY AND PHYSICAL (p. 457).

QUESTION 11
Choice C (dermatitis herpetiformis) is the correct answer. Dermatitis herpetiformis is an autoimmune disorder strongly associated with celiac disease (due to IgA immune complex deposition in the dermal papillae). It is characterized by a papulovesicular rash most commonly seen on the extensor surfaces, including both forearms and the scalp.   Management of the rash includes dapsone and a gluten-free diet.
DERMATOLOGY– DERMATITIS HERPETIFORMIS – MOST LIKELY (p. 405).

Choice A (*varicella zoster reactivation*) otherwise known as *"shingles"* is characterized by *grouped vesicles on an erythematous base usually along one dermatome.*

Choice B (*Molluscum contagiosum*) is a benign viral infection (poxvirdae family) most commonly seen in children, sexually active adults and patients with HIV infection. It is classically characterized by *multiple, dome-shaped, flesh-colored to pearly white, waxy papules with central umbilication. Curd-like material may be expressed* from the center of the papule if squeezed.

Choice D (coxsackie virus infection) is associated with hand foot and mouth disease and is usually seen in children less than 5 years of age.

Choice E (*pyogenic granuloma*) also known as lobular capillary hemangioma, is a *solitary, glistening, friable red nodule or papule often seen especially after trauma*. There is an increased incidence in pregnancy (and can be seen in the gingiva in these patients). The name is a misnomer because it is not pyogenic (pus forming) nor is it a granuloma.

QUESTION 12

Choice D (Aspirin and intravenous immunoglobulin) is the correct answer. Kawasaki disease is most common in children under the age of 5. It usually presents with fever rash, bilateral non-suppurative conjunctivitis and cervical lymphadenopathy. *Aspirin & intravenous immunoglobulin decreases cardiovascular complication risk.*

Choice A (Azithromycin) and Choice B (Penicillin VK) are not used in the management of Kawasaki as it is not due to bacterial infection.

Choice B (Aspirin) is used in the management of Kawasaki disease but studies have shown the combination of aspirin and intravenous immunoglobulin have been shown to decrease the cardiovascular complications associated with Kawasaki.

Choice E (Corticosteroids) can be used as a second line management in patients refractory to aspirin and intravenous immunoglobulin.

QUESTION 13

Choice E (mitral valve prolapse, tall stature, arachnodactyly, pectus carinatum, joint laxity, ectopia lentis) is the correct answer. CARDIOLOGY – MARFAN'S SYNDROME – HISTORY AND PHYSICAL EXAMINATION (online chapter)

Choice A (low set ears, flat facial features, upslanting palpebral fissures, single transverse palmar crease) are classically seen in patients with Trisomy 21 (Down syndrome).

Choice B (mitral valve prolapse, tall stature, hyperextensible joints, a long and narrow face, prominent forehead and chin, large ears, and macroorchidism) is associated with Fragile X syndrome.

Choice C (short stature, webbed neck, prominent ears, a broad chest with hypoplastic, widely-spaced nipples) is seen with Turner's syndrome.

Choice D (mitral valve prolapse, smooth and doughy skin, easy bruisability, positive Metenier's sign) is seen with Ehlers-Danlos syndrome.

QUESTION 14

Choice B is correct. This vignette describes infective endocarditis. *The most common cause of subacute endocarditis is Streptococcus viridans*, which is a part of the normal oral flora. In patients with poor dentition or gingivitis, transient bacteremia with S. viridans causes subacute endocarditis. Subacute endocarditis most commonly affects the *mitral*, aortic, tricuspid and pulmonic valves (in order of frequency).
CARDIOLOGY – INFECTIVE ENDOCARDITIS – LABS/DIAGNOSTIC (p. 52).

Choice A is not the most common combination.

Choice C is seen in patients who are IV drug abusers (which this patient has no evidence of drug use).

Choice D *(Staphylococcus epidermis) is most commonly seen post operative infective endocarditis*. Staph epidermis is often a contaminate if a blood culture isn't performed correctly, but in the setting of symptoms, it can be a pathogen.

Choice E (enterococcus) is most common cause of endocarditis in post genitourinary procedures.

QUESTION 15

Choice D is the correct answer. *Amiodarone contains iodine, which may lead to hypothyroid lab values* (as seen in this vignette). CARDIOLOGY – AMIODARONE – PHARMACOLOGY (p. 480).

Choice A (*digoxin*) is associated with a *narrow therapeutic index and can cause GI, cardiac and neurological side effects.*

Choice B (*spironolactone*) is associated with side effects of *hyperkalemia, teratogenicity & androgen inhibition.*

Choice C (*hydrochlorothiazide*) side effects include *hyperuricemia, hypercalcemia and hyponatremia.*

Choice E (*beta blocker*) side effects include *impotence, depression, and 3rd degree AV block, worsening of congestive (decompensated) heart failure* (although it is used for heart failure that is not congestive).

QUESTION 16

Choice E (Legionella pneumophila) is the correct answer. Legionella pneumophila is not associated with person to person transmission. It is *most commonly transmitted from contaminated water sources* such as air conditioners or cooling towers. Patients classically present with *gastrointestinal symptoms*, such as nausea, vomiting and diarrhea. *Liver function tests are often elevated* and patients may be *hyponatremic* in severe disease. PULMONARY – LEGIONELLA PNEUMONIA – MOST LIKELY (page 101)

Choice A [*Chlamydia pneumophila* (pneumoniae)] usually presents with *atypical symptoms and sinusitis.*

Choice B (*Mycoplasma pneumoniae*) is the *most common cause of "walking pneumonia".* Atypical presentations include *bullous myringitis* and pharyngitis.

Choice C (*Pseudomonas aeruginosa*) is most commonly seen *in hospital-acquired pneumonia.*

Choice D (*Klebsiella pneumoniae*) is most commonly seen in *alcoholics and debilitated patients.* It is also associated with *cavitary lesions* on chest radiographs and *purple colored "currant jelly' sputum* production.

QUESTION 17

Choice B (lacunar infarct) is the correct answer. *Lacunar infarcts are caused by ischemia to the penetrating arterioles (especially in the pons and the basal ganglia). Hypertension and diabetes mellitus are important risk factors.* It can present with *pure sensory symptoms, pure motor symptoms, ataxic hemiparesis, and dysarthria* including the *clumsy hand syndrome* (weakness of the hand especially when the patient is writing). Chronic infarctions can cause *vascular dementia* (the second most common cause of dementia). CT scan findings with lacunar infarcts are *small punched-out hypodense lesions especially near the pons and the basal ganglia.*
NEUROLOGY – LACUNAR INFARCT – MOST LIKELY DIAGNOSIS (p. 360).

Choice A (*Parkinson disease*) is associated with *bradykinesia, resting tremor, postural instability and rigidity.* It does not present with small punched out lesions on CT scan.

Choice C (*Anterior cerebral artery infarct*) would present with *contralateral hemiparesis greater in the lower extremity than the upper, urinary incontinence and personality changes* (including abulia) often with *speech preservation.*

Choice D (*Posterior cerebral artery infarct*) usually present with *visual changes, ipsilateral cranial nerve deficits and contralateral muscle weakness, comas and drop attacks.*

Choice E (*middle cerebral artery infarct*) usually presents with *weakness in the upper extremity and the face more prominent than the lower extremity. Middle cerebral artery syndromes are the most common ischemic stroke type.*

QUESTION 18
Choice A (*convex lens-shaped bleed that does not cross the suture line*) is the correct answer. Fractures to the *temporal bone* are the most common predisposing factor to *middle meningeal artery rupture*, leading to an *epidural hematoma.* Because the bleeding is between the skull and the dural layer, *it cannot cross the suture line* (the outer dural layer is continuous with the periosteum of the skull). It causes a *convex/lens-shape bleed* as the arterial high-flow separates the dura from the skull.
NEUROLOGY – EPIDURAL HEMATOMA – LABS/DIAGNOSTIC STUDIES (p 361).

Choice B (*concave crescent-shaped bleed that crosses the suture line*) describes the classic finding of subdural hematomas. *Subdural hematomas are usually the result of tearing of the bridging veins especially in patients >65 years of age.* Because subdural hematomas are located between the dura and the arachnoid space, they can expand along the inside of the skull, crossing the suture lines. The bleeding follows the curve of the brain, leading to *concave/crescent-shape* appearance of the bleed.

Choice C (bleeding into the brain parenchyma) describes intracerebral hemorrhages. The *most common causes of intracranial hemorrhage are uncontrolled hypertension and arteriovenous malformations.*

Choice D (bleeding into the subarachnoid space) describes subarachnoid hemorrhages.

Choice E (*punched-out lesions near the basal ganglia*) describes *lacunar infarcts.* Over a period of time, these can cause vascular dementia (the second most common type of dementia).

QUESTION 19
Choice A (*acetazolamide intravenous*) is the correct choice. This is a classic presentation of *acute angle closure glaucoma*, which is due to closure of the angle, leading to *increased intraocular pressure* and subsequent *swelling of the optic disc.* Closure of the angle can be exacerbated by things that cause pupil dilation (closing off the angle) such as *dark environments or medications like anticholinergics (such as choice C – atropine) & sympathomimetics.* *Acetazolamide is considered first line management* as it reduces the production of aqueous humor and reduced intraocular pressure. Choice B (pilocarpine ophthalmic drops) are often used in acute angle closure glaucoma but initiated once the pressure is lowered (to prevent spasm).
EENT – ACUTE ANGLE CLOSURE GLAUCOMA – CLINICAL INTERVENTION (p. 229).

Choice D (prednisone orally) can be used for certain ocular disorders, particularly with posterior uveitis.

Choice E (dexamethasone) is not indicated in acute angle closure glaucoma.

QUESTION 20
Choice C (*Esophageal adenocarcinoma*) is correct. Chronic acidic contents in the esophagus of someone with longstanding GERD leads to the development of Barrett's esophagus (Choice A), Barrett's is the precursor to esophageal adenocarcinoma. Dysphagia especially to solids, weight loss and anemia make malignancy the likely cause. GI/NUTRITION – ESOPHAGEAL CARCINOMA – MOST LIKELY (p. 132).

Choice B (*diffuse esophageal spasm*) is a motility disorder, so both solids and liquids will cause spasm of the esophagus. The patient will often complain of *odynophagia with stabbing chest pain that is worse with hot or cold foods AND liquids.* It is not classically associated with weight loss and anemia.

Choice D (*Squamous cell carcinoma*) is not usually seen in the context of GERD. It is more likely seen in patients who drink alcohol or smoke (this patient does neither), making Choice C the better answer. Squamous cell carcinoma is the most common cause of esophageal worldwide, adenocarcinoma is the most common in the US.

Choice E (*Mallory Weiss Tears*) are due to *repeated vomiting or retching, causing superficial mucosal tears.* They may present with upper gastrointestinal bleeding.

QUESTION 21

Choice D (provides rapid relief of symptoms by smooth relaxation of the prostate and bladder neck) is the correct answer. Tamsulosin is an alpha-1 blocker that blocks the alpha-1 receptors in the prostate. Of all the alpha-1 blockers, *tamsulosin is the most uroselective. The alpha-1 blockers may also be used in patients with BPH and hypertension,* as alpha-1 blockade also causes peripheral blood vessel dilation, leading to a reduction in blood pressure. GENITOURINARY – BENIGN PROSTATIC HYPERTROPHY – PHARMACOLOGY (p. 337).

Choice A (alpha-1 agonist stimulating the alpha receptors on the bladder neck) is incorrect as Tamsulosin is an alpha-1 antagonist.

Choice B (inhibits conversion of testosterone to dihydrotestosterone), Choice C (suppresses prostate gland growth) and choice E (reduces the size of the prostate, increasing outflow of urine) describes the mechanism of action of the *5-alpha reductase inhibitors such as finasteride and dutasteride.*

QUESTION 22

Choice D (acute tubular necrosis) is the correct answer. ATN is the most common type of intrinsic kidney injury in hospitalized patients and is associated with *oliguria and an increase in BUN and creatinine.* Because there is direct tubular injury, it is associated with *epithelial cell or muddy brown casts,* reflecting the tubular cell injury. Damage to the tubule leads to *isosthenuria, the inability to concentrate urine* or reabsorb sodium, *leading to a fractional excretion of sodium >2% and a low specific gravity. Common causes of ATN include prolonged prerenal azotemia, contrast dye and aminoglycosides (such as gentamicin).*
GENITOURINARY – ACUTE TUBULAR NECROSIS – MOST LIKELY (p. 320).

Choice A (obstructive uropathy) would cause a postrenal azotemia. Since there is no direct cellular injury, it is not associated with cast formation.

Choice B (*acute interstitial nephritis*) is associated with an allergic or inflammatory response in the interstitium and is also an intrinsic form of kidney injury. It is associated with *white blood cell casts. Penicillin is a common cause of acute interstitial nephritis.*

Choice C (*acute glomerulonephritis*) is another type of intrinsic kidney injury but is associated with the formation of *red blood cell casts and dysmorphic red blood cells.*

Choice E (*prerenal azotemia*) is caused by decreased renal perfusion. This causes activation of the renin-angiotensin-aldosterone system (RAAS) to reduce the hypo perfusion. The release of aldosterone causes increased renal sodium reabsorption, leading to a *fractional excretion of sodium of <1%.* The increased ADH from RAAS activation leads to a concentrated urine with a *high specific gravity.*

QUESTION 23

Choice C (Osteosarcoma) is the correct choice. Osteosarcoma is the *most common malignant bone tumor.* It usually presents in adolescents and most *commonly metastasizes to the lungs.* On X ray, it classically shows up as a *"sunburst" appearance or a "hair on end"* appearance. MUSCULOSKELETAL – OSTEOSARCOMA – MOST LIKELY (p. 197).

Choice A (*Osteochondroma*) *is the most common BENIGN bone tumor* and begins in childhood (however in small amount of cases, it may precede chondrosarcoma). It appears on radiographs as a *pedunculated growth that grows away from the growth plate.*

Choice B (*Ewing's sarcoma*) is a malignant bone tumor that classically shows up on radiograph as a layered periosteal *"onion peel"* appearance.

Choice D (*Chondrosarcoma*) would have a *punctuate or ring and arc appearance* on radiographs.

QUESTION 24
Choice D (conduct disorder) is the correct answer. Conduct disorder is characterized by social and academic difficulty, lack of guilt and remorse, and defiance of authority. Patients tend to cause fights in school, set fires, steal, and will often show cruelty to animals. *40% of them will develop antisocial personality disorder as an adult* (choice A). PSYCH/BEHAVIORAL – CONDUCT DISORDERS – MOST LIKELY (p. 386).

Choice A (antisocial personality disorder) is a diagnosis of adults. It is characterized by a sharp deviation from the norms, values and laws of society. These patients easily violate the rights of others, and lack remorse. They will often have a history of criminal activity.

Choice B (*attention deficit hyperactivity disorder*) is characterized by *short attention span, easy distractibility and impulsivity.*

Choice C (*oppositional defiant disorder*) is characterized by a *persistent pattern of negative, hostile and defiant behavior towards adults.*

Choice E (*Asperger syndrome*) is a type of *autism* in which there is *impaired social interaction with restricted behavior and normal communication skills.*

QUESTION 25
Choice E (stimulates pancreatic beta cell insulin release in a non-glucose dependent fashion) is the correct answer. This describes the primary mechanism of action of the sulfonylureas. ENDOCRINE – SULFONYLUREAS – PHARMACOLOGY (p. 305).

Choice A (*decreases hepatic glucose production with no effect on the pancreatic beta cells*) describes the mechanism of action of the *biguanides, such as metformin.*

Choice B (*delays intestinal absorption of glucose*) describes the primary mechanism of action of the *alpha glucosidase inhibitors,* such as acarbose and miglitol.

Choice C (*increases insulin sensitivity at the peripheral receptor sites of adipose and muscle tissues*) describes the mechanism of action of the *thiazolidinedione class,* such as pioglitazone and rosiglitazone.

Choice D (*lowers blood sugar by mimicking incretin*) describes the mechanism of action of *glucagon-like peptide 1 agonists* such as exenatide and liraglutide.

QUESTION 26
Choice B (decreased serum iron) is the correct answer. *Hereditary hemochromatosis is a disorder of excess iron deposition in the parenchyma cells* of the heart, liver, pancreas and endocrine organs. It can lead to *heart and liver failure as well as pancreatic insufficiency.* It is associated with an *increased serum iron, increased ferritin, increased transferrin saturation and positive hemosiderin deposition.* It is also associated with the *C282Y HFE genotype.* HEMATOLOGY – HEMOCHROMATOSIS – LABS/DIAGNOSTIC STUDIES (p. 468).

QUESTION 27

Choice D (pseudogout) is the correct choice. The radiographs show *chondrocalcinosis (calcification of the cartilage),* which is a manifestation of calcium pyrophosphate disease. *Arthrocentesis will show positively birefringent rhomboid-shaped crystals.* MUSCULOSKELETAL – PSEUDOGOUT – MOST LIKELY (p 204).

Choice A (*Gouty arthritis*) is associated with *rat bite lesions.* Arthrocentesis shows *negatively birefringent needle-shaped crystals.*

Choice B (Rheumatoid arthritis) is associated with symmetric arthritis and joint narrowing as well as osteopenia.

Choice C (Osteoarthritis) is associated with subchondral cysts, sclerosis of the bone, and osteophytes

Choice E (Paget's disease) is associated with areas of sclerosis and areas of lucency with bone that is larger and less compact than normal bone.

QUESTION 28

Choice D (Babesiosis) is the correct answer. Dubbed as the *"Malaria of the Northeast"* because it is a *parasitic infection* seen most commonly in the *Northeast United States that infects red blood cells.* It can present with fever, chills, arthralgias and a hemolytic anemia. The classic diagnostic test in suspected Babesiosis is a *peripheral smear to look for the pathognomonic tetrads* of the organisms in the red blood cells. Babesiosis is transmitted by the *Ixodes tick (the same tick that is responsible for Lyme disease and Ehrlichiosis).*
INFECTIOUS DISEASE – BABESIOSIS – MOST LIKELY (p 427).

Choice A (*Ehrlichiosis*) is also a tick borne disease but it *infects the white blood cells.*

Choice B (*Infectious Mononucleosis*) is caused by *Epstein-Barr virus.* It *affects B cells, often causing an atypical lymphocytosis >10% on peripheral smear & an exudative pharyngitis c̄ posterior cervical lymphadenopathy.*

Choice C (Malaria) also affects the red blood cells. She denies any travel history to an area where Malaria is endemic.

Choice E (Typhus) is a rickettsial illness, which causes two types of illness:
1) epidemic typhus (caused By Rickettsia prowazekii) transmitted by flying squirrels and human body louse. It presents with arthralgia, back pain, delirium fever, headache and a rash (that starts on the trunk and spreads to the extremities but spares the palms, soles and the face).
2) Murine (endemic) typhus presents with similar symptoms transmitted by rat fleas. Typhus characteristically spares the face, palms and soles.

QUESTION 29

Choice D (hidradenitis suppurativa) is the correct answer. Hidradenitis suppurativa is a chronic disease of the apocrine follicles, characterized by clusters of abscesses and/or epidermoid cysts, especially affecting the groin and the axilla. DERMATOLOGY – HIDRADENITIS SUPPURATIVA – BASICS (p 401).

Choice A (*carbuncle*) describes *interlocking furuncles with multiple openings* to the abscesses with cellulitis. They are larger and usually more painful than furuncles.

Choice B (*folliculitis*) is a *superficial hair follicle infection* characterized by *singular or clusters of small papules with surrounding erythema.*

Choice C *(furuncle)* is a *deeper infection of the hair follicle* (in contrast to folliculitis, which is superficial).   It is characterized by a *tender nodule with fluctuant abscess and a central plug*.

Choice E (*Molluscum contagiosum*) is a benign viral infection (poxvirdae family) most commonly seen in children, sexually active adults and patients with HIV infection. It is classically characterized by *multiple, dome-shaped, flesh-colored to pearly white, waxy papules with central umbilication. Curd-like material may be expressed* from the center of the papule if squeezed.

QUESTION 30
Choice C (biopsy of the lesion) is the correct choice. *Vulvar carcinoma* has a peak incidence in the sixth decade. The *most common presentation is vaginal pruritus.* On physical examination, *crusted white or red ulcerative lesions are usually seen.* Definitive diagnosis by biopsy is recommended in suspected cases of vulvar carcinoma. REPRODUCTIVE - VULVAR CARCINOMA – CLINICAL INTERVENTION (p 259).

Choice A *(podophyllin topical)* is *used to treat genital warts* caused by human papilloma virus. Genital warts usually present as *flesh-colored lesions that when larger, can have a "cauliflower' appearance* to them. They don't usually cause dyspareunia.

Choice B (acyclovir) is the management for herpes simplex lesions. These lesions may be associated with pruritus. Herpes presents as *grouped vesicles on an erythematous base.* It does not usually cause dyspareunia.

Choice D *(fluconazole)* is an anti-fungal used to *treat vulvovaginitis caused by Candia albicans.* These lesions are usually intensely pruritic, but they present with *vaginal discharge* (which is absent in this vignette). If it presents with additional intertrigo, it causes a beefy red rash with satellite lesions.

Choice E (*sodium bicarbonate sitz bath or douches*) is the treatment for *cytolytic vaginitis,* caused by the overgrowth of lactobacilli. Cytolytic vaginitis usually presents with vaginal pruritus & burning with a nonodorous white to opaque discharge.

QUESTION 31
Choice B (a patient with a serum beta hCG >5,000) is the correct answer. Some *contraindications to the use of methotrexate include serum beta hCG >5,000, ruptured ectopic pregnancy (including fluid/blood in the peritoneal cavity), history of tuberculosis, the presence of fetal heart activity.* In these instances, laparoscopic salpingostomy and removal is recommended. REPRODUCTIVE – ECTOPIC PREGNANCY – PHARMACOLOGY (p 267).

Methotrexate can be used safely in all the other choices. Indications for methotrexate use are ectopic pregnancies in a hemodynamically stable patient (choice A), early gestation, gestation tissue measuring less than 4 cm, no fetal heart activity seen (Choice C) and beta hCG less than 5,000 (Choice B) or patients with no evidence of tubal rupture (Choice D).

QUESTION 32
Choice B (propranolol) is the correct answer. *Essential familial tremor is an autosomal dominant.* It is manifested by an *intentional tremor that is an action tremor of hands, forearms neck, head and voice.* The tremor classically *relieved with alcohol ingestion.* Otherwise, the neurological exam is intact. *Propranolol is a beta-blocker that reduces the tremor.* NEUROLOGY– ESSENTIAL FAMILIAL TREMOR – HEALTH MAINTENANCE (p 352).

Choice A (prochlorperazine) is a dopamine antagonist and is not routinely used in the management of Essential familial tremor.

Choice C (entacapone) is a catechol-O-methyltransferase inhibitor that prevents dopamine breakdown. It is used in the management for Parkinson's disease.

Choice D (levodopa/carbidopa) is the drug of choice for Parkinson's disease. It increases CNS dopamine.

Choice E (verapamil) is not used in the management of essential tremor.

QUESTION 33
Choice D (cerumen impaction) is the correct answer.   There are two types of hearing loss: 1) conductive & 2) sensorineural. Cerumen impaction causes conductive hearing loss. Conductive hearing loss is associated with the physical examination findings of sound lateralizing to the affected ear with bone conduction greater than air conduction. All of the other choices are associated with sensorineural hearing loss.
EENT – CERUMEN IMPACTION – HISTORY AND PHYSICAL EXAMINATION (p 233).

QUESTION 34
Choice B (left middle cerebral artery occlusion) is the correct answer. The hallmark of *middle cerebral artery occlusions are contralateral hemiparesis (weakness) with arm & face more pronounced than the lower extremities.* Left hemisphere dominant lesions can cause aphasia. Due to bilateral innervation of the forehead, patients are usually able to raise the eyebrows. NEUROLOGY – MIDDLE CEREBRAL ARTERY OCCLUSION – MOST LIKELY (p 360).

Choice A (*Bell's Palsy*) is a cranial nerve VII palsy that leads to *isolated unilateral facial weakness. The arms and the legs are not involved in Bell's palsy* because only the facial nerve is involved. In these patients, they are *usually unable to lift the eyebrow on the affected side.*

Choice C (*left posterior cerebral artery occlusion*) will result in *visual hallucinations, and "crossed symptoms"* – meaning ipsilateral cranial nerve deficits and contralateral muscle weakness, comas and drop attacks are also seen in posterior.

Choice D (left *anterior cerebral artery occlusion*) would result in *contralateral hemiparesis (weakness) that tends to be greater in the leg than the arm,* is associated with *urinary incontinence and abulia* (lack of will), personality changes.

Choice E (right middle cerebral artery occlusion) would cause left-sided symptoms instead of right-sided symptoms.

QUESTION 35
Choice C (bird breeder) is the correct answer. Hypersensitivity pneumonitis is an inflammatory reaction to an organic antigen (ex birds). Acute pneumonitis is classically associated with rapid onset of fever, chills and productive cough with chest tightness occurring 4-8 hours after exposure. Lung biopsy isn't necessary but when it is performed, it reveals micronodular interstitial involvement with poorly formed noncaseating granulomas.
PULMONARY – HYPERSENSITIVITY PNEUMONITIS – HISTORY AND PHYSICAL (p 90).

Choice A (ship builder) and Choice E (demolition repair) are associated with *asbestosis.* Lung biopsy will often show *linear asbestos bodies with protein and iron deposition.*

Choice B (coal worker) is not associated with the clinical prodrome given in this vignette.

Choice D (sandblaster) is associated with silicosis.

QUESTION 36

Choice D (propranolol) is correct. *Nonselective beta-blockers reduce portal pressure and hypertension* and is the *treatment of choice to prevent recurrent esophageal variceal bleeding episodes.* It is not, however, used in the acute management of bleeds. GI/NUTRITION – ESOPHAGEAL VARICES – CLINICAL INTERVENTION (p 131).

Choice A (transjugular intrahepatic portosystemic shunt) can reduce the portal pressure but it is not the first line management.

All the other choices are used in the acute management of bleeds, not for prophylaxis

QUESTION 37

Choice C (IV fluids, toradol, metoclopramide and tamsulosin) is the correct answer as it is the management of choice for *symptomatic kidney stones <5 mm, (it is associated with >80% chance of spontaneous passage).* Tamsulosin is an alpha blocker that relaxes the bladder neck, promoting urinary flow and easier passage of stones. GENITOURINARY – NEPHROLITHIASIS – CLINICAL INTERVENTION (p 339).

Choice A (Metoclopramide, toradol and nephrolithotomy) are indicated in patients with larger stones, struvite stones or if other less invasive modalities fail.

Choice B (IV fluids, metoclopramide and shock wave lithotripsy) may be used in stones larger than 7-mm to break them up to allow easier passage.

Choice D (IV fluids and uretoscopy with stent) may be used in patients with an obstructed or at-risk kidney.

Choice E (Alkalinization of the urine) can be used to help to dissolve uric acid stones because acidic urine favors the formation of uric acid stones.

QUESTION 38

Choice E (55%) is the correct answer. Using the "rule of 9's", this patient has burns (other than 1st degree):
both legs: 18 x 2 = 36
abdomen: 9
Chest   9
Groin   1

                 55
DERMATOLOGY – BURNS – BASICS (p. 403).

QUESTION 39

Choice A (low set ears, flat facial features, upslanting palpebral fissures, single transverse palmar crease) is the correct answer. These findings are classically seen in patients with Trisomy 21.
PEDIATRICS – DOWN SYNDROME – HISTORY AND PHYSICAL EXAMINATION (p. 498).

Choice B (mitral valve prolapse, tall stature, hyperextensible joints, a long and narrow face, prominent forehead and chin, large ears, and macroorchidism) is seen with Fragile X syndrome.

Choice C (short stature, webbed neck, prominent ears, a broad chest with hypoplastic, widely-spaced nipples) is seen with Turner's syndrome.

Choice D (mitral valve prolapse, smooth and doughy skin, easy bruisability, positive Metenier's sign) is seen with Ehlers-Danlos syndrome.

Choice E (mitral valve prolapse, tall stature, arachnodactyly, pectus carinatum, joint laxity, ectopia lentis) is associated with Marfan's syndrome.

QUESTION 40

Choice D (Borderline personality disorder) is the correct answer. Borderline personality disorder is characterized by failed long-term relationships, mood swings & "black and white" thinking with no middle ground. They often engage in reckless activity and may indulge in self-harm. PSYCH/BEHAVIORAL – BORDERLINE DISORDER – MOST LIKELY (p 380).

Choice A (histrionic personality disorder) is characterized by dramatic, overemotional, seductive, "attention-seeking" behavior.

Choice B (Narcissistic personality disorder) is associated with grandiose, often excessive sense of self-importance in which the patients feel they are special, entitled and require extra attention but they have a fragile sense of self esteem.

Choice C (dependent personality disorder) is characterized by dependent, submissive behavior in which the patient needs constant reassurance, relies on others and has intense discomfort when alone.

Choice E (avoidant personality disorder) is characterized by the desire for relationships but avoids the due to an "inferiority complex". These patients tend to be very shy, timid lack confidence and are very sensitive to criticism.

QUESTION 41

Choice A (squaring of the vertebral bodies) is the correct answer. The vignette is a classic for ankylosing spondylitis that leads to *stiffness to the back that is improved with exercise.* The hallmark *bamboo spine (squaring of the vertebral bodies)* is seen in these patients, leading to the stiffness.
MUSCULOSKELETAL – ANKYLOSING SPONDYLITIS – LABS/DIAGNOSTIC STUDIES (p 213).

Choice B (osteomyelitis) is associated with periosteal reaction and bone destruction as time continues.

Choice C (wedge shaped vertebral bodies) is associated with a vertebral fracture.

Choice D (slipping of the vertebrae over another) is associated with spondylolisthesis

Choice E (defect fracture of the pars interticularis) is associated with spondylolysis (the precursor to spondylolisthesis).

QUESTION 42

Choice C (Psoriasis) is the correct answer. Psoriatic arthritis is a seronegative spondyloarthropathy that is associated with psoriasis. X ray changes of joint destruction leads to a *"pencil in cup" deformity* seen on radiographs (which sometimes can look like rheumatoid arthritis but is negative for rheumatoid factor). MUSCULOSKELETAL – PSORIATIC ARTHRITIS – HISTORY AND PHYSICAL (p 213).

QUESTION 43

Choice D (Adenosine) is correct. Adenosine is the drug of choice for narrow complex SVT. Adenosine temporarily blocks the AV node, thereby terminating the reentry of the impulse.
CARDIOLOGY – SUPRAVENTRICULAR TACHYCARDIA – CLINICAL INTERVENTION (p. 14).

Choice A (synchronized cardioversion) is the treatment of choice for unstable tachycardia

Choice B (*unsynchronized cardioversion*) is used in the treatment of *pulseless ventricular tachycardia or ventricular fibrillation*.

Choice C (*amiodarone*) is the treatment of choice for *wide complex tachycardia* not narrow tachycardias.

Choice E (*atropine*) is an *anticholinergic drug* that would *increase the heart rate* not decrease it.

QUESTION 44
Choice E (Patent ductus arteriosus) is the correct answer. Patent ductus arteriosus classically presents with a *continuous, machinery murmur* heard loudest at the left upper sternal border.
CARDIOLOGY – PATENT DUCTUS ARTERIOSUS – HISTORY AND PHYSICAL EXAMINATION (page 44)

Choice A *(Still's murmur) is the most common innocent murmur.* It presents with an *early to mid systolic, musical, vibratory, noisy, twanging high-pitched murmur.* It is loudest in the inferior aspect of the left lower sternal border and apex.

Choice B (*Graham Steell murmur*) is a *high-pitched early diastolic murmur* best heard at the left upper sternal border accentuated with deep inspiration. The murmur is due to *pulmonary hypertension* and increased velocity. Deep inspiration increases the murmurs on the right side of the heart (due to the increased flow to the right side during inspiration to allow oxygenation of the inspired air).

Choice C (*Austin Flint murmur*) is a *mid to late diastolic rumble heard at the apex* thought to be due to the mixture of the retrograde (backward) blood from *aortic regurgitation* mixing with the forward flow of blood into the left ventricle. It is not heard in all patients with aortic regurgitation however.

Choice D (*Atrial septal defect*) is associated with a systolic ejection crescendo-decrescendo murmur at the pulmonic area. It is also associated with a *widely fixed, split second heart sound (S2).*

QUESTION 45
Choice D (the presence of mobile protozoa on wet mount) is the correct choice. Trichomoniasis is a pear-shaped flagellated *protozoa* that is sexually transmitted, causing a *copious frothy yellow-green discharge and cervical petechiae (strawberry cervix).* REPRODUCTIVE – TRICHOMONIASIS – LABS/DIAGNOSTIC STUDIES (p. 260).

Choice A (*positive spirochetes on Darkfield microscopy*) is the diagnostic tool for *syphilis.* Syphilis can present with a chancre, maculopapular rash, condyloma lata or gumma.

Choice B (the presence of *clue cells on wet mount with few lactobacilli*) is classic for *bacterial vaginosis.*

Choice C (the presence of copious amounts of lactobacilli) is classic for cytolytic vaginitis.

Choice E (the presence of *hyphae and yeast with potassium hydroxide application*) is classic for *candida vulvovaginitis, which is associated with a thick, white curd-like discharge.*

QUESTION 46
Choice E (3 hour glucose tolerance test) is the correct answer. The *3-hour glucose tolerance test is considered the gold standard test for gestational diabetes.* It is usually done as the *second step if the screening 50g oral glucose challenge test is positive.* ENDOCRINE– GESTATIONAL DIABETES – HEALTH MAINTENANCE (p. 269).

Choice A (hemoglobin A1c) determines the glucose status of the patient in the preceding 3 months before evaluation and so is not part of the standard screening protocol in gestational diabetes. Gestational diabetes is glucose intolerance that occurs during pregnancy (due to the placental release of human placental lactogen). Human placental lactogen makes the pregnant mother relatively insensitive to insulin, allowing more glucose availability for the developing fetus.

Choice B (*50-g, 1-hour glucose challenge test*) is the *initial screening test for gestational diabetes* at 24-28 weeks gestation. If positive, a confirmatory test is done via 3-hour challenge test (choice E).

Choice C (random fasting plasma blood glucose levels) is not the gold standard for gestational diabetes.

Choice D (ACTH stimulation test) is used for suspected cases of adrenocortical insufficiency. These patients lack cortisol and would consequently be hypoglycemic, not hyperglycemic.

QUESTION 47

Choice B (Listeria monocytogenes bacteremia) is the correct answer. Listeria monocytogenes is a non spore-forming endotoxin producing *gram-positive bacilli*. It is the third most common cause of meningitis and has an *increased incidence in the elderly and the young. Listeria infections occurring during the third trimester of pregnancy is frequently associated with the induction of premature labor, stillbirth and increased risk of listeriosis in those newborns* that survive. *Maternal infection most commonly occurs in the consumption of cold deli meats and unpasteurized dairy products (such as some cheeses). IV ampicillin is the drug of choice* (often combined with gentamicin for synergistic effect). INFECTIOUS DISEASE – LISTERIOSIS – MOST LIKELY (p 422).

Choice A (Streptococcus agalactiae bacteremia) also known as *Group B Streptococcus* is a very *common cause of bacteremia and meningitis in the newborn* and will also show up as *gram-positive cocci*. It is *part of the normal vaginal flora* and would be possible if she had a vaginal delivery. In this vignette, she had a cesarean making it less likely. In addition, the mother also had symptoms, indicating she was also infected prior to the birth making GBS less likely.

Choice C (Salmonella bacteremia) and choice E (Shigella) are gram-negative bacilli. The bacteria in this vignette are gram-positive cocci.

Choice D (Neisseria meningitidis bacteremia) are gram-negative diplococci. The bacteria in this vignette are gram-positive cocci.

QUESTION 48

Choice A (widening of the mediastinum) is the correct answer. This is the classic description of cutaneous anthrax with an *erythematous papule that develops a painless black eschar*. If inhalation anthrax is also present, the extensive lymphadenopathy causes the *classic widened mediastinum on chest radiography*. Aortic dissection is a much more common cause of a widened mediastinum. All the other choices are nonspecific findings. Anthrax is transmitted from cattle, horses, goats, sheep swine and wool. INFECTIOUS DISEASE – ANTHRAX – MOST LIKELY (p. 425).

QUESTION 49

Choice D (pseudomonas aeruginosa) is the correct answer. Pseudomonas often proliferates in the soles of tennis shoes and has an increase incidence of infections in puncture wounds through tennis shoes.
INFECTIOUS DISEASE – PSEUDOMONAS – BASICS (p. 424).

Choice A (*Haemophilus ducreyi*) is the causative agent of *chancroid*.

Choice B (Enterococcus species) can be a cause of bacteremia, urinary tract infections in patients with indwelling catheters and patients in an inpatient setting as well as endocarditis.

Choice C (Streptococcus agalactiae) also known as Group B streptococcus is part of the vaginal flora and can cause infections in newborns via passage through the canal.

Choice E (Bartonella henselae) is the causative agent of cat scratch disease.

QUESTION 50

Choice D (Increased partial thromboplastin time) is the correct answer.   Thrombotic thrombocytopenic purpura is a disorder of platelets.   Platelets are part of the primary coagulation pathway.   Because the secondary coagulation is not involved, it is associated with a normal prothrombin time and partial thromboplastin time. HEMATOLOGY – THROMBOTIC THROMBOCYTOPENIC PURPURA – LABS/DIAGNOSTIC STUDIES (p 461).

Choice A (Decreased ADAMTS 13) is the pathologic cause of TTP. ADAMTS 13 is a von Willebrand factor cleaving protein. With low levels, there are large Von Willebrand multimers, leading to the pentad of microangiopathic hemolytic anemia and shistocyte formation (Choice C), thrombocytopenia, kidney failure, neurologic symptoms (Choice B) and fever.

QUESTION 51

Choice E (proteinuria of greater than 3.5g/day) is the correct choice. Nephrotic syndrome is defined as *proteinuria >3.5g/day in association with hypoalbuminemia, hyperlipidemia and edema.* All of the other choices are associated with nephritic syndrome (acute glomerulonephritis).   GENITOURINARY – NEPHROTIC SYNDROME – BASICS (p 317).

QUESTION 52

Choice D (chest pain lasting 55 minutes) is the correct answer. Acute coronary syndrome (which includes unstable angina, non ST elevation MI and ST elevation MI) is classically associated with *chest pain that lasts more than 30 minutes and is often not relieved with rest or multiple trials of sublingual nitroglycerin.* All of the other choices are nonspecific and can be seen in both stable and unstable angina.   CARDIOLOGY – UNSTABLE ANGINA – BASICS (p 23).

QUESTION 53

Choice C (pericardiocentesis) is the correct answer. The presentation of *Beck's triad: systemic hypotension, muffled heart sounds (pericardial effusion) and increased jugular venous distention* are hallmark for *pericardial tamponade.* The first line management is *pericardiocentesis.* Needle decompression removes the fluid in the pericardium that is reducing the cardiac output, improving hemodynamics. CARDIOLOGY – CARDIAC TAMPONADE – CLINICAL INTERVENTION (page 32).

Choice A (chest tube thoracostomy) can be used for pneumothorax or hemothorax.

Choice B (pericardial window) can be used to prevent recurrent pericardial effusions but rapid removal of the pericardial fluid via pericardiocentesis is the first line management.

Choice D (pericardiectomy) is used in the management of constrictive pericarditis.   The removal of the pericardium stops the pericardium from restricting ventricular filling.

Choice E (administration of IV furosemide) is not the management in this patient. The patient is hypotensive so any further reduction in blood volume may worsen the hemodynamics.

QUESTION 54

Choice B (pterygium) is the correct choice. A pterygium is a fleshy triangular mass that grows on the nasal side of the conjunctiva.
EENT – PTERYGIUM – HISTORY AND PHYSICAL EXAMINATION (p 224).

Choice A (*retinoblastoma*) is *most commonly seen in children* and would present with visual changes as well as with the *absence of a red reflex.*

Choice C (*pinguecula*) is a *painless nodule on the conjunctiva that does not grow.*

Choice D (hordeolum) is a painful localized lump on the eyelid margin.

Choice E (chemosis) is an allergic reaction of the conjunctiva, which presents with an edematous conjunctiva.

QUESTION 55
Choice B (Ludwig's angina) is the correct answer.   Ludwig's angina presents with swelling and erythema to the upper neck and chin and examination of the mouth will often reveal pus on the floor of the mouth.
EENT – LUDWIG'S ANGINA – BASICS (p 239).

Choice A (*Vincent's angina*) also known as *"trench mouth"* is an acute necrotizing ulcerative gingivitis causing *profuse gingival bleeding, severe gingival pain and interdental papilla with ulcerative necrosis.*

Choice C (acute herpetic tonsillopharyngitis) is the primary manifestation of Herpes Simplex Virus infection in adults. It presents as vesicles that rupture, leaving ulcerative lesions with grayish exudates in the posterior pharyngeal mucosa.

Choice D (*peritonsillar abscess*) is classically associated with *dysphagia, pharyngitis, a muffled "hot potato" voice, difficulty handling oral secretions and trismus. The abscess often will displace the uvula to the contralateral side.*

Choice E (infectious mononucleosis) is associated with posterior lymphadenopathy and exudative pharyngitis.

QUESTION 56
Choice E (pancreatic carcinoma) is correct.   The patient has pancreatic type pain (*abdominal pain radiating to the back*). The *weight loss and anorexia* is also more consistent with a malignancy. *Courvoisier's sign (a palpable nontender gallbladder) is a classic sign of pancreatic cancer* due to obstruction of the biliary tree from the malignancy, also causing jaundice. GI/NUTRITION – PANCREATIC CARCINOMA – MOST LIKELY (p 146).

Choice A (colorectal cancer) has a different presentation. *Right-sided colon cancer usually presents with bleeding and anemia, whereas left sided colon cancer presents later with changes in stool diameter.*

Choice B (*Acute cholecystitis*) is associated with a *large TENDER gallbladder* (Murphy's sign is sudden inspiratory arrest during palpation of the gallbladder due it being tender). Cholecystitis does not affect the rest of the biliary tree, so cholecystitis is not associated with jaundice.

Choice C (*Acute cholangitis*) is associated with the *triad of fever, right upper quadrant pain and jaundice.*

Choice D (Acute pancreatitis) presents classically with abdominal pain that radiates to the back.

QUESTION 57
Choice A (chronic hepatitis C infection) is the correct answer.   *Lichen planus* is an idiopathic, cell-mediated dermatologic rash classically associated with the *5P's: the rash is usually purple in color, polygonal (irregularly shaped and bordered, planar (plaques), pruritic, papular with fine scales.* Patients often have nail dystrophy.   Oral involvement may include *Wickham striae* (lesions with lacy white to gray striae). There is thought to be an increased incidence in patients with chronic Hepatitis C infection.
DERMATOLOGY – LICHEN PLANUS – HISTORY AND PHYSICAL (p 390).

Choice B (*Epstein Barr infection*) causes infectious mononucleosis and may cause a *maculopapular rash in patients with mononucleosis who are given ampicillin.*

Choice C (Group A beta hemolytic strep) can cause a diffuse erythematous rash with numerous small papular elevations, giving it a "sandpaper" feel. This rash can be seen in children with scarlet fever.

Choice D (Paramyxovirus) is associated with the development of *rubeola (measles).* The classic description is a Morbiliform (maculopapular) *brick-red rash* that *begins on the face and around the hairline*, progressing to the extremities. The rash of rubeola typically *lasts for 7 days.*

Choice E (Togavirus) is associated with the development of *rubella (German measles).* The classic description is a pink to *light red, spotted, maculopapular rash on the face* that progresses to the extremities. The rash of rubella typically *lasts about 3 days.*

QUESTION 58
Choice D (serotonin antagonist) is the correct answer. Serotonin blockade is the primary mode of *ondansetron and it is the antiemetic drug of choice for chemotherapy-related vomiting.* Serotonin, histamine, acetylcholine and dopamine can trigger the emetic centers of the brain and the GI tract. Blockage of these neurotransmitters are used in the treatment of emesis. GI/NUTRITION – ANTIEMETICS – PHARMACOLOGY (p 488).

Choice A (dopamine agonists) can cause vomiting.

Choice B (dopamine blockers) can be used in the management of emesis. Drugs that work in this fashion include metoclopramide, prochlorperazine, and promethazine.

Choice C (anticholinergic) and Choice E (antihistamine) describes the mechanism of action of the antihistamines such as meclizine, diphenhydramine. *Antihistamines have anticholinergic properties.*

QUESTION 59
Choice A (Toxic epidermal necrolysis) is the correct answer. *TEN is a cutaneous reaction that is most commonly seen after drug eruptions* (ex sulfa drugs, anticonvulsant medications) and certain infections (such as mycoplasma, HIV, herpes simplex virus infections) and malignancies. It can also be idiopathic. It usually begins with sore throat, myalgias and fever. It progresses to widespread *ulcerative lesions and blisters in the mucous membranes.* These symptoms progress with the development of erythematous, pruritic macules on the skin associated with *epidermal detachment and sloughing off of the skin (positive Nikolsky's sign).* *It involves more than 30% total body surface area involved.* Steven Johnson syndrome (Choice D) is a milder form that involves less than 10% of the total body surface area. DERMATOLOGY – TOXIC EPIDERMAL NECROLYSIS – MOST LIKELY (p 393).

Choice B (erythema multiforme major) is a type IV hypersensitivity reaction that classically presents with a dusty violet or red purpuric lesions with macules, vesicles or bullae in the center, giving it a classic target appearance *(target lesion).* There are two types. Erythema multiforme minor (choice E), which is characterized by the target lesion with the absence of mucosal involvement and Erythema multiforme major (the involvement of ≥1 mucous membranes, including oral, genital and ocular mucosa. The absence of target lesions in this vignette makes these two less likely.

Choice C (Morbiliform drug rash) is the most common type of cutaneous drug reaction. It is characterized by a generalized distribution of "bright-red" macules and papules that coalesce to form plaques.   It is not associated with the appearance of target lesions.

CHOICE 60

Choice C (acute stress disorder) is the correct answer. *Acute stress disorder meets most of the criteria for posttraumatic stress disorder but the symptoms occur less than 1 month from the event* (as in this vignette). The symptoms of PTSD occur in a patient exposed to a traumatic event with a response of helplessness, dissociative symptoms and avoidance of associated stimuli. The trauma is often experienced in recollections, nightmares that can resurface the feelings as if it were happening again. The fact the symptoms are less than 1 month makes this presentation acute stress disorder. PSYCH/BEHAVIORAL DISORDERS – ACUTE STRESS DISORDER – MOST LIKELY (p. 375).

Choice A (generalized anxiety disorder) is characterized by excessive anxiety or worries a majority of the days in a 6-month period.

Choice B (panic attack) is an acute episode of intense fear or discomfort developing abruptly often reaching a peak in 10 minutes.

Choice D (post traumatic disorder) occurs in a patient exposed to a traumatic event with a response of helplessness, dissociative symptoms and avoidance of associated stimuli. The trauma is often experienced in recollections, nightmares that can resurface the feelings as if it were happening again. The symptoms must be present for more than 1 month for the diagnosis to be made. This patient has symptoms for only 3 weeks.

Choice E (conversion disorder) is a loss of motor or sensory function suggestive of a physical disorder but caused by psychological factors.

QUESTION 61

Choice D (Serotonin syndrome) is the correct answer. *Serotonin syndrome is a potentially life-threatening condition due to increased serotonin activity.* It is usually due to the potentiation between 2 serotonergic drugs (in this case, the interaction between *Venlafaxine and the herb St. John's Wort*). Serotonin syndrome is characterized by *autonomic dysfunction including tachycardia, blood pressure fluctuations, hyperthermia, hyperreflexia, myoclonus, dilated pupils, agitation and a hyperactive GI tract* (due to the effect of serotonin on the enterochromaffin-like cells). *Management includes serotonin antagonists such as cyproheptadine* as well as *benzodiazepines for hyperthermia* (it reduces the hyperthermia-causing muscle contractions).
NEUROLOGY – SEROTONIN SYNDROME – MOST LIKELY (p 370).

Choice A (*Neuroleptic malignant syndrome*) is a condition seen due to decreased dopamine activity in patients on *dopamine antagonists* (such as anti-psychotic medications). It can also present with hyperthermia but these patients tend to be hyporeflexive, develop urinary incontinence, and they *lack the pupil findings and diarrhea that is classic for serotonin syndrome.*

Choice B (acute dystonia) describes the *reversible extrapyramidal symptoms that usually occur in hours to days after the initiation of dopamine-blocking antipsychotics* (especially 1st generation anti-psychotics). The extrapyramidal symptoms include intermittent spasms, trismus, protrusions of the tongue, facial grimacing, torticollis, and difficulty speaking.

Choice C (*Tardive dyskinesia*) is a *long-term complication of chronic dopamine antagonist use.* Repetitive, involuntary movements mainly of the extremities and the face such as *lip smacking, teeth grinding and rolling of the tongue* characterizes tardive dyskinesia.

Choice E (panic attack) is an acute episode of intense fear or discomfort, developing abruptly and often reaching a peak in 10 minutes.

QUESTION 62

Choice C (verapamil) is the correct answer. Verapamil is the first line for prophylaxis of cluster headaches. NEUROLOGY – CLUSTER HEADACHES – CLINICAL INTERVENTION (p 357).

Choice A (amitriptyline) can be used for prophylaxis of migraine headaches.

Choice B (lithium) is used in the management of bipolar disorders.

Choice D (propranolol) can be used in the prophylaxis of migraine headaches.

Choice E (aspirin) is not first line in the management of cluster headaches.

QUESTION 63

Choice C (increased oligoclonal bands) is the correct answer. *Multiple sclerosis is an autoimmune inflammatory demyelinating diseases of the CNS white matter* that usually present with *weakness, optic neuritis and upper motor neuron signs*. It is associated with *increased CNS IgG production* and increased T lymphocyte activation. Oligoclonal bands are bands of immunoglobulins produced by plasma cells, reflecting immunoglobulin production in the central nervous system. Up to 90% of patients with multiple sclerosis have oligoclonal bands present during active disease. NEUROLOGY– MULTIPLE SCLEROSIS – LABS/DIAGNOSTIC STUDIES (p. 356).

Choice A [increased white blood cells (primarily lymphocytes) with decreased glucose] are reflective of fungal or tuberculosis meningitis.

Choice B (high protein with normal white blood cell count), also called albuminocytological dissociation, is the classic CSF findings in patients with Guillain Barré syndrome.

Choice D [high protein with increased white blood cells (primarily polymorphonuclear neutrophils) with decreased glucose] is the classic CSF finding in bacterial meningitis.

Choice E [normal glucose with increased white blood cells (primarily lymphocytes)] are the classic findings in viral meningitis, aseptic meningitis

QUESTION 64

Choice D (Pyridoxine with doxylamine) Pyridoxine (vitamin B6) & doxylamine (an antihistamine) is the most effective management for hyperemesis gravidarum. REPRODUCTIVE – HYPEREMESIS GRAVIDARUM – CLINICAL (p 271).

Choice A (observation and reassurance that the vomiting is due to oversensitivity to the hormones of pregnancy) is the treatment for morning sickness. Hyperemesis gravidarum is a severe form of morning sickness. In this vignette the patient has severe weight loss and metabolic alkalosis (vomiting hydrochloric acid from the stomach). Due to the severity, medical management is warranted.

Choice B (promethazine) and Choice C (dimenhydrinate) are antihistamines that may also be used in the management of hyperemesis gravidarum but they are usually used as second line. Histamine receptors in the vomiting center help to trigger the act of vomiting, so antihistamines can be used as antiemetics.

Choice E (the administration of high protein foods with small frequent meal intake) is the preventative management or symptom reduction in patients with morning sickness or mild cases of hyperemesis gravidarum.

QUESTION 65

Choice C (Vibrio cholera) is correct answer. Vibrio cholera is associated worldwide with outbreaks. As a halophilic organism, it is most common in the Unites States in warm, salty waters (such as the Gulf coast) and associated with consumption of raw shellfish etc. It is a noninvasive organism, with stools described as grey in color with no fecal blood or pus. GI/NUTRITION – VIBRIO CHOLERA – MOST LIKELY (p 157).

Choice A (Campylobacter) is an invasive diarrhea and would be associated with a bloody diarrhea.

Choice B (Salmonella) is an invasive diarrhea commonly associated with the development of a bloody diarrhea. The diarrhea is often described as pea soup colored.

Choice D (Shigella) is an invasive diarrhea commonly associated with the development of a bloody diarrhea.

Choice E (Staphylococcus aureus) is noninvasive but it has a very short incubation period (1-6 hours from ingestion) before symptoms onset, so the delayed onset of symptoms would not be consistent with Staph aureus. Vomiting is also the predominant symptom in Staphylococcus aureus gastroenteritis and it is most commonly associated with dairy products such as meats, eggs, and mayonnaise.

QUESTION 66

Choice D (Zollinger Ellison Syndrome) is the correct answer. ZES is a neuroendocrine tumor (*gastrinoma)* that leads *gastrin hypersecretion* and *multiple peptic ulcer formation* (often refractory to treatment). The tumor can secrete histamine and other neuroendocrine hormones, leading to a secretory diarrhea that does not change with fasting. Secretin is an enzyme that is secreted by the duodenum that causes activation of pancreatic enzymes and inhibition of gastrin normally. *Gastrin secretion in gastrinomas is not inhibited by secretin. Gastrin levels are used as the screening test for ZES.* GI/NUTRITION – GASTRINOMAS – MOST LIKELY (p 135).

Choice A (H. pylori) is usually treated by triple therapy including a proton pump inhibitor and antibiotics. This leads to 90% healing of duodenal ulcers by 4 weeks and gastric ulcers by 6 weeks. Triple therapy often eradicates H. pylori infections. *Suspect either Zollinger Ellison or Gastric carcinoma in cases of refractory ulcers.*

Choice B is incorrect. Proton pump inhibitors work by inhibiting proton pump mediated hydrochloric acid secretion. One of the stimuli for gastrin production is hypochlorhydria. Because PPI's cause hypochlorhydria, gastrin levels are often elevated but would respond by decreasing in the setting of a secretin test.

Choice C (Atrophic Gastritis) is incorrect. Pernicious anemia is an autoimmune disorder in which there are antibodies against the parietal cell, leading to hypochlorhydria. The subsequent elevated gastrin levels (due to the G cell's attempt to increase hydrochloric acid production) is also responsive to secretin, and would lead to a decrease in gastrin production.

Choice E (Meckel's diverticulum) can cause ectopic gastric acid production and would be unaffected by secretin. But would classically present with abdominal pain, signs of obstruction and rectal bleeding.

QUESTION 67

Choice B (radical nephrectomy) is the correct answer.   Radical nephrectomy is the management of choice for localized renal cell carcinoma. GENITOURINARY – RENAL CELL CARCINOMA – CLINICAL INTERVENTION (p 338).

Choice A (chemotherapy) is not used in routine renal cell carcinoma as *renal cell carcinoma is often resistant to chemotherapy and radiation therapy* (Choice E)

Choice C (interleukin) may be used as adjunctive therapy in renal cell carcinoma.

Choice D (partial nephrectomy) is indicated in patients with bilateral kidney involvement or a patient with a solitary kidney to preserve renal function.

QUESTION 68
Choice E (Mallet Finger) is the correct choice. A *mallet finger is most commonly caused by a sudden blow to the finger with forced flexion*, which ends up *rupturing the extensor tendon*, leading to the *inability to extend the distal interphalyngeal (DIP) joint.* Sometimes when the extensor tendon ruptures, it may pull off a piece of the distal fracture, causing an avulsion fracture. MUSCULOSKELETAL – MALLET FINGER – MOST LIKELY (p 176).

Choice A (Jersey Finger) is the opposite of the Mallet finger. It is the inability to flex the distal interphalyngeal (DIP) joint due to avulsion of the flexor tendon (flexor digitorum profundus). The mechanism of injury is forced extension while the finger is in flexion.

Choice B (Boutonniere deformity) is a condition in where the PIP joint is in hyperflexion and the DIP joint is in hyperextension.

Choice C (Swan Neck deformity) is a condition where the PIP joint is in hyperextension and the DIP joint is in hyperflexion.

Choice D (Finger sprain) would cause pain (and possibly swelling) to the finger. The patient may not bend it due to pain but there is no loss of the ability to flex or extend the finger and it is not associated with a fracture.

QUESTION 69
Choice D (herniated disc at L4) is the correct answer. L4 disc herniation is associated with pain and paresthesias along the ANTERIOR aspect of the leg, weakness with ankle dorsiflexion and loss of knee jerk reflex. MUSCULOSKELETAL – HERNIATED DISC – HISTORY AND PHYSICAL (p 193).

Choice A (*vertebral compression fracture*) would cause *midline tenderness* at the L5 area.

Choice B (*herniated disc at S1*) is associated with pain and paresthesias along the *posterior aspect of the calf* and the *plantar surface of the foot with weakness with plantar flexion, loss of ankle jerk reflex and walking on toes more difficult than walking on the heels.*

Choice C (Lumbosacral strain) would cause pain and decreased range of motion but would *not be associated with neurological changes* such as paresthesias, numbness or weakness.

Choice E (Cauda Equina syndrome) is a complication of disc disease with compression at the *cauda equina leading to severe weakness and pain, saddle anesthesia, urinary or bowel incontinence*, loss of anal wink on physical examination. It is considered a surgical emergency.

QUESTION 70
Choice D (azithromycin) is correct. The fluid-filled blisters on the tympanic membrane is consistent with mycoplasma pneumonia. *The treatment of choice in general for Mycoplasma pneumoniae and empiric treatment for community acquired pneumonia is a macrolide or doxycycline*, but due to his age, choice A (doxycycline) would be inappropriate as tetracyclines have been known to cause permanent dental staining in children <8 year old. Had he been older, both A and D would have been acceptable. His age is the discriminating factor in this vignette.

Choice B is a fluoroquinolone and is not used in children under the age of 18 because it can interfere with articular cartilage formation and function (such as growth plate arrest). Even in adults, fluoroquinolones aren't used as first line empiric treatment for community acquired pneumonia. It reserved for treatment if there was a history of recent antibiotic use or in certain comorbid conditions.

Choice C (ceftriaxone) is inappropriate for the management of mycoplasma pneumonia. Ceftriaxone is a third generation cephalosporin (remember beta lactams work by inhibiting cell wall synthesis and mycoplasma pneumonia lacks a cell wall). This is why patients are given beta lactams with a macrolide for "atypical" additional coverage for organisms like mycoplasma, chlamydia and legionella.

Choice E is the management for community-acquired pneumonia in an admitted patient, not for outpatient treatment as ceftriaxone is given intravenously.

QUESTION 71
Choice A (chest tube thoracostomy) is the correct choice. The presence of a pneumothorax greater than 25-30% is treated with insertion of a chest tube.

Choice B (observation and oxygen therapy) is used for smaller pneumothoracies <20%

Choice C (insertion of a needle followed by chest tube) is the treatment for tension pneumothorax. There is no evidence of severe distress or a mediastinal shift on chest radiograph.

Choice D is adjunctive treatment for pneumothorax

Choice E (pleurodesis) is reserved for recurrent or malignant pleural effusions to obliterate the pleural space.

QUESTION 72
Choice A (bicuspid aortic valve) is the correct answer. Up to 70 percent of patients with coarctation of the aorta also have a bicuspid aortic valve. CARDIOLOGY – COARCTATION OF THE AORTA – BASICS (p 44).

QUESTION 73
Choice D (Takotsubo cardiomyopathy) is the correct answer. Takotsubo cardiomyopathy is a variant of dilated cardiomyopathy (often called the *Broken heart syndrome*). It is thought to follow an event that causes a *catecholamine surge* (ex emotional stress, family death, surgery). It is most common in menopausal women. They usually present with symptoms of acute coronary syndrome. *On ECG, it may show up as ST elevations* and/or T wave inversions with a mild elevation of cardiac enzymes. However, during the cardiac workup, the coronary arteries show no evidence of myocardial infarction. It classically shows up on *echocardiogram with left ventricular apical ballooning*. CARDIOLOGY – TAKOTSUBO CARDIOMYOPATHY – MOST LIKELY (p 36).

Choice A (unstable angina) is a type of acute coronary syndrome. It is not associated with apical ballooning.

Choice B (Brugada syndrome) is seen especially in Asian males. Often found incidentally, Brugada syndrome can lead to syncope, ventricular fibrillation and sudden cardiac death. The hallmark of Brugada syndrome is a right bundle branch pattern seen in V1 and V2 (it may often be incomplete), ST elevation in V1 through V3 (with a sharp down sloping pattern), and may have S waves in the lateral leads (I, aVL, V5 and V6). Management includes implantation of a cardioverter defibrillator to prevent sudden cardiac death.

Choice C (Takayasu arteritis) is a type of large vessel vasculitis that involves the aorta, the aortic arch and the pulmonary arteries. It may present with aneurysm formation, aortic dissection, lower extremity claudication and myocardial infarction. It most commonly affects young women.

Choice E (Restrictive cardiomyopathy) is increased ventricular rigidity leading to diastolic dysfunction with preserved systolic function. Because the ventricles are stiff and noncompliant, it leads to some back up of blood in the atria, leading to bilateral atrial enlargement evident on echocardiography.

QUESTION 74
Choice B (inhibits mast cell mediated degranulation in patients with exercise or cold air induced asthma) is the correct answer. This describes the mechanism of the mast cell modifiers nedocromil and cromolyn. PULMONARY – LEUKOTRIENE MODIFIERS – PHARMACOLOGY (p 78).

Choice A (blocks leukotriene-mediated neutrophil migration and smooth muscle contraction in patients with allergic asthma) describes the mechanism of action of leukotriene receptor antagonists such as montelukast, zafirlukast and zileuton.

Choice C (inhaled corticosteroid that blunts the immune system response) describes the mechanism of action of inhaled corticosteroids such as beclomethasone, flunisolide, and triamcinolone.

Choice D (anticholinergic that dilates the central airways in patients with acute asthma) describes the mechanism of action of ipratropium.

Choice E (beta 2 agonist that dilates the peripheral airways in patients with acute asthma) describes the mechanism of action albuterol, levalbuterol, terbutaline and epinephrine.

QUESTION 75
Choice E (cyclophosphamide) is the correct answer. Cyclophosphamide is associated with hemorrhagic cystitis and an increased risk of bladder cancer. Other side effects include: emesis, GI mucosal damage and syndrome of inappropriate anti diuretic hormone. HEMATOLOGY – CYCLOPHOSPHAMIDE – PHARMACOLOGY (p 495).

Choice A (cisplatin) is associated with emesis, neurotoxicity, renal failure and hypomagnesemia.

Choice B (doxorubicin) is associated with dilated cardiomyopathy, bone marrow suppression, gastrointestinal side effects and alopecia.

Choice C (gemcitabine) is associated with emesis, myelosuppression and hepatitis.

Choice D (5-fluorouracil) is associated with teratogenicity, dermatitis, photosensitivity, cardiotoxicity, and ocular toxicity.

QUESTION 76
Choice D (cimetidine) is the correct answer. Cimetidine is a histamine 2 receptor blocker. Compared to other drugs in this class, *cimetidine is associated with many side effects including: cytochrome P450 inhibition, and androgen inhibition (gynecomastia and impotence).* GI/NUTRITION – H2 BLOCKERS – PHARMACOLOGY (p 134).

Choice A *(misoprostol) is a prostaglandin E1 analog.* Side effects include cervical ripening & uterine contraction.

Choice B (sucralfate) is associated with many drug-drug interactions

Choice C (sorbitol) includes gastrointestinal side effects.

Choice E (omeprazole) is associated with diarrhea, headache, B12 deficiency, and hypomagnesemia.

QUESTION 77

Choice B (Tourette's syndrome) is the correct answer.   Tourette's syndrome is characterized by motor tics predominantly affecting the head, neck and face as well as repeating phrases (echolalia) or shouting out obscenities (coprolalia).   NEUROLOGY – TOURETTE'S SYNDROME – MOST LIKELY (p 354).

Choice A (Sydenham's chorea) is rapid, involuntary, jerky movements (as present in this vignette).   Sydenham's chorea is associated with rheumatic fever, which predominantly affects children ages 5-15 years old that had a recent Group A streptococcal infection.   It is not associated with coprolalia.

Choice C (Huntington's disease) is an autosomal dominant neurodegenerative disorder classically associated with the triad of ❶ initial behavioral changes then ❷ chorea and eventually ❸dementia.   The classic finding on CT scan is cerebral & caudate nucleus atrophy.   The caudate nucleus is part of the basal ganglia and as such can cause movement disorders such as chorea.   It typically manifests after 30 years of age (but may present at any age).

Choice D (Guillain Barré syndrome) is a demyelinating polyradiculopathy with symmetric lower extremity weakness that is usually greater than upper extremity weakness.   It is not classically associated with chorea.

QUESTION 78

Choice A (pyogenic granuloma) is the correct answer.   *Pyogenic granulomas* (also known as lobular capillary hemangioma) is a *solitary, glistening, friable red nodule or papule often seen especially after trauma.*   There is an increased incidence in pregnancy (and can be seen in the gingiva in these patients).   The name is a misnomer because it is not pyogenic (pus forming) nor is it a granuloma.   DERMATOLOGY – PYOGENIC GRANULOMA – MOST LIKELY (p 407).

Choice B (pyoderma gangrenosum) is a skin lesion commonly seen in patients with inflammatory diseases, such as Crohn's, ulcerative colitis, rheumatoid arthritis and spondyloarthropathies.   It is a misnomer as it is not infectious nor is it gangrenous.

Choice C (erythema nodosum) are painful, erythematous, inflammatory nodules seen especially on the anterior shins.   It is associated with estrogen exposure (ex pregnancy), sarcoidosis, tuberculosis, fungal infections (ex. Coccidiomycosis) as well as inflammatory disorders.

Choice D (malignant melanoma) lesions are associated with asymmetry, irregular borders, color variation, size usually >6 mm and may change in size and appearance rapidly.   It is the most common cause of skin cancer deaths.

Choice A (cellulitis) is an infection of the skin associated with warmth, tender erythema to the infected area with irregular borders.

QUESTION 79

Choice B (disseminated intravascular coagulation) is the correct answer.   DIC is a *pathological activation of the coagulation system, leading to widespread microthombi and a subsequent phase of severe thrombocytopenia.*   It is associated with thrombosis and widespread hemorrhages (ex. *spontaneous bleeding especially at venipuncture sites*).   Labs show an *increased PT, PTT and INR levels as well as a decreased fibrinogen level.*   It is common after gram-negative infections (such as Neisseria meningitis in this vignette).   Other causes include malignancies, obstetric complications, massive tissue injury, trauma, rocky mountain spotted fever, liver disease, aortic aneurysm and acute respiratory syndrome.   HEMATOLOGY – DISSEMINATED INTRAVASCULAR COAGULATION – MOST LIKELY (page 462)

Choice A (idiopathic thrombocytopenic purpura) is associated with an *isolated thrombocytopenia*.   Platelets are part of the primary coagulation pathway.   In ITP, there is no abnormality with the secondary pathway (clotting factors) so the PT, PTT and INR will be normal.

Choice C (*thrombotic thrombocytopenic purpura*) causes thrombocytopenia. Platelets are part of the primary coagulation pathway. In TTP, there is no abnormality with the secondary pathway (clotting factors) so the PT, PTT and INR should be normal.

Choice D (hemolytic uremic syndrome) causes thrombocytopenia. Platelets are part of the primary coagulation pathway. In HUS, there is no abnormality with the secondary pathway (clotting factors) so the PT, PTT and INR should be normal.

Choice E (Von Willebrand disease) causes ineffective platelet adhesion. Since Von Willebrand factor prevents Factor VIII degradation (which is part of the secondary intrinsic coagulation pathway), Von Willebrand disease is associated with a prolonged partial thromboplastin time (PTT). Prothrombin time (PT) and INR is usually unaffected.

QUESTION 80
Choice E (Noncontiguous, extranodal spread of the disease) is the correct answer. Non-Hodgkin lymphoma is associated with peripheral node involvement and *noncontiguous extranodal spread*. Burkitt's lymphoma is the only type of lymphoma associated with Epstein Barr Virus. All the other types on Non Hodgkin lymphoma are rarely associated with Epstein Barr Virus. All of the other choices are classically associated with Hodgkin lymphoma. HEMATOLOGY – NON-HODGKIN LYMPHOMA – HEALTH MAINTENANCE (Page 471).

QUESTION 81
Choice E (hyponatremia) is the correct answer. In diabetes insipidus, patients may develop hypernatremia if they are not able to maintain the increased water intake needed to offset the loss of large amounts of dilute urine. Diabetes insipidus is either central (no production of ADH) or nephrogenic (insensitivity to ADH). Both will lead to a large volume of dilute urine production with low specific gravity (Choice B), decreased urine osmolarity (Choice D) and an increased thirst due to the loss of volume. Unless severe, these patients are usually euvolemic. GENITORURINARY – DIABETES INSIPIDUS – BASICS (p 301).

QUESTION 82
Choice C (decreased calcium, decreased PTH levels, increased phosphate levels) is the correct answer. The symptoms the patient is experiencing correspond with hypocalcemia. *The most common cause of hypocalcemia is primary hypoparathyroidism. The most common cause of primary hypoparathyroidism is removal of the parathyroid glands during thyroid surgery.* Parathyroid hormone functions to increase serum calcium levels so decreased parathyroid hormone leads to hypocalcemia. In the kidney, parathyroid hormone is responsible for calcium reabsorption and phosphate excretion, so patients with primary hypoparathyroidism will develop increased serum phosphate. ENDOCRINE – HYPOPARATHYROIDISM – LABS/DIAGNOSTIC (p 291).

Choice A (*increased calcium, increased PTH levels, decreased phosphate levels*) is most commonly seen with *primary hyperparathyroidism*. Hyperparathyroidism presents with signs & symptoms of hypercalcemia.

Choice B (*decreased calcium, increased PTH levels, increased phosphate levels*) are the labs seen with *renal osteodystrophy*. In patients with chronic kidney disease, lack of vitamin D production leads to hypocalcemia. The resultant hypocalcemia will cause an increase in parathyroid hormone secretion in an attempt to increase calcium levels towards normal (secondary hyperparathyroidism – since the increased parathyroid hormone levels here are due to hypocalcemia). Because the kidney isn't working properly, renal phosphate excretion is diminished, leading to increased phosphate levels. The management of renal osteodystrophy includes phosphate binders (they supply calcium to manage the hypocalcemia while binding the excess phosphate). Please note that:

primary hyperparathyroidism:	secondary hyperparathyroidism of renal osteodystrophy:
↑PTH, ↑calcium & ↓phosphate	↑PTH, ↓calcium & ↑phosphate

QUESTION 83

Choice C (IV Ceftriaxone) is the correct answer. *Septic arthritis* is suggested in this vignette by the symptoms and the arthrocentesis *joint fluid analysis results of a white cell count greater than 50,000 with predominantly neutrophils.* The *most common cause of septic arthritis is Staphylococcus aureus*, which shows up as gram-positive cocci in clusters. *Neisseria gonorrhea is another common cause of osteomyelitis, particularly in young patients.* Neisseria gonorrhea is a gram-negative diplococcus (as seen in the gram stain in this vignette). IV Ceftriaxone is the drug of choice for septic arthritis caused by Neisseria gonorrhea.
MUSCULOSKELETAL – SEPTIC ARTHRITIS –CLINICAL INTERVENTION (p 196).

Choice A (IV Nafcillin) is an anti-staphylococcal penicillin and is used in suspected Staphylococcal or gram-positive infections. It is the drug of choice for suspected Staphylococcus aureus septic arthritis.

Choice B (IV Vancomycin) is used for gram-positive infections especially when methicillin-resistant Staphylococcus aureus (MRSA) is suspected. The gram stain in this vignette shows gram-negative diplococci.

Choice D (IV Penicillin G) can be used for non beta-lactamase producing gram-positive organisms, such as Staphylococcus aureus. It is the drug of choice for Neisseria meningitis (not Neisseria gonorrheae).

Choice E (IV Azithromycin) is not the first line treatment for septic arthritis.

QUESTION 84

Choice B (B. pertussis) is the correct choice. The coughing fits, whooping sound on inspiration and post tussive vomiting are hallmark of pertussis. PULMONARY – PERTUSSIS – MOST LIKELY (p 112).

Choice A (Haemophilus influenza type B) is more commonly seen with epiglottitis.

Choice C (Paramyxovirus) is associated with mumps, measles. RSV is included in the paramyxovirus family

Choice D (Parainfluenza type B) is associated with viral croup and a barking cough.

Choice E (Coxsackie virus) commonly cause hand foot and mouth syndrome in that age group especially Coxsackie A. Coxsackie B is more associated with myocarditis & pericarditis.

QUESTION 85

Choice A [Hampton's hump] is the correct choice. The vignette is a classic presentation of pulmonary embolism. *Hampton's hump* (wedge shaped infiltrate) and *Westermark's sign* (decreased vascular markings after the embolism) are both *classic* for PE (but are *not common*). *The most common X ray finding in pulmonary embolism is a normal X ray,* so a tachypneic patient with hypoxemia and a normal chest radiograph should raise the suspicion for possible pulmonary embolism.
PULMONARY – PULMONARY EMBOLISM – LABS/DIAGNOSTIC STUDIES (p 98).

Choice B (lung hyperinflation) is seen with obstructive disorders (due to air trapping).

Choice C (Kerley B) is classically seen with congestive heart failure.

Choice D (companion lines) is classically seen with pneumothorax

Choice E (reticular-nodular honeycombing pattern) is often seen in restrictive disorders or fibrotic disorders

QUESTION 86

Choice C (inhaled fluticasone) is the correct choice. Inhaled corticosteroids are the mainstay of treatment for the long-term management of chronic asthma.
PULMONARY – ASTHMA – PHRAMACOLOGY (p 78).

Choice A (*inhaled albuterol) is the treatment of choice for ACUTE exacerbation of asthma* not for long term asthma as it is short acting medication. The qualifier in this vignette is long-term management.

Choice B (inhaled salmeterol) is only used for long-term asthma. However its use has been associated with increased death from asthma and it is NEVER USED ALONE. It can be added to selected patients for long term asthma control in patients who need additional treatment after being placed on an inhaled corticosteroid.

Choice D (ipratropium and albuterol) can be used in patients for acute exacerbations. Albuterol is a beta 2 agonist that causes bronchodilation and ipratropium is an anticholinergic that also causes bronchodilation.

Choice E is used for the treatment of ACUTE exacerbation to reduce the inflammatory component of asthma and most patients with acute exacerbations should be placed on them. However, oral steroids are not first line in the management of long-term asthma.

QUESTION 87

Choice B is the correct answer. Whenever evaluating hepatitis, the quickest way is to look at surface antigen, surface antibody and the core antibody then look at the E if the person has acute or chronic to determine replication. Chronic hepatitis is defined as the presence of the Hepatitis B surface antigen (HBsAg) and the failure to develop the surface antibodies (HBsAb) in 6 months. Because the person has a chronic infection, the core antibody would be IgG (it would have already switched from making the acute IgM antibodies).

Choice A describes someone with a distant resolved infection. They developed the surface antibodies and the core antibodies.

Choice C denotes acute viral hepatitis, as the surface antigen is positive and the fact that the core is IgM (remember from immunology your body first starts making IgM pentamer antibodies before switching to IgG antibodies).

Choice D denotes successful Hepatitis B vaccination. The surface antibody is the only positive marker in vaccination. People often confuse this with someone with a distant resolved infection. But think of it this way, if you were infected with hepatitis B, then the virus would be destroyed by the macrophages, producing antibodies to surface proteins but also the viral core, so the core would be positive.

Choice E is the classic description of the window period. In someone who is infected, the window period describes the point where the surface antigen is disappearing (leading to a negative HBsAg) but the antibodies are not enough yet to be detected by testing (even though they will eventually increase). So the core IgM antibody is often the sole serologic marker in the window period.

QUESTION 88

Choice B (100% oxygen via nonrebreather mask) is the correct answer. The frequency of *"clusters" or bouts of headache, the stabbing periorbital pain and the ipsilateral manifestations of rhinorrhea, lacrimation etc. is hallmark for cluster headaches.* Cluster headache is one of the primary headaches (idiopathic). These headaches tend to be exacerbated at night and with alcohol. *High flow oxygen is the first line management in cluster headaches.* NEUROLOGY– CLUSTER HEADACHE – CLINICAL INTERVENTION (p 357).

Choice A (verapamil) is the first line management for prophylaxis of cluster headaches (to prevent a future bout). Since the question asked for current symptoms, oxygen is a better choice.

Choice C (carbamazepine) is first line for trigeminal neuralgia, not cluster headaches.

Choice D (sumatriptan) is a second line agent in terms of its use for cluster headaches.

Choice E (propranolol) may be used as prophylaxis in migraine headaches.

QUESTION 89

Choice D (Rh negative mother and Rh status father unknown) is the correct choice. In an Rh-negative mother & an Rh-positive father, there is a 50% chance the baby will be Rh-positive. *Rh alloimmunization occurs when the maternal antibodies of an Rh-negative mother binds to a fetus that is Rh-positive* (which he received from the father's genes). Rhogam (Rh immunoglobulin) is given to Rh-negative mothers if the father is R- positive or if the father's Rh type is unknown. REPRODUCTIVE – RH ALLOIMMUNIZATION – CLINICAL INTERVENTION (p 270).

QUESTION 90

Choice D (testicular torsion) is the correct answer. The *young age, negative Prehn's test* (no relief with elevation of the scrotum), *negative cremasteric reflex* are all suggestive of testicular torsion.
GENITOURINARY – TESTICULAR TORSION – MOST LIKELY (p 333).

Choice A (*torsion of the appendix of the testicle*) is classically associated with the presence of the *"blue dot"* sign, which is cyanosis of the appendix of the testicle.

Choice B (epididymitis) and choice C (orchitis) is classically associated with a positive Prehn's sign (relief of the scrotal pain with scrotal elevation) and a positive cremasteric reflex.

Choice E (*testicular cancer*) is not classically associated with testicular pain. The most common presentation of testicular is a nontender, palpable testicular mass

QUESTION 91

Choice B (anti-nuclear antibodies) is the correct choice. This is the classic description of systemic lupus erythematosus. *ANA is considered the screening test for SLE* (although it is not specific). Anti-double stranded DNA and anti-Smith antibodies are specific for SLE but not as sensitive as ANA. Patients with systemic lupus erythematosus often develop serositis (such as pleural effusions and pericarditis) and glomerulonephritis. MUSCULOSKELETAL – SYSTEMIC LUPUS ERYTHEMATOSUS – LABS/DIAGNOSTIC STUDIES (p 201).

Choice A (*Anti-Histone Ab*) is associated with *drug-induced lupus*. Drug-induced lupus may be seen with certain medications such as procainamide and isoniazid to name a few. The symptoms usually resolve after the discontinuation of the medications and is not associated with glomerulonephritis or the neurological symptoms seen in classic SLE. Keep in mind that patients may have more than one autoimmune disease and so the antibodies may overlap in clinical practice.

Choice C (anti-Ro antibodies) are seen in patients with Sjrogen's syndrome.

Choice D (Rheumatoid factor) is the screening test associated with rheumatoid arthritis.

Choice E (anti-mitochondrial antibodies) are associated with primary biliary cirrhosis.

QUESTION 92
Choice B (Complex regional pain syndrome) is the correct answer. Most commonly occurring after fractures or trauma *CRPS is autonomic dysfunction*, which initially leads to pain out of proportion to the injury. In its early stages, it is associated with autonomic changes, such as swelling, extremity color changes increased nail and hair growth. However in the later stages, it is associated with atrophic skin, hair, nail and muscle growth. MUSCULOSKELETAL – COMPLEX REGIONAL PAIN SYNDROME – MOST LIKELY (p 175).

Choice A (Mononeuritis multiplex) is a painful, asymmetrical, peripheral neuropathy affecting at least 2 nerve areas either simultaneously or sequentially (ex ulnar nerve and peroneal nerve). Eventually, it may become symmetrical. It is usually associated with vasculitis syndromes, autoimmune disorders, diabetes and amyloidosis (not trauma).

Choice C (Acute arterial insufficiency) is caused by acute arterial occlusion in a patient with chronic peripheral arterial disease. Classically associated with pain, paresthesias, pallor of the extremity, decreased pulses and poikilothermia.

Choice D (Raynaud's Phenomenon) is associated with vasculitis syndromes, autoimmune diseases and other vessel diseases. It is classically associated with tri-color changes of the extremities (red, white and blue) due to spasm.

Choice E (chronic peripheral arterial disease) is a manifestation of atherosclerotic vessel disease not trauma and would be associated with atrophic changes (such as decreased temperature, brittle nails and decreased hair growth – the opposite of what is seen in this vignette).

QUESTION 93
Choice B (gentamicin) is the correct answer. Certain drugs, such as beta blockers, fluoroquinolones and aminoglycosides may exacerbate myasthenia gravis. All the other choices can be used in the management of myasthenia gravis. NEUROLOGY – MYASTHENIA GRAVIS – HEALTH MAINTENANCE (p 355).

QUESTION 94
Choice B (begin IV phenytoin) is the correct answer. In the management of status epilepticus in which the patient is not responding to benzodiazepines, phenytoin is the next recommended step in the attempt to break the seizures followed by phenobarbital. NEUROLOGY – STATUS EPILEPTICUS – CLINICAL INTERVENTION (p 367).

Choice A (continue giving lorazepam until the seizure breaks) will not likely change the seizure if the patient is not responding to repeated doses.

Choice C (begin IV phenobarbital) is usually initiated after phenytoin fails to break the seizure.

Choice D (cool the patient to decrease the muscle contraction) is not the management of status epilepticus

Choice E (perform a prolactin level) is used to determine if someone is having a true epileptic seizures from non epileptic seizures. Prolactin elevations of at least threefold are associated with true epileptic seizures.

QUESTION 95
Choice E (piperacillin/tazobactam + gentamicin) is the correct answer. This patient acquired the infection in the hospital (nosocomial pneumonia). Despite the usual organisms, *you must cover for pseudomonas in nosocomial pneumonia.* Piperaclilin is an anti-pseudomonal penicillin and gentamicin is an anti-pseudomonal aminoglycoside.

Choice A (azithromycin) and Choice B (doxycycline) are both used for the treatment of community acquired pneumonia outpatient, not nosocomial pneumonia.

Choice C is the treatment of inpatient community acquired pneumonia (admitted to the hospital).

Choice D (Metronidazole) can be used to cover anaerobic organisms in suspected aspiration pneumonia.

QUESTION 96
Choice B (PaO2/FIO2 < 200mm Hg on ABG) is the correct choice. The hallmark of ARDS is *unresponsiveness to oxygen therapy and a low PaO2/FiO2 ratio.* The other component is *bilateral pulmonary infiltrates* (similar to heart failure). There is no cardiogenic pulmonary edema (so ARDS is associated with a normal or low pulmonary capillary wedge pressure) making choice A, D & E incorrect.

Choice C (Increased B-type natriuretic peptide) is associated with congestive heart failure

QUESTION 97
Choice E [Psychotherapy] is the correct answer. This is the classic description of obsessive-compulsive personality disorder. Psychotherapy is often considered first line therapy. Beta blockers (Choice A) may be used as adjunctive therapy if there is an anxiety component and SSRI's (Choice B) may be used as adjunctive therapy if there is a depression component.
PSYCH/BEHAVIORAL – OBSESSIVE-COMPULSIVE PERSONALITY DISORDER – HEALTH MAINTENANCE (p 381).

Choice C [Nortriptyline (Pamelor)] is used for depression disorders.

Choice D [Lithium] is used in the management of mania, bipolar disorders.

QUESTION 98
Choice C (Anorexia nervosa) is the correct answer. Anorexia nervosa is the refusal to maintain a normal body weight. These patients watch what they eat carefully to avoid becoming what they perceive is overweight. Despite their perception that they are overweight, they are, in actuality, underweight with a low BMI. Physical exam may reveal lanugo, salivary gland hypertrophy, and dental erosion.
PSYCH/BEHAVIORAL – ANOREXIA NERVOSA – MOST LIKELY (p 385).

Choice A (bulimia nervosa) is characterized by binge eating and purging. These patients tend to be normal weight or overweight.

Choice B (Munchausen syndrome) is an intentional, self-induced symptom or falsified physical or lab findings. This can include the seeking of multiple invasive procedures and operations even if the pose a serious life risk.

Choice D (binge eating disorder) is characterized by binge eating without the purging episodes characteristic of bulimia nervosa.

Choice E (conversion disorder) is a loss of motor or sensory neurologic function suggestive of a physical disorder but caused by psychological factors.

QUESTION 99

Choice B (positive anti-streptolysin titers) is the correct choice. This is a classic description of post streptococcus glomerulonephritis. It can occur with any infection, but Group A beta hemolytic streptococcus (Streptococcus pyogenes) infections such as strep pharyngitis or skin infections (this vignette describes the lesions of nonbullous impetigo). Glomerulonephritis is associated with hematuria and edema.
GENITOURINARY – POST STREP GLOMERULONEPHRITIS – LABS/DIAGNOSTIC (p 318).

Choice A (positive cytoplasmic anti-neutrophil cytoplasmic antibodies/C-ANCA) are seen in patients with *Wegener's granulomatosis* (granulomatosis with polyangiitis). The classic presentation is *necrotic upper respiratory tract involvement (including sinusitis), lower respiratory tract involvement, and rapidly progressing glomerulonephritis.*

Choice C (positive perinuclear anti-neutrophil cytoplasmic antibodies/P-ANCA) are associated with microscopic polyangiitis) and usually presents with signs and symptoms of vasculitis and lower respiratory tract involvement. P-ANCA can also be seen in Ulcerative Colitis, Churg-Strauss and Primary Sclerosing Cholangitis.

Choice D (positive anti glomerular basement membrane antibodies) are associated with Goodpasture syndrome. This classically presents with hemoptysis and glomerulonephritis.

Choice E (positive IgA deposits in the mesangium) presents usually after an upper respiratory tract or gastrointestinal infection.

QUESTION 100

Choice D (Prinzmetal's angina) is correct. Prinzmetal's angina is due to coronary vasospasm, leading to *transient* ST elevations, and a normal ECG in between episodes. The chest pain is classically nonexertional and often occurs at night and at rest. Ischemic disease would most likely show ECG changes (although 50% of patients with ischemic disease will have a normal resting ECG). A negative stress test and negative angiography are more likely seen in patients with Prinzmetal's angina, reflecting that the underlying problem is vasospasm not atherosclerosis. CARDIOLOGY – PRINZMETAL ANGINA – MOST LIKELY (p 27).

Choice A (*acute pericarditis*) is classically associated with chest pain that is *pleuritic* (sharp and worsened with inspiration), *persistent, postural* (relieved with sitting forward) and often associated with a *pericardial friction rub*. Pericarditis is also classically associated with *diffuse ST elevations* especially in the precordial leads, reflecting epicardial injury.

Choice B stable angina will often shows ST depressions (normal resting ECG in up to 50%) but a stress test would most likely induce chest pain or ST/T wave changes.

Choice C unstable angina would classically show ST depression and T wave inversions.

Choice E (Non ST elevation MI) would classically show ST depression and T wave inversions, as well as positive cardiac enzymes.

PHOTO CREDITS

PYOGENIC GRANULOMA
 Wellcome Trust Library / CustomMedical (Used with permission)

DERMATITIS HERPETIFORMIS 1
 Wellcome Trust Library / CustomMedical (Used with permission)

DERMATITIS HERPETIFORMIS 2
Science Photo Library / CustomMedical (Used with permission)

ANTHRAX
By Photo Credit: Content Providers(s): CDC [Public domain], via Wikimedia Commons

NEISSERIA GONORRHEA
 Mike Peres RBP SPAS / CustomMedical (Used with Permission)

1. A 36-year-old male is complaining of left thumb pain after falling onto his left thumb, causing forced hyperabduction of his thumb. On physical examination, there is increased laxity with varus stress testing of the left thumb. The following radiographs are obtained:

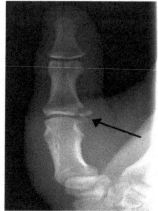

   Which of the following is the most likely diagnosis?
   a.   Rolando Fracture
   b.   Boxer's Fracture
   c.   Bennett's fracture
   d.   Skier's Thumb
   e.   Thumb dislocation

2. A 53-year-old male with a history of chronic bronchitis states he has had an increase in the production of mucus with a change in the quality of the mucus. He also complains of low-grade fever and sharp chest pain that worsens with inspiration. A chest radiograph is obtained and shows an infiltrate. Which of the following is the most likely the etiologic agent of his symptoms?
   a. Mycoplasma pneumoniae
   b. Staphylococcus aureus
   c. Haemophilus influenzae
   d. Pseudomonas aeruginosa
   e. Histoplasma capsulatum

3. A 20-year old female with a history of headaches presents to the clinic with a right-sided, pulsatile, throbbing headache associated with nausea, vomiting and photophobia. The patient states that prior to the onset of the headache, she experienced impairment of her speech and flashing lights that lasted for about 10 minutes. She states she experienced similar symptoms before. There are no neurologic deficits on physical examination and there is no papilledema seen on fundoscopic examination. Which of the following is the most likely diagnosis?
   a. common migraine
   b. cluster headache
   c. tension headache
   d. pseudotumor cerebri
   e. classic migraine

4. Which of the following is not a significant risk factor for the development of ovarian cancer?
   a. the presence of the BRCA 1 gene
   b. a history of infertility
   c. a history of nulliparity
   d. a history of Turner's syndrome
   e. a history of combined oral contraceptive use

5. A 35-year-old female presents with positive pain and paresthesias to the thumb, index and middle fingers. She states at times she has difficulty opening jars. Tinel's and Phalen's signs are positive. There is no evidence of thenar atrophy. Which of the following is considered the first line treatment?
   a. cubital tunnel release surgery
   b. carpal tunnel release surgery
   c. steroid injection into the affected area
   d. volar splint and naprosyn
   e. oral corticosteroids

6. A 44-year-old male presents to the urgent care center with a headache. In which of the following medical conditions is the use of sumatriptan contraindicated in the management of migraine headache?
   a. history of tension headache
   b. history of coronary artery disease
   c. history of cluster headache
   d. history of chronic obstructive pulmonary disorder
   e. history of obesity

7. A 62-year-old male with a history of type I diabetes mellitus and longstanding hypertension presents with abnormal gait, right sided weakness more pronounced in the right leg than in the right arm, abulia and urinary incontinence. The patient is able to raise both eyebrows and his speech is relatively preserved. Which of the following is the most likely diagnosis?
   a. Bell's palsy
   b. left middle cerebral artery occlusion
   c. left posterior cerebral artery occlusion
   d. left anterior cerebral artery occlusion
   e. right middle cerebral artery occlusion

8. A 23-year-old college student is seeking medical attention because he has been "down in the dumps" for the last 4 years. He states he has been feeling hopeless and "blue" every day for the last 4 years. He states he always has a constant state of tiredness. He states he has no goals or aspirations after graduating college and feels this way every day. He seems to have no enthusiasm about any aspect of his life although he is able to maintain a 4.0 grade average in school. Which of the following is the most likely diagnosis?
   a. Major depressive disorder
   b. Cyclothymia
   c. Persistent depressive disorder (Dysthymia)
   d. Bipolar disorder type I
   e. Social phobia

9. A 57-year-old male with a longstanding history of diabetes mellitus and early onset Alzheimer's dementia goes for his yearly physical to a new clinic. A urine dipstick is significant for 2+ protein but is otherwise normal. Upon looking at his old records. He had 1+ protein on dipstick last year. Which of the following is the next most appropriate test to perform in this patient?
   a. cystoscopy
   b. intravenous pyelogram
   c. spot urine albumin: creatinine ratio
   d. urine cytology
   e. 24 hour urine creatinine clearance collection

10. A 40-year-old female is brought into the emergency room by her sister after she had been "acting strange". Her sister said she was acting paranoid and confused all day. She states her sister kept complaining that she feels as if she is "being cut up by a butcher knife". She states her sister mentioned that she had recently seen her psychiatrist, who increased the dose of her medication but she was unsure the name of her sister's medication. On physical examination, her vital signs are as follows: temperature 102°F, heart rate of 120 beats per minute, respiratory rate of 20 breaths per minute, oxygen saturation of 98% on room air, with fluctuations in her blood pressure. She is diaphoretic and has noticeable stiffness of her neck and arms. Her neurologic exam is positive for decreased deep tendon reflexes and her pupils are normal. She had 2 episodes of urinary incontinence since her arrival but no diarrhea. Her ECG is normal. Which of the following is the most likely diagnosis?
   a.   amphetamine toxicity
   b.   serotonin syndrome
   c.   neuroleptic malignant syndrome
   d.   opiate toxicity
   e.   acute dystonia

11. In a hemodynamically stable patient with the following electrocardiogram, which of the following is considered the management of choice if vagal maneuvers fail to decrease the heart rate?

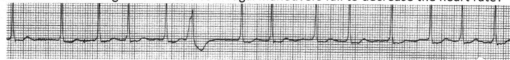

   a.   adenosine
   b.   unsynchronized cardioversion
   c.   synchronized cardioversion
   d.   amiodarone
   e.   verapamil

12. A 50-year-old obese female is complaining of multiple episodes of sharp, right upper quadrant pain that is worsened with fatty and fried foods. The patient states the pain radiates to the right shoulder. On physical examination, there is right upper quadrant tenderness, causing the patient to hold their breath in mid-inspiration. There is no fever or jaundice. Which of the following is the most appropriate test at this time?
   a.   Hepatobiliary iminodiacetic acid (HIDA) scan
   b.   Endoscopic retrograde cholangiopancreatography (ERCP)
   c.   Ultrasound of the gallbladder
   d.   Abdominal radiograph
   e.   Prothrombin and albumin levels

13. A 37-year-old male is being evaluated for psychotherapy. During the interview, he is found to have a very constricted, cold affect. He states he has a lack of emotional response to praise or criticism by his bosses or peers. He tends to prefer to be alone and states his family calls him a "hermit" because he stays home all the time. He seems to have problems sustaining long-term relationships because his partners feel he has no enjoyment in their relationships and he states he has difficulty "seeing the point of wasting my time interacting with other people". Which of the following is the most likely diagnosis?
   a.   social phobia
   b.   schizoid personality disorder
   c.   schizotypal personality disorder
   d.   schizophrenia
   e.   paranoid personality disorder

14. A 43-year-old male presents to the ophthalmology clinic with pain to the lower left eyelid that started 4 days ago and has become increasingly painful. On physical examination, there is tenderness and inflammation around the nasal side of the lower lid and medial canthus. There is no ocular pain with eye movements. Which of the following is the most likely diagnosis?
- a. blepharitis
- b. hordeolum
- c. chalazion
- d. dacrocystitis
- e. septal cellulitis

15. A 72-year-old Caucasian woman with a history of Hashimoto's thyroiditis presents to the emergency room with altered mental status. Her vital signs are as follows: blood pressure 100/60 mmHg, Heart rate: 50 beats per minute, respiratory rate 9 breaths/minute and oxygen saturation of 98% on room air. Myxedema coma is suspected. Which of the following is not considered part of the routine management in this patient?
- a. administration of IV dexamethasone
- b. administration of IV levothyroxine
- c. administration of IV normal saline
- d. rapid rewarming of the patient
- e. obtain a TSH level and free T4 level

16. A 6-year-old girl presents to the clinic with a rash and joint pain. Her mother states her symptoms started two weeks ago with fever, sore throat and an erythematous rash that her mother states felt like "sandpaper" which spontaneously resolved. She became concerned because she developed this new rash, which did not look like the previous rash. On physical examination, there is a macular, erythematous, nonpruritic, annular rash with rounded, sharply demarcated edges, no central clearing and the rash blanches with pressure. The rash is seen on the back and the chest, but spares the face. In addition, there is the presence of firm, painless lumps on the dorsum of the hands and shins. Which of the following is the most likely diagnosis?
- a. erythema migrans
- b. erythema nodosum
- c. erythema marginatum
- d. erythema multiforme
- e. erythema infectiosum

17. Which of the following is the first line management of melasma (chloasma)?
- a. topical hydroquinone
- b. topical corticosteroids
- c. topical diphenhydramine
- d. topical ketoconazole
- e. oral hydroxychloroquine

18. A 7-year-old girl presents to the pediatric clinic with sore throat, nonproductive cough and fever for 48 hours. On physical examination, her temperature is 39°C (102.2°F), there are positive exudates on her tonsils as well as positive anterior cervical lymphadenopathy. There is also an erythematous, blanching, "sandpaper rash" and a strawberry tongue. How many of the Centor criteria are present in this patient?
- a. two
- b. three
- c. five
- d. six
- e. seven

19. A 42-year old male with a history of HIV infection presents to the emergency room with headache and neck stiffness. A head CT shows no evidence of acute intracranial bleed, brain masses or mass effect. A lumbar puncture is performed and shows the following:

    Opening pressure: mildly increased
    Protein: increased
    Glucose: decreased
    WBC count: increased with predominantly lymphocytes

    Based on the findings which of the following would be ordered to determine the most likely diagnosis?
    a. Tzanck smear
    b. Lactate dehydrogenase levels
    c. India ink preparation
    d. Antistreptolysin titers
    e. Cold agglutinin test

20. Which of the following is not seen in anemia of chronic disease?
    a. Normochromic red blood cells
    b. Mean corpuscular volume of 90 fl (normal 80 – 100 fl)
    c. Decreased serum ferritin
    d. Decreased serum iron
    e. Decreased total iron binding capacity

21. A 60-year-old male with a history of benign prostatic hypertrophy is diagnosed with hypertension. He begins hypertensive therapy to help with both conditions and develops dizziness when he tries to stand. His wife states that she took his blood pressure at the time and recorded it as 90/60 mm Hg. Which of the following medication was the patient most likely prescribed?
    a. lisinopril
    b. prazosin
    c. verapamil
    d. nicardipine
    e. metoprolol

22. A patient being managed for peptic ulcer disease develops dark-colored stools and a dark colored tongue. Which of the following medications is the most likely cause of these symptoms?
    a. sucralfate
    b. bismuth salicylate
    c. cimetidine
    d. misoprostol
    e. diphenoxylate

23. A 14-year-old male comes in for a wellness visit. On cardiac examination, there is a systolic ejection crescendo-decrescendo murmur best heard at the left upper sternal border with a loud first heart sound and a widely fixed split second heart sound that does not vary with respirations. Blood pressure in the right arm is 120/80 and the left arm 125/80. Carotid and femoral pulses are 2+. Which of the following is the most likely diagnosis?
    a. coarctation of the aorta
    b. patent ductus arteriosus
    c. atrial septal defect
    d. aortic stenosis
    e. aortic regurgitation

24. In addition to bimanual pelvic examination and transvaginal ultrasonography, which of the following is the most useful tumor biomarker for epithelial cell ovarian cancer?
    a. Carcinogenic embryonic antigen
    b. CA-125
    c. beta subunit of the human chorionic gonadotropin
    d. human placental lactogen
    e. alpha fetoprotein

25. A 57-year-old male with no significant past medical or smoking history was found to have an incidental peripheral mass on chest radiograph. Biopsy of the lesion shows a malignancy. Based on the patient's history, which of the following is the most likely diagnosis?
    a. bronchioloalveolar carcinoma
    b. small cell (oat cell) carcinoma
    c. large cell (anaplastic) carcinoma
    d. adenocarcinoma
    e. squamous cell carcinoma

26. Which of the following is the most common physical exam finding in a patient with suspected acute pulmonary embolism?
    a. respiratory rate >20/min
    b. accentuated second heart sound
    c. pulse rate of >100
    d. sweating
    e. cyanosis

27. Which of the following is not recommended in the management of gastroesophageal reflux disease?
    a. elevate the head of the bed after eating to reduce reflux of esophageal contents
    b. smoking cessation
    c. avoid recumbency immediately after eating
    d. reduce alcohol intake
    e. increase fat intake to increase gastrointestinal transit

28. A 34-year-old male is brought into the clinic because his family is concerned. The family states they noticed for the last few months he has had some behavioral and cognitive changes. They began to worry because he developed rapid involuntary arrhythmic movements of his hands and face with facial grimacing. A CT scan is performed and shows cerebral and caudate nucleus atrophy. Which of the following is the most likely diagnosis?
    a. Parkinson's disease
    b. Tourette's syndrome
    c. Sydenham's chorea
    d. Tardive dyskinesia
    e. Huntington's disease

29. A 68-year-old male with longstanding history of uncontrolled diabetes mellitus is thought to have proliferative retinopathy.   Which of the following fundoscopic eye examination findings most reliably depicts proliferative retinopathy?
   a. new abnormal blood vessels
   b. papilledema
   c. flame-shaped hemorrhages
   d. hard exudates in a circinate pattern
   e. cotton wool spots

30. A 36-year-old male presents with a 4-week history of pain along the radial side of the right wrist that radiates to the forearm. He states the pain is worse with gripping. A positive Finkelstein test is seen on physical examination. Which of the following is the most likely diagnosis?
   a. Flexor tenosynovitis
   b. DeQuervain's tenosynovitis
   c. Carpal tunnel syndrome
   d. Cubital Tunnel syndrome
   e. Lateral epicondylitis

31. A 40-year-old woman presents to the clinic complaining of intermittent pain and tingling sensation to the left arm and hand, especially on part of the ring finger and the entire pinky finger. She states that, on occasion, she has had swelling of the arm on abduction. On physical exam, there is a loss of the left radial pulse when the head is rotated to the left side. Which of the following tests are positive in this patient?
   a. Thompson test
   b. Apley test
   c. Ober Test
   d. Adson test
   e. Hawkins test

32. A 31-year-old female at 15-weeks gestation presents to the clinic with increased urgency, frequency and painful urination. She is afebrile and does not have any costovertebral angle tenderness. A urinalysis with microscopic examination is performed showing >10 white blood cells/high powered field, positive nitrites and positive hematuria.   Which of the following is the management of choice?
   a. doxycycline
   b. trimethoprim-sulfamethoxazole
   c. nitrofurantoin
   d. ciprofloxacin
   e. clindamycin

33. A 40-year-old male with a history of refractory hypertension despite dieting, lifestyle changes, and compliance with two antihypertensive medications comes to the clinic for intermittent episodes of severe headache, sweating and palpitations. His vital signs are: pulse rate of 130 beats per minute, respiratory rate of 20 breaths/minute, blood pressure 189/112 mm Hg, temperature 38.5° C, and 98% oxygen saturation on room air. Renal angiogram is negative for renal artery stenosis or fibromuscular dysplasia. Which of the following is the most appropriate next step in the evaluation of this patient?
   a. check plasma renin levels
   b. echocardiography
   c. overnight dexamethasone suppression test
   d. 24-hour urine vanillylmandelic acid levels
   e. ACTH stimulation test

34. A 63-year old male with a history of heart failure is on lisinopril and metoprolol for his heart failure. He states for the last three days, he has had increasing fatigue and weakness. On physical examination, there is no increased jugular venous pressure and the lungs are clear to auscultation bilaterally. The following ECG is obtained:

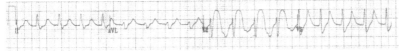

Which of the following is the best next step in the management of this patient?
   a. Oral sodium polystyrene sulfonate
   b. IV sodium bicarbonate
   c. IV calcium gluconate
   d. IV potassium chloride
   e. IV Dextrose

35. A 37-year-old male construction worker presents with a nonproductive cough. Recently, he brought a house in Pittsburgh. He has been digging up the soil in the backyard in August in preparation for an in ground pool. He cleaned out the attic and stated he removed an old bat nest. He is worried he may have been exposed to rabies although he doesn't recall being bitten and didn't see any bats there. He is not exhibiting any signs of rabies encephalitis. A chest radiograph is obtained and shows an atypical infiltrate. Blood cultures are negative. Which of the following is the most likely diagnosis?
   a. Pneumocystis jirovecii pneumonia
   b. Haemophilus influenza pneumonia
   c. Histoplasma capsulatum pneumonia
   d. Influenza virus pneumonia
   e. Severe acute respiratory syndrome

36. A 43-year-old male presents with fever, headache and mild neck stiffness. On physical examination, there are no focal neurological motor or sensory deficits and cranial nerve exam is unremarkable. A head CT scan is performed, which is negative for intracranial bleed, brain masses or mass effect. A lumbar puncture is performed and shows the following:
   Opening pressure: mildly increased
   Protein: normal
   Glucose: normal
   WBC count: increased with predominantly lymphocytes
Which of the following is the most likely etiologic agent?
   a. Enterovirus
   b. Herpes Simplex Virus
   c. Rhabdovirus
   d. Arbovirus
   e. Varicella Zoster Virus

37. Which of the following is the etiologic agent for oral hairy leukoplakia?
   a. Herpes simplex virus
   b. Yersinia pestis
   c. Flavivirus
   d. Hantavirus
   e. Epstein Barr Virus

38. A 34-year-old female has well demarcated, round macules with fine scaling and areas of hypopigmentation that do not tan when exposed to sunlight. A Woods lamp test shows yellow-green fluorescence. A potassium hydroxide preparation is performed, showing hyphae with a "spaghetti and meatball" appearance. Which of the following is the most likely diagnosis?
   a. pityriasis rosea
   b. pityriasis versicolor
   c. non bullous impetigo
   d. melasma
   e. lichen planus

39. A 60-year-old male presents to the clinic for routine screening and is found to have a white blood cell count of 60,000/mcL (normal 5,000 – 10,000/mcL). The white blood cells are well differentiated. On genetic testing, there is the presence of a translocation between chromosome 9 and 22 (Philadelphia chromosome). Which of the following is the most likely diagnosis?
   a. acute myelogenous leukemia
   b. chronic lymphocytic leukemia
   c. acute lymphocytic leukemia
   d. multiple myeloma
   e. chronic myelogenous leukemia

40. A 65-year-old male is being treated for a recent diagnosis of small cell (oat cell) carcinoma. A few weeks into the treatment, he develops sharp chest pain worse with inspiration, shortness of breath, hemoptysis, fever and chills. A chest radiograph shows an upper lobe consolidation. He is placed on isolation and the first acid-fast bacilli smear is positive. Which of the following is the treatment of choice?
   a. isoniazid + vitamin B6 for 12 months
   b. place a PPD and look for positivity
   c. isoniazid + vitamin B6 for 9 months
   d. isoniazid, rifampin, pyrazinamide and ethambutol (total duration of treatment for 6 months).
   e. CT scan without IV contrast

41. In which of the following patients can tincture of opium and loperamide be used most safely?
   a. Enterotoxigenic E. coli
   b. Shigella
   c. Campylobacter
   d. Yersinia
   e. Salmonella

42. A 32-year-old woman presents with diarrhea & weight loss despite an increased appetite. On physical examination, her skin is warm, moist and soft. She has protruding eyeballs with lid lag but there are no visual changes. There are dark brown patches on her anterior shins bilaterally. A radioactive uptake scan shows diffuse, increased uptake of iodine. Which of the following would be most specific for the suspected diagnosis?
   a. increased TSH and increased free T4 levels
   b. positive thyroid stimulating antibodies
   c. positive thyroid peroxidase antibodies
   d. positive thyroglobulin antibodies
   e. biopsy showing papillary thyroid carcinoma

43. A 34-year-old male skyscraper window washer is involved in an accident in which the scaffold fell rapidly about 10 stories. He is now complaining that he is unable to move his right leg although his leg was not trapped. He seems genuinely concerned about his physical ailment though he has no pain and denies hitting his leg during the fall. He states he has been anxious because he thought he was going to die during the accident.   On physical examination, there is no physical evidence of leg trauma and he has a normal nerve conduction study to the lower legs.   Which of the following is the most likely diagnosis?

    a. panic disorder
    b. post traumatic stress disorder
    c. functional neurologic disorder (conversion disorder)
    d. illness anxiety disorder (hypochondriasis)
    e. Munchausen syndrome

44. A 45-year-old male is diagnosed with early-onset Parkinson disease. He has a resting pill rolling tremor of the hands but does not have cogwheel rigidity, slowness of movement or other Parkinsonian symptoms. Which of the following medications is recommended for his current symptoms at this time?

    a. levodopa/carbidopa
    b. benztropine
    c. entacapone
    d. propranolol
    e. carbamazepine

45. Which of the following describes Auspitz sign?

    a. Clustered, white lesions on the buccal mucosa with a surrounding erythematous rim opposite the lower 1st and 2nd molars
    b. Sloughing off of the skin when the skin is lightly stroked
    c. Localized subcutaneous anaphylactoid reaction after stroking the skin
    d. Skin lesions appearing in the on the lines of trauma
    e. Punctate bleeding spots when the plaques of psoriasis are unroofed

46. Which of the following bests describes guttate psoriasis?

    a. raised, dark-red plaques with thick silvery-white scales
    b. small, erythematous discrete papules with fine scales and confluent plaques
    c. generalized erythematous rash involving most of the skin especially at body folds with the absence of plaques
    d. uniformly swollen "sausage" digits and joint stiffness
    e. deep yellow non-infected pustules that evolve into red macules on the palms and the soles

47. Which of the following lab values is most consistent with alcohol hepatitis?

    a. increased alkaline phosphatase with gamma glutamyl transpeptidase (GGT)
    b. increased alanine aminotransferase levels (ALT) >1000
    c. increased alanine aminotransferase levels (ALT) >1000 with positive smooth muscle antibodies
    d. increased alanine aminotransferase (ALT) and increased aspartate transaminase (AST) <500.
    e. increased aspartate transaminase (AST): increased alanine aminotransferase (ALT) > 2:1

48. Which of the following is a class II anti-arrhythmic drug that antagonizes the alpha-1, beta-1 and beta-2 receptors?

    a. atenolol
    b. propranolol
    c. metoprolol
    d. nadolol
    e. carvedilol

49. A 50-year-old male with no past medical history presents with substernal chest pain. He is found to have an anterolateral myocardial infarction on electrocardiogram. A coronary angiogram is performed, showing a critical occlusion of the left main coronary artery. Which of the following is the most appropriate management of this patient?
    a. percutaneous transluminal coronary angioplasty with stent
    b. coronary artery bypass graft
    c. percutaneous transluminal coronary angioplasty without stent
    d. initiation of an angiotensin converting enzyme inhibitor
    e. aspirin and clopidogrel for at least 6 months

50. Which of the following describes a 35-year-old woman with 4 pregnancies, history of 3 births and 1 miscarriage?
    a. G3P4A1
    b. G4P3A0
    c. G4P3A1
    d. G3P4A1
    e. G4P4A1

51. A 24-year-old male presents to the emergency room after being hit in the right eye with a baseball. He is complaining of blurred vision, decreased visual acuity and decreased sensation to the anteromedial cheek. There is noticeable ecchymosis of the soft tissues surrounding the eye and subcutaneous emphysema. Which of the following motions would most likely result in worsening of the diplopia in this patient?
    a. shining a light into the right eye
    b. shining a light into the left eye
    c. having the patient look upwards
    d. palpation of the upper portion of the eye
    e. covering the right eye and having the patient read a Snellen chart

52. A 33-year-old left-hand dominant tennis player complains of left elbow pain. Which of the following would most likely be seen if the patient is suffering from Tennis Elbow?
    a. Pain and tenderness of the pronator teres
    b. Pain and tenderness of the flexor carpi radialis
    c. Lateral elbow pain with tenderness at the lateral epicondyle
    d. Pain with wrist flexion against resistance
    e. Pain worse with pulling activities

53. A 10-year-old male is brought into the emergency room for fever and limping. The child denies any recent trauma. On physical examination, there is significant bone tenderness. A radiograph of the right tibia and fibula shows a positive periosteal reaction. A blood culture is obtained with the gram stain as below. The organism shows beta lactamase positivity.
    Which of the following is the management of choice?
    a. IV Penicillin G aqueous
    b. IV Ampicillin
    c. IV Gentamicin
    d. IV Nafcillin
    e. IV Aztreonam

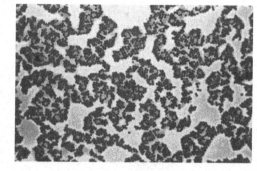

54. A 43-year-old male is being evaluated after presenting with petechiae. A CBC with peripheral smear is performed and is consistent with a hemolytic anemia & a platelet count of 85,000 (normal is 150,000 – 450,000/mcL). Other labs are performed, consistent with thrombotic thrombocytopenic purpura. Which of the following is the first line management of a patient with thrombotic thrombocytopenic purpura?
    a. plasmapheresis
    b. splenectomy
    c. corticosteroids
    d. transfusion of platelets
    e. cyclophosphamide

55. A patient with leukostasis due to acute myelogenous leukemia is being managed via chemotherapy. In addition to IV fluids, which of the following is the management of choice if tumor lysis syndrome develops as a complication of the chemotherapy?
    a. hydroxyurea
    b. chemotherapy
    c. allopurinol
    d. deferoxamine
    e. imatinib

56. A 20-year-old male presents to the clinic for trauma to his right testicle. An ultrasound is performed, revealing a traumatic hydrocele and a right testicular mass. A biopsy of the mass confirms a pure seminomatous germ cell tumor. Which of the following lab values are most consistent with pure seminomatous germ cell testicular tumors?
    a. normal alpha fetoprotein and normal beta human chorionic gonadotropin
    b. normal alpha fetoprotein and increased beta human chorionic gonadotropin
    c. normal alpha fetoprotein and decreased beta human chorionic gonadotropin
    d. increased alpha fetoprotein and increased beta human chorionic gonadotropin
    e. increased alpha fetoprotein and normal beta human chorionic gonadotropin

57. A 56-year-old female presents to the emergency room with worsening dyspnea. Her home medications include hydrochlorothiazide, carvedilol and lisinopril. Physical examination reveals an S3 gallop and rales are heard throughout both lung fields. Chest radiographs shows cardiomegaly. An echocardiogram shows a dilated cardiac chamber, thin ventricular walls, and an ejection fraction of 40% (normal ejection fraction 55-60%). Blood pressure is 180/96 mmHg. Which of the following is not part of the routine management of this patient?
    a. Temporary discontinuation of carvedilol
    b. IV furosemide
    c. Elevated the head of the bed to position the patient to sit up
    d. IV morphine
    e. IV verapamil

58. On cardiac examination, a high-pitched early diastolic murmur is best heard at the left sternal border that is accentuated with deep inspiration, consistent with a Graham Steell murmur. Which of the following valvular abnormalities are most commonly associated with the Graham Steell murmur?
    a. Tricuspid regurgitation
    b. Pulmonary regurgitation
    c. Aortic regurgitation
    d. Aortic stenosis
    e. Pulmonary stenosis

59. A 65-year old female is brought into the emergency room. She states she was at her son's softball game and when it became crowded, she felt a sudden onset of intense fear followed by chest pain, palpitations, diaphoresis, tremors, a choking sensation and dizziness. An electrocardiogram is obtained, showing normal sinus rhythm at 98 beats per minute with negative cardiac enzymes. Which of the following is considered first line treatment for the acute symptoms?

   a. Diazepam (Valium)
   b. Fluoxetine (Prozac)
   c. Buspirone (Buspar)
   d. Imipramine (Tofranil)
   e. Lithium (Lithobid)

60. A 43-year-old male is seen in the neurology clinic for difficulty swallowing, abnormal speech with hoarseness and progressive weakness over the last 6 months. On physical examination, he has decreased strength and difficulty lifting his hands over his head. His tongue is atrophic with fasciculations. He has increased deep tendon reflexes and a positive Babinski's sign with muscle atrophy of the head neck and the torso. Which of the following is the most likely diagnosis?

   a. Cerebral palsy
   b. Parkinson's disease
   c. Multiple sclerosis
   d. Amyotrophic lateral sclerosis
   e. Guillain-Barré syndrome

61. Which of the following organisms are associated with an increased incidence of urinary tract infections in young, sexually active women?

   a. Proteus mirabilis
   b. Enterobacteriaceae
   c. Candida albicans
   d. Staphylococcus saprophyticus
   e. Pseudomonas aeruginosa

62. A 10-year-old male is being evaluated for a well visit. He is below the weight percentile for his age. He has been complaining of bulky, fatty, foul-smelling stools as well as intermittent constipation. The patient also has had a lifetime history of recurrent pulmonary infections. Which of the following would be elevated in this patient?

   a. lactate dehydrogenase
   b. alpha-1 antitrypsin
   c. chloride during sweat test testing
   d. angiotensin converting enzyme
   e. serum sodium levels

63. A 47-year-old male with no significant past medical history has recently relocated to New York City from Sacramento California. He is being evaluated for fever, nonproductive cough, headache and joint pains. He has had bilateral ankle and knee swelling for 1 week. 4 days ago, he developed a "painful red rash on both of his shins". There are no verrucous lesions present. Lab tests reveal an elevated immunoglobulin M precipitin antibody test. Which of the following is the most likely diagnosis?

   a. Histoplasma capsulatum
   b. Coccidioides immitis
   c. Aspergillus fumigatus
   d. Cryptococcus neoformans
   e. Blastomyces dermatitidis

64. A 19-year-old female presents to the dermatology clinic with a generalized, pruritic rash. On physical examination, there are bilateral, symmetric, round, oval, salmon-colored macules with white circular scaling along the cleavage lines in a Christmas tree pattern along the trunk. There is also a larger, solitary macule on the upper trunk of which the patient states appeared before the other lesions. The rash spares the face. Which of the following is the most likely diagnosis?
    a. psoriasis
    b. pityriasis rosea
    c. pityriasis versicolor
    d. lichen planus
    e. seborrheic dermatitis

65. A 22-year-old female presents to the dermatology clinic complaining of comedogenic acne with very small amounts of pustules. There are no nodular or cystic lesions seen. Which of the following is the best initial management?
    a. benzoyl peroxide
    b. minocycline orally
    c. spironolactone
    d. isotretinoin
    e. cephalexin

66. A 32-year-old male with a history of poorly controlled hypertension despite being on combination hypertension medications presents with headache, proximal muscle weakness, fatigue and polyuria. His vital signs show a blood pressure of 140/110. On physical examination, there are decreased deep tendon reflexes and facial flushing. There is no presence of edema. An electrocardiogram shows prominent U waves. An aldosterone to renin ratio test is >20. Which of the following is the most likely diagnosis?
    a. secondary hyperaldosteronism
    b. congestive heart failure
    c. renal artery stenosis
    d. primary hyperaldosteronism
    e. hypoaldosteronism

67. Which of the following tests are used to distinguish between the different causes of Cushing's syndrome?
    a. fluid deprivation test
    b. low dose dexamethasone suppression test and ACTH levels
    c. CRH stimulation test
    d. ACTH stimulation test
    e. High dose dexamethasone suppression test and ACTH levels

68. A 30-year-old female presents with cyclical menstrual pain, dysmenorrhea, painful sexual intercourse and painful bowel movements. Which of the following is the most likely diagnosis?
    a. endometriosis
    b. premenstrual syndrome
    c. mittelschmertz
    d. adenomyosis
    e. endometrial carcinoma

69. A 36-year-old long distance runner complains of right lateral knee pain whenever she runs. She states that the knee pain is worse at the beginning of her run, especially if she runs downhill. On physical examination, there is positive lateral condyle tenderness and she resists adduction when her leg is placed parallel to the table in neutral position due to pain. Which of the following is the most likely diagnosis?
   a. Osgood-Schlatter's disease
   b. Legg-Calve Perthe disease
   c. Chrondromalacia
   d. Rheumatoid Arthritis
   e. Iliotibial band syndrome

70. Which of the following is the most useful diagnostic tool in patients with a negative Coombs test and a peripheral smear showing microcytic, hyperchromic, sphere-shaped cells?
   a. Ristocetin activity test
   b. Schilling test
   c. Mixing study
   d. Osmotic fragility test
   e. Flow cytometry testing

71. Which of the following is used in the management of patients with moderate Type I Von Willebrand disease?
   a. aspirin
   b. hydroxyurea
   c. desmopressin
   d. plasmapheresis
   e. intravenous immunoglobulin

72. A 52-year-old postmenopausal woman status post hysterectomy 1 year ago presents to the office complaining of hot flashes and painful sexual intercourse due to vaginal dryness. Which of the following is the most effective management of her symptoms?
   a. tamoxifen
   b. estradiol
   c. clomiphene
   d. raloxifene
   e. progesterone

73. A 28-year-old male presents to the clinic for a yearly physical. A urine dipstick is positive for blood. The patient denies any symptoms but admits to being a smoker. Which of the following is the next most appropriate step in the management of this patient?
   a. urinalysis and urine culture
   b. cystoscopy
   c. intravenous pyelogram
   d. urine cytology
   e. bladder biopsy

74. Which of the following is not considered to be an increased risk factor for bladder cancer?
   a. history of smoking cigarettes
   b. history of cyclophosphamide use
   c. Caucasian male with type II diabetes mellitus on pioglitazone
   d. a history of working as a beautician
   e. an African American female with a history of hypertension

75. On physical examination of a newborn, there is the presence of a wide pulse pressure and a murmur consistent with patent ductus arteriosus. Which of the following is primarily used to close a patent ductus arteriosus?
    a. indomethacin
    b. corticosteroids
    c. prostaglandins
    d. high flow oxygen
    e. low flow oxygen

76. During cardiac examination, a systolic crescendo-decrescendo murmur is best heard at the right upper sternal border and radiates to the carotids that decreases in intensity with the Valsalva maneuver. An electrocardiogram shows left ventricular hypertrophy. Which of the following physical exam findings are most consistent with the suspected diagnosis?
    a. a weak, delayed peripheral pulse
    b. the presence of an opening snap
    c. the presence of bounding pulses
    d. the presence of an ejection click
    e. the presence of a wide pulse pressure

77. A 3-week-old infant is brought into the pediatric emergency room for projective, nonbilious vomiting. On physical examination, there is a nontender, hard, olive-shaped mass palpated after the child vomited. Which of the following is the recommended next step in the evaluation of the suspected diagnosis?
    a. Abdominal radiograph
    b. Ultrasound
    c. Upper GI series
    d. CT scan of the abdomen
    e. Intravenous pyelogram

78. A 43-year-old male being medically managed for peptic ulcer disease has a yearly examination. A complete blood count (CBC) shows a decreased hemoglobin with a mean corpuscular volume (MCV) of 105 /fL (normal 80 – 100 /fL). Vitamin B12, folate and liver function tests are within normal limits. The patient denies any alcohol abuse. Which of the following is the most likely causative agent responsible for the CBC findings?
    a. chlorpropramide
    b. sitagliptin
    c. glyburide
    d. rosiglitazone
    e. metformin

79. A 64-year-old Vietnam veteran is diagnosed with posttraumatic stress disorder and is undergoing psychotherapy. He believes it has been helpful but his psychiatrist feels he needs some medical intervention to relieve some of the stress and feelings associated with the traumatic event. Which of the following is considered to be the first line management in this patient?
    a. Paroxetine (Paxil)
    b. Lithium (Lithobid)
    c. Phenelzine (Nardil)
    d. Amitriptyline (Elavil)
    e. Imipramine (Tofranil)

80. Which of the following medications is the first line medication for the long-term management of schizophrenia?
   a.   Lithium (Lithobid)
   b.   Lorazepam (Ativan)
   c.   Fluoxetine (Prozac)
   d.   Clomipramine (Anafranil)
   e.   Olanzapine (Zyprexa)

81. Which of the following best describes the pathophysiology of Parkinson disease?
   a. idiopathic excess production of acetylcholine in the basal ganglia
   b. idiopathic dopamine excess in the mesolimbic pathway
   c. idiopathic depletion of dopamine in the basal ganglia
   d. idiopathic malfunction of dopamine in the mesocortical pathway
   e. drug induced dopamine antagonism

82. A 7-year-old male is brought into the clinic by his mother because his teacher noticed that the child had brief staring episodes and eyelid twitching with a sudden return to normal activity. The teacher stated the child seemed unaware of these episodes. An electroencephalogram is performed, which shows bilateral symmetric 3Hz spike and wave action. Which of the following is the recommended first line medical management for this patient?
   a. carbamazepine
   b. gabapentin
   c. ethosuximide
   d. valproic acid
   e. lamotrigine

83. Which of the following electrocardiogram findings would most likely be seen in a patient with severe chronic bronchitis?
   a. ST elevations in leads I, avL, V5 and V6
   b. depth of the S wave in lead V1 + height of the R wave in V6 >35mm
   c. positive QRS complex in Lead I, negative QRS complex in lead aVF
   d. electric alternans
   e. negative QRS complex in Lead I, positive QRS complex in lead aVF

84. Which of the following patients would most likely present with the following ABG?

pH: 7.56	Normal 7.34 – 7.45
PCO$_2$: 23 mm Hg	Normal 35 - 45
PO$_2$: 70 mm Hg	Normal 75 - 100
HCO$_3$: 21 mEq/L	Normal 22 – 28

   a. a patient with morphine overdose
   b. a patient with prolonged, retracted vomiting from chemotherapy
   c. a patient with history of anxiety disorder with prolonged hyperventilation
   d. an uncontrolled type I diabetic
   e. a patient with vibrio cholera with profound diarrhea

85. Which of the following is an adverse reaction of Lansoprazole?
   a. abortifacent due to the induction of uterine contractions
   b. macrocytic anemia
   c. gynecomastia
   d. tardive dyskinesia
   e. induction of the cytochrome P450 syndrome

86. Which of the following most accurately describes a pilonidal cyst?
   a. an abscess of the apocrine sweat glands
   b. an abscess of the gluteal cleft
   c. a cyst containing soft, cheese-like material
   d. a painless lump of adipose tissue in between the skin and the muscular layer
   e. a cyst that contains more than 1 germ cell layer

87. A 35-year-old intravenous injection drug user has a full workup during rehab, which reveals chronic hepatitis C with an increased viral load. Which of the following is the management of choice?
   a. lamivudine
   b. adefovir
   c. adefovir plus lamivudine
   d. interferon beta 1
   e. pegylated alpha-2 interferon plus ribavirin

88. A 44-year-old male with a history of longstanding HIV infection presents to the clinic with fever, body aches, and headache for the last 10 days. A CT scan of the head shows a ring-enhancing lesion. Which of the following is the most common predisposing factor?
   a. Sheep exposure
   b. Cat exposure
   c. Rodent and flea exposure
   d. Decaying wood near waterways
   e. Unpasteurized milk

89. A 4-year-old girl presents to the clinic with a high fever of 3 days duration. Her mother states that despite having high fever, she has been pretty active. She developed a pink maculopapular rash beginning on the trunk and the back that later progressed to the face. Which of the following is the most likely diagnosis?
   a. rubella
   b. rubeola
   c. fifth's disease
   d. roseola
   e. coxsackie virus A

90. A 45-year-old male with a history of diabetes mellitus is complaining of excruciating testicular and perineal pain. His vitals are as follows: temperature 104° F, blood pressure 120/70, pulse rate of 120 beats per minute, respiratory rate of 22 beats per minute and an oxygen saturation of 100% on room air. On physical examination, there is erythema, edema and warmth of the penis and scrotum extending to the pubic symphysis and a small hemorrhagic bulla. Which of the following is the most likely diagnosis?
   a. testicular torsion
   b. torsion of the appendix of the testicle
   c. epididymitis
   d. necrotizing fasciitis
   e. varicocele

91. Which of the following best describes the pathophysiology of psoriasis?
   a. Malassezia furfur overgrowth
   b. Type I IgE hypersensitivity reaction of the dermis and subcutaneous tissues
   c. Keratin hyperplasia in the stratum basale and spinosum due to T-cell activation
   d. Type II hypersensitivity reaction in the basement membrane
   e. Autoimmune disruption of the desmosome layer

92. A 43-year-old firefighter comes in for evaluation after fighting a four-alarm fire. On physical examination, there is soot in his mouth and singed nasal hairs. He is complaining of a headache, dizziness, nausea and body aches. On physical examination, he appears flushed. Which of the following tests would give the most information about his need for oxygen?
   a. pulse oximetry
   b. serum bicarbonate levels
   c. carboxyhemoglobin levels
   d. lead levels
   e. hemoglobin levels

93. A 40-year-old male presents to the dermatology clinic for conjunctivitis and a papulopustular rash on the face. He states the rash is getting worse. The rash is also associated with flushing and stinging if he consumes alcohol, hot chocolate, buffalo wings, and if he takes hot baths, especially in the winter. On physical examination, there are telangiectasias seen on the nose. In addition to lifestyle changes, which of the following is the first line management of choice?
   a. Moh's excision
   b. Hydroquinone
   c. Metronidazole topically
   d. Clonidine orally
   e. Corticosteroids orally

94. Which of the following is the most common benign ovarian neoplasm?
   a. dermoid cystic teratomas
   b. struma ovarii
   c. serous cystoadenomas
   d. Brenner tumor
   e. Fibroadenoma

95. A 30-year-old female presents with menorrhagia. A transvaginal ultrasound is performed, which showed a thickened endometrial stripe of 6-mm. A biopsy is performed, showing hyperplasia without atypia. The patient wishes to preserve the possibility of fertility. Which of the following is the management of choice at this time?
   a. estrogen only
   b. progesterone orally
   c. hysterectomy
   d. clomiphene
   e. Uterine ablation

96. A 34-year-old female presents with soft, shallow, painful ulcerations in the groin area surrounded by small papules. There are no vesicles present. Which of the following is the most likely causative organism?
   a. Herpes simplex virus
   b. Neisseria gonorrhea
   c. Human papilloma virus
   d. Haemophilus ducreyi
   e. Lactobacilli

97. Which of the following is most commonly seen as a consequence of thrombocytopenia?
   a. petechiae
   b. delayed bleeding after surgery
   c. large hematomas
   d. bleeding into the joints after minor trauma (hemarthrosis)
   e. prolonged partial thromboplastin time (PTT)

98. Which of the following is decreased in patients with Hemophilia A?
   a. Protein C
   b. Protein S
   c. Factor VIII
   d. Lupus anticoagulant
   e. Factor IX

99. Which of the following is the most common clinical presentation in patients sickle cell trait?
   a. Episodic hematuria
   b. Hepatomegaly
   c. Splenomegaly
   d. Bone marrow hyperplasia
   e. Asplenic crisis

100. A 32-year old male is complaining of sore throat, runny nose and cough. On physical examination, his thyroid gland is tender to palpation. DeQuervain's thyroiditis is suspected. Which of the following is most commonly associated with DeQuervain's (subacute) thyroiditis?
   a. increased diffuse uptake on radioactive uptake scan
   b. positive thyroid stimulating antibodies
   c. positive thyroid peroxidase antibodies
   d. positive thyroglobulin antibodies
   e. increased erythrocyte sedimentation rate

QUESTION 1

Choice D (Skier's thumb) is the correct choice. Skier's thumb is an injury to the ulnar collateral ligament (Gamekeeper's thumb is the chronic version). It is most often due to forced thumb abduction, leading to increased laxity on valgus stress of the thumb. Sometimes, the ulnar collateral ligament can pull of a piece of the bone at its insertion site when it ruptures, causing a small avulsion fracture at the base of the proximal phalanx. MUSCULOSKELETAL – SKIER'S THUMB – MOST LIKELY (p 177).

Choice A (Rolando's Fracture) is a comminuted form of Choice C (Bennett's Fracture). A Bennett's fracture is a facture at the base of the first metacarpal bone.

Choice B (Boxer's fracture) is a fracture of the 4th or the 5th metacarpal head or neck.

Choice E (Thumb dislocation) would show displacement of the bone, not a fracture.

QUESTION 2

Choice C [Haemophilus influenzae] is the correct choice. H. flu is the second most common cause of community acquired pneumonia (after Streptococcus pneumoniae). Patients with underlying pulmonary disease such as COPD (as seen in this patient), bronchiectasis, cystic fibrosis, diabetics, children and elderly are at increased risk to develop H. flu pneumonia. PULMONARY – PNEUMONIA – BASICS (p 101).

Choice A (*Mycoplasma*) is the most common cause of *walking pneumonia*.

Choice B (*S. aureus*) usually occurs after viral infections and is associated with cavitations.

Choice D is commonly seen in hospital acquired pneumonia or structural abnormalities such as bronchiectasis.

Choice E (Histoplasma capsulatum) usually has a classic story of someone from the Ohio and Mississippi river valley area (such as Pittsburg) exposed to bird or bat droppings.

QUESTION 3

Choice E (classic migraine) is the correct answer.   The classic migraine is a migraine with aura. Auras are subjective sensations that precede the migraine.   Most migraine sufferers don't present with the aura.
NEUROLOGY – CLASSIC MIGRAINE – MOST LIKELY (p 358).

Choice A (*common migraine*) is a migraine headache without the preceding auras. This is the most common type of migraines in regards to the frequency.

Choice B (*cluster headache*) presents with *"clusters"* or bouts of headache described as stabbing, periorbital pain with *ipsilateral manifestations of rhinorrhea, lacrimation* etc.

Choice C (*tension headache*) is classically bilateral and described as a tight band-like headache. It is not associated with the nausea and vomiting symptoms seen here in this vignette.

Choice D (*pseudotumor cerebri*) is due to *increased intracranial pressure*. They may also develop nausea and vomiting but will also often develop visual changes. The chronicity of the headaches in the story makes migraines a more likely diagnosis.

QUESTION 4

Choice E (history of combined oral contraceptive use) is the correct choice. In ovarian cancer, combined oral contraceptives reduce the risk of ovarian cancer by reducing the number ovulatory cycles.
REPRODUCTIVE – OVARIAN CANCER – HEALTH MAINTENANCE (p 254).

All the other choices are associated with increased risk due to the increased number of ovulatory cycles in those disorders. Increased ovulatory cycles are a risk factor for the development of ovarian cancer.

QUESTION 5

Choice D (volar splint and Naprosyn) is the correct choice.   This is a classic description of Carpal tunnel syndrome. Tinel's and Phalen's sign are often positive in carpal tunnel syndrome and it can cause thumb weakness and thenar atrophy in addition to the classic pain and paresthesias along the median nerve distribution.
MUSCULOSKELETAL – CARPAL TUNNEL SYNDROME – CLINICAL INTERVENTION (p 179).

Choice A (Cubital tunnel release surgery) is used in the management for cubital tunnel not carpal tunnel. Cubital tunnel syndrome causes ulnar nerve neuropathy.

Choice B (carpal tunnel release surgery) is used in patients refractory to conservative treatment.

Choice C (steroid injection into the affected area) is used for patients that are unresponsive to lifestyle changes, volar splint and NSAID's.

Choice E (oral corticosteroids) is not used in the management of carpal tunnel syndrome.

QUESTION 6
Choice B (prior history of coronary artery disease) is the correct answer. Sumatriptan causes vasoconstriction, which could potentially decrease the bloody supply to the heart, leading to coronary ischemia.
NEUROLOGY – MIGRAINE HEADACHE – HEALTH MAINTENANCE (p 358).

QUESTION 7
Choice D (left anterior cerebral artery occlusion) is the correct answer. *Anterior cerebral artery* syndromes result in *contralateral hemiparesis (weakness) that tends to be greater in the leg than the arm*, is associated with *urinary incontinence*, abulia (lack of will) & personality changes. NEUROLOGY – ANTERIOR CEREBRAL ARTERY OCCLUSION – MOST LIKELY (p 360).

Choice A (*Bell's Palsy*) is a cranial nerve VII palsy that leads to *isolated unilateral facial weakness*. The arms and the legs are not involved in Bell's palsy because only the facial nerve is involved. With *Bell's palsy, patients are usually unable to lift the eyebrow on the affected side.*

Choice B (Left *middle cerebral artery occlusion*) would cause contralateral hemiparesis (weakness) with *arm & face weakness more pronounced than in the lower extremities.* Left hemisphere dominant lesions can cause aphasia. Due to bilateral innervation of the forehead, patients are usually able to raise the eyebrows. Choice E (right middle cerebral artery occlusion) would cause left-sided symptoms as described in choice B but the symptoms would be on the left side instead of the instead of the right-sided.

Choice C (left *posterior cerebral artery occlusion*) will result in *visual hallucinations, and "crossed symptoms" –* meaning *ipsilateral cranial nerve deficits* and *contralateral muscle weakness. Comas and drop attacks* are also seen in posterior cerebral artery occlusion.

QUESTION 8
Choice C (dysthymia) is the correct answer. Dysthymia is defined as a mild form of chronic depression in which the severity of the mood does not meet the criteria for major depression and the depressed mood is continuous (greater than 2 years in adults or > 1 year in children). PSYCH – DYSTHYMIA – MOST LIKELY DIAGNOSIS (p 376).

Choice A (Major depressive disorder) is defined as depressed mood and anhedonia for almost every day for most of the days for at least 2 weeks. Patients with major depressive disorder have moments when they are not severely depressed. This patient is still able to fully function despite his symptoms whereas patients with MDD tend to have clinical distress or impairment in occupational, educational or social functioning

Choice B (Cyclothymia) is a variant of bipolar in which a patient alternates between dysthymia and mild elevation of the mood (that does not meet the criteria for mania). This patient has had 4 years of chronically depressed mood.

Choice D (Bipolar type I) is characterized by major depressive disorder alternating with manic episodes.

Choice E (Social phobia) is defined as persistent fear of social or performance situations in which the patient is subject to the scrutiny of others. These exposures may prompt a panic attack.

QUESTION 9

Choice C (spot urine albumin: creatinine ratio) is the correct answer. Spot ratio is the preferred method for evaluating the severity of proteinuria. It is more specific than a 24-hour urine protein collection (which is also used in proteinuria quantification). GENITOURINARY – PROTEINURIA – LABS/DIAGNOSTIC STUDIES (p 323).

Choice A (cystoscopy) is used for the evaluation of hematuria to visualize the bladder.

Choice B (intravenous pyelogram) is used to assess the kidney bladder and the ureter.

Choice D (urine cytology) is used to assess a patient with possible bladder cancer.

Choice E (24 hour urine creatinine collection) is used to estimate glomerular filtration rate in patients with chronic kidney disease.

QUESTION 10

Choice C (neuroleptic malignant syndrome) is the correct answer. Neuroleptic malignant syndrome is a life-threatening complication of dopamine inhibition. It most commonly occurs 1 – 2 weeks after initiation or increasing the dose of dopamine antagonists (especially 1st generation antipsychotics). *Symptoms include autonomic instability, incontinence, hypersalivation, hyperthermia, lead pipe rigidity, hyporeflexia and possible rhabdomyolysis.* Management includes dopamine agonist (such as Bromocriptine or Amantadine) as well as Dantrolene to reduce fever and muscle rigidity. NEUROLOGY – NEUROLEPTIC MALIGNANT SYNDROME – MOST LIKELY (p 370).

Choice A (amphetamine toxicity) can also present with hyperthermia but usually presents with increased motor activity, headache, tremor, flushing, hyperthermia, cold sweats, nausea, vomiting, and seizures, *SYMPATHETIC STIMULATION:* sweating, tachycardia (arrhythmias), *pupillary dilation* (the pupils are normal in this patient) as well as peripheral vasoconstriction (which can cause *hypertension and potentially* myocardial infarction).

Choice B (*serotonin syndrome*) usually presents with *autonomic instability, tremors and hyperthermia* as in NMS but characteristics that are absent in NMS that are present serotonin syndrome includes *mydriasis, diarrhea & abdominal cramps* (from serotonin's effect on the enterochromaffin cells of the GI tract). Those specific symptoms are absent in this vignette.

Choice D (*Opioid toxicity*) presents with *pupillary constriction* (narcotics are miotics), *respiratory depression, bradycardia, hypotension*, coma, nausea and vomiting.

Choice D (*acute dystonia*) is *reversible extrapyramidal symptoms* that usually occur in *hours to days after the initiation of a dopamine blocking antipsychotics* (especially 1st generation anti-psychotics). The extrapyramidal symptoms include intermittent spasms, trismus, and protrusions of the tongue, facial grimacing, torticollis, and difficulty speaking.

QUESTION 11

Choice E is the correct answer. The rhythm strip shows atrial fibrillation. Beta blockers or calcium channel blockers are used for the first line management of atrial flutter or atrial fibrillation. CARDIOLOGY – ATRIAL FIBRILLATION - CLINICAL INTERVENTION (p 13).

Choice A (adenosine) is indicated as first line in regular, narrow QRS complex tachycardias (not including atrial flutter).

Choice B (unsynchronized cardoversion) is indicated in pulseless ventricular tachycardia or ventricular fibrillation.

Choice C (synchronized cardioversion) is indicated in unstable tachyarrhythmia.

Choice D (amiodarone) is used for wide QRS complex tachycardia.

QUESTION 12

Choice C (ultrasound of the gallbladder) is correct. This is a classic presentation of acute cholecystitis, making *ultrasound the best initial test in the evaluation of suspected cholecystitis*. Ultrasound findings in acute cholecystitis include the presence of gallstones, thickened gall bladder and a positive sonographic Murphy's sign while performing the test. Although afebrile in this vignette, patients with acute cholecystitis can be febrile due to the infection. The referred pain to the right shoulder is known as Boas sign (not to be confused with pain that radiates the left shoulder – Kehr's sign). Both are caused by phrenic nerve irritation. Boas sign is associated with acute cholecystitis and Kehr's sign is usually associated with splenic injury most commonly, ectopic pregnancy, or kidney stones.

Choice A *(HIDA scan) is the gold standard* test but remember, gold standard tests are most often not the initial tests done. If the question asked for gold standard, then HIDA scan would have been correct.

Choice B (ERCP) is indicated in suspected biliary tract disease. In acute cholecystitis, the stone is in the cystic duct but bile is still able to flow through the bile ducts (this is why there are no long-term serious sequelae in patients who have a cholecystectomy as the bile can still flow without the gall bladder). In biliary duct diseases, patients usually develop jaundice with the blocking of the biliary tract.

Choice D (abdominal X ray) are indicated in other disorders, such as small bowel obstruction. Most gallstones are radiopaque (since they are predominantly made of cholesterol) and often won't be seen on abdominal radiographs.

Choice E (PT and albumin levels) are helpful in cases where end stage liver disease is suspected.

QUESTION 13

Choice B (schizoid personality disorder) is the correct answer. Schizoid personality disorder is characterized by a long pattern of *voluntary social withdrawal* and often appears lonely with a *very "cold", flattened affect.* They tend to exhibit *hermit-like behavior* and the inability to form long-term relationships because they don't see any point in sharing their time with others. Patients with schizoid personality classically tend to lack the odd eccentric behavior such as the "magical thinking" seen in schizotypal disorder or in schizophrenia.
PSYCH/BEHAVIORAL – SCHIZOID PERSONALITY DISORDER – MOST LIKELY (p 379).

Choice A (social phobia) is defined as persistent fear of social or performance situations in which the patient is subject to the scrutiny of others. These exposures may prompt a panic attack.

Choice C (schizotypal personality disorder) is characterized by odd, eccentric behavior and peculiar thought patterns suggestive of schizophrenia but without psychosis or delusions. Schizotypal may avoid people because of the fear of the social interaction. They tend to have eccentric behavior and don't tend to have the flattened effect seen with schizoid. The absence of the eccentric behavior in this vignette makes this diagnosis less likely.

Choice D (schizophrenia) is characterized by hallucinations and delusions.

Choice E (paranoid personality disorder). The reason for the avoidance of relationships in patients with paranoid personality disorder is they have a distrust and suspiciousness of others not because they lack the desire or need to interact with others (which is characteristic of schizoid). They can also appear cold.

QUESTION 14

Choice D (dacrocystitis) is the correct choice. Dacrocystitis is an infection of the lacrimal gland and presents with signs of infection and inflammation along the nasal side of the eyelids.
EENT – DACROCYSTITIS – MOST LIKELY DIAGNOSIS (p 224).

Choice A (Blepharitis) presents with erythematous eyelid margins (red-rimming) and flaking of the eyelids

Choice B (Hordeolum) is a local infection of the eyelid margin and presents with a tender, swollen, erythematous lump on the eyelid margin.

Choice C (chalazion) is a painless lump on the eyelid margin.

Choice E (septal cellulitis) would present with soft tissue signs of cellulitis, ocular pain, visual changes and ocular pain with eye movements.

QUESTION 15

Choice D (rapid warming of the patient) is the correct answer.   Passive warming using a warm room and blankets are part of the supportive therapy. Rapid warming is contraindicated in patients with myxedema coma as it may precipitate shock. All of the other choices are part of the routine management of myxedema coma.
ENDOCRINE - MYXEDEMA COMA – CLINICAL INTERVENTION (p. 288).

QUESTION 16

Choice C (erythema marginatum) is the correct answer. This is a classic description of rheumatic fever. *Rheumatic fever is a complication of Group A Beta Hemolytic Streptococcus (Streptococcus pyogenes).*   In this vignette she had a recent throat infection.   *The Jones criteria include carditis, Sydenham's chorea, erythema marginatum (seen here), subcutaneous nodules (seen here) and arthritis (seen here).* Erythema marginatum is described as a macular, erythematous, nonpruritic, enlarging annular rash with rounded, sharply demarcated edges, no central clearing and blanches with pressure.
CARDIOLOGY – ERYTHEMA MARGINATUM – HISTORY AND PHYSICAL EXAM (p 39).

Choice A (*erythema migrans*) is associated with Lyme disease. The rash of erythema migrans is an expanding, warm, *annular, erythematous rash* with *central clearing* and inner erythema, giving it the *"bull's-eye' or target* appearance. In comparison to the multiple lesions seen in erythema marginatum, erythema migrans is classically one lesion around the site of the tick bite (but it can be multiple in some cases).

Choice B (*erythema nodosum*) describes *painful, erythematous, inflammatory nodules seen especially on the anterior shins.* Erythema nodosum is associated with increased estrogen exposure (ex pregnancy), sarcoidosis, tuberculosis, fungal infections (ex Coccidiomycosis) as well as inflammatory disorders.

Choice D (*erythema multiforme*) is seen as a type IV hypersensitivity reaction that classically described as dusty *violet or red purpuric macules with vesicles or bullae in the center, giving it a classic target appearance.*

Choice E (*erythema infectiosum*) is also known as fifth's disease. The rash of erythema infectiosum classically presents with an *erythematous rash with circumoral pallor, giving it a "slapped cheek" appearance.* The rash then progresses to lacy reticular rash on the extremities (especially the upper extremities) and spares the palms and soles.

QUESTION 17
Choice A (topical hydroquinone) is the correct answer. Chloasma (melasma) is hypermelanosis especially seen in sun exposed areas. It is classically associated with hyperpigmented areas, which are unchanged under black light (Wood's lamp). It is most commonly seen with increased estrogen exposure, such as women who use oral contraceptives and in pregnancy. Sunscreen is also an effective part of management in these patients.
DERMATOLOGY – CHLOASMA – CLINICAL INTERVENTION (p 401).

Choice B (topical corticosteroids) is not used in the management of chloasma.

Choice C (topical diphenhydramine) may be used for localized itching but does not treat the hypermelanosis.

Choice D (topical ketoconazole) is used in the management of fungal infections.

Choice E (oral hydroxychloroquine) can be used for certain skin disorders, such as the photosensitive rashes and the malar rashes. It is also use in the prophylactic prevention of malaria.

QUESTION 18
Choice B (three) is the correct answer. The Centor criteria are used to determine the need for antibiotics in possible streptococcal pharyngitis. The 4 criteria are "LEAF"
L ymphadenopathy (cervical)
E xudates on the pharynx and/or tonsils
A bsence of cough
F ever (greater than $38°C/100.4°F$)
This patient qualifies for 3: 1) fever 2) exudates and 3) lymphadenopathy. The patient has a nonproductive cough so that does not meet the fourth criteria. INFECTIOUS DISEASE – STREP PHARYNGITIS – LABS/DIAGNOSTIC STUDIES (p 418).

QUESTION 19
Choice C (India ink) is the correct answer. Cryptococcal meningitis is the most common cause of fungal meningitis. The CSF findings of *decreased glucose & elevated white blood cell count with lymphocytosis* are characteristic of *fungal or tuberculosis meningitis.* India ink and the Cryptococcal antigen examination of the cerebrospinal fluid are diagnostic tests used in suspected cases of Cryptococcal meningitis.
INFECTIOUS DISEASE – CRYPTOCOCCUS MENINGITIS – LABs/DIAGNOSTIC STUDIES (p 416).

Choice A (Tzanck smear) tests for multinucleated giant cells in herpes simplex virus, varicella zoster virus and cytomegalovirus. *Viral meningitis is associated with an increased white cell count, lymphocytosis and a normal glucose* (glucose was decreased in this vignette).

Choice B (Lactate dehydrogenase levels) is a non-specific test that measures tissue damage and can be seen with many diseases.

Choice D (Antistreptolysin titers) is seen with Group A beta hemolytic streptococcal infections.

Choice E (Cold agglutinin test) is used to detect cold autoimmune hemolytic disease or diseases that can induce cold autoimmune hemolytic disease, such as mycoplasma pneumonia infections and infectious mononucleosis.

QUESTION 20
Choice C (decreased serum ferritin) is the correct answer. Anemia of chronic disease is associated with a decreased serum iron (choice D) due to increased storage of iron in ferritin, leading to an increased serum ferritin. It results in a normocytic anemia (although early anemia of chronic disease may be microcytic). It is also associated with a decreased total iron binding capacity (choice E).
HEMATOLOGY – ANEMIA OF CHRONIC DISEASE – LABS/DIAGNOSTIC STUDIES (p 456).

QUESTION 21

Choice B (prazosin) is the correct answer. Prazosin is an alpha-1 antagonist that is used in the management of hypertension in patients with benign prostatic hypertrophy. Alpha-1 blockade in the peripheral vessels causes vasodilation. Alpha-1 receptors blockade also causes relaxation of the prostate and the bladder neck. It is not used as first line management for essential hypertension because of the side effects of first dose hypotension, orthostatic hypotension and reflex tachycardia and nasal congestion. CARDIOLOGY – ALPHA BLOCKERS – PHARMACOLOGY (p 46).

QUESTION 22

Choice B (bismuth salicylate) is the correct answer. Side effects of bismuth salicylates include darkening of the tongue and the stool as well as constipation. GI/NUTRITION – SALICYLATES – PHARMACOLOGY (p 487).

Choice A (sucralfate) may reduce the bioavailability of some drugs, such as histamine 2 receptor blockers, proton pump inhibitors and fluoroquinolones if given simultaneously with sucralfate.

Choice C (cimetidine) is a histamine-2 receptor blocker with a special side effect profile compared to other histamine-2 receptor blockers. *Cimetidine* specifically has many drug interactions due to *inhibition of the cytochrome P450 system* so it may increase the levels of theophylline, warfarin and phenytoin. Other side effects include *androgen inhibition, leading to impotence and gynecomastia.*

Choice D (misoprostol) is a prostaglandin E1 analog that increased bicarbonate and mucous secretions and reduces acid production.

Choice E (diphenoxylate) is an opioid agonist used as an anti diarrheal.

QUESTION 23

Choice C (atrial septal defect) is correct. Atrial septal defect classically presents with a systolic murmur, prominent S1 and a widely fixed, split S2 sound. CARDIOLOGY – ATRIAL SEPTAL DEFECT – MOST LIKELY (p 44).

Choice A (coarctation of the aorta) is classically associated with a systolic ejection murmur that radiates to the back or scapula, delayed weak femoral pulses & asymmetrical blood pressure measurements between arms of >20 mmHg.

Choice B (*patent ductus arteriosus*) is classically associated with a *continuous machinery murmur.*

Choice D (*aortic stenosis*) is classically associated with a *systolic ejection crescendo murmur that radiates to the neck and is associated with a weak, delayed upstroke of the peripheral pulses.*

Choice E (aortic regurgitation) is a diastolic murmur(not systolic).

QUESTION 24

Choice B (CA-125) is the correct answer. 90% of ovarian cancers are epithelial cell tumors (especially in postmenopausal women). CA-125 is a glycoprotein that is normally produced by ovarian cells. It also produced by other organs (such as the pancreas) so CA-125 isn't specific to ovarian cancer. CA-125 overproduction occurs in ovarian cancer and its elevation in a patient treated for ovarian cancer may suggest tumor recurrence. REPRODUCTIVE – OVARIAN CANCER – HEALTH MAINTENANCE (p 254).

Choice A (Carcinogenic embryonic antigen) is used as a tumor marker for pancreatic, gastric, lung, breast and medullary thyroid carcinomas. Other non-cancerous conditions that associated with an elevated CEA level include smoking, COPD and inflammatory bowel disease. CEA is normally produced in gastrointestinal tissues during fetal development with cessation of CEA production prior to birth.

Choice C (beta subunit of the human chorionic gonadotropin) is a tumor marker for germ cell tumors. Germ cell ovarian tumors are not as common as epithelial ovarian tumors and are associated with a much younger age group (especially women <30y). Beta HCG can be elevated in testicular cancers, choriocarcinomas, hydatidiform molar pregnancies, islet cell tumors and teratomas.

Choice D (human placental lactogen) may be elevated in placenta site trophoblastic tumors.

Choice E (alpha fetoprotein) may be elevated in germ cell tumors. They may be elevated in some ovarian tumors but CA-125 is more widely used since 90% of ovarian tumors being epithelial cell in origin.

QUESTION 25
Choice D [adenocarcinoma] is the correct choice. Adenocarcinoma is the most common lung tumor in smokers, non smokers & in women. It causes 35% of cancers PULMONARY – LUNG CANCER – HEALTH MAINTENANCE (p 92).

Choice A bronchoalveolar carcinoma is relatively rare.

Choice B (small cell) is associated with smoking. It causes 13% of all lung cancers.

Choice C (large cell) represents only 10 % of malignancies.

Choice E (squamous cell) is also associated with smoking. It causes 20% of all lung cancers.

QUESTION 26
Choice A [tachypnea] is the correct choice. Tachypnea is the most common sign seen in pulmonary embolism (97%). Accentuated heart sounds seen in 55%, tachycardia in 44%, sweating in 20% and cyanosis in 18%.

QUESTION 27
Choice E (increase fat intake to increase gastrointestinal transit) is the correct answer. Fatty foods decrease gastrointestinal transit so patients with GERD are told to reduce fatty food intake to improve symptoms. All of the other choices are recommended to reduce the symptoms of GERD. GI/NUTRITION– GASTROESOPHAGEAL REFLUX DISEASE (page 128).

QUESTION 28
Choice E (Huntington's disease) is the correct answer. Huntington's disease is an autosomal dominant neurodegenerative disorder classically associated with the *triad of* ❶ initial *behavioral changes* then ❷ *chorea* and eventually ❸*dementia.* The classic finding on *CT scan is cerebral & caudate nucleus atrophy.* The caudate nucleus is part of the basal ganglia and as such can cause movement disorders such as chorea.
NEUROLOGY – HUNTINGTON'S DISEASE – MOST LIKELY (p. 354).

Choice A (*Parkinson's disease*) classically causes the triad of ❶ *resting tremor* ❷*bradykinesia* and ❸ *rigidity.*

Choice B (*Tourette's syndrome*) often becomes reduce in childhood but may persist in adulthood. It is characterized by *motor tics predominantly affecting the head, neck and face.*

Choice C (Sydenham's chorea) are *rapid, involuntary, jerky movements* (as present in this vignette) but is associated with rheumatic fever which predominantly affects children ages 5-15 years old that had a *recent Group A streptococcal infection.*

Choice D (*Tardive dyskinesia*) is a complication of long-term dopamine antagonist therapy. The extrapyramidal symptoms associated with tardive dyskinesia is classified by *repetitive involuntary movement mostly involving the extremities and the face, such as lip smacking, teeth grinding, rolling of the tongue.*

QUESTION 29

Choice A (new, abnormal blood vessels) is the correct answer. Diabetic retinopathy is due to retinal ischemia. In proliferative retinopathy, new abnormal blood vessels are formed via angiogenesis but these fragile blood vessels are prone to bleeding, causing visual loss. *It is this abnormal, new blood vessel formation that distinguishes proliferative diabetic retinopathy from nonproliferative diabetic retinopathy.* EENT – PROLIFERATIVE DIABETIC RETINOPATHY – HISTORY AND PHYSICAL (p 226).

Choice B (papilledema) can be seen in optic neuritis, acute angle closure glaucoma or malignant hypertension.

Choice C (flame shaped hemorrhages) is a nonspecific finding that can be seen in both diabetic and hypertensive retinopathy. Flame shaped hemorrhages are found in the nerve fiber layer with the ganglion cells shaping the blood flowing around them into the characteristic flame shape.

Choice D (hard exudates) are caused by leaky, damaged capillaries and are lipid residues. Hard exudates can be seen with both diabetic and hypertensive retinopathy.

Choice E (cotton wool spots) are fluffy white microinfarctions of the nerve fiber layer and can be seen with both hypertensive and diabetic retinopathy.

QUESTION 30

Choice B (DeQuervain's Tenosynovitis) is the correct choice. It is associated with pain along the radial side of the wrist and the forearm. A *positive Finkelstein test* (pain with ulnar deviation or thumb extension) is classically seen with it. MUSCULOSKELETAL – DEQUERVAINS TENOSYNOVITIS – HISTORY AND PHYSICAL (p 179).

Choice A (*Flexor Tenosynovitis*) is an infection of the flexor tendons that can rapidly lead to loss of the finger. It is classically associated with *the 4 Kanavel's signs (1. The finger held in flexion, 2. Diffuse swelling of the affected tendon, 3. Tenderness over the affected tendon & 4. Pain on passive extension of the finger).*

Choice C (*Carpal Tunnel syndrome*) causes *pain or paresthesias along the median nerve* that is often *worse at night* and may be associated with *thenar atrophy and thumb motion deficits.*

Choice D (*Cubital tunnel syndrome*) causes symptoms along the *ulnar nerve.*

Choice E (*Lateral epicondylitis*) will occur along the lateral aspect of the elbow and is associated with lateral elbow tenderness.

QUESTION 31

Choice D (Adson test) is the correct choice. This presentation is classic for *Thoracic outlet syndrome.* This condition is an *idiopathic compression of the brachial plexus, subclavian artery or vein.* The *Adson test* is the loss of the radial pulse when the head is turned to the affected side due to vascular compression. MUSCULOSKELETAL – THORACIC OUTLET SYNDROME – HISTORY AND PHYSICAL (p 167).

Choice A (*Thompson test*) is associated with *Achilles tendon rupture if it is positive.*

Choice B (*Apley test)* is used to assess shoulder range of motion (abduction and external rotation).

Choice C (*Ober test*) is done for *iliotibial band syndrome* affecting the knee.

Choice E (*Hawkins test*) is done to assess *rotator cuff injuries.*

QUESTION 32

Choice C (nitrofurantoin) is the correct answer. In the management of acute cystitis in pregnancy, treatment choices include nitrofurantoin, amoxicillin, cephalexin, and cefpoxidime.
GENITOURINARY – URINARY TRACT INFECTIONS – PHARMACOLOGY (p 335).

Choice A (doxycycline), Choice B (trimethoprim-sulfamethoxazole) and choice D (ciprofloxacin) are contraindicated in pregnancy due to their teratogenic effects. Fluoroquinolones, however, are the drug of choice for urinary tract infections for nonpregnant patients.

Choice E (clindamycin) covers primarily gram-positive organisms and anaerobes, so it would be ineffective in the management of gram negative uropathogens, which are the most common cause of cystitis.

QUESTION 33

Choice D (24-hour urine vanillylmandelic acid levels) is the correct answer. This vignette describes the classic signs of *pheochromocytoma*, which is a *neuroendocrine tumor that secretes catecholamines*, causing *palpitations, headache, excessive sweating and hypertension.* *Elevated 24-hour measurements of the metabolites of epinephrine (such as vanillylmandelic acid)* are characteristic of pheochromocytoma.
ENDOCRINE – PHEOCHROMOCYTOMA – LABS/DIAGNOSTIC STUDIES (p 299).

Choice A (plasma renin levels) are elevated in renal artery stenosis. In this patient, there is no evidence of renal artery stenosis, such as abdominal bruits.

Choice B (echocardiography) is indicated if the hypertension was thought to be due to coarctation of the aorta, which would be associated with a systolic murmur and blood pressure differences in the arm and the leg.

Choice C (overnight dexamethasone suppression test) is indicated if Cushing's syndrome is suspected.

Choice E (ACTH stimulation test) is indicated if adrenal insufficiency is suspected. Adrenal insufficiency is associated with hypotension not hypertension.

QUESTION 34

Choice C (IV calcium gluconate) is the correct answer. Calcium gluconate stabilizes the cardiac membrane, so in patients with positive ECG findings (such as peaked T waves seen on this ECG or sine waves), severe symptoms, or potassium levels greater than 6.5 mEq/L, calcium gluconate should be given to prevent arrhythmias. Certain medications (such as beta blockers and ACE inhibitors seen in this vignette) may work synergistically to cause hyperkalemia in some patients. GENITOURINARY– HYPERKALEMIA – CLINICAL INTERVENTION (p 331).

Choice A (Oral sodium polystyrene sulfonate) can also be an adjunct in the management of hyperkalemia, but requires a bowel movement to get rid of the potassium via the GI tract. It does not cause a rapid reduction of potassium levels.

Choice B (IV sodium bicarbonate) can be used in severe cases of hyperkalemia and severe metabolic acidosis but it is not first line management of hyperkalemia.

Choice D (IV potassium chloride) is used to treat hypokalemia not hyperkalemia.

Choice E (IV Dextrose) may be given with insulin as part of the treatment of hyperkalemia. Insulin shifts potassium into the cells and the dextrose prevents hypoglycemia from the insulin treatment.

QUESTION 35

Choice C (Histoplasma capsulatum pneumonia) is the correct answer. Histoplasma capsulatum is associated with *soil containing bat and bird droppings especially in the Mississippi and Ohio river valley areas.* It is usually asymptomatic or may cause an atypical pneumonia. In immunocompromised patients, it may become disseminated. Pittsburgh fits the perfect location, he was digging up soil and there was a bat nest in his house, which puts him at increased risk for Histoplasma infection. PULMONARY – HISTOPLASMOSIS PNEUMONIA – MOST LIKELY (p 101).

Choice A (Pneumocystis jirovecii pneumonia) is classically seen in immunocompromised patients.

Choice B (Haemophilus influenza pneumonia) usually causes a lobar infiltrate. It is the second most common cause of community-acquired pneumonia (after Streptococcus pneumoniae).

Choice D (Influenza virus pneumonia) usually presents with severe body aches. Influenza has the highest incidence in the fall and the winter, making this diagnosis less likely.

Choice E (Severe acute respiratory syndrome) known as SARS is caused by Coronavirus. Coronavirus can also cause an atypical pneumonia. They usually present with nonspecific flu-like symptoms and often an atypical pneumonia that would show up as ground glass opacities or a lobar consolidation on CT scan.

QUESTION 36

Choice A (enterovirus) is the correct answer. The *CSF findings of a normal glucose, an increased white blood cell count and lymphocytosis is the hallmark of aseptic (viral) meningitis.* These findings can also be seen in encephalitis, but the absence of neurological deficits makes viral meningitis the more likely diagnosis. The enteroviruses (such as echovirus and coxsackie virus) are the most common cause of viral meningitis. NEUROLOGY – VIRAL MENINGITIS – MOST LIKELY (p 365).

Choice B (Herpes Simplex Virus) can cause viral meningitis but Enterovirus is the most common cause. However, *HSV infection is the most common cause of encephalitis*, which presents with the same CSF findings. However, since encephalitis is an infection of the brain tissue, it is *classically associated with neurological deficits* and may have brain hemorrhaging as well on CT scan of the head.

Choice C (Rhabdovirus) is the causative agent of Rabies. It causes encephalitis. Encephalitis presents with the same CSF findings as viral meningitis but as encephalitis is an infection of the brain tissue, it is classically associated with neurological deficits.

Choice D (Arbovirus) and choice E (Varicella Zoster Virus) can cause either viral meningitis or encephalitis but are not the most common causes.

QUESTION 37

Choice E (Epstein Barr Virus) is the causative agent of oral hairy leukoplakia.
EENT – ORAL HAIRY LEUKOPLAKIA – BASICS (p 238).

QUESTION 38

Choice B (pityriasis versicolor) is the correct answer. *Pityriasis versicolor (also known as tinea versicolor) presents classically with well demarcated round/oval macules with fine scaling.* The lesions may be hyperpigmented or hypopigmented. The involved skin frequently *fails to tan with sun exposure. Wood's lamp (black light) will often reveal yellow-green immunofluorescence* (hence the name tinea versicolor due to the enhanced color variation). Examination of scrapings with potassium hydroxide reveal budding hyphae with a "spaghetti and meatball" appearance. DERMATOLOGY – TINEA VERSICOLOR – LABS/DIAGNOSTIC STUDIES (p 391).

Choice A (*pityriasis rosea*) is classically associated with a *herald patch* (a solitary salmon-colored macule) on the trunk that precedes the development of a generalized exanthem with multiple, smaller, bilateral, symmetric round and oval salmon-colored macules with a white circular (collarette) scale along the cleavage lines in a *Christmas tree pattern* along the trunk, sparing the face. The *herald patch* of pityriasis rosea can resemble pityriasis versicolor but with potassium hydroxide, hyphae are not seen (as in pityriasis versicolor). *PR often has a collarette scale* in which the scale is seen around the periphery of the lesion, whereas PV has a fine scale.

Choice C (*non bullous impetigo*) is most commonly caused by Staphylococcus aureus and Group A beta hemolytic Streptococcus (Strep pyogenes). Vesicles or pustules that develop characteristic *honey-colored crusts* characterize it. Wood's lamp is not used in the workup of impetigo.

Choice D (*melasma) is hypermelanosis* especially seen in sun exposed areas. It is classically associated with hyper pigmented areas, which are unchanged under black light (Wood's lamp).

Choice E (*lichen planus*) is classically associated with the *5P's: the rash is usually purple in color, polygonal (irregularly-shaped, planar (plaques), pruritic & papular with fine scales.* Patients often have nail dystrophy. Oral involvement may include *Wickham striae* (lesions with lacy white to gray striae). Wood's lamp is not used in the evaluation of lichen planus.

QUESTION 39

Choice E (chronic myelogenous leukemia) is the correct answer. Chronic myelogenous leukemia is most commonly seen in patients older than 50 years of age. It is associated with a *strikingly elevated white blood cell count,* increased LDH, an increased leukocyte alkaline phosphatase score. The white blood cells tend to be well differentiated (mature cells). Most patients are asymptomatic until they develop a blastic crisis. *The Philadelphia chromosome is classically associated with CML* (although in small amount of cases it can be seen in ALL and rarely in AML). HEMATOLOGY – CHRONIC MYELOGENOUS LEUKEMIA – MOST LIKELY (Page 466).

Choice A (acute myelogenous leukemia) is classically associated with the Auer rod, a linear intracellular inclusion.

Choice B (chronic lymphocytic leukemia) is associated with smudge cells (fragile, well differentiated white blood cells that often smudge during slide preparation).

Choice C (acute lymphocytic leukemia) most commonly presents in children. It has a peak incidence between 2 to 5 years of age.

Choice D (multiple myeloma) is associated with a monoclonal protein spike on hemoglobin electrophoresis and Bence-Jones (light chain) proteins on urine electrophoresis.

QUESTION 40

Choice D [isoniazid, rifampin, pyrazinamide and ethambutol (total duration of treatment for 6 months)] is the correct choice. The patient has pulmonary symptoms, a positive AFB smear, and an upper lobe consolidation all consistent with active tuberculosis infection. The management of choice is initiation of 4 drugs "RIPE" or "RIPS". *The total treatment duration for active tuberculosis is 6 months* (the drugs are discontinued basis of the sensitivities determined by cultures). PULMONARY – TUBERCULOSIS – CLINICAL INTERVENTION (p 108).

Choice A is the treatment for latent TB infection in patients with HIV or granuloma on chest X ray.

Choice B is incorrect because a positive PPD only tells you someone is infected. It does not tell you if they are infectious to other people or if they have active disease. PPD is a screening test for infection.

Choice C is the treatment for latent TB infection in the general population.

Choice E may be used in situations if active tuberculosis is suspected but the chest radiograph is negative. There is a positive chest radiograph and a positive acid fast bacilli seen on sputum smear in this vignette.

QUESTION 41

Choice A (Enterotoxigenic E. coli) is the correct answer. All of the other choices cause an invasive diarrhea so anti-motility agents are contraindicated in invasive diarrheas. Decreased gastrointestinal motility could lead to increased bacterial toxicity. GI/NUTRITION – ENTEROTOXIGENIC E COLI – BASICS (p 157).

QUESTION 42

Choice B (positive thyroid stimulating antibodies) is the correct answer. The patient has *ophthalmopathy, pretibial myxedema and hyperthyroid symptoms.* In addition to a *diffuse radioactive iodine uptake scan,* these are indicative of Graves' disease. *Thyroid stimulating antibodies* are the hallmark antibodies of Graves. These antibodies stimulates the TSH receptor on the thyroid gland, causing thyroid gland growth and hyperthyroidism. *Graves disease is the most common cause of hyperthyroidism in the United States.*
ENDOCRINE – GRAVES DISEASE – LABS/DIAGNOSTIC STUDIES (p 286).

Choice A (increased TSH and increased free T4 levels) is associated with TSH-secreting adenomas. TSH-secreting adenomas are the other reason for a diffuse, increased radioactive iodine uptake scan but would more likely be associated with visual changes & headaches in addition to hyperthyroid symptoms. *The presence of ophthalmopathy is much more highly suggestive of Graves.*

Choice C (positive thyroid peroxidase antibodies) and Choice D (positive thyroglobulin antibodies) are classically associated with the autoimmune thyroid inflammation such as Hashimoto's, silent lymphocytic thyroiditis or post-partum thyroiditis. They are sometimes present in patients with Graves' disease but they are not specific for it. These disorders are associated with decreased diffuse uptake on radioactive iodine uptake scan.

Choice E (biopsy showing papillary thyroid carcinoma) is incorrect because most thyroid carcinomas do not produce large amounts of thyroid hormone and are not classically associated with significant thyroid function test abnormalities.   Thyroid malignancies are associated with cold nodules with no uptake on radioactive iodine uptake.

CHOICE 43

Choice C (functional neurological disorder/conversion disorder) is the correct answer. Conversion disorder is a loss of motor or sensory neurologic function suggestive of a physical disorder but caused by psychological factors. PSYCH/BEHAVIORAL – CONVERSION DISORDER – MOST LIKELY (p 384).

Choice A (panic disorder) is defined as recurrent panic attacks that are not due to a pharmacologic substance, medical condition or other mental disorder.

Choice B (post traumatic disorder) occurs in a patient exposed to a traumatic event with a response of helplessness, dissociative symptoms and avoidance of associated stimuli. The trauma is often experienced in recollections, nightmares that can resurface the feelings as if it were happening again.   The symptoms must be present for more than 1 month for the diagnosis to be made.

Choice D (hypochondriasis) is the preoccupation with the fear or belief that one has a serious, undiagnosed disease despite reassurance.

Choice E (Munchausen syndrome) is an intentional, self-induced symptom or falsified physical or lab findings.

QUESTION 44

Choice B (benztropine) is the correct answer.   Due to the relative dopamine depletion seen in Parkinson disease, acetylcholine is allowed to excite the nerves without inhibition, leading to tremors. *Anticholinergic medications, such as benztropine will reduce the tremor in younger patients in which tremor is the predominant symptom.* (notice it sounds like atropine, an anticholinergic used in asthma). Although levodopa/carbidopa (Choice A) is more effective for all of the symptoms, using it early on in someone so young will lead to an earlier wearing off effect after years of use. NEUROLOGIC – PARKINSON'S DISEASE – PHARMACOLOGY (p 353).

Choice C (entacapone) can also be used in the management of Parkinsonism. It is not first line however.

Choice D (propranolol) and choice E (carbamazepine) are not routinely used in the management of Parkinson's disease.

QUESTION 45

Choice E (Punctate bleeding spots when the plaques of psoriasis are unroofed) is the correct answer.   This describes Auspitz sign, which is classically associated with plaque psoriasis. DERMATOLOGY – PSORIASIS – HISTORY AND PHYSICAL (p 391).

Choice A (Clustered, white lesions on the buccal mucosa with an erythematous rim opposite the lower 1st and 2nd molars) describes Koplik's spots seen with rubeola (measles).

Choice B (Sloughing off of the skin when the skin is lightly stroked) describes Nikolsky sign. *Nikolsky sign is removal of the epidermis with slight pressure applied to the skin.* A positive Nikolsky's sign can be seen in toxic epidermal necrolysis, Steven-Johnson syndrome, pemphigus vulgaris, and staphylococcal scalded skin syndrome.

Choice C (Localized subcutaneous anaphylactoid reaction after stroking the skin) describes Darier's sign. Darier's sign is associated with urticarial pigmentosa and mastocytosis.

Choice D (Skin lesions appearing on the lines of trauma) describes Koebner's phenomenon.   Koebner's phenomenon can be seen in many diseases such as psoriasis, lichen planus, vitiligo, and some infectious diseases.

QUESTION 46

Choice B (small, erythematous discrete papules with fine scales) is the correct answer.   This is the classic description of guttate psoriasis. DERMATOLOGY – GUTTATE PSORIASIS – HISTORY AND PHYSICAL (p 391).

Choice A (*raised, dark-red plaques with thick silvery-white scales*) describes *plaque psoriasis. Plaque psoriasis is the most common variant of psoriasis.*

Choice C (generalized erythematous rash involving most of the skin especially at body folds with the absence of plaques) describes inverse psoriasis.

Choice D (*uniformly swollen "sausage" digits and joint stiffness*) describes *psoriatic arthritis.* X rays will often show bone erosions described as "pencil in cup" deformities. Psoriatic arthritis is an inflammatory arthritis associated with psoriasis.

Choice E (deep yellow non-infected pustules that evolve into red macules on the palms and the soles) describes pustular psoriasis.

QUESTION 47

Choice E (increased aspartate transaminase (AST): increased alanine aminotransferase (ALT) > 2:1) is the correct answer. AST levels are greater than ALT levels in alcoholic hepatitis because AST is primarily found in the mitochondria of hepatocytes. Alcohol causes direct mitochondrial damage. The AST levels are usually <500 in alcohol hepatitis. GI/NUTRITION – ALCOHOLIC HEPATITIS – LABS/DIAGNOSTIC STUDIES (p 140).

Choice A [*increased alkaline phosphatase with gamma glutamyl transpeptidase (GGT)*] is associated with *cholestasis* (such as gallstones in the biliary tree).

Choice B [increased alanine aminotransferase levels (ALT) >1000] is associated with viral, toxic or acute inflammatory hepatitis.

Choice C [increased alanine aminotransferase levels (ALT) >1000 with *positive smooth muscle antibodies*] is associated with *autoimmune hepatitis*.

Choice D [increased alanine aminotransferase (ALT) and increased aspartate transaminase (AST) > 2:1 with levels <500] is associated with chronic hepatitis.

QUESTION 48

Choice E (Carvedilol) is correct. Carvedilol and Labetalol block the peripheral alpha-1, beta-1 and beta 2 receptors. CARDIOLOGY – ANTIARRHYTHMICS – PHARMACOLOGY (p 480).

Choice A (atenolol) and C (metoprolol) are cardioselective beta blockers, which preferentially affect the beta -1 receptor only, leading to its cardioselective effects.

Choice B (propranolol) and Choice D (nadolol) are nonselective beta blockers that have both beta 1 and beta 2 receptor blocking qualities

QUESTION 49

Choice B (coronary artery bypass graft) is the correct answer. Coronary artery bypass graft is the definitive management of patients with coronary artery disease if the occlusion involves the left main coronary artery, occlusion involving 3 or more coronary arteries and/or decreased left ventricular ejection fraction. CARDIOLOGY – CORONARY BYPASS GRAFT – LABS/DIAGNOSTIC STUDIES (p 22).

Choice A (percutaneous transluminal coronary angioplasty with stent) and Choice C (percutaneous transluminal coronary angioplasty without stent) can be used as definitive management of coronary artery disease in patients with occlusion of coronary vessels (not involving the left main coronary artery), less than 3 coronary vessel involvement and in patients with normal or near normal left ventricular ejection fraction.

Choice D (initiation of an angiotensin converting enzyme inhibitor) is part of the long-term management of ST elevation myocardial infarction once the patient is stabilized. ACE inhibitors do not directly treat the occlusion but are used to prevent the long-term progression from ST elevation myocardial infarction to heart failure.

Choice E (aspirin and clopidogrel for at least 6 months) does not reestablish perfusion. They prevent the progression of clot formation.

QUESTION 50

Choice C (G4P3A1) is the correct answer. Gravida = the number of pregnancies (regardless if carried to term). Para = number of births (>20 weeks gestations) including viable or nonviable births (including still births). Abortus = number of pregnancies that were lost for whatever reason (including miscarriages, abortions) etc. The vignette describes a woman with 4 pregnancies (G4) 3 births (P3) & 1 miscarriage (A1). REPRODUCTIVE – PREGNANCY – BASICS (p 250).

QUESTION 51

Choice C (having the patient look upwards) is the correct choice. This is a classic description of *orbital floor fracture*. Due to *entrapment of the inferior rectus muscle, patients may develop diplopia, inability to look upward or may have worsening of symptoms on upward gaze*. EENT – ORBITAL FLOOR FRACTURE – HISTORY AND PHYSICAL EXAM (p 225).

QUESTION 52

Choice C (lateral elbow pain with lateral epicondyle tenderness) is the correct choice. Tennis elbow is inflammation of the tendon insertion of the extensor carpi radialis brevis muscle and is associated with lateral tenderness at the insertion site. MUSCULOSKELETAL – TENNIS ELBOW – HISTORY & PHYSICAL (p 172).

Choice A (Pain and tenderness of the pronator teres), Choice B (pain and tenderness of the flexor carpi radialis), Choice D (pain with wrist flexion against resistance) and Choice E (pain worse with pulling activities) are all associated with medial epicondylitis (Golfer's elbow).

QUESTION 53

Choice D (IV Nafcillin) is the correct answer. Staphylococcus aureus is the most common cause of osteomyelitis in both adults and children. The positive *periosteal reaction* indicates bony destruction in osteomyelitis. The periosteal reaction can also be seen in a healing fracture or in some bone malignancies, such as Ewing's sarcoma. The *gram stain shows gram-positive (purple) cocci in clusters, indicative of Staphylococcus aureus.* First line management is an anti-staphylococcal penicillin (such as Nafcillin). The mechanism of action of penicillin is to inhibit cell wall synthesis via the beta lactam ring structure of penicillin, leading to rapid bacterial cell death. Some bacteria have developed an enzyme called beta lactamase (penicillinase) that can break the beta lactam ring, rendering these antibiotics ineffective. The *anti staphylococcal penicillins (Nafcillin, Dicloxacillin, Oxacillin) are the only penicillin group that are active against beta lactamase without adding an inhibitor.* INFECTIOUS DISEASE – OSTEOMYELITIS – PHARMACOLOGY (p 195 & 411).

Choice A (IV Penicillin G aqueous) can be used for non beta lactamase producing gram-positive organisms, such as Staphylococcus aureus but it is not reliably effective against beta lactamase producing organisms.

Choice B (IV Ampicillin) is an aminopenicillin that has good gram positive and gram-negative coverage. It is not used for beta lactamase producing bacteria by itself. Sulbactam, a beta lactamase inhibitor, can be added to Ampicillin to inhibit beta lactamase. The combination of ampicillin/sulbactam is marketed as the drug Unasyn.

Choice C (IV Gentamicin) is an aminoglycoside, which reliably covers gram-negative organisms. As single coverage, it is not indicated for gram-positive coverage as its gram positive coverage is less reliable. When added to other medications, such as penicillin, there is enhanced, synergistic gram-positive coverage of aminoglycosides.

Choice E (IV Aztreonam) is a monobactam antibiotic that is used for gram-negative coverage (including pseudomonas). It is not indicated in gram-positive infections.

QUESTION 54

Choice A (plasmapheresis) is the correct answer. First line management of thrombotic thrombocytopenic purpura is *plasmapheresis* (plasma exchange therapy). Plasmapheresis removes excess the excess ADAMTS 13 antibodies and replaces ADAMTS 13, which reduces the disease burden. It is usually continued until 48 hours after the serum LDH and platelet count normalizes.
HEMATOLOGY – THROMBOTIC THROMBOCYTOPENIC PURPURA – CLINICAL INTERVENTION (Page 461).

Choice B (splenectomy) can be used in cases that are refractory to plasmapheresis and corticosteroids.

Choice C (corticosteroids) may be added as additional therapy in cases where plasmapheresis has not been effective or in severe cases. Corticosteroids and Cyclophosphamide (Choice E) are immunosuppressive drugs that help to blunt the immune response.

Choice D (transfusion of platelets) is not routinely used in the management of thrombocytopenia. Platelet transfusion may paradoxically cause thrombi formation. Platelet transfusion may be indicated in severe thrombocytopenia, in patients with severe bleeding or patients that need an invasive procedure.

QUESTION 55
Choice C (allopurinol) is the correct answer. Tumor lysis syndrome is a condition in which large amounts of cancer cells are destroyed in a short period of time by chemotherapy (Choice B). This leads to large amounts of potassium, and nucleic acid release into the systemic circulation. The breakdown of the nucleic acids leads to uric acid formation and subsequent hyperuricemia. The increased uric acid and phosphate levels can lead to renal failure. *Management includes allopurinol and aggressive IV hydration.*
HEMATOLOGY– TUMOR LYSIS SYNDROME – CLINICAL INTERVENTION (Page 466).

Choice A (hydroxyurea) is used in the management of severe pain crisis in sickle cell disease, polycythemia vera, refractory chronic myelogenous leukemia and some solid tumors.

Choice D (deferoxamine) is a chelating agent used in iron overload states, such as hereditary hemochromatosis and thalassemia.

Choice E (Imatinib) is an oral chemotherapeutic agent used in Philadelphia chromosome-positive CML (and in relapsed or refractory Philadelphia-positive ALL)

QUESTION 56
Choice A (normal alpha fetoprotein and normal beta human chorionic gonadotropin) is the correct answer. Pure **S**eminomas are "**S**imple (normal alpha fetoprotein and normal beta human chorionic gonadotropin) and **S**ensitive (sensitive to radiation). GENITOURINARY – TESTICULAR CANCER – BASICS (p 334).

Choice C (increased alpha fetoprotein and increased beta human chorionic gonadotropin) are seen with pure nonseminomas or mixed tumors. Nonseminomatous tumors are usually resistant to radiation treatment.

QUESTION 57
Choice E is the correct answer. Nondihydropyridine calcium channel blockers are not used in the management of systolic heart failure. Systolic heart failure is diagnosed by echocardiogram evidence of dilated thin chamber walls and decreased ejection fraction. In systolic heart failure, calcium channel blockers will often exacerbate the symptoms. Calcium channel blockers however can be used in diastolic dysfunction.
CARDIOLOGY – HEART FAILURE – CLINICAL INTERVENTION (p 28).

Choice A (discontinue carvedilol temporarily) is often done in the setting of acute decompensated (congestive heart failure). Although beta blockers reduce mortality in heart failure, their dose is either decreased or temporarily discontinued to prevent exacerbation of the heart failure.

Choice C, D are often used in the management of congestive heart failure. Remember *LMNOP (Lasix, Morphine, Oxygen, and position the patient to sit up).*

QUESTION 58

Choice B (Pulmonary regurgitation) is the correct answer. The Graham Steell murmur is a high-pitched early diastolic murmur best heard at the left upper sternal border accentuated with deep inspiration. The murmur is due to pulmonary hypertension & increased velocity. Deep inspiration increases the murmurs on the right side of the heart (due to the increased flow to the right side during inspiration to allow oxygenation of the inspired air). CARDIOLOGY – PULMONARY REGURGITATION – HISTORY AND PHYSICAL (page 37).

Choice A (Tricuspid regurgitation) is a holosystolic murmur best heard at the xyphoid.

Choice C (Aortic regurgitation) is a diastolic, blowing murmur best heard at the left upper sternal border as well but since it is a left sided murmur, inspiration would decrease the intensity of the murmur of aortic regurgitation. Left sided murmurs are heard maximally at end expiration (not inspiration). This is because during expiration, there is increase blood flow to the left side of the heart.

Choice D (Aortic stenosis) is a systolic crescendo-decrescendo murmur best heard at the right upper sternal border.

Choice E (Pulmonary stenosis) is a harsh systolic murmur at the left upper sternal border that may radiate to the neck. It will also be heard maximally during inspiration as seen in this vignette but it is systolic not diastolic.

QUESTION 59

Choice A [Diazepam (Valium)] is the correct answer. A panic attack is defined as an episode of intense fear or discomfort with four or more physical symptoms developing abruptly. Benzodiazepines are first line medication for acute panic attacks. PSYCH/BEHAVIORAL – PANIC ATTACKS - PHARMACOLOGY (p 374).

Choice B [Fluoxetine (Prozac)] and Choice D [Imipramine (Tofranil)] may be used in the long-term management of panic disorder but are not first line for acute attacks.

Choice C [Buspirone (Buspar)] can be used in the long-term management of anxiety disorder.

Choice E [Lithium (Lithobid)] is used for psychosis, mania and bipolar disorders. They are not indicated in panic attacks.

QUESTION 60

Choice D (amyotrophic lateral sclerosis) is the correct answer. *ALS is idiopathic necrosis of both lower and upper motor neurons with progressive motor degeneration* (often with normal sensory function). The patient often presents with loss of the ability to initiate or control motor movements. *The hallmark of ALS is the mixed presence of both upper motor neuron and lower motor lesion signs.* In this vignette the patient has increased deep tendon reflexes and a positive Babinski sign (indicative of upper motor neuron involvement). Muscle atrophy and fasciculations are indicative of lower motor neuron involvement. NEUROLOGY– AMYOTROPIC LATERAL SCLEROSIS – MOST LIKELY (p 370).

Choice A (cerebral palsy) is a group of syndromes that cause postural and motor malfunction. They are often associated with spastic syndromes, diskinetic syndromes, ataxic syndromes and atonic syndromes. They would have presented early on in life.

Choice B (*Parkinson's disease*) is associated with the *bradykinesia, resting tremor, postural instability and rigidity*. Patients with Parkinson's disease usually have normal deep tendon reflexes.

Choice C (*Multiple sclerosis*) is auto immunologic inflammation of central nervous system white matter and classically presents with *optic neuritis, sensory deficits, spinal cord symptoms and Charcot's triad of nystagmus, staccato speech and intentional tremor.*

Choice E (*Guillain Barré syndrome*) classically presents with *symmetrical lower extremity weakness that progress to the upper extremities.*

QUESTION 61
Choice D (staphylococcus saprophyticus) is the correct answer. In addition to E. coli (which is the most common organism), Staphylococcus saprophyticus has an increased incidence in young, sexually active women. GENITOURINARY – URINARY TRACT INFECTIONS – BASICS (p 335).

QUESTION 62
Choice C (chloride sweat test) is the correct answer. In patients with cystic fibrosis, the *defect in the chloride transport leads to increased viscosity of secretions,* such as the protective mucus (leaving patients prone to multiple infections and the development of *bronchiectasis*) as well as digestive enzymes (leading to *decreased fat absorption, malabsorption and growth delays*). PULMONARY – CYSTIC FIBROSIS – LABS/DIAGNOSTIC (p 84).

Choice A (LDH) is often elevated in patients with Pneumocystis jirovecii pneumonia.

Choice B (*alpha-1 antitrypsin deficiency*) is a genetic disorder in which patients are prone to developing *emphysema and bronchiectasis.*

Choice E is incorrect. Pulmonary infections may often cause SIADH, leading to increased water retention causing hypOnatremia (decreased sodium levels)

QUESTION 63
Choice B (Coccidioides immitus) is the correct answer. Coccidioides grows in the soil in arid desert regions of Southwestern United States. It has 3 common presentations: 1) primary pulmonary disease, 2) valley fever: fever, arthralgias with pain and swelling to the ankles, erythema nodosum (described in this vignette), erythema multiforme and 3) disseminated. In early disease, an IgM antibody tube precipitin test is often positive. INFECTIOUS DISEASE – COCCIDIODOMYCOSIS – MOST LIKELY (p 418).

Choice A (Histoplasma capsulatum) is associated with soil containing bat and bird droppings especially in the Mississippi and Ohio river valley areas. It is usually asymptomatic or may cause an atypical pneumonia. In immunocompromised patients, it may become disseminated.

Choice C (Aspergillus fumigatus) most commonly affects the lungs, sinuses and the central nervous system. Beta-D glucan and galactomannan levels are elevated in the chronic or disseminated forms of Aspergillosis.

Choice D (Cryptococcus neoformans) commonly causes pneumonia and meningioencephalitis. It is diagnosed via Cryptococcal antigen in the CSF and via India ink staining.

Choice E (Blastomyces dermatitidis) is a pyogranulomatous fungal infection most commonly seen in immunocompetent men who live or work in close proximity to waterways. It is especially prevalent in the soil and in decaying wood. It usually presents with pulmonary symptoms, cutaneous wart-like lesions, prostatitis in men and may present in disseminated form.

QUESTION 64
Choice B (pityriasis rosea) is the correct answer. *Pityriasis rosea is classically associated with a herald patch* (a solitary salmon-colored macule) on the trunk that precedes the development of a generalized exanthem with *multiple, smaller, bilateral, symmetric round and oval salmon-colored macules with a white circular (collarette) scale along the cleavage lines in a Christmas tree pattern* along the trunk, sparing the face. DERMATOLOGY – PITYRIASIS ROSEA – HISTORY AND PHYSICAL EXAMINATION (p 391).

Choice A (*psoriasis*) has different forms. The most common type is plaque psoriasis, which classically presents as *raised, dark-red plaques or papules with thick silver-white scales* especially on the extensor surfaces.

Choice C (*pityriasis versicolor*) also known as *tinea versicolor* presents classically with *well demarcated round/oval macules with fine scaling.* The lesions may be hyperpigmented or hypopigmented. The involved skin frequently *fails to tan with sun exposure.*

Choice D (*lichen planus*) is an idiopathic cell-mediated dermatologic rash classically associated with the *5Ps: the rash is usually purple in color, polygonal (irregular shape and bordered), planar (plaques), pruritic, papular with fine scales.* Patients often have nail dystrophy. Oral involvement includes *Wickham striae* (lesions with lacy white to gray striae). Choice E (seborrheic dermatitis) classically presents with erythematous plaques with fine white scales common in the scalp, face, eyebrows, beard, nasolabial folds, chest and intertriginous regions of the groin.

QUESTION 65
Choice A (benzoyl peroxide) is the correct answer. For mild acne (comedones with small amounts of pustules and papules). The initial management includes benzoyl peroxide, topical retinoid, topical antibiotics and, in some cases, oral contraceptive therapy in women. DERMATOLOGY - ACNE – CLINICAL INTERVENTION (p 394).

Choice B (minocycline orally), Choice C (spironolactone), and Choice E (cephalexin) are indicated for moderate acne (defined as comedones with larger amounts of papules and pustules). Or in mild acne in which the conventional treatments are ineffective.

Choice D (isotretinoin) is indicated in severe, recalcitrant nodular or cystic acne that is not responsive to conventional therapy such as all the other choices listed.

QUESTION 66
Choice D (primary hyperaldosteronism) is the correct answer. Primary hyperaldosteronism is an autonomous increase in aldosterone (renin independent). Aldosterone functions to absorb sodium in exchange for potassium and hydrogen ions so hyperaldosteronism is associated with sodium retention (leading to hypertension), hypokalemia (prominent U waves on ECG, polyuria & weakness associated with hypokalemia) and metabolic alkalosis. An increased aldosterone: renin ratio distinguishes primary hyperaldosteronism from secondary hyperaldosteronism. ENDOCRINE – PRIMARY HYPERALDOSTERONISM – MOST LIKELY (p 299).

Choice A (secondary hyperaldosteronism) is increased levels of aldosterone as a direct consequence of a primary elevation in renin levels and thus, is associated with an aldosterone: renin ratio <20. Conditions in which renin is elevated including Choice B (congestive heart failure) and Choice C (renal artery stenosis) will cause secondary hyperaldosteronism.

Choice E (hypoaldosteronism) is associated with hyperkalemia. Hyperkalemia can present with peaked T waves on ECG. The prominent U waves in this vignette suggests hypokalemia.

QUESTION 67
Choice E (High dose dexamethasone suppression test and ACTH levels) is the correct answer. A high dose dexamethasone test (along with ACTH levels) are used to distinguish the causes of Cushing's syndrome. ENDOCRINE – CUSHING'S SYNDROME – LABS/DIAGNOSTIC STUDIES (p 298).

Choice A (fluid deprivation test) is the screening test for diabetes insipidus.

Choice B (low dose dexamethasone suppression test and ACTH levels) are used as screening tests for Cushing's syndrome. If positive, then a high dose suppression test is done to help distinguish possible etiologies.

Choice C (CRH stimulation test) is used in adrenal insufficiency to help distinguish between the causes of adrenal insufficiency

Choice D (ACTH stimulation test) is used as the screening test for adrenal insufficiency.

QUESTION 68

Choice A (Endometriosis) is the correct answer.   Endometriosis is associated with the classic triad of cyclic premenstrual pelvic pain, dysmenorrhea and dyspareunia (painful intercourse), which is described in this vignette. Patients may also sometimes have dyschezia (painful bowel movements). REPRODUCTIVE – ENDOMETRIOSIS – MOST LIKELY (p 249).

Choice B (*premenstrual syndrome*) is described as a *cluster of physical, behavioral or mood changes that occur during the luteal phase of the menstrual cycle (7-14 days before the onset of menses* and relieved 2-3 days after the onset of menses). It may cause discomfort but is not associated with functional impairment. If there is functional impairment, it is termed premenstrual dysphoric disorder.

Choice C (*mittelschmertz*) otherwise known as *"ovulation pain"* is lower abdominal or pelvic pain that occurs *during ovulation* (mid cycle) not right before menstruation.

Choice D (*adenomyosis*) is a condition of islands of endometrial tissue within the myometrium (the muscular layer of the uterine wall) producing hyperplasia of the myometrium & an *enlarged tender, symmetric, soft uterus.*

Choice E (endometrial carcinoma) most commonly presents with postmenopausal bleeding or premenopausal menorrhagia.

QUESTION 69

Choice E (iliotibial band syndrome) is the correct choice.   ITBS is *inflammation of the iliotibial band bursa* due to lack of flexibility. It is the *most common cause of knee pain in runners*. It is associated with *LATERAL knee pain* and tenderness. On physical examination a *positive Ober test* (described in the vignette) is usually seen. MUSCULOSKELETAL – ILIOTIBIAL BAND SYNDROME– MOST LIKELY (p 187).

Choice A (*Osgood Schlatter disease*) presents in children and usually causes pain on the *ANTERIOR aspect of the knee that is worse with kneeling*. On physical examination, *the tibial tubercle is usually enlarged*, causing a palpable bump. The pain usually resolves when growth is complete.

Choice B (*Legg Calve Perthe*) is *avascular necrosis of the femoral head* seen in children.

Choice C (*Chondromalacia*) causes *ANTERIOR knee pain behind or around the patella*.

QUESTION 70

Choice D (Osmotic fragility test) is the correct answer. Hereditary spherocytosis is due to a defect in the red blood cell membrane, leading to sphere-shaped red blood cells and increased cell fragility. Both hereditary spherocytosis and autoimmune hemolytic anemia are associated with microcytosis and spherocytosis. A negative Coombs test distinguishes hereditary spherocytosis from autoimmune hemolytic anemia.
HEMATOLOGY – HEREDITARY SPHEROCYTOSIS – LABS/DIAGNOSTIC STUDIES (page 459).

Choice A (Ristocetin activity test) is used in the diagnosis of von Willebrand disease. Ristocetin is an antibiotic that causes platelet aggregation in vitro. Hypoactivity & decreased platelet activity in vitro with Ristocetin is associated with Von Willebrand deficiency.

Choice B (Schilling test) is a test used in the diagnostic work up of pernicious anemia.

Choice C (*Mixing study*) is used to *distinguish factor deficiencies from conditions associated with coagulation factor inhibitors* (such as antiphospholipid syndrome).

Choice E (Flow cytometry testing) is the best screening test for suspected cases of paroxysmal nocturnal hemoglobinuria.

QUESTION 71

Choice C (Desmopressin) is the correct answer.   *Desmopressin (DDAVP) is used in the management of Von Willebrand disease and Hemophilia A. Desmopressin is a synthetic anti-diuretic hormone* (arginine vasopressin) that also increases von Willebrand factor and factor VIII levels. It has no effect on Factor IX. *Desmopressin is also used in the management of central diabetes insipidus* (a disease where there is a lack of anti diuretic hormone production). Desmopressin can also be used in certain cases of nocturnal enuresis since it inhibits diuresis.
HEMATOLOGY – VON WILLEBRAND DISEASE – CLINICAL INTERVENTION (p 463).

Choice A (Aspirin) is not used in Von Willebrand disease. *The use of aspirin* in patients with Von Willebrand disease is associated with *worsening of the already prolonged bleeding time*.

Choice B (hydroxyurea) is used in the management of severe pain crisis in sickle cell disease, polycythemia vera, refractory CML and some solid tumors.

Choice D (Plasmapheresis) also known as plasma exchange therapy is used to remove and/or replace certain components of the blood. It is used in the management of thrombotic thrombocytopenic purpura, hemolytic uremic syndrome, antiphospholipid antibody syndrome, multiple sclerosis, Goodpasture syndrome, myasthenia gravis, multiple sclerosis and Eaton-Lambert syndrome.

Choice D (Factor VIII Concentrates) is used in the management of hemophilia A.

Choice E (Intravenous immunoglobulin) is a blood product made from pooled IgG antibodies that is used to treat some autoimmune diseases such as: idiopathic (immune) thrombocytopenic purpura, Guillain-Barre syndrome. It is also used to treat Kawasaki disease.

QUESTION 72

Choice B (estradiol) is the correct answer. Hot flashes and vaginal dryness are seen in postmenopausal as a direct consequence of decreased estrogen, so estrogen therapy is the most effective management for these symptoms. However, keep in mind that in postmenopausal women with an intact uterus, estrogen therapy alone (unopposed estrogen) may lead to endometrial hyperplasia and possibly endometrial cancer. These risks must be explained to the patient if they have an intact uterus.   *Other medications used to treat hot flashes, vasomotor insufficiency and similar symptoms include progesterone, clonidine, SSRIs and gabapentin.*
REPRODUCTIVE – MENOPAUSE – PHARMACOLOGY (p 251).

Choice A (*Tamoxifen*) is an estrogen antagonist in the breast but is also an estrogen agonist in the bone and endometrium. *Tamoxifen can cause hot flashes as an adverse reaction.*

Choice C (clomiphene) is used to stimulate ovulation in anovulatory women. It is not indicated in the management of postmenopausal symptoms.

Choice D (*raloxifene*) is an estrogen antagonist in the breast and the endometrium. *Raloxifene, like Tamoxifen, can cause hot flashes as an adverse reaction.*

Choice E (progesterone) can be used to treat hot flashes but estrogen is more effective than progesterone.

QUESTION 73

Choice A (urinalysis and urine culture) is the correct answer. In the evaluation of hematuria, urinalysis and urine culture is the first step in the evaluation, as the most common causes are genitourinary infection and nephrolithiasis in patients younger than 40 years of age. GENITOURINARY – HEMATURIA – LABS/DIAGNOSTIC STUDIES (p 341).

Choice B (cystoscopy), Choice C (intravenous pyelogram) and Choice D (urine cytology) are used in patients over the age of 40 or in whom malignancy is suspected. Due to his age in this vignette, a urinalysis and urine culture would be the first step in the evaluation of the hematuria.

Choice E (bladder biopsy) would be done as a follow up study if the cystoscopy, intravenous pyelogram or urine cytology show positive findings suggesting a bladder malignancy.

QUESTION 74

Choice E (an African American female with a history of hypertension) is the correct answer. Bladder cancer is 3 times more common in white males. Other risk factors include smoking (Choice A), history of cyclophosphamide use (Choice B), pioglitazone (Choice C), a history of working as a beautician with dye exposure (Choice D), occupational exposure to rubber and leather, schistosomiasis infections and chronic bladder infection are other risk factors. GENITOURINARY – BLADDER CANCER – HEALTH MAINTENANCE (p 338).

QUESTION 75

Choice A (indomethacin) is the correct answer. A ductus arteriosus remains patent due to prostaglandin release. Indomethacin can be given to close a patent ductus arteriosus. Indomethacin is a non steroidal anti-inflammatory that exerts its effects by prostaglandin inhibition. CARDIOLOGY – PATENT DUCTUS ARTERIOSUS – CLINICAL INTERVENTION (p 44)

Choice C (prostaglandins) can be used if the ductus arteriosus needs to remain patent. In some cyanotic heart diseases (such as coarctation of the aorta and tetralogy of Fallot), the ductus arteriosus may be intentionally left patent by giving prostaglandin E analogs because the PDA allows for some mixture of the blood, improving oxygenation in these cyanotic patients until a more definitive procedure can be done.

All the other choices are not used specifically to close the patent ductus arteriosus.

QUESTION 76

Choice A (a weak, delayed peripheral pulse) is the correct answer. Aortic stenosis is characterized by a systolic crescendo-decrescendo murmur that is best heard at the right upper sternal border and radiates to the carotids. The stenotic aortic valve decreases the amount of blood that can be ejected from the ventricle leading to pulsus parvus et tardus (a weak and delayed pulse) and a fixed cardiac output. CARDIOLOGY – AORTIC STENOSIS – HISTORY AND PHYSICAL EXAMINATION (p 43).

Choice B (the presence of an *opening snap*) is seen with *mitral stenosis* classically (as well as tricuspid stenosis).

Choice C (the presence of *bounding pulses*) and choice E (the presence of a *wide pulse pressure*) is classically associated with *aortic regurgitation*.

Choice D (the presence of an *ejection click*) is classically seen with *mitral valve prolapse*.

QUESTION 77

Choice B (ultrasound) is the correct answer. The *nonbilious vomiting* and the *olive-shaped mass is consistent with pyloric stenosis. Ultrasound is the preferred initial step* in children because it does not involve radiation. GI NUTRITION – PYLORIC STENOSIS – LABS/DIAGNOSTIC STUDIES (p 136).

Choice A (Abdominal radiograph) may be used in children if obstruction (such as Hirschsprung's disease is suspected.

Choice C (*Upper GI series*) can be used in the diagnosis of pyloric stenosis. The *"string sign"* is the classic finding as the contrast passes through the narrowed, stenotic pyloris. This procedure however involves radiation.

Choice D (CT scan of the abdomen) may be used to rule out other diagnoses.

Choice E (Intravenous pyelogram) is a test used to evaluate the kidneys, ureter and the bladder.

QUESTION 78

Choice E (metformin) is the correct answer. Metformin is a biguanide that is associated with *acute kidney injury, gastrointestinal side effects, lactic acidosis and megaloblastic anemia*. In this vignette there is an elevated mean corpuscular volume with normal B12, folate and liver function (all can also produce a macrocytic anemia), making metformin the likely answer. ENDOCRINE – METFORMIN – PHARMACOLOGY (p 305).

Choice A (chlorpropramide) and choice C (glyburide) are sulfonylureas. *Side effects of sulfonylureas include hypoglycemia, gastrointestinal upset, disulfuram reaction, sulfa allergies, weight gain and dysrhythmias.*

Choice B (sitagliptin) is a dipeptidylpeptidase inhibitor. Side effects include: pancreatitis, renal failure and gastrointestinal symptoms.

Choice D (rosiglitazone) thiazolidinedione. Side effects include: fluid retention, congestive heart failure, hepatotoxicity and increased incidence of myocardial infarctions. Pioglitazone may cause bladder cancer.

CHOICE 79

Choice A [Paroxetine (Paxil)] is the correct answer. Selective serotonin reuptake inhibitors are the medical management of choice for post traumatic stress disorder. PSYCH/BEHAVIORAL – POST TRAUMATIC STRESS DISORDER (p 374).

Choice B [Lithium (Lithobid)] is not indicated in the routine management of posttraumatic stress disorder.

Choice C [Phenelzine (Nardil)] is a MAO-inhibitor that can be potentially used in PTSD but it is not the first-line agent.

Choice D [Amitriptyline (Elavil)] and Choice E [Imipramine (Tofranil)] are tricyclic antidepressants that can also be used to treat PTSD but they are not first line agents.

QUESTION 80

Choice E [Olanzapine (Zyprexia)] is the correct answer. Olanzapine is a second generation antipsychotic. The second-generation antipsychotics are the most effective neuroleptic drugs. Psychosis and the positive symptoms of schizophrenia are thought to be the result of excess dopamine receptors in the mesolimbic pathway. The antipsychotic medications 1st & 2nd generation works by blocking dopamine. Ziprasidone is a benzisoxazole drug that is often also used as a first line agent. PSYCH/BEHAVIORAL – SCHIZOPHRENIA – PHARMACOLOGY (p 382).

Choice A [Lithium (Lithobid)] may be used as an adjunctive medication if the symptoms are not controlled with first-line medications.

Choice B [Lorazepam (Ativan)] is a benzodiazepine that may be used as an adjunctive medication to anti-psychotic medications in patients with acute symptoms who are still agitated with anti-psychotics.

Choice C [Fluoxetine (Prozac)] and Choice D [Clomipramine (Anafranil)] are antidepressants medications.

QUESTION 81

Choice C (idiopathic depletion of dopamine in the basal ganglia) is the correct answer. Parkinson disease is idiopathic dopamine depletion due to failure to inhibit acetylcholine in the basal ganglia and is associated with cytoplasmic inclusions (Lewy bodies) and loss of pigment cells in the basal ganglia. NEUROLOGY – PARKINSON'S DISEASE – BASICS (p 353).

Choice A (idiopathic excess production of acetylcholine in the basal ganglia) is not the cause of Parkinson disease. Parkinson is a relative dopamine production problem not an excess of acetylcholine.

Choice B (idiopathic dopamine excess in the mesolimbic pathway) is thought to be the etiology for the positive symptoms of schizophrenia such as delusions and hallucinations.

Choice D (idiopathic malfunction of dopamine in the mesocortical pathway) is thought to be the cause of the negative symptoms of schizophrenia.

Choice E (drug-induced dopamine antagonism) causes Parkinsonism (symptoms that may include bradykinesia, tremor and rigidity). There are many causes of Parkinsonism.

QUESTION 82

Choice C (ethosuximide) is the correct answer. The presentation in this vignette is classic for absence (petit mal) seizures. *Absence seizures classically begins in childhood and is associated with brief impairment of consciousness followed by brief staring episodes, eyelid twitching and the absence of convulsions as well as the absence of a post-ictal phase.* The classic EEG finding in absence seizures is *bilateral symmetric 3Hz spike and wave action. The drug of choice for absence seizures is ethosuximide.* Ethosuximide blocks the calcium channels, which elevates the stimulation threshold for nerve impulses. It is only used in absence seizures (not for grand mal seizures). NEUROLOGY – PETIT MAL SEIZURES – PHARMACOLOGY (p 367).

Choice A (carbamazepine) is indicated in the long-term management of generalized seizure disorders, bipolar disorder and trigeminal neuralgia. It is not routinely used in absence seizures.

Choice B (gabapentin) can be used in partial seizures, grand mal seizures and neuropathic pain syndromes (such as in diabetic neuropathy or post herpetic neuralgia).

Choice D (valproic acid) is second line in the management of absence seizures. It is also used in partial seizures, grand mal seizures and sometimes in the acute manic phase of bipolar disorder

Choice E (lamotrigine) can also be used in absence seizures (it is not first-line). Lamotrigine is also used in complex-partial seizures and grand mal seizures.

QUESTION 83

Choice E (negative QRS complex in Lead I, positive QRS complex in lead aVF) is the correct choice. Severe chronic bronchitis causes severe hypoxemia, which leads to hypoxemic vasoconstriction of the pulmonary circulation, leading to pulmonary hypertension. The right side of the heart has to overcome the higher pressure by *right ventricle hypertrophy, eventually leading to right axis deviation from the increased muscle on the right side (ECG findings described as above), right atrial enlargement and eventually right heart failure. These changes are called cor pulmonale* (which can be seen with any cause of pulmonary hypertension). PULMONARY – CHRONIC BRONCHITIS – LABS/DIAGNOSTIC STUDIES (p 80 & 81).

Choice A (ST elevations in leads I, avL, V5 and V6) is seen with a lateral wall myocardial infarction (often involving the left circumflex artery)

Choice B describes left ventricular hypertrophy (which can be cause by longstanding SYSTEMIC hypertension, aortic stenosis etc).

Choice C describes left axis deviation (which can be a result of left ventricular hypertrophy or inferior wall MI to name a few)

Choice D is seen with large pericardial effusions (as the heart swings to and fro in the pericardial fluid).

QUESTION 84
Choice C [hyperventilation]. is the correct choice. This is an example of a 2-step question. The first step is to determine the acid base disorder and the second is to determine which choice correlates with the answer in step 1. To determine the acid base, first look at the pH to determine if it is acidosis or alkalosis. The pH here is 7.56 (normal pH is 7.35 – 7.45) so the patient is *alkalotic.* The next step is to look at the pCO_2 to see if it correlates. The patient's PCO_2 is 23 (normal PCO_2 is 35-45 mmHg) so a number less than 35 is consistent with respiratory alkalosis, meaning the primary disorder is respiratory alkalosis (the bicarb is 21 and if the primary disorder was metabolic, then the bicarb would have been increased). The bicarb is low in an attempt to try to compensate. Now that you determine the acid base disorder, choice C (hyperventilation) will cause patient to blow off CO_2.
PULMONARY – RESPIRATORY ALKALAOSIS – LABS/DIAGNOSTIC STUDIES (p 116 & 117).

Choice A (morphine overdose) would cause respiratory depression, leading to a respiratory acidosis.

Choice B would cause a metabolic alkalosis (vomiting leads to loss of H+ from the GI tract from the hydrochloric acid as well as the contraction alkalosis from extracellular fluid depletion).

Choice D (uncontrolled type I diabetic) would develop DKA (high anion gap metabolic acidosis).

Choice E (diarrhea) can lead to a loss of sodium bicarbonate and the kidney tries to preserve volume by holding onto sodium chloride, leading to a non anion gap metabolic acidosis.

CHOICE 85
Choice B (macrocytic anemia) is the correct choice. Proton pump inhibitors work by inhibiting parietal cell hydrochloric acid secretion. Parietal cells also secrete intrinsic factor, which is necessary for B12 absorption in the small intestine, leading to a B12 deficiency manifested by a macrocytic anemia.
GI/NUTRITION – PROTON PUMP INHIBITORS – PHARMACOLOGY (p 134).

Choice A (abortifacent by causing uterine contractions) describes the side effects of misoprostol, a prostaglandin analog used in the prevention of NSAID-induced gastric ulcers. Prostaglandins are essential for the production of the protective factors of the stomach (bicarbonate and mucus). Misoprostol is used in medical abortions, because it causes uterine contractions, detaching the embryo from the placenta.

Choice C (gynecomastia) is a side effect of cimetidine, which has anti-androgenic effects.

Choice D (tardive dyskinesia) is a common side effect of dopamine receptor blockers.

Choice E is incorrect. Proton pump inhibitors are inhibits (not induces) the cytochrome P450.

QUESTION 86
Choice B (gluteal cleft) is correct. A pilonidal cyst (or abscess) is a cyst near the gluteal cleft.
DERMATOLOGY – PILONIDAL CYSTS – MOST LIKELY (p 154).

Choice A (an abscess of the apocrine sweat glands) describes hidradenitis suppurativa

Choice C (a cyst containing soft, cheese-like material) describes epidermal or sebaceous cysts.

Choice C (a painless lump of adipose tissue in between the skin and the muscular layer) describes lipomas.

Choice D (a cyst that contains more than 1 germ cell layer) describes teratomas.

QUESTION 87
Choice E (pegylated alpha interferon + ribavirin) is the correct choice. This is the treatment of choice for chronic hepatitis. GI/NUTRITION – HEPATITIS C – CLINICAL INTERVENTION (p 141).

Choice A (lamivudine) and Choice B (adefovir) are used in the management of hepatitis B.

Choice D (interferon beta) is used in the treatment of multiple sclerosis.

QUESTION 88
Choice B (cat exposure) is the correct answer. Toxoplasmosis is a parasitic infection that is most commonly transmitted from the soil, cat feces (cat litter) or by undercooked meat infected with the parasite. It is associated with flu-like symptoms in immunocompetent patients. In immunosuppressed patients, it presents with encephalitis and chorioretinitis. It is part of the congenital ToRCH syndrome. INFECTIOUS DISEASE – TOXOPLASMOSIS – HEALTH MAINTENANCE (p 428).

Choice A (Sheep exposure) is associated with diseased such as Anthrax, Brucellosis and Q fever.

Choice C (Rodent and flea exposure) is associated with plague and murine typhus.

Choice D (Decaying wood near waterways) is associated with blastomycosis and histoplasmosis

Choice E (Unpasteurized milk) is associated with Brucellosis and (in some cases) Listeriosis.

QUESTION 89
Choice D (Roseola) is the correct answer. Roseola is the only childhood exanthema that starts on the trunk and then goes to the face. DERMATOLOGY – ROSEOLA - MOST LIKELY (p 434).

Choice A (*Rubella*) is associated with a *light red to pink spotted rash that lasts about 3 days*. It is usually self-limiting in children but it can cause *transient photosensitivity and arthritis* (especially in young women).

Choice B (Rubeola) is the cause of *measles*. The rash of measles is classically described as *a brick-red rash starting on the face and spreading to the trunk lasting 7 days*. It is often preceded by a *prodrome of cough, runny nose and conjunctivitis*.

Choice C (*fifth's disease*) otherwise known as erythema infectiosum is associated with *coryza, fever and the appearance of an erythematous rash with circumoral pallor giving the classic "slapped cheek" appearance*. This rash is often followed by a *lacy, reticular rash on the extremities* (especially the upper extremities and the rash often spares the palms and the soles).

Choice E (*coxsackie virus A*) is the causative agent of *hand, foot and mouth disease*. Hand foot and mouth disease classically presents with vesicular lesions on a reddened based with an erythematous halo in the oral cavity followed by vesicular rash involving the palms and the soles.

QUESTION 90

Choice D (necrotizing fasciitis) is the correct answer. Necrotizing fasciitis is a rapidly progressing infection that classically presents with erythema and extreme pain out of proportion to physical examination findings. This is followed by the development of hemorrhagic bullae with progression to gangrene and possibly septic shock if antibiotics and surgical debridement are not started early. *Fournier's gangrene is necrotizing fasciitis of the penis and scrotum in patients with impaired immunity* (such as diabetes mellitus, which is present in this vignette). INFECTIOUS DISEASE – NECROTIZING FASCIITIS – MOST LIKELY (p 419).

Choice A (testicular torsion) can present with scrotal pain and edema but is not associated with penile pain or increased warmth as it is localized to the testicle and is associated with decreased blood flow. A blue dot sign would be seen on the testicle with Choice B (torsion of the appendix of the testicle), which is a tender nodule with blue discoloration. Neither of these conditions classically presents with fever and chills.

Choice C (epididymitis) is associated with testicular pain and swelling and may present with fever. It is not associated with hemorrhagic bullae (so necrotizing fasciitis should be suspected).

Choice E (varicocele) is varicosities in the testicle classically described as "a bag of worms" on palpation of the scrotum. It is not usually associated with fever and chills.

QUESTION 91

Choice C (Keratin hyperplasia in the stratum basale and spinosum due to T-cell activation) is the correct answer. Psoriasis is a chronic, multisystemic inflammatory immune disorder. It causes keratin hyperplasia in the stratum basale and spinosum due to T-cell activation. This leads to greater epidermal thickness and continuous turnover of the dermis. DERMATOLOGY – PSORIASIS – BASICS (p 391).

Choice A (overgrowth of Malassezia furfur) is associated with the development of pityriasis (tinea) versicolor.

Choice B (Type I IgE hypersensitivity reaction of the dermis and subcutaneous tissues) describes the pathophysiology of urticaria, a dermatologic allergic response.

Choice D (Type II hypersensitivity reaction in the basement membrane) describes the pathophysiology of bullous pemphigoid. This leads to subepidermal blistering (and the reason why it is classically associated with a negative Nikolsky's sign).

Choice E (Autoimmune disruption of the desmosome layer) describes the pathophysiology of pemphigus vulgaris. The desmosome disruption leads to a positive Nikolsky's sign).

QUESTION 92

Choice C (carboxyhemoglobin levels) is the correct answer. 100% oxygen via nonrebreather is recommended for anyone with a carboxyhemoglobin level of greater 10%. DERMATOLOGY – SMOKE INHALATION INJURIES – LABS/DIAGNOSTIC TESTS (p 404).

Choice A (pulse oximetry) is not reliable in suspected carbon monoxide poisoning because most pulse oximeters cannot distinguish between oxygen on hemoglobin and carboxyhemoglobin. Carbon monoxide has over 200 times more affinity for hemoglobin than oxygen, so the oxygen saturation seen on most pulse oximeters can be misleadingly high.

Choice B (serum bicarbonate levels) are not reliable for detecting carbon monoxide.

Choice D (lead levels) are used in suspected lead poisoning cases. This is an acute event in the vignette.

Choice E (hemoglobin levels) are not significantly affected in acute carbon monoxide poisoning.

QUESTION 93

Choice C (metronidazole topically) is the correct answer. This is the classic description of Rosacea. Rosacea has an unclear etiology but is associated with vasomotor instability with acne-like lesion formation. *Triggers include alcohol, hot or cold weather, hot drinks, spicy foods and hot baths.* It manifests clinically as a *papulopustular rash similar to acne, facial flushing, telangiectasia, skin coarsening and conjunctivitis. Topical metronidazole is the first line choice for the treatment of the acne-like rash.* Rosacea is differentiated from acne vulgaris by the absence of comedones in Rosacea. DERMATOLOGY – ROSACEA – CLINICAL INTERVENTION (p 395).

Choice A (Moh's excision) is used in the management of some dermatological cancers, such as basal cell carcinoma and squamous cell carcinoma.

Choice B (Hydroquinone) is a bleaching agent used for dark spots or hyperpigmentation disorders, such as melasma (chloasma).

Choice D (Clonidine orally) can be used in the management of the flushing symptoms of rosacea (which is absent in this vignette).

Choice E (Corticosteroids orally) is not used in the first line management of rosacea.

QUESTION 94

Choice A (dermoid cystic teratomas) is the correct choice. Of all the benign neoplasms listed in the choice, dermoid cystic teratomas account for between 10-20 percent of all ovarian neoplasms in general and are the most common benign ovarian neoplasm specifically. REPRODUCTIVE – OVARIAN NEOPLASMS – BASICS (p 255).

QUESTION 95

Choice B (progesterone orally) is the correct answer. Endometrial hyperplasia (thickening of the lining of the uterus) can, in some cases, lead to endometrial cancer if not treated. During the first part of the menstrual cycle, the hormone estrogen causes the endometrial lining to grow and thicken to prepare the uterus for possible egg implantation. This is called the proliferative phase.   After ovulation, progesterone production causes the secretory phase, which matures the endometrium. If no pregnancy occurs, progesterone levels fall, causing the shedding of the built up endometrium (menstruation). In situations where there is unopposed estrogen, the absence of progesterone means the endometrium does not shed but keeps proliferating, leading to abnormal growth and thickening. Replacing the lost progesterone cyclically (Choice B) can reverse the hyperplasia by inducing shedding of the uterus when the progesterone levels drop.
REPRODUCTIVE – ENDOMETRIAL HYPERPLASIA – CLINICAL INTERVENTION (p 250).

Choice A (estrogen only) will worsen the condition of unopposed estrogen, making this an incorrect choice.

Choice C (hysterectomy) is the management of endometrial hyperplasia with or without atypia in patients who does not wish to preserve fertility.

Choice D (clomiphene) is used to induce ovulation by increasing LH and FSH release. It used in anovulatory patients.

Choice E (uterine ablation) is used primarily to treat excessive menstrual blood loss.

QUESTION 96

Choice D (Haemophilus ducreyi) is the correct choice. Chancroid, an uncommon sexually transmitted infection in the United States, is caused by H. ducreyi. Chancroid is associated with painful genital ulcers with bubo formation and painful lymphadenopathy. INFECTIOUS DISEASE – CHANCROID – HISTORY AND PHYSICAL EXAMINATION (p 423).

Choice A (Herpes simplex virus) most commonly presents with painful grouped vesicles on an erythematous base and may often be preceded by pain or paresthesias prior to the eruption of the vesicles.

Choice B (Neisseria gonorrhea) is associated with penile or vaginal discharge
Choice C (human papilloma virus) is associated with genital warts, which are painless.
Choice E (Lactobacilli) overgrowth is associated with cytolytic vaginitis.

QUESTION 97

Choice A (petechiae) is the correct answer. Thrombocytopenia is a platelet disorder of the primary coagulation pathway. It classically presents with petechiae and mucocutaneous bleeding. All the other choices are associated with factor deficiencies affecting the secondary (coagulation protein) pathway.
HEMATOLOGY – THROMBOCYTOPENIA – BASICS (Page 463).

QUESTION 98

Choice C (Factor VIII) is the correct choice. Hemophilia is an X-linked recessive disorder causing lack of Factor VIII. Choice E (Factor IX) is associated with Hemophilia B. HEMATOLOGY – HEMOPHILIA A – BASICS (p 462).

QUESTION 99

Choice A (episodic hematuria) is the correct answer. Sickle cell trait is usually asymptomatic. Patients may develop anemia under extreme exertion or dehydration but the only presentation of the trait is occasional episodic painless hematuria. They may have isosthenuria (the inability to concentrate the urine). All of the other choices are associated with sickle cell anemia. HEMATOLOGY – SICKLE CELL TRAIT – BASICS (page 457)

QUESTION 100

Choice E (increased ESR) is the correct choice. DeQuervain's thyroiditis is thyroid inflammation most commonly seen after a viral illness. The hallmark of DeQuervain's thyroiditis is the presence of thyroid tenderness and pain as well as an elevated erythrocyte sedimentation rate. ENDOCRINE – DEQUERVAIN'S THYROIDITIS – LABS (p)287.

Choice A (increased diffuse uptake on radioactive uptake scan) is not seen with DeQuervain's. The thyroid inflammation associated with DeQuervain's causes release of preformed hormone from leakage of inflamed thyroid tissue. The increase in T3 and T4 will lead to suppression of pituitary TSH production (as a result of the negative feedback loop) so there is no new hormone production, leading to *diffuse decreased uptake on radioactive iodine uptake scan.* A diffuse increased uptake is associated with Graves' disease and TSH secreting adenoma, both of those are associated with increased new hormone production.

Choice B (positive thyroid stimulating antibodies) is associated with Graves' disease.

Choice C (positive thyroid peroxidase antibodies) and choice D (positive thyroglobulin antibodies) are associated with autoimmune thyroid disorders such as Hashimoto's, post-partum thyroiditis and silent (lymphocytic) thyroiditis. Although DeQuervain's thyroiditis is associated with viral illnesses, it is not autoimmune.

PHOTO CREDITS
Gram stain: Le Beau / CustomMedical

Gamekeeper's thumb
By James Heilman, MD (Own work) [CC BY-SA 3.0 (http://creativecommons.org/licenses/by-sa/3.0) or GFDL (http://www.gnu.org/copyleft/fdl.html)], via Wikimedia Commons.

1. A 75-year-old female presents to the eye clinic with gradual onset of central vision loss, especially affecting her detail and color vision. Which of the following would most likely be seen on fundoscopic examination based on the most likely diagnosis?
    a. the presence of papilledema
    b. the presence of drusen bodies
    c. the presence of AV nicking
    d. the presence of clumped pigment cells in the anterior vitreous
    e. the presence of the retina hanging in the vitreous

2. A 34-year-old female is complaining of sudden onset of right foot pain after an inversion injury. A radiograph is obtained, which shows a transverse fracture through the diaphysis of the fifth metatarsal. The cuneiforms are in alignment with the metatarsals. Which of the following is the most likely diagnosis?
    a. Pseudo Jones fracture
    b. Charcot's joint
    c. Jones Fracture
    d. Lisfranc Injury
    e. Fleck fracture

3. A 33-year-old male was involved in a motor vehicle accident. A CT scan of the abdomen and pelvis is performed to rule out traumatic injury. The CT scan shows incidental cysts in the liver and the kidney. Which of the following is the patient at significantly increased risk for developing?
    a. CNS lymphoma
    b. Subarachnoid hemorrhage
    c. Ischemic stroke
    d. Alzheimer's disease
    e. Glioblastoma multiforme

4. In evaluation of a pediatric patient, a mid-systolic, musical, vibratory, noisy, high-pitched murmur is heard loudest in the inferior aspect of the left lower sternal border and apex. There is no wide, fixed splitting of the second heart sound. Which of the following is the most likely diagnosis?
    a. Venous hum
    b. Patent ductus arteriosus
    c. Still's murmur
    d. Graham-Steele murmur
    e. Atrial septal defect

5. Hypertensive crisis induced by tyramine-containing foods such as aged cheese and wines are most commonly seen with which of the following medications?
    a. Venlafaxine (Effexor)
    b. Amitriptyline (Elavil)
    c. Phenelzine (Nardil)
    d. Citalopram (Celexa)
    e. Duloxetine (Cymbalta)

6. A 72-year old male presents with a resting "pill-rolling" tremor of the hands, a festinating, shuffling gait with lack of arm movements, and slow initiation of certain movements. He has a fixed facial expression and seborrhea of the skin.   Which of the following is the most effective management in this patient?
   a. Prochlorperazine
   b. Levodopa/carbidopa
   c. Benztropine
   d. Amantadine
   e. Metoclopramide

7. Which of the following medications is used as first line management to reduce pulmonary arterial pressure in patients who are diagnosed with idiopathic pulmonary hypertension?
   a. beta blockers
   b. ACE inhibitors
   c. calcium channel blockers
   d. corticosteroids
   e. diuretics

8. A 43-year-old male presents with painless rectal bleeding and a positive Meckel's scan. Which of the following embryologic structure is most commonly involved?
   a. Neural tube
   b. Auerbach's plexus
   c. Meissner's plexus
   d. Vitelline duct
   e. Processus vaginalis

9. A 25-year-old male who works as a dog groomer is bitten by a dog while clipping the dog's nails. Which of the following medications is the first line management to prevent cellulitis?
   a. clindamycin
   b. doxycycline
   c. amoxicillin/clavulanic acid
   d. trimethoprim-sulfamethoxazole
   e. ciprofloxacin

10. Which of the following is the first line management of choice for torsades de pointes in a patient with a palpable pulse?
   a. Unsynchronized cardioversion
   b. Procainamide
   c. Amiodarone
   d. IV Magnesium sulfate
   e. Adenosine

11. Which of the following is recommended in the management of severe, recalcitrant nodular, cystic acne that is not responsive to conventional medication therapy?
   a. benzoyl peroxide
   b. topical retinoid
   c. spironolactone
   d. isotretinoin
   e. cephalexin

12. A 54-old-woman is believed to be in menopause. Which of the following lab values are most consistent with menopause?
    a. increased estrogen, increased LH, increased FSH
    b. decreased estrogen, decreased LH, decreased FSH
    c. increased estrogen, decreased LH, increased FSH
    d. decreased estrogen, increased LH, decreased FSH
    e. decreased estrogen, increased LH, increased FSH

13. Which of the following is the most appropriate next step in the management of a 40-year-old woman with Pap smear cytology showing atypical squamous cells of undetermined significance and a positive acetic acid test?
    a. repeat the Pap smear in 6 weeks and test for human papilloma virus
    b. retest for human papilloma virus in 6 months after cryotherapy
    c. colposcopy with biopsy
    d. repeat cytology in 1 year
    e. perform genotype of the human papilloma virus to see is HPV 16 or 18 is present

14. Which of the following is the most common hematologic malignancy seen in children?
    a. acute myelogenous leukemia
    b. chronic lymphocytic leukemia
    c. acute lymphocytic leukemia
    d. multiple myeloma
    e. chronic myelogenous leukemia

15. A 34-year-old female is found to have an increased partial thromboplastin time (PTT). A mixing study is performed and there is no correction of the increased partial thromboplastin time. Which of the following is the most likely diagnosis?
    a. Hemophilia A
    b. Hemophilia B
    c. Antiphospholipid syndrome
    d. Factor VIII deficiency
    e. Von Willebrand deficiency

16. A 41-year-old male presents to the clinic for evaluation of a "mass" in the neck. On physical examination, there is a small, mobile, rubbery, non-tender nodule. A radioactive iodine uptake is performed and shows a cold nodule. Which of the following is the next appropriate step?
    a. obtain thyroglobulin levels
    b. fine needle aspiration
    c. thyroidectomy
    d. obtain CT scan of the neck and soft tissues
    e. administration of radioactive iodine to reduce the size of the thyroid gland

17. Which of the following medications is not used in the routine management of severe hypercalcemia?
    a. furosemide
    b. intravenous normal saline
    c. calcitonin
    d. bisphosphonates
    e. hydrochlorothiazide

18. Vitamin C, E and Zinc are used to slow down the progression of which of the following disorders?
  a. glaucoma
  b. retinal detachment
  c. macular degeneration
  d. central retinal artery occlusion
  e. pinguecula

19. An 8-year-old boy presents to the pediatric office with a painless limp that his mother noticed about 2 weeks ago which seemed to worsen towards the end of the day. A pelvic film shows a positive crescent sign, consistent with Legg-Calvé-Perthes disease. Which of the following would be classically seen on physical exam of the leg in this patient?
  a. Loss of abduction and internal rotation
  b. Loss of abduction and external rotation
  c. Loss of external rotation only
  d. Loss of adduction and internal rotation
  e. Loss of adduction and external rotation

20. A 10-month-old infant who recently emigrated from Panama goes for his first well-child visit in the United States. On physical examination, the scrotum is small in size and there is right-sided inguinal fullness. Which of the following is considered the best management in this patient at this time?
  a. observation for possible descent of the testicle with orchiopexy performed if the testicle has not descended after 12 months of age
  b. administration of papaverine prior to orchiopexy
  c. orchiectomy
  d. CT scan of the abdomen and pelvis to see the position of the testicle
  e. Orchiopexy

21. Which of the following is the most common chemotherapeutic agent that can also be used intrapleurally for pleurodesis in a patient with recurrent malignant pleural effusions?
  a. doxorubicin
  b. bleomycin
  c. vincristine
  d. 5 Fluorouracil
  e. methotrexate

22. A 32-year-old male is diagnosed with major depressive disorder. Which of the following is considered to be the first line medical management?
  a. tetracyclic compounds
  b. nonselective MAO inhibitors
  c. serotonin and norepinephrine reuptake inhibitors
  d. tricyclic antidepressants
  e. selective serotonin reuptake inhibitors

23. Which of the following is associated with international travel & feco-oral transmission and high, spiking fever?
  a. Hepatitis A
  b. Hepatitis B
  c. Hepatitis C
  d. Hepatitis D
  e. Hepatitis E

24. A 70-year-old male sandblaster presents to your office with progressive shortness of breath especially with exertion. Which of the following chest radiograph findings is most commonly associated with this clinical presentation based on his occupation?

      a. pleural thickening (plaques)
      b. small upper lobe nodules with hyperinflation of the lower lobes
      c. eggshell calcifications of the hilar and mediastinal lymph nodes
      d. pleural effusion
      e. the presence of a companion line

25. In a patient with suspected diverticulitis, which of the following is the most common site of the development of diverticula?

      a. Sigmoid colon
      b. Terminal ileum
      c. Transverse colon
      d. Rectum
      e. Ascending colon

26. Which of the following organisms is most commonly associated with gas gangrene?

      a. Staphylococcus aureus
      b. Clostridium perfringens
      c. Bacillus anthracis
      d. Coxiella burnetii
      e. Haemophilus ducreyi

27. In evaluation of a patient with dizziness. An electrocardiogram shows a constant PR interval of 0.24 seconds with occasional dropped narrow QRS complexes. Which of the following is the most likely diagnosis?

      a. third degree heart block
      b. first degree heart block
      c. second degree heart block Mobitz I
      d. second degree heart block Mobitz II with aberrancy
      e. second degree heart block Mobitz II

28. A 42-year-old female presents with a dark red, raised rash covered with thick silvery-white scale on the nape of her neck and in her scalp. Physical examination of the hands shows pitting of the nails and yellow-brown discolorations under the nail bed. Which of the following is the most likely diagnosis?

      a. pyoderma gangrenosum
      b. psoriasis
      c. pityriasis rosacea
      d. lichen planus
      e. lichen simplex chronicus

29. A 26-year-old woman at 35-weeks gestation is found to have a positive non stress test. A contraction stress test is also done, showing repetitive late decelerations of the fetal heartbeat and the presence of 3 contractions a minute. Which of the following is considered to be the management of choice at this time?

      a. repeat non stress testing in 1 week
      b. repeat contraction test within 24 hours
      c. administer terbutaline
      d. administer magnesium sulfate
      e. prompt delivery of the fetus

30. A 7-year old male presents with symptoms consistent with hemolytic uremic syndrome. Which of the following is the most common antecedent infection?
   a. Campylobacter jejuni
   b. Parvovirus B-19
   c. Enterohemorrhagic Escherichia coli 0157:H7
   d. Group A beta hemolytic streptococci
   e. Enterotoxigenic Escherichia coli

31. A 23-year-old male is found to have severe hypertension and workup reveals an adrenal tumor consistent with Conn's syndrome. Which of the following medications is considered the medical management of choice in this patient?
   a. labetalol
   b. hydrochlorothiazide
   c. spironolactone
   d. methyldopa
   e. nitroglycerin

32. A 29-year-old janitor presents to the emergency room with left eye pain and redness after a bleach solution splashed into his eye. Which of the following is the next most appropriate step in the management?
   a. check the visual acuity then irrigate the eye with hypotonic saline
   b. check the pH of the eye and then irrigate with lactated ringers
   c. irrigate the eye with lactated ringers and then check the pH of the eye
   d. initiate antibiotic eye drops and then irrigate the eye
   e. perform a fundoscopic exam and then irrigate the eye if there are any sings of abrasions or ulcerations

33. Which of the following rheumatologic diseases is closely associated with giant cell arteritis and classically presents with achy, stiff proximal joints especially involving the shoulder, hip and neck?
   a. polymyositis
   b. dermatomyositis
   c. Sjrogen's syndrome
   d. fibromyalgia
   e. polymyalgia rheumatica

34. A 32-year-old male is found to have a stage I nonseminomatous germ cell tumor. Which of the following is the management of choice?
   a. orchiectomy with retroperitoneal lymph node dissection
   b. orchiectomy followed by radiation
   c. orchiopexy with retroperitoneal lymph node dissection
   d. debulking chemotherapy with orchiectomy and post surgical radiation
   e. chemotherapy

35. A 43-year-old male is being evaluated by his psychiatrist for frequent attacks of psychosis despite being on two different types of medications. Which of the following medications has been shown to decrease psychotic episodes in patients with resistance to first line medications?
   a. Risperidone (Risperdal)
   b. Clozapine (Clozaril)
   c. Aripiprazole (Abilify)
   d. Amitriptyline (Elavil)
   e. Fluoxetine (Prozac)

36. A 23-year-old obese African-American female presents to the emergency room with a severe headache that is intensified with straining. The headache is associated with nausea vomiting and ringing of the ears. She states she has been having some blurred vision as well. On physical exam, there is blurring of the optic disc with optic disc swelling. Which of the following is the next appropriate step in the management of this patient?
    a. administration of sumatriptan
    b. obtain a CT scan without contrast
    c. obtain an MRI of the pituitary gland
    d. perform a lumbar puncture
    e. perform an electroencephalogram

37. A 40-year-old African-American woman with a 4-month history of nonproductive cough presents to the clinic with progressive shortness of breath. A chest X ray is obtained and shows bilateral hilar lymphadenopathy. Which of the following is the management of choice in this patient?
    a. azithromycin
    b. oral prednisone
    c. inhaled fluticasone
    d. ceftriaxone and azithromycin
    e. levofloxacin

38. Which of the following liver function tests is most consistent with Dubin-Johnson syndrome?
    a. increased alkaline phosphatase with increased GGT
    b. increased AST:ALT 2:1 with AST <500
    c. isolated increased direct bilirubin
    d. isolated increased indirect bilirubin
    e. increase prothrombin time and decreased albumin

39. A 32-year-old female went to a winter retreat in a cabin and spent some time in a wooden sauna. She developed small pink and red papules with some pustules that are pruritic, especially around the hair follicles and around the bikini lines. Skin scrapings are negative for burrows or mites. Which of the following is the most likely causative agent?
    a. Sarcoptes scabiei
    b. Poxviridae
    c. Pediculus humanis capiti
    d. Tricophyton
    e. Pseudomonas aeruginosa

40. A pregnant female at 20 weeks gestation presents with right leg swelling measured 4 cm bigger compared to the left leg after a 7-hour trip from North Carolina to New York. She is not experiencing any shortness of breath or chest pain. Which of the following is the most next appropriate step in the evaluation of this patient?
    a. venography of the lower extremity
    b. Helical CT scan
    c. D-dimer evaluation
    d. Venous duplex ultrasound of the lower extremities
    e. Ventilation-perfusion scan

41. A 10-year-old boy presents to the pediatric clinic with small red itchy bumps on his hands after a camping trip. On physical examination, there are many fluid-filled blisters in a straight line. In addition to diphenhydramine, which of the following is recommended for the management in severe cases?

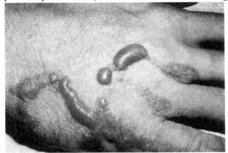

    a. topical mupirocin
    b. topical ketoconazole
    c. topical metronidazole
    d. topical corticosteroids
    e. oral griseofulvin

42. A 43-year-old female is complaining of unintentional leakage of urine, which is preceded by an overwhelming urge to urinate. In addition to lifestyle changes, which of the following is considered the first line medical management of this condition?
    a. pilocarpine
    b. pseudoephedrine
    c. oxybutynin
    d. mirabegron
    e. imipramine

43. A 20-year-old male with Hemophilia B slips on ice and sustains a Grade III ankle sprain with a hematoma to the ankle. Which of the following is used in the routine management of this patient?
    a. Platelet transfusion
    b. Desmopressin (DDAVP)
    c. Plasmapheresis
    d. Factor VIII Concentrates
    e. Factor IX concentrates

44. Which of the following best describes the dawn phenomenon in newly diagnosed diabetics placed on insulin therapy?
    a. it is caused by nocturnal hypoglycemia followed by a rebound early morning hyperglycemia
    b. it causes hypoglycemia in the morning at 8 am upon awakening due to insulin surges
    c. it is associated with a progressive rise of serum glucose from bedtime to morning when the NPH evening dose is administered before dinner
    d. it is caused by decreased insulin sensitivity due to the nightly surge in glucagon and cortisol during nighttime fasting
    e. it is caused by an insulin producing tumor associated with multiple endocrine neoplasia

45. Which of the following symptoms most reliably distinguishes pyelonephritis from acute cystitis?
    a. urinary frequency
    b. hematuria
    c. costovertebral angle tenderness
    d. suprapubic pain
    e. pyuria

46. A 43-year-old woman is complaining of left proximal forearm pain. She states she occasionally gets weakness and tingling sensations to the left first three and a half fingers. The pain is not increased at night and is not reproducible if both of her wrists are flexed for 60 seconds. Which of the following is the most likely diagnosis?
   a. cubital tunnel syndrome
   b. carpal tunnel syndrome
   c. pronator syndrome
   d. tarsal tunnel syndrome
   e. Charcot's joint

47. Which of the following is the best initial treatment modality for a patient with neuroleptic malignant syndrome?
   a. cyproheptadine
   b. diazepam
   c. bromocriptine
   d. acetaminophen
   e. promethazine

48. A 53-year-old male presents to the clinic with sudden onset of stabbing, "jolting" pain shooting from the corner of the right side of his mouth to the angle of his jaw and the right ear. He states the pain is episodic, lasting about 15 seconds, making him wince in pain. The pain is exacerbated with eating, shaving or drafts of wind. There is no associated lacrimation, nasal congestion, rhinorrhea, or miosis. Which of the following is the first line medication for the most likely diagnosis?
   a. 100% oxygen via nonrebreather
   b. sumatriptan
   c. verapamil
   d. toradol and metoclopramide
   e. carbamazepine

49. An 18-year-old college student presents to the school clinic with a 5-day history of runny nose, sneezing and a productive cough. She denies chest pain or shortness of breath. Her vital signs are all within normal limits. On physical examination, her lungs are clear to auscultation bilaterally with no adventitious breath sounds. A chest radiograph shows no infiltrates or other abnormalities. An ECG shows normal sinus rhythm with no ST or T wave changes. A D-dimer is within normal limits. Which of the following is the most likely diagnosis?
   a. sarcoidosis
   b. acute pulmonary embolism
   c. typical bacterial pneumonia
   d. acute bronchitis
   e. chronic bronchitis

50. A 34-year-old female is found to have "saw tooth" waves on ECG with a ventricular rate of 140 beat per minute. The QRS complexes are narrow. There is no associated chest pain or shortness of breath. Her blood pressure is 140/90 mm Hg. Which of the following is the next appropriate management?
   a. Atropine
   b. Amiodarone
   c. Synchronized cardioversion
   d. Verapamil
   e. Radiofrequency ablation

51. A 63-year-old female with a history of bronchiectasis develops an increased cough with increased sputum. Mycobacterium avium complex is suspected. Which of the following is the first line management?
- a. Penicillin VK
- b. Clarithromycin plus ethambutol
- c. Doxycycline
- d. Vancomycin plus Ceftriaxone
- e. Nafcillin plus Gentamicin

52. A 40-year-old male presents to the emergency room with a generalized, pruritic rash consistent with urticaria. On physical examination there are clear lung fields and no evidence of uvula or pharyngeal edema. Which of the following is the management of choice?
- a. topical corticosteroids
- b. diphenhydramine oral
- c. fluconazole oral
- d. clonidine oral
- e. observation

53. A 32-year-old female with pelvic pain is found to have a 3-mm ovarian cyst with no evidence of ovarian torsion on ultrasound. CA-125 levels are normal. Which of the following is the most appropriate management at this time?
- a. rest, NSAIDs and repeat ultrasound in 6 weeks
- b. rest, NSAIDs and schedule for biopsy
- c. laparoscopy
- d. total abdominal hysterectomy/salpingo-oophorectomy
- e. oophorectomy

54. A 60-year-old male presents to the clinic with headache, dizziness, tinnitus, blurred vision and increasing pruritus over the last 2 weeks that he states worsens when he takes hot showers. On physical examination, his face appears flushed. In assessing his vision, a fundoscopic exam shows engorged retinal veins with no evidence of papilledema. His hemoglobin and hematocrit are both increased. Which of the following is most likely associated with the suspected diagnosis?
- a. JAK2 mutation
- b. HFE C282Y genotype
- c. Translocation of chromosomes 9 and 22
- d. Human Leukocyte Antigen – B27
- e. Menin gene

55. A 43-year-old male is placed on lithium therapy for bipolar disorder. Approximately one month after initiating therapy, the patient states he has increased thirst and frequent urination. He states he drinks about 8 liters of water a day and urinates about 8 liters as well. Which of the following test is most reliable to distinguish lithium-induced nephrogenic diabetes insipidus from central diabetes insipidus?
- a. fluid deprivation test
- b. arginine vasopressin challenge test
- c. high dose dexamethasone suppression test
- d. oral glucose tolerance test
- e. fluid challenge test

56. In addition to behavioral modification, which of the following medications is considered first-line medical management of attention deficit hyperactivity disorder?
   a. Fluoxetine
   b. Amitriptyline
   c. Tranylcypromine
   d. Methylphenidate
   e. Bromocriptine

57. A 43-year-old male with a history of hypertension and myocardial infarction presents to the emergency room with episodes of drop attacks, nystagmus, left-sided homonymous hemianopsia, left-sided muscle weakness and right-sided facial nerve palsy. Which of the following is the most likely diagnosis?
   a. Bell's palsy
   b. left middle cerebral artery occlusion
   c. left posterior cerebral artery occlusion
   d. left anterior cerebral artery occlusion
   e. right posterior cerebral artery occlusion

58. A 6-year-old girl is brought to the emergency department for acute onset of a severe barky cough that began 2 days ago. Her mother states she has had a week of runny nose, coughing and nasal congestion. On examination, there is inspiratory stridor and some intercostal retractions. Which of the following radiologic findings are most consistent with the suspected diagnosis?
   a. thumbprinting sign
   b. air bronchograms
   c. companion lines
   d. steeple sign
   e. diffuse bilateral pulmonary infiltrates

59. Which of the following physical exam findings are most consistent with acute anterolateral myocardial infarction?
   a. increased jugular venous pressure
   b. sinus bradycardia
   c. a fourth heart sound (S4)
   d. peripheral edema
   e. anterior wall chest tenderness

60. Which of the following is used in addition to IV ceftriaxone in a 25-year-old in the empiric management of bacterial meningitis?
   a. IV gentamicin
   b. IV aztreonam
   c. IV Clindamycin
   d. IV Vancomycin
   e. IV Azithromycin

61. A 67-year-old Caucasian male presents with a rash on the face. A biopsy is done, showing epidermal and dermal cells with large pleomorphic, hyperchromatic nuclei consistent with squamous cell carcinoma in situ. Which of the following is the most likely diagnosis?
   a. Caplan syndrome
   b. Bowen's disease
   c. Sezary's disease
   d. Peutz Jegher's syndrome
   e. Sturge-Weber syndrome

62. A 27-year-old woman comes into the fertility clinic because she has not menstruated in the last 2 years. On physical examination, the patient is obese with physical evidence of hirsutism. Further testing shows evidence of insulin resistance. Which of the following is the most likely diagnosis?
    a. metabolic syndrome
    b. polycystic ovarian syndrome
    c. hydatidiform mole
    d. adrenocortical insufficiency
    e. endometrial adenocarcinoma

63. Which of the following is the recommended management of refractory idiopathic (immune) thrombocytopenic purpura?
    a. platelet transfusion
    b. bone marrow transplant
    c. hydroxyurea
    d. splenectomy
    e. fresh frozen plasma

64. A 28-year-old sexually active female presents to the clinic with a 4 day history of burning on urination, increased urgency and frequency. A urinalysis is performed and is positive for nitrites and hematuria. A urine culture is performed. Which of the following would most likely grow out of the culture?
    a. Chlamydia trachomatis
    b. Escherichia coli
    c. Klebsiella species
    d. Enterococcus faecalis
    e. Enterobacteriaceae

65. Which of the following is thought to be the cause of the positive symptoms associated with schizophrenia (such as psychosis)?
    a. excess dopamine receptors in the mesolimbic pathway
    b. dopamine dysfunction in the mesocortical pathway
    c. idiopathic dopamine depletion in the substantia nigra
    d. increased CNS grey matter with decreased size of the ventricles
    e. dopamine antagonism in the central nervous system

66. A 28-year-old male presents to the clinic with a 3 month history of persistent, nonproductive cough & shortness of breath that is worsened with exertion. Chest radiographs are positive for bilateral hilar lymphadenopathy. Which of the following biopsies would be most consistent with the suspected diagnosis?
    a. tissue infiltrated with streptococcus pneumoniae
    b. tissue infiltrated with caseating granulomas
    c. tissue infiltrated with cells consistent with squamous cell carcinoma
    d. tissue infiltrated with noncaseating granulomas
    e. tissue with enlarged alveoli and enlarged small airways

67. Which of the following medications is the best initial management for the long-term management of heart failure?
    a. dobutamine
    b. nesiritide
    c. lisinopril
    d. digoxin
    e. spironolactone

68. A 38-year-old male presents to the urgent care center in rural Utah with acutely swollen & extremely painful lymph nodes in the groin, axilla and the cervical regions & multiple flea bites. Cultures from the nodes show gram negative rods with increased staining at the ends, giving it a "safety pin appearance" seen below: Which of the following is the most likely etiologic agent?

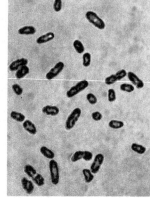

      a. Yersinia pestis
      b. Bacillus anthracis
      c. Ehrlichia chaffeensis
      d. Coxiella burnetii
      e. Brucella melitensis

69. A 43-year-old male with a history of HIV infection presents to the clinic with multiple dome-shaped, flesh colored pearly-white papules with central umbilication. Squeezing the papules produces a curd-like material from the center. There is no surrounding erythema or telangiectasia. Which of the following is the most likely diagnosis?

      a. sebaceous cysts
      b. Molluscum contagiosum
      c. basal cell carcinoma
      d. acne vulgaris
      e. Kaposi sarcoma

70. A 32-year-old sexually active male presents with a yellow-green penile discharge. In addition to azithromycin, the patient should receive which of the following medications?

      a. Clindamycin 300mg orally every 12 hours for 7 days
      b. Metronidazole 2g orally x 1 dose
      c. Ceftriaxone 250mg IM x 1 dose
      d. Vancomycin 125mg orally every 6 hours for 7 days
      e. Ampicillin/sulbactam 1000mg IV x 1 dose

71. A 35-year-old female presents to the clinic with a 6-month history of headaches, decreased frequency in menstruation, decrease in libido and a 4-day onset of bilateral, milky nipple discharge. CT scan shows a pituitary microadenoma that is not compressing the optic chiasm. Which of the following is the most appropriate management at this time?

      a. transsphenoidal resection of the tumor
      b. cabergoline orally
      c. somatostatin
      d. octreotide
      e. pegvisomant

72. Which of the following is not classically increased in patients with primary erythrocytosis (polycythemia vera)?

      a. platelets
      b. red blood cells
      c. lymphocytes
      d. hematocrit
      e. basophils

73. A patient presents with T wave flattening and prominent U waves on ECG.   Which of the following medications is most likely responsible for the ECG findings?
    a. spironolactone
    b. ibuprofen
    c. enalapril
    d. losartan
    e. furosemide

74. Which of the following is the first line medical management of hypertrophic cardiomyopathy?
    a. digoxin
    b. propranolol
    c. nitroglycerin
    d. furosemide
    e. lisinopril

75. Which of the following is classically the first sign of a tetanus infection?
    a. an annular expanding rash with central clearing at the site of inoculation
    b. trismus
    c. increased deep tendon reflexes
    d. increased muscle rigidity
    e. pain and paresthesias at the site of inoculation

76. A 10-year-old boy is brought to the clinic because his mother was told by his barber to "go to the doctor".   His mother states the child has been scratching his head and she noticed thinning of the hair in the area.   There is no flaking of the scalp.   On examination, the following rash is seen:

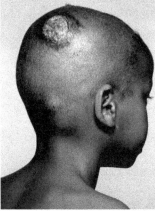

Which of the following is considered the management of choice?
    a. Griseofulvin
    b. Fluconazole
    c. Selenium sulfide
    d. Caspofungin
    e. Hydrocortisone

77. Which of the following is the most important risk factor for the development of cervical carcinoma?
    a. nulliparity
    b. late onset of sexual activity
    c. human papilloma virus infection
    d. unopposed estrogen use
    e. early onset menopause

78. A 36-year-old pregnant female presents to the clinic with palpitations, anxiety and weight loss. Lab values show a thyroid stimulating hormone (TSH) level of 0.3 (normal is 0.9 – 5.0). Which of the following is the most appropriate management at this time?
   a. levothyroxine
   b. methimazole
   c. propylthiouracil
   d. triiodothyronine
   e. radioactive iodine ablation of the thyroid

79. Which of the following is the first line management for acute pain crisis in patients with sickle cell disease?
   a. folic acid
   b. red blood cell transfusion
   c. IV normal saline and oxygen
   d. IV Penicillin G
   e. hydroxyurea

80. A 33-year-old female with a history of fibromuscular dysplasia develops hypertension that is refractory to beta blocker and hydrochlorothiazide therapy. On physical examination, an abdominal bruit is auscultated. Which of the following is the most definitive diagnosis based on the history and physical exam findings?
   a. renal biopsy
   b. renal ultrasound
   c. renogram
   d. renal angiogram
   e. aldosterone: renin ratio >20

81. Which of the following is the first line management of choice for lymphogranuloma venereum?
   a. azithromycin
   b. cephalexin
   c. Penicillin VK
   d. Penicillin G
   e. Clindamycin

82. A 28-year-old female is diagnosed bacterial vaginosis. Which of the following is most consistent with bacterial vaginosis?
   a. a "fishy" smell with potassium hydroxide preparation and the presence of clue cells
   b. the presence of a strawberry cervix and yellow-green frothy discharge
   c. white "curd-like" vaginal discharge
   d. whitening of the lesion with acetic acid application
   e. grouped vesicles on an erythematous base

83. A 41-year-old male presents with a history of recurrent kidney stones, polyuria, nocturia and constipation. Physical examination reveals decreased deep tendon reflexes. An ECG is obtained and shows a shortened QT interval. Which of the following is the most likely etiology of this constellation of symptoms?
   a. malignancy
   b. primary hyperparathyroidism
   c. secondary hyperparathyroidism
   d. Lithium toxicity
   e. Milk alkali syndrome

84. Which of the following is not seen in hereditary spherocytosis?
   a. Hyperchromic red blood cells
   b. Positive osmotic fragility test
   c. Coombs positivity
   d. Increased red blood cell distribution width
   e. microcytic anemia

85. Which of the following is not considered part of the routine management of benign prostate hypertrophy?
   a. observation if mild symptoms
   b. finasteride
   c. tamsulosin
   d. transurethral resection of the prostate
   e. oxybutynin

86. A 43-year-old sexually active male develops a maculopapular rash on his palms and soles. Lab testing reveals a positive rapid plasma reagent test and FTA test. Which of the following is the management of choice?
   a. Azithromycin
   b. Penicillin G
   c. Doxycycline
   d. Ceftriaxone
   e. Podophyllin

87. A 26-year-old woman presents to the clinic for a breast mass she palpated. She states she first noticed the mass 3 months ago. She states the mass seems to increase and decrease in size in relation to her menstruation. On physical examination, there are two tender, mobile, well demarcated breast masses palpated. There are no inflammatory changes to either breast or nipple discharge. Which of the following is the most likely diagnosis?
   a. mastitis
   b. breast abscess
   c. fibrocystic breast disorder
   d. fibroadenoma of the breast
   e. Paget's disease of the breast

88. Which of the following is not classically associated with chronic primary adrenocortical insufficiency?
   a. metabolic alkalosis
   b. isovolemic hypotonic hyponatremia
   c. hyperkalemia
   d. hypoglycemia
   e. hypotension

89. A 32-year-old male presents with perineal pain, and back pain. Acute prostatitis is suspected. Which of the following is not considered part of the routine management in the evaluation of this patient?
   a. urine culture
   b. urinalysis
   c. rectal exam
   d. gonorrhea and chlamydia cultures
   e. prostate massage to increase the bacterial yield on urinalysis

90. A 54-year-old male with chronic diarrhea has evidence of colitis on colonoscopy. A CT scan is done and shows multiple liver abscesses. Stool ova and parasites testing is positive. Which of the following is the most likely etiologic agent?
    a. Acanthamoeba lentica
    b. Entamoeba histolytica
    c. Babesia microti
    d. Plasmodium falciparum
    e. Toxoplasma gondii

91. Which of the following describes the mechanism of action of clomiphene?
    a. a gonadotropin releasing hormone analog
    b. estrogen antagonist in the breast and estrogen agonist in the endometrium
    c. estrogen antagonist in the breast and endometrium
    d. progesterone receptor agonist
    e. partial estrogen receptor agonist that stimulates ovulation

92. A 43-year-old male presents with frequent headaches and visual changes. On physical examination, there is loss of outer vision in both the right and left visual fields. A pituitary MRI shows the presence of a macroadenoma. Which of the following is the most likely etiology?
    a. prolactinoma
    b. TSH secreting adenoma
    c. Cushing's disease
    d. Somatotropinoma
    e. FSH/LH secreting adenoma

93. A 40-year old male is being evaluated for infertility after trying to conceive with is wife for approximately two years. On physical examination there is nontender, left testicular swelling that is worse with the Valsalva maneuver. The mass does not transilluminate and has a "bag of worms" feeling on palpation. Which of the following is the most likely diagnosis?
    a. hydrocele
    b. spermatocele
    c. testicular cancer
    d. testicular torsion
    e. varicocele

94. In which of the following patients is administering the measles mumps rubella (MMR) vaccine contraindicated?
    a. an adult immigrant from another country
    b. A patient with a history of HIV and a CD4 count of $100/mm^3$
    c. A patient with sickle cell disease with functional asplenia
    d. A patient who is receiving the varicella zoster vaccine on the same day
    e. A patient with a history of cirrhosis

95. A 43-year-old male with a history of HIV infection presents with a cough. He states he has been having low-grade fever and shortness of breath when he ambulates more than three city blocks. His last CD4 count was 145/mm^3 (normal 500/mm^3 to 1,200/mm^3). On ambulation around the hospital, the nurse notes desaturation on pulse oximetry. An arterial blood gas shows a PaO$_2$ of 70 mm Hg. Lactate dehydrogenase levels are 2,453 IU/L (normal 105 -333 IU/L). A chest X ray is obtained and bronchoalveolar lavage reveals cysts with Toluidine staining:

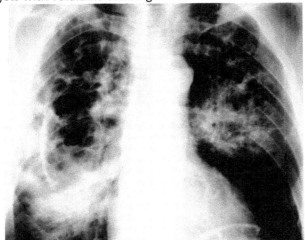
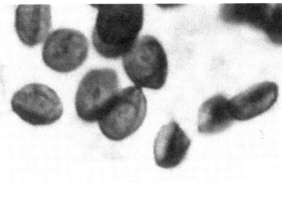

Which of the following is the recommended first-line management of choice?
    a. azithromycin
    b. trimethoprim-sulfamethoxazole plus corticosteroids
    c. itraconazole plus corticosteroids
    d. doxycycline
    e. fluconazole

96. A patient is given IV magnesium for status asthmaticus. Which of the following would be seen if the patient develops hypermagnesemia as a complication of treatment for asthma?
    a. positive Trousseau's sign
    b. Torsades de pointes
    c. Decreased deep tendon reflexes
    d. Serum potassium levels < 3.5 mEq/L (Normal 3.5 – 5 mEq/L)
    e. Serum calcium levels < 8.5 mEq/L (Normal 8.5 – 10 mEq/L)

97. Which of the following contraception agents has a 10-year duration of action?
    a. tubal ligation
    b. Paragard copper intrauterine device
    c. levonorgestrel (Mirena) intrauterine device
    d. Essure
    e. Medroxyprogesterone acetate (Depo-Provera)

98. A 45-year-old male is complaining of headaches and gradual enlargement of his hands, feet and skull along with weight gain and new onset of diabetes mellitus. Which of the following is the best screening test for the suspected diagnosis?
    a. insulin-like growth factor
    b. CRH stimulation test
    c. High dose dexamethasone suppression test
    d. Thyroid stimulating hormone test
    e. Low dose dexamethasone suppression test

99. A 16-year-old girl from Panama develops fever, cough, anorexia and the onset of a light red, spotted maculopapular rash with transient photosensitivity and joint pain. Which of the following is the most likely diagnosis?
   a. rubella
   b. rubeola
   c. fifth's disease
   d. mumps
   e. hand foot and mouth disease

100. Which of the following medications is associated with an increased risk for the development of diabetes insipidus?
   a. ibuprofen
   b. lithium
   c. carbamazepine
   d. chlorpropramide
   e. hydrochlorothiazide

QUESTION 1
Choice B (the presence of drusen bodies) is the correct choice. Macular degeneration is the most common cause of permanent legal blindness and visual loss in the elderly. The macula is responsible for central vision and color vision. *Drusen bodies (caused by waste products from the retinal pigment epithelium) are a hallmark of macular degeneration.* EENT – MACULAR DEGENERATION – HISTORY AND PHYSICAL EXAM (p 225).

Choice A (the presence of papilledema) is seen with malignant hypertension.

Choice C (the presence of AV nicking) is seen with hypertensive retinopathy.

Choice D (the presence of clumped pigment cells in the anterior vitreous) and Choice E (the presence of the retina hanging in the vitreous) are both associated with retinal detachment.

QUESTION 2
Choice C (Jones Fracture) is the correct choice. A Jones fracture is a fracture through the diaphysis of the fifth metatarsal. MUSCULOSKELETAL – JONES FRACTURE – BASICS (p 191).

Choice A (Pseudo Jones Fracture) is a fracture at the base (tuberosity) of the fifth metatarsal. Pseudo jones fractures are located more proximal than Jones fracture.

Choice B (Charcot Joint) is a destructive neuropathic joint arthropathy associated with diabetes mellitus.

Choice D (Lisfranc injury) is associated with disruption between the articulation of the metatarsals and their respective cuneiforms. A *Fleck Fracture* (Choice E), which is a fracture at the base of the second metatarsal bone, makes a Lisfranc injury highly suspicious.

QUESTION 3
Choice B (subarachnoid hemorrhage) is the correct answer. Renal and extrarenal cysts characterize adult polycystic kidney disease. *Other extrarenal manifestations include mitral valve prolapse, diverticulosis and berry aneurysms* (which puts patients at risk for developing subarachnoid hemorrhage from berry aneurysm rupture). All of the other choices are not increased in patient with polycystic kidney disease.
GENITOURINARY – POLYCYSTIC KIDNEY DISEASE – HEALTH MAINTENANCE (p 322).

QUESTION 4

Choice C (Still's murmur) is the correct answer. Still's murmur is the most common innocent (functional) murmur (thought to be due to vibration of the valve leaflets). It is usually heard from 2 years of age to preadolescence. It presents clinically with an *early to mid-systolic musical, vibratory, noisy, twanging high-pitched murmur*. It is heard loudest in the inferior aspect of the left lower sternal border & apex. The murmur may radiate to the carotids. CARDIOLOGY – STILL MURMUR – HISTORY AND PHYSICAL EXAMINATION (pediatrics online chapter).

Choice A (Venous hum) is the second most common innocent murmur. It is due to the sound of blood flowing from the neck into the thorax. It presents with a grade I or II, harsh systolic ejection murmur (may be continuous – if heard in diastole, it is the only non pathologic diastolic murmur). It localizes to the upper left sternal border.

Choice B (*Patent ductus arteriosus*) presents with a *continuous machinery murmur* best heard at the pulmonic area and associated with a *wide pulse pressure (bounding pulses)*.

Choice D (*Graham-Steell murmur*) is a high-pitched, early diastolic murmur heard best at the left sternal edge in the second intercostal space with the patient in full inspiration. This murmur is most commonly associated with *pulmonary hypertension*.

Choice E (*Atrial septal defect*) produces a systolic ejection crescendo decrescendo flow murmur at the pulmonic area. It is associated with a *widely fixed split second heart sound (S2)*.

QUESTION 5

Choice C [Phenelzine (Nardil)] is the correct answer. MAO-inhibitors block the breakdown of neurotransmitters (such as dopamine, serotonin, epinephrine and norepinephrine) by inhibiting the enzyme monoamine oxidase. When a patient on MAO-inhibitors eat certain foods that contain tyramine, MAO-inhibitors prevent the breakdown of tyramine. Tyramine acts as a catecholamine-releasing agent, leading to hypertensive crisis. Foods that are rich in tyramine include aged or fermented cheeses, wine, beer, aged foods, smoked meats, chocolates, coffee and tea. PSYCH/BEHAVIORAL – MAO INHIBITORS – PHARMACOLOGY (p 492).

QUESTION 6

Choice B (Levodopa/carbidopa) is the correct answer. Levodopa/carbidopa is the most effective management in Parkinson's disease. Parkinson's disease is idiopathic dopamine depletion due to failure to inhibit acetylcholine in the basal ganglia. It is associated with cytoplasmic inclusions (*Lewy bodies*) and loss of pigment cells in the basal ganglia. Levodopa is converted into dopamine, correcting the dopamine depletion and Carbidopa reduces the amount of levodopa needed. NEUROLOGY – PARKINSON'S DISEASE – PHARMACOLOGY (p 353).

Choice A (Prochlorperazine) and Choice E (metoclopramide) are dopamine antagonists. Since they block dopamine, they may exacerbate Parkinson symptoms.

Choice C (Benztropine) is an anticholinergic medication that reduces tremors and is primarily used in younger patients in which tremor is the predominant symptom.

Choice D (Amantadine) may help early on in the disease course of patients with mild symptoms. Amantadine increases presynaptic dopamine release and improves long-term levodopa induced dyskinesias.

QUESTION 7

Choice C (calcium channel blockers) are considered the first line management in idiopathic pulmonary hypertension. Not all patients may respond to this therapy however, but given the choices, it is the best initial management. Other medications used to treat this disorder include phosphodiesterase inhibitors (such as sildenafil), prostacyclins, endothelin receptor antagonists, and oxygen therapy.

PULMONARY – PULMONARY HYPERTENSION – CLINICAL INTERVENTION (p 117).

QUESTION 8

Choice D (Vitelline duct) is correct. *Meckel's diverticulum is a congenital outpouching of the intestine due to a persistent vitelline duct (yolk stalk) and may secrete gastric or pancreatic enzymes*, leading to the painless rectal bleeding (from erosion by the ectopic enzyme release in the bowel).

Choice A (Neural tube) is associated with congenital spinal bifida.

Choice B (Auerbach's plexus) is associated with two disorders. *Acquired decrease of the Auerbach's plexus is responsible for achalasia. Congenital absence of Auerbach's plexus in the gut is the cause of Hirschsprung's disease.* Hirschsprung's disease often presents with meconium ileus in newborns.

Choice C (Meissner's Plexus) is a secondary plexus (submucosal) plexus of the GI tract.

Choice E (process vaginalis) is associated with indirect hernias.

QUESTION 9

Choice C (amoxicillin/clavulanic acid) is the correct answer. *Amoxicillin/clavulanic acid is the drug of choice for bite wounds because it has good gram positive, gram negative and anaerobic coverage* (which covers the oral flora). INFECTIOUS DISEASE – DOG BITES – PHARMACOLOGY (p 419).

Choice A (clindamycin) and Choice E (ciprofloxacin) are used together in patients who are penicillin allergic in the management of dog and human bites. The clindamycin covers gram positive and anaerobic organisms. The fluoroquinolone is primarily used for gram-negative coverage. In patients under the age of 18, Choice D (trimethoprim-sulfamethoxazole) can be substituted for fluoroquinolones in dual therapy. Single therapy with any of these three agents is not recommended in the prophylaxis of dog bite wounds.

Choice B (doxycycline) monotherapy can be used as an alternative to penicillin in cat bites but not dog bites.

QUESTION 10

Choice D (IV Magnesium) is the correct answer. *IV Magnesium is the first line treatment for torsades de pointes.* CARDIOLOGY – TORSADES DE POINTES – CLINICAL INTERVENTION (p 15).

Choice A (*Unsynchronized cardioversion*) otherwise known as *defibrillation*, is indicated in *ventricular tachycardia without a pulse or ventricular fibrillation.*

Choice B (*Procainamide*) and Choice C (*Amiodarone*) are used in the management of *stable wide-complex tachycardia.*
Choice E (*Adenosine*) is used in the management of *narrow complex tachycardia with a regular rhythm.*

QUESTION 11

Choice D (isotretinoin) is the correct answer. The *indication for oral isotretinoin include severe, recalcitrant nodular or cystic acne that is not responsive to conventional therapy* such as all the other choices listed. *Isotretinoin has many potential side effects such as being highly teratogenic, has many psychological side effects.* Isotretinoin can also cause *hepatitis, increased triglycerides and hypercholesterolemia.*
DERMATOLOGY – CYSTIC ACNE – CLINICAL INTERVENTION (p 394).

QUESTION 12

Choice E (decreased estrogen, increased LH, increased FSH) is the correct answer.   Menopause (the cessation of menstruation) is due to the cessation of estrogen and progesterone production by the ovaries.   Since the ovaries are under the hypothalamus-pituitary-ovary axis, decreased levels of estrogen and progesterone are sensed by the pituitary gland via the positive feedback loop, causing an elevation in pituitary LH and FSH secretion (remember positive feedback in the H-P-O axis means low levels of ovarian hormones will cause an increase in pituitary hormones in attempt to increase the ovarian hormones).   REPRODUCTIVE – MENOPAUSE – LABS/DIAGNOSTIC STUDIES (p 251).

Choice A (increased estrogen, increased LH, increased FSH) would be seen in a FH/LSH secreting pituitary adenoma. The normal response to elevated levels of estrogen would be to decrease LH and FSH secretion via the negative feedback loop.   These tumors secrete pituitary LH and FSH in an autonomous fashion and do not respond to the H-P-O axis. These types of tumors are very rare.

Choice B (decreased estrogen, decreased LH, decreased FSH) can be seen in either hypothalamic or pituitary failure.

QUESTION 13

Choice C (colposcopy with biopsy) is the correct choice.   This vignette describes atypical squamous cells of undetermined significance (ASCUS) with positive HPV infection (HPV becomes whitened when acetic acid is applied to the lesions).   HPV positive lesions have a higher risk of progression to cervical carcinoma so in women greater than 25 years of age with HPV-positive ASCUS, the recommendations are to either perform colposcopy with biopsy or to repeat the PAP in 1 year and to perform colposcopy if it is still positive at that time.   All of the other choices are not the management of HPV positive ASCUS. REPRODUCTIVE – PAP SMEAR RESULTS – CLINICAL INTERVENTION (p 256).

QUESTION 14

Choice C (acute lymphocytic leukemia) is the correct answer.   Acute leukemia is the most common form of cancer in children with the peak incidence occurring between 2 – 5 years of age.
HEMATOLOGY – ACUTE LYMPHOCYTIC LEUKEMIA – BASICS (Page 466)

QUESTION 15

Choice C (antiphospholipid syndrome) is the correct answer. *Antiphospholipid syndrome is a condition of increased arterial and venous thrombi formation as well as frequent miscarriages.* It is due to the presence of antiphospholipid antibodies. Despite being a prothrombotic state, the presence of antiphospholipid antibodies may cause a paradoxical increase in the partial thromboplastin time in vitro. This occurs because the antibodies bind to the phospholipid component of the PTT reagent in vitro, causing a false elevation in the PTT. Lupus anticoagulant is a type of antiphospholipid antibody but its name is a misnomer (as it is a procoagulant). A mixing study is performed to distinguish between factor deficiencies (ex. hemophilia, von Willebrand disease) from the present of factor inhibitors (such as phospholipid antibodies).   *No correction of the PTT with mixing studies indicate a clotting factor inhibitor.*   HEMATOLOGY – ANTIPHOSPHOLIPID SYNDROME – MOST LIKELY (page 463)

Choice A (Hemophilia A), choice B (Hemophilia B), choice D (Factor VII deficiency) and choice E (Von Willebrand deficiency) are examples of factor deficiencies. Only 50% of coagulation factors are needed to cause coagulation. If the blood of a patient with a factor deficiency is "mixed" with the normal blood, it will lead to correction of the partial thromboplastin time (PTT) in vitro.

QUESTION 16

Choice B (fine needle aspiration) is the correct answer. *Fine needle aspiration with biopsy is the best test to evaluate a suspicious nodule.* Cold nodules are usually benign but may also indicate malignancy.
ENDOCRINE – THYROID NODULE – LABS/DIAGNOSTIC STUDIES (p 289).

Choice A (thyroglobulin levels) are often ordered prior to and after surgical removal of confirmed thyroid cancer.

Choice C (thyroidectomy) is used to treat confirmed thyroid carcinoma.

Choice D (obtain CT scan of the neck and soft tissues) may be used to evaluate extent of the disease and to see if there is any local metastasis.

Choice E (administration of radioactive iodine to reduce the thyroid gland) is not part of the workup or management of a suspected malignancy.

QUESTION 17
Choice E (hydrochlorothiazide) is the correct answer. Hydrochlorothiazide works as a diuretic in the distal collecting tubule by inhibiting the Na^+/Ca^+ pump. This leads to the loss of sodium (causing diuresis) with the retention of calcium, which can lead to hypercalcemia in some patients. *Hydrochlorothiazides are not used in hypercalcemia because they can cause worsening of the hypercalcemia.* All the other choices can be used in the management of severe hypercalcemia. GENITOURINARY – HYPERCALCEMIA – CLINICAL INTERVENTION (p 292).

QUESTION 18
Choice C (macular degeneration) is the correct answer. Vitamin C, Vitamin E & Zinc are used to slow down the progression of macular degeneration. EENT – MACULAR DEGENERATION – HEALTH MAINTENANCE (p 225).

QUESTION 19
Choice A (loss of abduction and internal rotation) is the correct choice. This is a classic presentation of Legg Calve Perthe disease, which can be associated with loss of abduction and internal rotation on physical examination. MUSCULOSKELETAL – LEGG CALVE PERTHES DISEASE – HISTORY AND PHYSICAL EXAM (p 181).

QUESTION 20
Choice E (orchiopexy) is the correct answer. In patients with cryptorchidism, *orchiopexy is recommended in children as early as 6 months of age and before 1 years old* because testicles rarely descend spontaneously after 3 months of age. GENITOURINARY – CRYTPORCHIDISM – CLINICAL INTERVENTION (p 334).

Choice A (observation for possible descent of the testicle with orchiopexy performed if the testicle has not descended after 12 months of age) is not recommended in a 10-month old. Observation may only be an option in children less than 6 months of age. Orchiopexy is recommended between 6 months of age and before 1 year to reduce the risk of testicular cancer and for viability of the testicle.

Choice B (administration of papaverine prior to orchiopexy) is not correct. Papaverine is used in impotence. In patients with cryptorchidism, injection of beta human chorionic gonadotropin may be given prior to orchiopexy to promote descent of the testicles.

Choice C (orchiectomy) is usually done if the *testicle is not viable or if the testicle is found later in life.*

Choice D (CT scan of the abdomen and pelvis to see position of the testicle) is not the recommended step in this patient.

QUESTION 21
Choice B (bleomycin) is the correct answer. Bleomycin is chemotherapeutic agent can also be used intrapleurally for pleurodesis in a patient with recurrent malignant pleural effusions. Talc may also be used. Bleomycin has been used in Hodgkin and Non Hodgkin lymphoma, testicular tumors and squamous cell carcinoma. HEMATOLOGY – BLEOMYCIN – PHARMACOLOGY (p 496).

Choice A (doxorubicin) is used in the management of acute myeloid leukemia, acute lymphoblastic leukemia and other solid tumors.

Choice C (vincristine) is used in the management of leukemias.

Choice D (5 Fluorouracil) is used in the management of superficial basal cell cancer and actinic keratosis. It is also used in the management of metastatic colon and breast cancers.

Choice E (methotrexate) is used in the management of Non Hodgkin lymphoma, trophoblastic tumors (choriocarcinoma and hydatidiform molar pregnancy), lung, breast, head and neck cancers as well as osteosarcomas.

QUESTION 22

Choice E (selective serotonin reuptake inhibitors) are the first line medications in the management of major depressive disorder. They have the advantages of easy dosing, lower incidence of side effects and low toxicity in cases of overdose. All of the other classes are options in patients with depression but are not the first line due to their side effect profiles and potential toxicities (especially with the tricyclic antidepressants the non-selective MAO inhibitors). PSYCH/BEHAVIORAL – DEPRESSSION – CLINICAL INTERVENTION (p 376 & 377).

QUESTION 23

Choice A (Hepatitis A) is the correct answer. International travel is the most common predisposing factor. Hepatitis A is transmitted feco-oral and is the only viral hepatitis associated with high spiking fever. GI/NUTRITION – HEPATITIS A – BASICS (p 141).

QUESTION 24

Choice C (eggshell calcifications) is the correct choice. This patient has silicosis (occupation working with sand and quartz). *Eggshell calcifications are classic for silicosis* (they can also be seen in sarcoidosis). PULMONARY – SILICIOSIS – LABS/DIAGNOSTIC STUDIES (91).

Choice A (*pleural plaques*) are classic for *asbestosis*. Occupations asbestos exposure include *demolition of old buildings (asbestos was used as a fire retardant), ship building and pipe insulation*. These patients are at increased risk for development of mesothelioma, lung cancer and tuberculosis.

Choice B (*small upper lobe nodules with hyperinflation of the lower lobes*) is classically associated with *coal workers pneumoconiosis*. The pneumoconiosis disorders are associated with progression to restrictive lung disease (coal workers is the exception as it is associated with obstructive commonly).

Choice D (pleural effusion) is not a disease but a sign of an underlying disease.

Choice E (companion line) is associated with pneumothorax as it marks the edge of the lung.

QUESTION 25

Choice A (Sigmoid colon) is correct. Because the sigmoid colon is most commonly involved (and is located in the left lower quadrant), patients with diverticulitis most commonly present with left lower quadrant pain. GI/NUTRITION – DIVERTICULITIS – BASICS (p 148).

QUESTION 26

Choice B (Clostridium perfringens) is the correct answer. INFECTIOUS DISEASE – GAS GANGRENE – BASICS (p 421).

Choice A (Staphylococcus aureus) commonly causes skin and soft tissue infections. Staphylococcus aureus is usually pus forming and is not classically gas forming.

Choice C (Bacillus anthracis) is the causative agent of anthrax

Choice D (Coxiella burnetii) is the causative agent of Q fever.

Choice E (Haemophilus ducreyi) is the causative agent of chancroid.

QUESTION 27
Question E (second degree Mobitz II) is correct answer. Second degree heart block Mobitz II is defined by a constant (or prolonged) PR interval *with occasional dropped QRS complexes.*   A normal PR interval is between 0.12 – 0.20 seconds. CARDIOLOGY – HEART BLOCKS – BASICS (p 13).

Choice A (third degree) is associated with AV dissociation. The atrial impulses (p waves) are not associated with ventricular impulses (QRS complexes).

Choice B (*first degree*) is associated with a *prolonged PR interval* as in this question, however, *all impulses are conducted to the ventricles, so there should be no occasional dropped QRS complex.*

Choice C (*second Mobitz I*) is associated *occasional dropped QRS* (as seen in this question) however, it is associated with *progressive lengthening of the PR interval prior to the dropped QRS complexes.*

Choice D (aberrancy) is associated with *wide QRS complex* as the depolarization occurs from cell to cell, taking longer for the impulse to be conducted in the ventricles.

QUESTION 28
Choice B (psoriasis) is the correct answer.   Plaque psoriasis is the most common type of psoriasis. *Plaque psoriasis classically presents as raised, dark-red plaques or papules with thick silver-white scales* especially on the extensor surfaces. Involvement of the nails is also common and may present with *pitting of the nails* and *yellow-brown discolorations under the nail bed.* DERMATOLOGY – PSORIASIS – MOST LIKELY (p 391).

Choice A (pyoderma gangrenosum) is a skin lesion commonly seen in patients with inflammatory diseases, such as Crohn's, ulcerative colitis, rheumatoid arthritis and spondyloarthropathies. It is a misnomer as it is not infectious nor is it gangrenous.

Choice C (*pityriasis rosacea*) is classically associated with a *herald patch* (a solitary salmon-colored macule) on the trunk that precedes the development of a *generalized exanthem with multiple, smaller, bilateral, symmetric, round and oval salmon-colored macules with a white circular (collarette) scale* along the cleavage lines in a Christmas tree pattern along the trunk, sparing the face.

Choice D (*lichen planus*) is an idiopathic cell-mediated dermatologic rash classically associated with the *5P's: the rash is usually purple in color, polygonal (irregular shape and bordered, planar (plaques), pruritic, popular with fine scales.* Patients often have nail dystrophy.   Oral involvement may include *Wickham striae* (lesions with lacy white or gray striae).

Choice E (lichen simplex chronicus) also known as neurodermatitis is skin thickening in patients with eczema secondary to repetitive rubbing or scratching.

QUESTION 29
Choice E (prompt delivery of the fetus) is the correct answer. The woman has signs of fetal distress both on non-stress and with the fetal response to stress test during contractions, making prompt delivery the recommended management. REPRODUCTIVE– PREMATURE DELIVERY – CLINICAL INTERVENTION (p 268).

QUESTION 30
Choice C (Enterohemorrhagic Escherichia coli 0157:H7) is the correct answer. Hemolytic uremic syndrome is most commonly seen in children. *Enterohemorrhagic Escherichia coli 0157:H7 is the organism most commonly associated with the development of hemolytic uremic syndrome.* Other common organisms include *Shigella and Salmonella gastritis.* In adults, it can be due to infectious causes as well as in patients with HIV, systemic lupus erythematosus and antiphospholipid antibody syndrome.
HEMATOLOGY – HEMOLYTIC UREMIC SYNDROME – HEALTH MAINTENANCE (p 468).

Choice A (*Campylobacter jejuni*) is the most common antecedent for *Guillain Barré syndrome.*

Choice B (*Parvovirus B-19*) causes *erythema infectiosum (fifth's disease).*

Choice D (Group A beta hemolytic streptococci) can cause the following:
* Noninvasive infections: strep pharyngitis, skin infections: cellulitis, impetigo, erysipelas, scarlet fever
* Invasive infections: toxic shock syndrome, necrotizing fasciitis, meningitis bacteremia, pneumonia, acute glomerulonephritis (rheumatic fever is a complication of strep infections but not directly caused by it).

Choice E (*Enterotoxigenic Escherichia coli*) is the *most common cause of traveler's diarrhea.*

QUESTION 31
Choice C (spironolactone) is the correct answer. Conn syndrome is an adrenal aldosteronoma that secretes aldosterone autonomously, causing the symptoms of hyperaldosteronism, including hypernatremia and hypokalemia. *Spironolactone is considered the treatment of choice because spironolactone blocks the aldosterone receptor* and therefore blocks the effects of excess aldosterone. ACE inhibitors and calcium channel blockers have may also be used. ENDOCRINE – HYPERALDOSTERONISM – CLINICAL INTERVENTION (p 299).

QUESTION 32
Choice C (irrigate the eye and then check the pH) is the correct choice. *In ocular chemical exposures, irrigation to remove the chemical from the eye is the first and most important step* before any other assessment. After irrigation, the pH is checked to assure that the chemical has been completely removed from the eye to prevent further damage and then visual acuity can be assessed. EENT – CHEMICAL EYE EXPOSURE – CLINICAL INTERVENTION (p 228).

QUESTION 33
Choice E (polymyalgia rheumatica) is the correct answer. *Polymyalgia rheumatica is classically associated with giant cell arteritis* and in any patient diagnosed with polymyalgia rheumatica with head or neck symptoms, giant cell arteritis should be ruled out as a secondary condition. MUSCULOSKELETAL – POLYMYALGIA RHEUMATICA – BASICS (p 202).

QUESTION 34
Choice A (orchiectomy with retroperitoneal lymph node dissection) is the correct answer as it is the treatment of choice for stage I nonseminomatous germ cell tumors.
GENITOURINARY– TESTICULAR CANCER – CLINICAL INTERVENTION (p 334).

Choice B (orchiectomy followed by radiation) is the management of low grade seminomatous testicular tumors.

Choice C (orchiopexy with retroperitoneal lymph node dissection) is not recommended in the management of testicular cancer because testicle removal is recommended.

Choice D (debulking chemotherapy with orchiectomy and post-surgical radiation) is the management of high grade seminomas.

Choice E (chemotherapy) is the management of some metastatic, higher grade tumors.

QUESTION 35

Choice B [Clozapine (Clozaril)] is the correct answer. *Clozapine has been shown to decrease psychotic episodes in patients with resistance to other medications in patients with schizophrenia.*
PSYCH/BEHAVIORAL – SCHIZOPHRENIA – PHARMACOLOGY (p 493).

QUESTION 36

Choice B (obtain a CT scan without contrast) is the correct answer. The neurologic symptoms and the blurred optic disc can be either idiopathic intracranial pressure or increased intracranial pressure from mass effect (ex a cranial tumor). A head CT is performed first to rule out in intracranial lesion before a lumbar puncture can be performed to prevent herniation from the removal of the CSF fluid during lumbar puncture in cases with mass effect. CSF findings in intracranial hypertension include increased opening pressure with an otherwise normal CSF analysis.
NEUROLOGY – PSEUDOTUMOR CEREBRI – LABS/DIAGNOSTIC STUDIES (p 358).

Choice A (administration of sumatriptan) is used in the management of migraines. Migraines are not associated with papilledema.

Choice C (obtain an MRI of the pituitary) is done to rule out pituitary masses.

Choice D (perform a lumbar puncture) is done after ruling out mass effect from an intracranial lesion to prevent herniation from the removal of the CSF fluid during lumbar puncture.

Choice E (perform an electroencephalogram) can be done to rule out seizure disorder, sleep disorders and in patients in a coma. It can be used as part of the diagnostic workup but is not first line.

QUESTION 37

Choice B (oral prednisone) is the correct choice. The clues here are a young African-American (it could have also have been Northern European), longstanding nonproductive cough and bilateral hilar lymphadenopathy, which all indicate sarcoidosis. 40% of patients with sarcoidosis spontaneously resolve without treatment and 40% respond to treatment. Since the pathophysiology of sarcoidosis is a systemic inflammatory granulomatous disorder, steroids are the drug of choice because they blunt the immune response, decrease granuloma formation and reduce fibrosis.
PULMONARY – SARCOIDOSIS – CLINICAL INTERVENTION (p 87).

Choice A is used to treat community acquired pneumonia and atypical pneumonia (legionella, mycoplasma and chlamydophila).

Choice C is incorrect because inhaled corticosteroids have local effects. Sarcoidosis is a systemic disorder so it needs a systemic treatment.

Choice D is used for the management of inpatient community acquired pneumonia

Choice E is used for the management of inpatient (or outpatient) community acquired pneumonia

QUESTION 38

Choice C (Isolated direct bilirubin) is the correct choice. Dubin-Johnson syndrome is caused by a hereditary genetic mutation, which prevents hepatocytes from secreting conjugated bilirubin, leading to an *isolated direct (conjugated) bilirubinemia.* Think *D* (Direct) = *D*ubins. Rotor syndrome is a milder form of the disease.
GI/NUTRITION – DUBIN JOHNSON SYNDROME – LABS/DIAGNOSTIC STUDIES (p 138).

Choice A (increased alkaline phosphatase with increased GGT) is classically associated with cholestasis (biliary tract obstruction).

Choice B (increased AST:ALT 2:1 with AST <500) is classically associated with alcoholic hepatitis.

Choice D (isolated increased indirect bilirubin) is associated with Gilbert's syndrome or Criggler-Najjar syndrome.

Choice E (increase prothrombin time and decreased albumin) is associated with end stage liver disease.

QUESTION 39
Choice E (Pseudomonas aeruginosa) is the correct answer. This is the classic description of *hot tub folliculitis*, which is caused by Pseudomonas aeruginosa. It is commonly seen in patients who bathe in a *contaminated spa, swimming pool or hot tub*. It manifests as *small red papules that may be pustular*. It is usually *self-limiting and resolves within 2 weeks without treatment*. *Ciprofloxacin can be used in persistent or severe cases.*
INFECTIOUS DISEASE – HOT TUB FOLLICULITIS – MOST LIKELY (p 424).

Choice A (Sarcoptes scabiei) causes *scabies*. It usually manifests as *linear burrows or intensely pruritic macules or papules*. It is transmitted directly from skin to skin or via fomites.

Choice B (Poxviridae) causes Molluscum contagiosum.

Choice C (Pediculus humanis capiti) causes head lice.

Choice D (Tricophyton) is one of the fungal agents associated with tinea.

QUESTION 40
Choice D is correct answer. In patients with moderate to high risk of deep venous thrombosis, an *ultrasound is considered the first line diagnostic test of choice.* CARDIOLOGY – DEEP VENOUS THROMBOSIS – LABS (p 61).

Choice A (*Venography) is gold standard* (but is only usually done if noninvasive tests such as ultrasound fail to diagnose deep venous thrombosis.

Choice B (CT scan) is indicated in symptoms of pulmonary embolism: tachycardia, chest pain, shortness of breath, etc. The patient is pregnant, so a study without radiation would be preferred and she has no signs of PE.

Choice C (D dimer) is only helpful in low risk factors to rule out DVT if negative. If D dimer is positive then an ultrasound must be done.
Choice E (V/Q scan) is done if pulmonary embolism is suspected and there is a contraindication to CT scan (ex increased creatinine).

QUESTION 41
Choice D (topical corticosteroids) is correct answer. It is the recommended management of Poison Ivy. The rash of Poison Ivy initially begins as an erythematous, pruritic rash with the development of papules, plaques, vesicles and or bullae arranged commonly in *linear or streak-like configurations* where a portion of the plant has made contact with the skin. DERMATOLOGY – POISON IVY – CLINICAL INTERVENTION

Choice A (topical *mupirocin*) is the *treatment of choice for localized, nonbullous impetigo* and as part of *eradicating MRSA from the nares.*

Choice B (topical ketoconazole) is used in the management of fungal infections.

Choice C (topical metronidazole) is used in the management of acne rosacea.

Choice E (oral griseofulvin) is used in the management of tinea capitus.

QUESTION 42

Choice C (oxybutynin) is the correct choice. The vignette describes urge incontinence. *Urge incontinence* is the overwhelming urge to urinate due *detrusor muscle overactivity (overactive bladder)*. Detrusor muscle contraction is stimulated by muscarinic acetylcholine receptors so *anticholinergics (such as oxybutynin) reduces bladder over activity*. GENITOURINARY – URGE INCONTINENCE – PHARMACOLOGY (p 342).

Choice A (pilocarpine) is a cholinergic drug that will increase urination, making the urge incontinence worse.

Choice B (pseudoephedrine) is a sympathomimetic used to treat stress incontinence, not urge incontinence.

Choice D (mirabegron) is a beta-3 agonist that also relaxes the bladder and can be used to treat urge incontinence but is not the first line agent.

Choice E (imipramine) is a tricyclic antidepressant drug that has anticholinergic properties. As such, it may also be used to treat urge incontinence, but it is not first line.

QUESTION 43

Choice E (Factor IX concentrates) is the correct answer. Hemophilia B is a deficiency of Factor IX. HEMATOLOGY – HEMOPHILIA B – CLINICAL INTERVENTION (page 463)

Choice A (Platelet transfusion) is not used in the management of Hemophilia. Hemophilia B is a coagulation factor IX deficiency, which affects the secondary coagulation pathway. Platelets are part of the primary coagulation pathway. Platelet transfusion is usually reserved for management of severe thrombocytopenia: ex. platelet count of <10,000/mcL in patients with signs of clinically significant mucocutaneous or other bleeding.

Choice B (*Desmopressin/DDAVP) is used in the management of Von Willebrand disease and Hemophilia A only*. Desmopressin is a synthetic anti-diuretic hormone (arginine vasopressin) that increases Von Willebrand factor and factor VIII levels. It has no effect on Factor IX. Desmopressin is also used in the management of central diabetes insipidus (a disease where there is a lack of anti-diuretic hormone production). Desmopressin can also be used in certain cases of nocturnal enuresis since it inhibits diuresis. It has no role in Hemophilia B.

Choice C (Plasmapheresis) also known as plasma exchange therapy is used to remove and/or replace certain components of the blood. It is used in the management of thrombotic thrombocytopenic purpura, hemolytic uremic syndrome, antiphospholipid antibody syndrome, multiple sclerosis, Goodpasture syndrome, myasthenia gravis, multiple sclerosis and Eaton-Lambert syndrome. It has no role in the management of hemophilias.

Choice D (Factor VIII Concentrates) is used in the management of hemophilia A. It has no role in hemophilia B

QUESTION 44

Choice D is the correct answer. The Dawn phenomenon is caused by decreased insulin sensitivity due to the *nightly surge in glucagon and cortisol during nighttime fasting*. It manifests by normal evening serum glucose levels, and increased levels during the late night/early morning as well as elevated levels upon awakening. ENDOCRINE – DAWN PHENOMENON – BASICS (p. 304).

Choice A describes the Somogyi effect. The *Somogyi effect is caused by nocturnal hypoglycemia followed by a rebound early morning hyperglycemia*. It manifests as normal evening serum glucose levels followed by late night/early morning hypoglycemia followed by hyperglycemia upon awakening.

Choice C describes insulin waning.   It is associated with a progressive rise of serum glucose from bedtime to morning when the evening NPH dose is administered before dinner (due to inadequate insulin dosing).

Choice B and Choice E are associated with an insulinoma. Insulinomas secrete insulin and are associated with hypoglycemia not hyperglycemia.

QUESTION 45
Choice C (costovertebral angle tenderness) is the correct answer. Nausea, vomiting, fever, chills and costovertebral angle tenderness are more commonly seen in pyelonephritis compared to acute cystitis. All the other choices can be seen in both disorders. GENITOURINARY – PYELONEPHRITIS – BASICS (p 335).

QUESTION 46
Choice C (Pronator syndrome) is the correct choice. Pronator syndrome is median nerve compression at the level of the proximal forearm. *Patients develop symptoms similar to carpal tunnel syndrome but the symptoms usually predominate in the hand and the forearm* (compared to the wrist as seen with carpal tunnel syndrome). *Pronator syndrome is not associated with pain at night as seen in carpal tunnel syndrome* (Choice B).
MUSCULOSKELETAL – PRONATOR SYNDROME – MOST LIKELY (179).

Choice A (Cubital tunnel syndrome) causes nerve compression of the ulnar nerve at the elbow.

Choice D (Tarsal tunnel syndrome) is seen in the foot due to tibial nerve compression.

QUESTION 47
Choice C (bromocriptine) is the correct answer. *Neuroleptic malignant syndrome* is a condition seen due to *decreased dopamine activity in patients on dopamine antagonists* (such as anti-psychotic medications). Bromocriptine is a dopamine agonist, replenishing the dopamine, which reverses the symptoms of NMS.
NEUROLOGY– NEUROLEPTIC MALIGNANT SYNDROME – CLINICAL INTERVENTION (p 370).

Choice A (*cyproheptadine*) is a *serotonin antagonist used in the management of serotonin syndrome*, which is caused by serotonin excess when multiple serotonin agonists or serotonin reuptake inhibitors are used together.

Choice B (diazepam) can be used to reduce hyperthermia in patients with serotonin syndrome.

Choice D (acetaminophen) is not helpful to reduce the fever as the hyperthermia is caused by muscle contractions.

Choice E (promethazine) is a dopamine antagonist that can cause neuroleptic malignant syndrome.

QUESTION 48
Choice E (carbamazepine) is the correct answer. *The stabbing, shooting pain exacerbated with chewing and drafts of wind are hallmark of trigeminal neuralgia. Carbamazepine is the drug of choice for trigeminal neuralgia*, although its mechanism of action in trigeminal neuralgia is unknown. Gabapentin is sometimes used in the management of trigeminal neuralgia. NEUROLOGY – TRIGEMINAL NEURALGIA – PHARMACOLOGY (p. 359).

Choice A (100% oxygen via nonrebreather) is the treatment of choice for *cluster headaches*, which presents with *"clusters" of bouts of headache, the stabbing periorbital pain and the ipsilateral manifestations of rhinorrhea, lacrimation etc.*

Choice B (sumatriptan) is the treatment used in migraine, tension and cluster headaches.

Choice C (verapamil) is the drug of choice for prophylaxis of cluster headaches.

Choice D (toradol and metoclopramide) is used in the management of mild to moderate migraine headaches.

QUESTION 49
Choice D [Acute bronchitis] is the correct choice. The viral like presentation, normal chest radiograph and the normal lung exam indicates acute bronchitis (which is most commonly viral in nature).
PULMONARY – ACUTE BRONCHITIS – MOST LIKELY (p 111).

Choice A (sarcoidosis) classically shows up on radiographs as Stage I (bilateral lymphadenopathy), Stage II lymphadenopathy + interstitial pattern, Stage III: interstitial only & Stage IV: fibrosis.

Choice B (pulmonary embolism) can also present with a normal chest X ray and a normal physical exam, but would classically present with an elevated D dimer, tachypnea (94%), tachycardia, abnormal ECG findings (ST/T wave changes) or chest pain.

Choice C (typical bacterial pneumonia) would classically produce an infiltrate on chest radiograph.

Choice E (chronic bronchitis) is associated with longstanding smoking and would have an abnormal baseline chest radiographs.

QUESTION 50
Choice D (Verapamil) is the correct answer. The saw tooth pattern is consistent with atrial flutter with rapid ventricular rate. Based on the blood pressure and symptoms, the patient is stable. The management of choice for stable atrial flutter includes vagal maneuvers, calcium channel blockers and beta blockers. Verapamil is a calcium channel blocker (nondihydropyridine). CARDIOLOGY – ATRIAL FLUTTER – CLINICAL INTERVENTION (p 13).

Choice A (Atropine) is used for symptomatic bradycardia. It is an anticholinergic that is used to increase the heart rate.

Choice B (Amiodarone) is used for stable, wide complex tachycardia.

Choice C (Synchronized cardioversion) is used in the management of unstable tachycardia.

Choice E (Radiofrequency ablation) is the definitive management of atrial flutter. It is not used as first line in patients who are symptomatic at the time of presentation. The patient is usually stabilized first.

QUESTION 51
Choice B (Clarithromycin plus ethambutol) is the correct answer. The management of mycobacterium is to use clarithromycin plus another agent such as ethambutol or rifampin.
PULMONARY – MYCOBACTERIUM AVIUM COMPLEX – PHARMACOLOGY (p 431).

Choice A (Penicillin VK) can be used for gram positive and oral anaerobic infections.

Choice C (Vancomycin + Ceftriaxone) is the empiric management of choice for bacterial meningitis.

Choice E (Nafcillin + Gentamicin) is the empiric management of choice for disorders such as endocarditis or septic arthritis when the causative agent is unknown.

QUESTION 52

Choice B (diphenhydramine oral) is the correct answer. Urticaria is a type I (IgE-mediated) hypersensitivity reaction. Allergen-bound *IgE stimulates mast cell proinflammatory chemokine release, such as histamine*, leading to an immune reaction and localized edema (wheals). *Diphenhydramine is an antihistamine* that can be used in the management of urticaria to reduce the pruritus and wheal formation. Oral or intravenous corticosteroids may be added to antihistamines in patients with severe or persistent urticaria to blunt the immune response. This patient has no wheezing, uvula swelling or pharyngeal edema, indicating this is a mild reaction. Most cases of urticaria can resolve spontaneously so observation (Choice E) can be a choice in very mild cases especially if not associated with pruritus. DERMATOLOGY – URTICARIA – CLINICAL INTERVENTION (p 393).

Choice A (topical corticosteroids) wouldn't be able to reduce the generalized rash as it only works locally. Oral or intravenous corticosteroids may be added to the antihistamines in patients with severe or persistent urticaria to blunt the immune response.

Choice C (fluconazole oral) is an antifungal agent.

Choice D (clonidine oral) is used for the flushing symptoms in patients with acne rosacea

QUESTION 53

Choice A (rest, NSAIDs and repeat ultrasound in 6 weeks) is the management of choice for small, uncomplicated ovarian cysts. Symptomatic treatment for the pain and repeat ultrasound between 6-12 weeks to assess if the cyst is not growing is the mainstay of treatment for these patients.
REPRODUCTIVE – OVARIAN CYST – CLINICAL INTERVENTION (p 254).

Choice B (rest, NSAIDs and schedule for biopsy) may be indicated if CA-125 levels were elevated or for lesions highly suspicious of ovarian cancer.

Choice C (laparoscopy) or laparotomy is the management of choice for persistent symptomatic ovarian cysts, large cysts or complicated cysts.

Choice D (total abdominal hysterectomy/salpingo-oophorectomy) and choice E (oophorectomy) are not the treatment for uncomplicated ovarian cysts.

QUESTION 54

Choice A (JAK2 mutation) is the correct answer. The *JAK2 mutation is associated with Polycythemia vera* (primary erythrocytosis). It causes an increase primarily in red blood cell mass (but can lead to an increase in all the myeloid cell lines). HEMATOLOGY – POLYCYTHEMIA VERA – MOST LIKELY (page 467)

Choice B (HFE C282Y genotype) is associated with hereditary hemochromatosis.

Choice C (Translocation of chromosomes 9 and 22) known as the Philadelphia chromosome is seen in chronic myelogenous leukemia (CML).

Choice D (Human Leukocyte Antigen – B27) is associated with seronegative spondyloarthropathies.

Choice E (Menin gene) is associated with multiple endocrine neoplasia type I

QUESTION 55

Choice B (arginine vasopressin challenge test) is the correct answer. Lithium can induce diabetes insipidus (DI). Diabetes insipidus is caused by either a decrease in production of arginine vasopressin/antidiuretic Hormone/ADH (as seen in central DI) or an insensitivity of the kidney to ADH (as seen in nephrogenic DI). After a fluid deprivation test is done as a screening test for DI, a confirmatory vasopressin test distinguishes nephrogenic from central DI. If there is a progressive increase in urine osmolarity after exogenous vasopressin is given (indicating ADH-induced concentration of urine), then central DI is diagnosed. If the urine remains dilute after the administration of vasopressin, it means the kidneys are not sensitive to ADH (nephrogenic DI). GENITOURINARY – NEPHROGENIC DIABETES INSIPIDUS – LABS/DIAGNOSTIC STUDIES (p 325).

Choice A (fluid deprivation test) is the screening test for someone suspected of having diabetes insipidus. It does not distinguish between central and nephrogenic diabetes insipidus.

Choice C (high dose dexamethasone suppression test) is used in the setting of Cushing's syndrome to differentiate the causes.

Choice D (oral glucose tolerance test) is done in patients suspected of having diabetes mellitus.

Choice E (fluid challenge test) is done in patients with suspected prerenal azotemia. If the urine output returns or increase after a fluid challenge, then prerenal acute kidney injury is likely.

QUESTION 56

Choice D (Methylphenidate) is the correct answer. Methylphenidate is a sympathomimetic that blocks norepinephrine and dopamine uptake as well as increases the release of those neurotransmitters, improving the attention span. BEHAVIORAL – ADHD – PHARMACOLOGY (p 386).

Choice A (Fluoxetine), choice B (Amitriptyline) and choice C (Tranylcypromine) are antidepressants.

Choice E (Bromocriptine) is a dopamine agonist. It is not used in ADHD.

QUESTION 57

Choice E (right posterior cerebral artery occlusion) is the correct answer. A right posterior cerebral artery occlusion can result in *visual hallucinations, and "crossed symptoms" – meaning ipsilateral (in this case right) cranial nerve deficits and contralateral (in this case left) muscle weakness.* Comas and drop attacks are also seen in posterior. NEUROLOGY – POSTERIOR INFARCTION SYNDROME – MOST LIKELY (p 360).

Choice A (*Bell's Palsy*) is a *cranial nerve VII palsy that leads to isolated unilateral facial weakness.* The arms and the legs are not involved in Bell's palsy because only the facial nerve is involved. In these patients, they are usually *unable to lift the eyebrow on the affected side.*

Choice B (Left *middle cerebral artery occlusion*) would cause *contralateral hemiparesis (weakness) with arm & face more pronounced than the lower extremities.* Left hemisphere dominant lesions may cause aphasia. Due to bilateral innervation of the forehead, patients are usually able to raise both eyebrows.

Choice C (left posterior cerebral artery occlusion) can result in visual hallucinations, and "crossed symptoms" – meaning ipsilateral (left) cranial nerve deficits and contralateral (right) muscle weakness, comas and drop attacks are also seen in posterior. The patient in this vignette has the opposite sides affected.

Choice D (left anterior cerebral artery occlusion) would result in contralateral hemiparesis (weakness) that tends to be greater in the leg than the arm. It is associated with urinary incontinence and abulia (lack of will), personality changes.

QUESTION 58
Choice D (Steeple sign) is the correct choice. A barking, seal like cough is classic for viral croup (which is most commonly associated with parainfluenza virus). PULMONARY – VIRAL CROUP – LABS/DIAGNOSTIC (p 111).

Choice A (thumbprinting) is seen with epiglottitis.

Choice B (air bronchograms) are often seen with infant respiratory distress syndrome.

Choice C (companion lines) are seen with pneumothorax.

Choice E can also be seen with infant respiratory distress, adult respiratory distress and congestive heart failure

QUESTION 59
Choice C [a fourth heart sound (S4)] is the correct answer. A fourth heart sound is the most consistent physical exam finding in patients with myocardial infarction.
CARDIOLOGY – ACUTE MYOCARDIAL INFARCTION – HISTORY AND PHYSICAL EXAMINATION (p 23).

Choice A (Increased jugular venous pressure) may indicate decreased forward flow (such as seen with obstructive shock, pericardial tamponade, cardiogenic shock or congestive heart failure).

Choice B (sinus bradycardia) may be seen in inferior wall myocardial infarctions because the right coronary artery supplies the sinoatrial and atrioventricular nodes in a majority of cases.

Choice B (peripheral edema) may indicate congestive heart failure.

Choice E (anterior wall chest tenderness) is not classically associated with myocardial infarction as the chest pain is not classically reproducible by palpation.

QUESTION 60
Choice D (IV Vancomycin) is the correct answer. In the empiric management of bacterial meningitis when the organism is not known, IV vancomycin primarily covers gram-positive organisms (including MRSA). Ceftriaxone primarily covers the gram-negative organisms (although it does have some gram positive coverage as well). Ceftriaxone has excellent CNS penetration.
NEUROLOGY – MENINGITIS – PHARMACOLOGY (p 365).
Choice A (IV gentamicin) covers primarily gram-negative organisms, so if it is used with ceftriaxone, there is not strong gram-positive coverage. In addition, gentamicin has poor CNS penetration, so its use in meningitis would be limited.

Choice B (IV aztreonam) primarily covers gram-negative organisms, so if used with ceftriaxone, there would be no strong gram-positive coverage of organisms such as Streptococcus pneumonia (the most common cause of meningitis over the age of 18) and Listeria monocytogenes (the 3rd most common cause of bacterial meningitis overall). Listeria monocytogenes is seen with an increased incidence in the young and the elderly.

Choice C (IV Clindamycin) is not used as first line for suspected meningitis.

Choice E (IV Azithromycin) is not used in the routine management of bacterial meningitis.

QUESTION 61

Choice B (Bowen's disease) is the correct answer. Bowen's disease is the name for squamous cell carcinoma in situ. DERMATOLOGY – SQUAMOUS CELL CARCINOMA – BASICS (p 397).

Choice A (Caplan syndrome) is the development of rheumatoid arthritis in patients with coal workers pneumoconiosis.

Choice C (Sezary's disease) is a type of cutaneous lymphoma.

Choice D (Peutz Jegher's syndrome) is a hereditary intestinal polyposis syndrome that is associated with the development of hyperpigmented macules on the lips and the oral mucosa and colon cancer.

Choice E (Sturge Weber syndrome) is a rare congenital skin and neurologic disease associated with port-wine stain dermatologic lesions of the face, seizures, mental retardation and cerebral tumors.

QUESTION 62

Choice B (polycystic ovarian syndrome) is the correct choice. *The triad of amenorrhea, obesity and hirsutism is classic for polycystic ovarian syndrome.* Polycystic ovarian syndrome is due to dysfunction of the hypothalamus-pituitary-ovarian axis and an increase in androgen production in women (due to increased insulin from insulin resistance and luteinizing hormone). REPRODUCTIVE – POLYCYSTIC OVARIAN SYNDROME – MOST LIKELY (p 255).

Choice A (metabolic syndrome) is the constellation of at least 3 of the 5 following: central obesity, hypertension, elevated fasting plasma glucose, high serum triglycerides and low HDL levels.

Choice C (molar pregnancy) also known as gestational trophoblastic disease, occurs in ovulating patients. It usually presents as painless vaginal bleeding with or without severe, persistent hyperemesis gravidarum.

Choice D (adrenocortical insufficiency) causes lack of androgen production (the opposite of what is seen in this vignette). Patients are usually hypotensive as well (due to lack of aldosterone).

Choice E (endometrial adenocarcinoma) usually presents with abnormal vaginal bleeding not amenorrhea.

QUESTION 63

Choice D (splenectomy) is the correct answer. *Splenectomy is used to treat refractory immune thrombocytopenic purpura.* Removal of the spleen is definitive management of the splenic destruction of the platelets. HEMATOLOGY – IDIOPATHIC THROMBOCYTOPENIC PURPURA – CLINICAL (page 462)

Choice A (platelet transfusion) is reserved for management of severe thrombocytopenia: ex. platelet count of <10,000/mcL in patients with signs of clinically significant mucocutaneous or other bleeding.

Choice B (bone marrow transplant) is not used in the management, as there is normal marrow production of megakaryocytes and platelets in ITP. The site of platelet destruction occurs primarily in the spleen.

Choice C (Hydroxyurea) is used in the management of severe pain crisis in sickle cell disease, polycythemia vera, refractory CML and some solid tumors.

Choice E (fresh frozen plasma) is indicated in the management of patients with coagulation protein (factor) deficiencies (especially when the specific factor concentrates or not available). Thrombocytopenia is a platelet disorder (primary coagulation pathway). The secondary coagulation pathway (clotting factor pathway) is not affected.

QUESTION 64
Choice B (Escherichia coli) is the correct answer. *Escherichia coli is the most common organism in uncomplicated and complicated urinary tract infections* (causes up to 80% of all cases) as well as in prostatitis in men >40 years of age.   GENITOURINARY – URINARY TRACT INFECTIONS – MOST LIKELY (p 335).

QUESTION 65
Choice A (excess dopamine receptors in the mesolimbic pathway) is the correct answer. Excess dopamine receptors in the mesolimbic pathway are thought to cause the positive symptoms, which explain why dopamine antagonists are the mechanism of action of many of the anti-psychotics.
PSYCH/BEHAVIORAL – SCHIZOPHRENIA – BASICS (p 382).

Choice B (dopamine dysfunction in the mesocortical pathway) describes the theory thought to explain the development of the negative symptoms of schizophrenia.

Choice C (idiopathic dopamine depletion in the substantia nigra) describes the pathophysiology of Parkinson's disease.

Choice D (increased CNS grey matter with decreased size of the ventricles) is not seen in schizophrenia. Schizophrenia is associated with an increase in the size of the ventricles as a result of decreased CNS grey matter.

QUESTION 66
Choice D (noncaseating granuloma) is the correct choice. The bilateral hilar lymphadenopathy is classic for sarcoidosis. Noncaseating granulomas are seen in sarcoidosis. PULMONARY – SARCOIDOSIS – LABS/DIAGNOSTIC (p 86).

Choice A would be seen in lobar pneumonia.

Choice B would be seen with tuberculosis. These granulomas undergo caseous necrosis in the center to provide an acidic, hypoxemic environment (which inhibits mycobacterium tuberculosis growth).

Choice E describes emphysema (permanent dilation of the terminal airspaces).

QUESTION 67
Choice C (lisinopril) is the correct answer. The basic *pathophysiology of heart failure is a combination of a pathologic increase in preload, afterload as well as decreased contractility.* This leads to the activation of the renin angiotensin aldosterone system, which over a long period of constant stimulation promotes deterioration. Angiotensin converting enzyme inhibitors reduces preload and afterload, decreases aldosterone production, potentiates other vasodilators (such as bradykinin) and increases exercise tolerance. *Unless contraindicated, all patients with heart failure should be on an ACE inhibitor for long-term management (with diuretics often added for symptomatic edema).* CARDIOLOGY – HEART FAILURE – PHARMACOLOGY (p 29).

Choice A (dobutamine) is used in the short-term management of severe congestive heart failure.

Choice A (nesiritide) is primarily used in the emergent management of severe heart failure.

Choice D (digoxin) can be used in a subset of patients with heart failure but it is not first line.

Choice E (spironolactone) can also be used in the management of heart failure but is not first line.

QUESTION 68

Choice A (Yersinia pestis) is the correct answer.   *Yersinia pestis causes plague* and is transmitted by infected *rodents and their fleas.* It has 3 major forms: 1) *bubonic*: the most common form, is associated with acutely swollen, extremely painful nodes. 2) *septicemic*: which is associated with disseminated intravascular coagulation and gangrene and 3) *pneumonic* is associated with pulmonary infiltrates and pulmonary hemorrhage. *Yersinia pestis is a gram-negative rod with a bipolar staining, giving it a safety pin appearance.*
INFECTIOUS DISEASE – YERSINIA INFECTIONS – MOST LIKELY (p 425).

Choice B (Bacillus anthracis) is the causative agent of anthrax. It usually presents in the cutaneous form with an erythematous papule that progresses to a *black eschar.*

Choice C (Ehrlichia chaffeensis) is one of the causative agents of Ehrlichiosis.

Choice D (Coxiella burnetii) is the causative agent of Q fever.

Choice E (Brucella melitensis) is the causative agent of Brucellosis.

QUESTION 69

Choice B (Molluscum contagiosum) is the correct answer.   Molluscum contagiosum is a benign viral infection (poxviridae family) most commonly seen in children, sexually active adults and patients with HIV infection. It is classically characterized by *multiple dome-shaped flesh-colored to pearly white waxy papules with central umbilication. Curd-like material* may be expressed from the center of the papule if it is squeezed.
DERMATOLOGY– MOLLUSCUM CONTAGIOSUM – HISTORY AND PHYSICAL (p 399).

QUESTION 70

Choice C (ceftriaxone) is the correct choice.   Because many patients are coinfected with both gonorrhea and chlamydia, empiric treatment for both is recommended.
INFECTIOUS DISEASE – GONORRHEA/CHLAMYDIA – PHARMACOLOGY (p 422).

QUESTION 71

Choice B (cabergoline) is the correct answer.   Prolactin suppresses FSH and LH release, leading to decrease in menstruation and decrease in libido from the subsequent testosterone reduction. *The first line management of prolactinomas are dopamine agonists (*such as *cabergoline or Bromocriptine).* Dopamine inhibits prolactin, leading to a reduction in the tumor size via inhibition. ENDOCRINE – PROLACTINOMA – CLINICAL INTERVENTION (p 300).

Choice A (transsphenoidal resection of the tumor) is the treatment of choice for all other types of pituitary adenoma. Prolactinomas are the exception, in which medical management is the initially management. Transsphenoidal resection may be indicated if there is compression of the optic chiasm, compressive macro prolactinomas or other complications (which is not seen in this vignette).

Somatostatin (Choice C), Octreotide (choice D) and Pegvisomant (Choice E) are used in the management of somatostatinomas (tumors that secrete growth hormone).

QUESTION 72

Choice C (lymphocytes) is the correct answer.   Polycythemia vera is an acquired myeloproliferative disorder with *overproduction of the myeloid cell lines,* which causes primarily an *increase in the red blood cell line* (but may also include the platelet lines and the myeloid white blood cells). The lymphocyte line however is unaffected as lymphocytes are not formed via the myeloid differentiation pathway. All the other choices can be elevated in polycythemia vera. HEMATOLOGY – POLYCYTHEMIA VERA – BASICS (Page 467).

QUESTION 73

Choice E (furosemide) is the correct answer. Furosemide is a loop diuretic which works at the thick ascending loop of Henle at the $Na^+/K^+/Cl^-$ cotransporter in which it promotes sodium as well as potassium loss, leading to possible hypokalemia. The classic ECG change in hypokalemia is T wave flattening and prominent U waves. GENITOURINARY – HYPOKALEMIA – MOST LIKELY (p 331).

Choice A (spironolactone) is a potassium-sparing diuretic that works at the distal tubule and collecting duct as an aldosterone antagonist, leading to enhanced sodium excretion and enhanced potassium retention, possible leading to hyperkalemia, not hypokalemia.

Choice B (ibuprofen) and other NSAIDs can cause hyperkalemia by reducing aldosterone release as well as lowering prostaglandin-mediated renin secretion. These two things can lower urinary potassium excretion, possibly causing hyperkalemia (not hypokalemia)

Choice C (enalapril) is an angiotensin converting enzyme inhibitor. By blocking angiotensin converting enzyme, it decreased aldosterone production, possibly leading to hyperkalemia (not hypokalemia)

Choice D (losartan) is an angiotensin II receptor blocker, leading to decreased aldosterone effect, possibly leading to hyperkalemia (not hypokalemia)

QUESTION 74

Choice B (propranolol) is the correct answer. Two things that make the obstruction in *hypertrophic cardiomyopathy worse* are 1) *decreased left ventricular volume* (because it increases systolic anterior motion of the mitral valve against the hypertrophied septum) and 2) *increased contractility.* Propranolol is the first line management (due to beta-1 blockade reduction of contractility). Because beta-blockers decrease heart rate, they prolong ventricular filling times, leading to increased left ventricular volume. Calcium channel blockers (the non-dihydropyridines verapamil and diltiazem) and disopyramide may also be used in the medical management. CARDIOLOGY – HYPERTROPHIC CARDIOMYOPATHY – CLINICAL INTERVENTION (page 37).

Choice A (digoxin) is a positive inotrope that should be used with caution in patients with significant hypertrophic cardiomyopathy (as it increases contractility).

Choice C (nitroglycerin), Choice D (furosemide) and choice E (lisinopril) may produce decreased left ventricular filling or hypotension and should be used in caution in patients with severe hypertrophic cardiomyopathy. Dihydropyridine calcium channel blockers may also be used with caution (not the case with non dihydropyridines).

QUESTION 75

Choice E (pain and paresthesias at the site of inoculation) is the correct answer. Tetanus infection is caused by Clostridium tetani, which produces a neurotoxin called tetanospasmin. Tetanospasmin blocks neuron inhibition, leading to increased muscle spasm and muscle contractions. Pain and paresthesias at the inoculation site is usually the first sign of tetanus infection followed by the early symptoms: local muscle spasms, neck and jaw stiffness dysphagia and hyperirritability. Late symptoms are due to increased muscle stimulation without inhibition including: Choice B (trismus), Choice C (increased deep tendon reflexes), Choice D (increased muscle rigidity) and risus sardonicus (facial spasms resembling a sinister smile). INFECTIOUS DISEASE – TETANUS – HISTORY AND PHYSICAL EXAMINATION (p 421).

Choice A (an annular expanding rash with central clearing at the site of inoculation) describes erythema migrans, the classic rash of Lyme disease.

QUESTION 76

Choice A (Griseofulvin) is the correct answer. Tinea capitus has a varied presentation but is associated with an annular, scaling lesion with broken hair shafts. There is often alopecia around the area. *Griseofulvin is teratogenic (even in males) and commonly associated with the development of hepatitis (so LFTs should be evaluated before prior to, during and after treatment with griseofulvin).*
DERMATOLOGY – TINEA CAPITUS – CLINICAL INTERVENTION (p 400).

Choice B (Fluconazole) is a second line treatment for tinea capitus.

Choice C (Selenium sulfide) is used in pityriasis versicolor and seborrheic dermatitis

Choice D (Caspofungin) is used for severe, life-threatening fungal infections.

Choice E (Hydrocortisone) are used for dermatitis and immune disorders.

QUESTION 77

Choice C (human papilloma virus) is the correct answer. The most common predisposing factor for cervical cancer is the presence of HPV infection (99.7% of the cervical cancer is associated with HPV). Other risk factors include early onset of sexual activity, increased number of sexual partners, smoking and diethylstilbestrol usage.
REPRODUCTIVE – CERVICAL CANCER – HEALTH MAINTENANCE (p 258).

QUESTION 78

Choice C (propylthiouracil) is the correct answer. Propylthiouracil is safer in pregnancy than methimazole (Choice B) in the medical management of hyperthyroidism. ENDOCRINE – HYPERTHYROID – CLINICAL INTERVENTION (p 286).

Choice A (levothyroxine) is a synthetic version of the thyroid hormone T4. Levothyroxine is indicated in the management of hypothyroidism not hyperthyroidism.

Choice D (triiodothyronine) is a synthetic version of the thyroid hormone T3. Triiodothyronine is indicated in the management of hypothyroidism not hyperthyroidism.

Choice E (radioactive iodine ablation of the thyroid) is contraindicated in the management of hyperthyroidism in pregnant patients because it will destroy the fetal thyroid gland as well lead to cretinism.

QUESTION 79

Choice C (IV hydration and oxygen) is the correct answer. IV hydration and oxygen is the first line management of sickle cell crisis. Pain medication is also commonly administered.
HEMATOLOGY – SICKLE CELL DISEASE - CLINICAL INTERVENTION (p. 457).

Choice A (Folic acid) is part of the long-term management of many types of anemia (folic acid is needed for red blood cell synthesis).

Choice B (Red blood cell transfusion) may be needed in severe sickle cell disease during acute chest syndromes, splenic sequestration crisis and certain preoperative situations.

Choice D (IV Penicillin G) may be used in certain infections seen in patients with sickle cell disease such as Neisseria meningitidis and Streptococcus pneumoniae.

Choice E (Hydroxyurea) can be used in severe pain crisis and in long-term management in some cases to reduce the frequency of pain crisis.

QUESTION 80

Choice D (renal angiogram) is the correct answer. *Renal angiogram is the definitive diagnosis (gold standard) in renal artery stenosis.* The most common cause of renovascular hypertension is atherosclerosis in the elderly and fibromuscular dysplasia in young women. The stenosed renal artery leads to activation of the renin-angiotensin-aldosterone system, leading to refractory hypertension and a renal artery bruit heard when listening to the abdomen from the turbulent blood flow through the stenosed renal artery.
GENITOURINARY– RENAL ARTERY STENOSIS – LABS/DIAGNOSTIC STUDIES (p 339).

Choice A (renal biopsy) is used to diagnose malignancies, and in certain cases, some causes of nephrotic or nephritic syndromes.

Choice B (renal ultrasound) is part of the evaluation of patients with suspected renal artery stenosis but is not the definitive diagnosis (gold standard).

Choice C (*renogram) is the best noninvasive test for the evaluation of suspected renal artery stenosis* but is not the definitive diagnosis (gold standard).

Choice E (aldosterone: renin ratio >20) is suggestive of primary hyperaldosteronism. Renal artery stenosis is associated with secondary hyperaldosteronism and would be associated with a low aldosterone: renin ratio.

QUESTION 81

Choice A (azithromycin) is the correct answer. Lymphogranuloma venereum are genital/rectal lesions with suppuration caused by Chlamydia trachomatis [the same organism that causes the much more common chlamydia urethritis/cervicitis, pelvic inflammatory disease and reactive arthritis (Reiter's syndrome)]. First line management of chlamydia trachomatis is azithromycin or doxycycline.
INFECTIOUS DISEASE – LYMPHOGRANULOMA VENEREUM – CLINICAL INTERVENTION (p 422).

QUESTION 82

Choice A (a "fishy" smell with potassium hydroxide and the presence of clue cells) is the correct answer. These findings are classic for bacterial vaginosis. *Bacterial vaginosis is caused by an overgrowth of normal flora (especially Gardnerella vaginalis).* It produces a *thin, homogenous watery grey-white "fishy, rotten"* smell worse with potassium hydroxide application with *clue cells.* REPRODUCTIVE – BACTERIAL VAGINOSIS – LABS/DIAGNOSTIC STUDIES (p 260).

Choice B (the presence of a *strawberry cervix and yellow-green frothy discharge*) is associated with *trichomoniasis.*

Choice C (*white "curd-like" vaginal discharge*) is associated with *candida vulvovaginitis.*

Choice D (*whitening of the lesion with acetic acid application*) is associated with *human papilloma virus infections* (genital warts).

Choice E (grouped vesicles on an erythematous base) is associated with herpes simplex infections.

QUESTION 83

Choice B (primary hyperparathyroidism) is the correct answer. The vignette is describing symptoms of hypercalcemia. ECG findings associated with hypercalcemia include a shortened QT interval, prolonged PR interval and QRS widening. The most common cause of hypercalcemia is primary hyperparathyroidism.
ENDOCRINE – HYPERPARATHYROIDISM – MOST LIKELY (p 291).

Choice A (malignancy) is the second most common cause of hypercalcemia. 90% of all hypercalcemia are due to either primary hyperparathyroidism or malignancy.

Choice C (secondary hyperparathyroidism) is associated with hypocalcemia not hypercalcemia. In situations with persistent hypocalcemia (the primary problem), the hypocalcemia-stimulated increase in parathyroid hormone attempts to increase the calcium levels back to normal. Hypocalcemia in secondary hyperparathyroidism will result in muscle spasms and a prolonged QT interval.

Choice D (Lithium toxicity) and Choice E (milk alkali syndrome) are associated with hypercalcemia as well but neither are the most common cause of hypercalcemia.

QUESTION 84
Choice C (Coombs positivity) is the correct answer. Coombs positivity is associated with autoimmune hemolytic anemia. All of the other choices are associated with hereditary spherocytosis.
HEMATOLOGY – HEREDITARY SPHEROCYTOSIS – BASICS (page 459).

QUESTION 85
Choice E (oxybutynin) is the correct answer. Oxybutynin is an anticholinergic medication that is used in the medical management of urge incontinence. Anticholinergics and antihistamines (which have anticholinergic effects) can increase urinary retention, especially in patients with benign prostatic hypertrophy.
GENITOURINARY– BENIGN PROSTATIC HYPERTROPHY – CLINICAL INTERVENTION (p 337).

Choice A (observation if mild symptoms) is part of the treatment of BPH.

Choice B (finasteride) is a 5-alpha reductase inhibitor, which inhibits conversion of testosterone to dihydrotestosterone, thereby suppressing prostate growth and reducing the need for surgery. It has been shown to improve the clinical course of BPH.

Choice C (tamsulosin) is an alpha-1 blocker that is used to induce smooth muscle relaxation of the prostate and the bladder neck, improving urinary outflow in patients with symptomatic BPH (obstructive symptoms).

Choice D (transurethral resection of the prostate) may be used in severe cases of BPH to remove excess prostate tissue and relieve obstruction.

QUESTION 86
Choice B (Penicillin G) is the correct answer. A positive rapid plasma reagent test and a maculopapular rash are seen in secondary syphilis. The management of choice for syphilis is Penicillin G. In some cases of patients with penicillin allergies, penicillin desensitization may be required for adequate treatment.
INFECTIOUS DISEASE – SYPHILIS – PHARMACOLOGY (p 426).

Choice A (Azithromycin) can be used in patients with penicillin allergy in early latent syphilis, but doxycycline may be a better second line alternative. It is important to note that these second line drugs are less well studied. Sometimes, penicillin desensitization may be preferred rather than using the second line agents.

Choice C (Doxycycline) is often the preferred agent in patients with true penicillin allergy in both early and late latent syphilis. It is important to note that these second line drugs are less well studies and sometimes penicillin desensitization may be preferred than using the second line agents.

Choice D (Ceftriaxone) can be used in patients with penicillin allergy in early latent syphilis, but doxycycline may be a better second line alternative. It is important to note that these second line drugs are less well studied. Sometimes penicillin desensitization may be preferred than using the second line agents.

Choice E (Podophyllin) is used in the management of external condyloma acuminata (genital warts). Note that condyloma acuminata (genital warts) are different than condyloma lata (which is seen in secondary syphilis).

QUESTION 87
Choice C (fibrocystic breast disorder) is the correct answer. Fibrocystic breast disorder is the presence of fluid-filled breast cyst(s) due to the exaggerated response of breast tissue to hormones. The hallmark of this disorder are *cysts that increase or decrease with menstrual hormonal* changes and may be *tender to palpation.*
REPRODUCTIVE – FIBROCYSTIC BREAST DISORDER – MOST LIKELY (p 277).

Choice A (mastitis) is an infection of the breast in lactating woman due to break in the skin from nipple trauma from a suckling infant. It is classically unilateral and may be associated with breast tenderness, warmth, swelling and nipple discharge.

Choice B (breast abscess) is a complication of mastitis and is associated with induration and fluctuance (due to the pus).

Choice D (fibroadenoma of the breast) is the second most common breast disorder after fibrocystic disorders. It is distinguished from fibrocystic disorder because *fibroadenomas do not change in size with menstrual hormonal changes.* In fibroadenoma, fine needle aspiration with biopsy would show collagen and glandular tissue arranged in a "swirl" (compared to the straw-colored fluid seen in fibrocystic disorders with fine needle aspiration).

Choice E (*Paget's disease of the nipple) is associated with a chronic, eczematous, itchy scaling rash on the nipples and the areola and is a type of breast cancer.*

QUESTION 88
Choice A (metabolic alkalosis) is the correct answer. Adrenocortical insufficiency is associated with metabolic acidosis. Aldosterone normally causes sodium reabsorption in exchange for excretion of potassium and hydrogen ions (to maintain electric neutrality). The absence of aldosterone will cause renal retention of potassium causing hyperkalemia (Choice C) and hydrogen ions (metabolic acidosis). The lack of sodium retention and lack of cortisol will lead to hypotension (Choice E), isovolemic hypotonic hyponatremia (choice B) and hypoglycemia (Choice D).
ENDOCRINE – ADRENOCORTICAL INSUFFICIENCY – BASICS (p 296).

QUESTION 89
Choice E (prostate massage to increase the bacterial yield on urinalysis) is the correct answer. The perineal pain and back pain are suggestive of acute prostatitis. Prostatic massage is often employed in chronic prostatitis because urine cultures are often negative and the prostatic massage increases the bacterial yield. *In acute prostatitis, prostatic massage is contraindicated as it can promote bacteremia.* All of the other choices are part of the routine workup in a patient with suspected prostatitis.
GENITOURINARY – ACUTE PROSTATITIS – HISTORY AND PHYSICAL EXAM (p 336).

Choice A (urine culture) and choice B (urinalysis) are done to determine the cause as well as sensitivity of the organism to common antibiotics used in the empiric management of prostatitis.

Choice C (rectal exam) is part of the workup in suspected cases. *In acute prostatitis, rectal examination reveals a tender, boggy prostate. Chronic prostatitis is associated with a non-tender boggy prostate.*

Choice D (gonorrhea and chlamydia cultures) are recommended as they are the most common causes of acute prostatitis in young men under the age of 35.

QUESTION 90
Choice B (Entamoeba histolytica) is the correct answer. Amebiasis is classically associated with diarrhea and the development of hepatic abscesses. Stool ova and parasite testing will be positive In Entamoeba infections. GI/NUTRITION– AMEBIASIS – MOST LIKELY (p 159).

Choice A (Acanthamoeba lentica) can cause keratitis especially in contact lens wearers. It commonly shows up as a cornea stromal ring infiltrates when examining the eye.

Choice C (Babesia microti) is the causative agent of babesiosis.

Choice D (Plasmodium falciparum) is one of the Plasmodium species responsible for malaria.

Choice E (Toxoplasma gondii) is associated with toxoplasmosis. It can cause a mono-like illness, encephalitis and chorioretinitis.

QUESTION 91
Choice E (partial estrogen receptor agonist that stimulates ovulation) is the correct choice. Clomiphene is a partial estrogen receptor agonist that is used in some patients with infertility due to induce ovulation. REPRODUCTIVE – CLOMIPHENE – PHARMACOLOGY (p 266).

Choice A (a gonadotropin releasing hormone analog) describes the mechanism of action of Leuprolide. Normally, gonadotropin releasing hormone is released in a pulsatile fashion, so if given in a pulsatile fashion, leuprolide can induce ovulation. However, if given continuously (instead of in a pulsatile fashion), leuprolide will cause down regulation of luteinizing hormone & follicle stimulating hormone, ultimately leading to a decrease in estrogen & testosterone.

Choice B (estrogen antagonist in the breast and estrogen agonist in the endometrium) describes the mechanism of action of Tamoxifen.

Choice C (estrogen antagonist in the breast and endometrium) describes the mechanism of action of Raloxifene.

Choice E (progesterone receptor agonist) describes the mechanism of action of progestin.

QUESTION 92
Choice A (prolactinoma) is the correct answer. Prolactinomas are pituitary adenomas that can cause neurological symptoms such as headache and visual changes. *Prolactinomas are the most common pituitary tumor* compared to all of the other choices. ENDOCRINE – PITUITARY TUMORS – BASICS (p 300).

QUESTION 93
Choice E (varicocele) is the correct answer. Varicoceles are varicosities of the pampiniform plexus and the internal spermatic vein. They most commonly occur on the left side and have the consistency of *"a bag of worms"* on testicular palpation. They do not transilluminate. Dilation is often worse when the patient is upright or with the Valsalva maneuver (due to the increased flow to varicosities). *Varicoceles are the most common surgically correctable cause of infertility* (in this vignette, this couple had trouble conceiving). GENITOURINARY – VARICOCELE – MOST LIKELY (p 333).
Choice A (hydrocele) normally transilluminates. Communicating hydroceles may worsen with Valsalva maneuver as well.

Choice B (spermatocele) are freely movable and also transilluminates easily.

Choice C (testicular cancer) does not transilluminate but is associated with a palpable testicular mass.

316

Choice D (testicular torsion) is associated with testicular pain, nausea, and vomiting.

QUESTION 94
Choice B (A patient with a history of HIV and a CD4 count of 100/mm^3) is the correct answer. The Measles Mumps Rubella (MMR vaccine) is a live attenuated vaccine. *It is the only safe live attenuated vaccine to be given in patients with HIV (as long as the CD4 count is greater than 200/mm^3).* The MMR vaccine is safe to administer in all of the other cases.   INFECTIOUS DISEASE – MMR VACCINATION – HEALTH MAINTENANCE (online chapter).

QUESTION 95
Choice B (trimethoprim-sulfamethoxazole plus corticosteroids) is the correct answer. Pneumocystis jiroveci is a yeast-like fungus that is the most common opportunistic infection in patients who are immunocompromised (ex. patients with *HIV with a CD4 count under 200/mm^3*).   It classically presents with *fever, dyspnea, oxygen desaturation on ambulation, an extremely elevated LDH level, bilateral diffuse interstitial infiltrates* (as seen on this radiograph). *The management of choice in PCP pneumonia is trimethoprim-sulfamethoxazole.* The addition of corticosteroids have been shown to improve function in patients with a PaO$_2$ <70 mmHg.   Although pneumocystis jirovecii is a yeast like fungus, it doesn't respond to antifungal therapy. The name Pneumocystis is derived from the characteristic cysts seen in the lung tissue of affected patients.
INFECTIOUS DISEASE – PCP PNEUMONIA – CLINICAL INTERVENTION (p 416).

Choice A (azithromycin) and Choice D (doxycycline) are used as first line empiric OUTpatient management for community acquired bacterial pneumonia.

Choice C (itraconazole plus corticosteroids) and Choice E (fluconazole) are incorrect because Pneumocystis jirovecii is a yeast like fungus that does not respond to antifungal medications.

QUESTION 96
Choice C (decreased deep tendon reflexes) is the correct answer. Magnesium is needed to make parathyroid hormone, so patients with hypermagnesemia are often also hypercalcemic (and hyperkalemic). Hypercalcemia is associated with an increased threshold for muscle contraction, leading to decreased muscular contraction and decreased deep tendon reflexes.
GENITOURINARY – HYPERMAGNESEMIA – HISTORY AND PHYSICAL EXAMINATION (p 330).

Choice A (positive Trousseau's sign) is associated with hypocalcemia and hypomagnesemia.

Choice B (Torsades de pointes) is associated with hypomagnesemia.

Choice D [Serum potassium levels < 3.5 mEq/L (Normal 3.5 – 5 mEq/L)] is associated with hypomagnesemia. Magnesium normally inhibits the ROMK channels, which decreases potassium excretion. Magnesium deficiency, therefore, causes renal potassium wasting by increasing distal potassium excretion, so hypomagnesemia is associated with hypokalemia and hypermagnesemia is associated with hyperkalemia.

Choice E (Serum calcium levels < 8.5 mEq/L (Normal 8.5 – 10 mEq/L) would be seen in hypomagnesemia. Magnesium is needed to make parathyroid hormone, so hypomagnesemia is associated with hypocalcemia.

QUESTION 97
Choice B (Paragard copper intrauterine device) is the correct choice. The copper intrauterine device Paragard has a 10-year length of action. REPRODUCTIVE – CONTRACEPTION – HEALTH MAINTENANCE (p 266).

Choice A (tubal ligation) is permanent contraception.   It is a form of sterilization.

Choice C (Levonorgestrel/Mirena) is an intrauterine device that has a 5-year duration of action.

Choice D (Essure) is a permanent condition (also a form of sterilization). It involves chemical or coils that scar the Fallopian tubes.

Choice E (Medroxyprogesterone acetate/Depo-Provera) has a 3-month duration.

QUESTION 98
Choice A (insulin-like growth factor) is the correct answer. The symptoms describe in this vignette are classic for a growth hormone secreting somatostatinoma. Insulin-like growth factor 1 production is stimulated by growth hormone and can be elevated despite the levels of growth hormone, which can fluctuate through the day. ENDOCRINE – SOMATOTROPINOMA – LABS/DIAGNOSTIC STUDIES (p 300).

Choice B (CRH stimulation test) is used in evaluation of adrenal insufficiency.

Choice C (High dose dexamethasone suppression test) and choice E (Low dose dexamethasone suppression test) are used in the evaluation of Cushing's syndrome.

Choice D (Thyroid stimulating hormone test) is the initial test in the evaluation of suspected thyroid disorders.

QUESTION 99
Choice A (rubella) is the correct answer. Rubella is associated with a *light red to pink spotted rash that lasts about 3 days.* It usually self-limiting in children but it c*an cause transient photosensitivity and arthritis (especially in young women).* INFECTIOUS DISEASE – RUBELLA – MOST LIKELY (p 435).

Choice B (Rubeola) is the cause of *measles.* The rash of measles is classically described as a *brick-red rash starting on the face and spreading to the trunk lasting 7 days.* It is often preceded by a prodrome of cough, runny nose and conjunctivitis.

Choice C (fifth's disease) otherwise known as erythema infectiosum is associated with coryza, fever and the appearance of an erythematous rash with circumoral pallor giving the classic *"slapped cheek" appearance.* This rash is often followed by a *lacy, reticular rash on the extremities* (especially the upper extremities and the rash often spares the palms and the soles).

Choice D (mumps) is associated with parotid gland swelling.

Choice E (hand foot and mouth disease) classically presents with vesicular lesions on a reddened based with an erythematous halo in the oral cavity followed by vesicular rash involving the palms and the soles.

QUESTION 100
Choice B (lithium) is the correct answer. Lithium therapy has been shown to cause diabetes insipidus. Other side effects of lithium therapy include hypothyroidism, hyperparathyroidism (hypercalcemia). All the other choices can cause syndrome of inappropriate ADH secretion (SIADH).
ENDOCRINE – DIABETES INSIPIDUS – BASICS (p 493).

PHOTO CREDITS

POISON IVY
  Beckman / CustomMedical (Used with Permission)

TINEA CAPITUS
  Wellcome Trust Library / CustomMedical (Used with Permission)

ANTHRAX
  J. Cavallini / CustomMedical (Used with Permission)

PCP cysts
      By User InvictaHOG on en.wikipedia [Public domain], via Wikimedia Commons

PCP PNEUMONIA
  T. Youssef / CustomMedical (Used with Permission)

Well you finally made it to the end!!!!

I just personally want to say thank you for purchasing this book as part of your study arsenal.

Dwayne A. Williams

Please check out the website **pancepreppearls.com** to claim your **20 AAPA-approved Category 1 self assessment credits for the PANCE/PANRE question book,** for radiology case studies, blogs, videos and more!!!!

ALSO, CHECK OUT THE BOOK THAT STARTED IT ALL....
PANCE PREP PEARLS!!!

A MEDICAL STUDY AND REVIEW
GUIDE FOR THE PANCE, PANRE
& MEDICAL EXAMINATIONS

2nd edition

PANCE PREP PEARLS

By Dwayne A. Williams

AWESOME FEATURES
Bold and italicized essentials of each topic
frequently asked with emphasis on high-yield
information. Simple yet effective layouts to
maximize learning and increase retention of
difficult topics.

VARIATIONS
Clinical correlation bullet
points, same as before, to help
connect related topics in
different systems.

ALSO AVAILABLE

CYTOCHROME P450 INDUCERS

John was **wor**thy when referred & <u>**inducted**</u> into sainthood for giving up **chronic alcohol** use & placing himself **on a real** fast, **fend**ing off **greasy carbs**, leading to **less warfare** with **theo**logians.

drugs that induce CP450 system can lead to decreased levels of certain drugs ex. warfarin (less warfare), theophylline (theologians) and phenytoin

INDUCERS OF THE P450
- **St. Johns Wort**
- **rifampin** (referred)
- **chronic alcohol use**
- **sulfonylureas** (self on a real)
- **Phenytoin**
- **Phenobarbital** (fend)
- **Griseofulvin** (greasy)
- **Carbamazepine** (carbs)

Made in USA - North Chelmsford, MA
1152186_9781508682172
08.20.2021 1146